READING ACTS

READING THE NEW TESTAMENT SERIES

Charles H. Talbert

READING ACTS

A LITERARY AND
THEOLOGICAL COMMENTARY
ON THE ACTS OF THE APOSTLES

A Crossroad Book
The Crossroad Publishing Company
New York

1997
The Crossroad Publishing Company
370 Lexington Avenue, New York, NY 10017

Library of Congress Cataloging-in-Publication Data

Talbert, Charles H.
    Reading Acts : a literary and theological commentary on the Acts
of the Apostles / Charles H. Talbert.
        p.   cm. – (Reading the New Testament series)
    Includes bibliographical references.
    ISBN 0-8245-1669-9 (pbk.)
    1. Bible. N.T Acts–Commentaries.   I. Title.   II. Series..
BS2625.3.T36   1997
226.6'07–dc21   97-10324
                                                                   CIP

Leander E. Keck,
Doktorvater,
with appreciation

CONTENTS

EDITOR'S PREFACE

"Reading the New Testament" is a commentary series that aims to present cutting-edge research in popular form that is accessible to upper-level undergraduates, seminarians, seminary-educated pastors, and educated laypeople, as well as to graduate students and professors. The volumes in this series do not follow the word-by-word, phrase-by-phrase, verse-by-verse method of traditional commentaries. Rather they are concerned to understand large thought units and their relationship to an author's thought as a whole. The focus is on a close reading of the final form of the text. The aim is to make one feel at home in the biblical text itself. The approach of these volumes involves a concern both for *how* an author communicates and *what* the religious point of the text is. Care is taken to relate both the *how* and the *what* of the text to its milieu: Christian (New Testament and non-canonical), Jewish (scriptural and postbiblical), and Greco-Roman. This enables both the communication strategies and the religious message of the text to be clarified over against a range of historical and cultural possibilities. Moreover, a section of commentary on a large thought unit will often contain a brief excursus on some topic raised by the material in the unit, sometimes sketching Old Testament, postbiblical Jewish, Greco-Roman, New Testament, and noncanonical Christian views on the subject. Throughout, the basic concern is to treat the New Testament texts as religious documents whose religious message needs to be set forth with compelling clarity. All other concerns are subordinated to this. It is the hope of all participants in this project that our efforts at exposition will enable the New Testament to be understood better and communicated more competently.

Charles H. Talbert, General Editor

AUTHOR'S PREFACE

This volume was completed during the summer and fall semester, 1995. Research for the book has occupied me off and on much of my teaching career. Several incentives toward meeting my deadline were given me during the 1990s: an invitation to contribute to a Festschrift for Gerhard Schneider in 1991; an invitation to participate in the 8th Annual Biblical Symposium at Florida Southern College in Lakeland, Florida, in 1994; and an invitation to have a part on the program of the Luke-Acts Seminar of the Society of Biblical Literature in 1995. Special assistance in my final preparations was offered by four Wake Forest undergraduates who undertook individualized research projects under my supervision in the summers of 1994 and 1995. Daniel Hilty, John H. Hayes, Craig Joseph, and Jennifer Trafton did splendid work, which is acknowledged at appropriate points in the commentary. I am, of course, indebted to a long history of Lukan scholarship. A special debt is owed to H. J. Cadbury, Martin Dibelius, Kirsopp Lake, Ernst Haenchen, Hans Conzelmann, Richard Pervo, Robert Tannehill, Luke Johnson, and the team that has put together the multivolume set *The Book of Acts in Its First Century Setting.*

Explanations should be offered for two practices in the commentary. First, in references to the Deity, I follow the lead of Marie Isaacs, *Sacred Space: An Approach to the Theology of the Epistle to the Hebrews* (Sheffield: JSOT Press, 1992), 67 n. 1: "The capitalization of personal pronouns for God adopted throughout this work is intended to signal that God is above gender—*not* that the deity is male." Second, I stand within and write from the standpoint of historic Christianity. Therefore, I use the designations B.C. and A.D.

Gratitude must be expressed to the publishers who have graciously allowed me to use material from two prior publications. (1) "The Acts of the Apostles: Monograph or *Bios*?" in *History, Literature and Society in the Books of Acts,* ed. Ben Witherington III (Cambridge: Cambridge University

Press, 1996), 58-72; and (2) "Once Again: The Gentile Mission in Luke-Acts," in *Der Treue Gottes Trauen,* ed. C. Bussmann and W. Radl (Freiburg: Herder, 1991), 99-110.

Finally, my appreciation must go to my wife, Betty, for her patience and support throughout the process.

Christmas, 1996
Charles H. Talbert

ACKNOWLEDGMENTS

Quotations from the Bible are from the New American Bible, with revised New Testament, or are translated by the author, unless otherwise specified. Quotations from the church fathers are normally taken from *The Ante-Nicene Fathers*. Excerpts from Greek and Latin authors are usually from the Loeb Classical Library. Material from the Cynic epistles is taken from *The Cynic Epistles*, ed. A. J. Malherbe (Missoula, Mont.: Scholars Press, 1977). Quotations from the Old Testament pseudepigrapha are normally taken from James Charlesworth, ed., *The Old Testament Pseudepigrapha*, 2 vols. (Garden City, N.Y.: Doubleday, 1983, 1985). Material from the apocryphal New Testament is ordinarily taken from M. R. James, *The Apocryphal New Testament* (Oxford: Clarendon, 1955). Citations from the Mishnah are from *The Mishnah*, trans. Herbert Danby (Oxford: Clarendon, 1933); those from the Tosefta are from *The Tosefta*, trans. J. Neusner (New York: Ktav, 1981); those from the Babylonian Talmud are from *The Babylonian Talmud*, ed. I. Epstein (London: Soncino, 1948).

INTRODUCTION

A nswers to the usual introductory questions do not yield sufficient harvest to enable an intelligent reading of Acts. (1) Authorship—The early
tradition speaks of Luke as the author: for example, the Muratorian Canon;
Irenaeus, *Against Heresies* 3.14.1; Clement of Alexandria, *Miscellanies*
5.12; Eusebius, *Church History* 3.4; Jerome, *Commentary on Isaiah* 3.6,
Epistle 53.9; *Lives of Illustrious Men* 7. There is every likelihood that this
tradition represents an early Christian inference from the internal evidence
of Acts read in light of its canonical context. (a) The "we-sections" of Acts
(16:10-17; 20:5-15; 21:1-18; 27:1-28:16), taken at face value, imply that a
companion of Paul who accompanied him to his imprisonment in Rome
wrote them (and the rest of Acts?). (b) Col 4:14; 2 Tim 4:11; and Phlm 24
have Paul in prison (in Rome?) and Luke with him (in 2 Tim 4:11, only
Luke). Taking the two together, the inference is that Luke was the companion of Paul and the author of Acts (Cadbury 1979, 263). If the external tradition is questionable and the document is itself anonymous, the issue of
authorship is moot.

   (2) Date—Dating the Acts is equally difficult. The document must have
been composed later than the events of Acts 28 (the early 60s?). It must have
been written before the time of Justin Martyr. *1 Apology* 50.12 reads as follows:

> afterwards, when He had risen from the dead and appeared to them, and had
> taught them to read the prophecies in which all these things were foretold as
> coming to pass, and when they had seen Him ascending into heaven, and had
> believed, and had received power sent thence by Him upon them, and went to
> every race of men, they taught these things, and were called apostles.

This quote indicates Justin knew not only Acts' distinctive plot but also its
connection to Luke 24:25-27, 32. "Not until Justin Martyr can a knowledge
and use of Luke's two works be established" (Haenchen, 8). Acts, then, can

have been written anytime between the early sixties and the early second century. Although arguments aiming at greater precision have been put forward, they have not been compelling.

(3) Sources—Both source critics and form critics have expended incredible energy on the issue of the sources of Acts with very little to show for their efforts. The conclusion of Jacques Dupont after his survey of the problem sums up the matter.

> The predominant impression is certainly very negative. Despite the most careful and detailed research, it has not been possible to define any of the sources used by the author of Acts in a way that will meet with widespread agreement among the critics. (p. 166)

To say that Acts was written by an unknown author between the early sixties and the early second century using unknown sources does not advance the cause of interpretation very far. Some other tack must be taken.

The approach in this volume is to ask how ancient Mediterranean auditors would have heard Acts when it was read in their presence. This approach must be divided into two parts: (1) how Acts would have been heard in its precanonical context, and (2) how Acts would have been heard in its canonical context. We begin with the former question.

To have heard Acts read in its precanonical context would have involved hearing Acts as volume two of a narrative of which the Third Gospel was volume one. Justin Martyr, *1 Apology* 50.12, clearly knew the two volumes as parts of one whole. Modern scholars, for the most part, also regard Luke and Acts as parts of one whole: Luke-Acts. Several lines of evidence have supported this conclusion. (1) The prefaces of Luke (1:1-4) and Acts (1:1-2) present a strong case for unity. Josephus, *Against Apion*, offers an apt analogy. This work consists of two books, each beginning with a preface involving a dedication. *Against Apion* 1.1 §§ 1-5 runs,

> I suppose that, by my books of the Antiquities of the Jews, most excellent Epaphroditus, I have made it evident . . . that our Jewish nation is of very great antiquity. . . . However, since I observe a considerable number of people giving ear to the reproaches that are laid against us by those who bear ill will to us. . . . I therefore have thought myself under an obligation to write somewhat briefly about these subjects . . . to instruct all those who are desirous of knowing the truth. . . .

Book two begins with a secondary preface (2.1 §§ 1-7). It reads,

> In the former book, most honored Epaphroditus, I have demonstrated our antiquity, and confirmed the truth of what I have said. . . . I have also made a refutation of . . . our enemies. I shall now therefore begin a confutation of the remaining authors. . . .

The similarities to the prefaces of Luke and Acts are striking and argue that the two Lukan books are, likewise, parts of one whole.

(2) The architecture of Luke-Acts argues for its unity. Just as Cedric H. Whitman's *Homer and the Heroic Tradition* countered successfully the claims that the works of Homer were not a unity by discerning the formal patterns or architectonic designs that control the arrangement of the material in its larger units, so the delineation of the architecture of Luke-Acts has argued for its unity (Talbert 1974).

(3) Likewise major efforts have been made to show the narrative unity of Luke-Acts from its plot (Tannehill) and its theological themes (Korn). Both approaches argue persuasively that each book is vital to the interpretation of the other. Taken together, such arguments support Cadbury's designation of the Third Gospel and Acts as Luke-Acts. Any modern reading of Acts in its precanonical context must, like Justin, take the two volumes together as two parts of one story.

To have heard Luke-Acts read as a continuous whole would have been to hear it as a narrative of fulfillment. When, in Luke 1:1, the author says that he is composing a "narrative of the things that have been fulfilled (*peplērophorēmenōn*) among us," he gives a clue to the nature of the upcoming narrative. Luke-Acts is an account of the life of Jesus and the beginnings of the early church told as the fulfillment of prophecy (Talbert 1982, 234–40). What is being actualized in the various prophecies' fulfillment is the plan of God that stands behind the events narrated. The issue is: is the plan of God that lies behind the events of Luke's narrative the background against which the evangelist paints his portrait(s), or is it the foreground?

In antiquity it was widely believed that a divine necessity controlled human history, shaping the course of its events. Polybius, for example, believed a divine providence ruled the world. This belief he expounded in his *Histories*. Nevertheless, this was only the backdrop against which he pursued his dual purpose: (a) providing useful training and experience for the practical politician (e.g., 3.6.6ff.), and (b) teaching the reader how to bear the vicissitudes of Fortune by describing what had befallen others (e.g., 1.35–36; 2.35.5ff.). Moreover, Josephus, in his *Antiquities*, shares in this cultural belief, although as a Jew he would have viewed the divine necessity as deriving from the personal will of God, who is a living person and not a neutral necessity (e.g., 10.8.2–3 § 142). Nevertheless, this was but the background against which he pursued his aim: to legitimate the Jews by an appeal to their antiquity. So when one recognizes that the narrative of Luke-Acts is a working out of the divine plan, one must ask: what aim is the author pursuing against this background? The obvious answer is that in the Third Gospel it is Christology (explicitly stated in Acts 1:1); in the Acts, ecclesiology (Talbert 1988). Reading Luke-Acts in a precanonical context, then, means reading a unified narrative in which the plan of God functions as the background for all that takes place.

When one concentrates on the foreground of Luke-Acts, three matters come to mind. First, what is the plot of Luke and Acts? The plot of Luke is simply put: conceived, empowered, and guided by the Holy Spirit, Jesus both embodies the Way and makes provision for others to follow in it, thereby fulfilling the divine plan. Here the focus is on Jesus but against the background of the divine plan. The plot of Acts is equally straightforward: between the ascension and parousia, empowered by the Holy Spirit, the Messianists bear an unstoppable, universal witness to Jesus by word and deed, thereby fulfilling the divine plan. Here the focus is on the church but against the background of the divine plan.

Second, what is the picture of Jesus and the church in Luke and Acts? Actually there are two sides to the one picture. On the one hand, Jesus is the messianic king and the Messianists are his people. Prophecies promise that the child to be born will be given the throne of David and will reign over the house of Jacob (Luke 1:32; 1:69; 2:11; 2:26). Jesus' exodus (Luke 9:31) is regarded as his departure to receive his kingdom (Luke 19:12,15). This kingdom is a gift of his Father (22:29). It is received in connection with his exaltation (Acts 2:36). Those who acknowledge Jesus' messiahship (e.g., Acts 4:10; 17:3; 18:5) are the reconstituted tabernacle of David (Acts 15:16–17), his people. This much seems clear on a cursory reading.

On the other hand, what has not so often been recognized is that the church is depicted as a Jewish philosophical school and Jesus as its founder (Talbert 1974, 89–99; Mason 1993). (1) Jews were sometimes regarded by outsiders as a nation of philosophers: Aristotle (so Josephus, *Against Apion* 1.22 § 179) and Theophrastus (so Porphyry, *On Abstinence* 2.26). Ancient Judaism of the Diaspora often portrayed itself in philosophical terms: Aristobulus (so Eusebius, *Preparation for the Gospel* 13.12.1, 4, 8; 4 Macc 1:1; 5:4, 7, 23, 35; Philo, *Moses* 2.216; *On the Contemplative Life* 2, 16, 26). (a) Judaism is a philosophical culture (Josephus, *Antiquities* Preface 4 § 25), whose philosophy is contained in the Law (Josephus, *Against Apion* 2.4 § 47). (b) Moses is depicted as a philosopher–king in the Platonic sense (*Republic* 5.473D) by Philo, *Life of Moses* 2.2 (Sandmel, 48). (c) Moses is said to be the inventer of philosophy (Artapanus, so Eusebius, *Preparation for the Gospel* 9.27.4) and is the teacher and source of Greek philosophy (Aristobulus, so Eusebius, *Preparation for the Gospel* 13.12.1f.). Pythagoras, Socrates, and Plato with great care follow and copy him (Aristobulus, so Eusebius, *Preparation for the Gospel* 13.13.4).

(2) It should be no surprise, then, to find Josephus portraying Pharisees (*War* 2.8.13 § 162; *Life* 38 § 191; 39 § 197), Sadducees (*War* 2.8.13 § 164;

Antiquities 20.9.1 § 199), and Essenes (*War* 2.8.3 § 122; 2.8.7 § 137,142) as Jewish philosophical schools, as *haireseis* (*War* 2.8.2 § 119; 2.8.14 § 166; *Life* 2 § 10; *Antiquities* 13.6.9 §§ 171-72) (Mason 1991, 126-28; 1993, 1-28; 1995, 153-56). This can be seen from several strands of evidence. First, in *Antiquities* 18:1.2-5 §11-22, *philosophia* is substituted for *hairesis*. Josephus regards them as equivalents. Second, *hairesis* is a term used for Greek philosophical schools by Greek writers: for example, Polybius 5.93.8; Dionysius of Halicarnassus, *Composition* 2; Diogenes Laertius, *Lives of Eminent Philosophers* 1.19; 7.191. Third, Philo, in *On Noah's Work as a Planter* 151, uses *hairesis* for the Greek schools, while in his *Contemplative Life* 129, he uses it for the Jewish Therapeutae. Fourth, Josephus actually claims the *hairesis* of Essenes follows Pythagorean teachings (*Antiquities* 15.10.4 § 371), and Pharisees are like the Stoics (*Life* 2 § 12). Finally, in Josephus's description of these three groups, they are shown to be involved in a philosophical discussion about fate and free will (*War* 28.14 §§ 162-66; *Antiquities* 13.5.9 §§ 171-73; 18.1.2-6 §§ 11-25). Josephus describes Pharisees, Sadducees, and Essenes as Jewish philosophical schools akin to Greek schools of Stoics and Pythagoreans, for example.

(3) Some early Christians presented Christianity as the true philosophy: for example, in the second century Justin, *Dialogue* 1-8. Some pagans viewed Christianity as a philosophical school: for example, in the second century Galen, *On the Pulse* 2.4. It is often overlooked that in Acts not only are Pharisees (15:5; 26:5) and Sadducees (4:1) designated "schools" (*haireseis*) by the narrator but also Messianists are so designated by their Jewish counterparts (24:5, 14; 28:22). In Acts, establishment Jews designate Messianists as one Jewish philosophical school alongside others, namely, Pharisees and Sadducees.

(4) This verbal designation of early Messianists as a Jewish philosophical school is reinforced, on the one hand, by various philosophical echoes in the narrative of Acts. Three examples suffice. First, Acts 5:29 (cf. 4:19) has the apostles say, "We must obey God rather than men." This echoes Socrates' similar sentiment at his defense (Plato, *Apology* 29D–"I shall obey God rather than you, and while I have life and strength I shall never cease from the practice and teaching of philosophy"). The early apostles speak like Socrates, the philosophic ideal. Second, the portrait of Paul in Acts has been seen as echoing various components of the tradition about Socrates: for example, divine call (Plato, *Apology* 20e-22a); mission (Plato, *Apology* 23b); divine guidance (Xenophon, *Memorabilia* 1.2-5); tribulations (Seneca, *Epistle* 104.27-28); persecution (Diogenes Laertius 2.21); trial (Diogenes Laertius 2.20); prison (Epictetus 2.6.27); death (Seneca, *Epistle* 104.22) (Alexander, 58-63). Such echoes have been seen especially focused in the episode of Paul's visit to Athens in Acts 17 (Sandnes). Third,

Paul's defense before Agrippa in Acts 26:26 has been seen to echo numerous facets of philosophic argument: for example, madness due to great learning; the impossibility of sudden conversion (Malherbe). In Acts, then, the church is portrayed as a Jewish philosophical school.

The evidence of Acts is reinforced on the other hand by the Lukan prologue. Several terms in Luke 1:1-4 evoke philosophical echoes. (a) The term *paradidomi* ("deliver," 1:2) is a technical term for the passing on of tradition in the schools. (b) The word *asphaleia* ("certainty," 1:4) is a favorite one for the true philosophy: for example, Plutarch, *Superstition* 171E, uses *asphalōs* to characterize philosophy as distinct from superstition; Justin, *Dialogue* 8:1, says that his youthful quest for the true philosophy ended only when he found a philosophy that was secure (*asphalē*). (c) The term *plērophoreō* ("fulfill," 1:1) used in association with "certainty" is significant. Justin, *Dialogue* 1-8, in describing his conversion to Christianity as the true philosophy was so prompted by the fulfillment of prophecy. An ancient auditor would have heard echoes of the philosophical tradition in Luke 1:1-4. If so, then even if Jesus in the Third Gospel is not called a philosopher (but rather a prophet—e.g., Luke 4:24; 7:16; 7:39; 13:33; 24:19; cf. Acts 3:22-23; 7:37), he is inevitably seen as the founder of the Messianist school.

How do the two sides of the coin fit together? In Philo's thought about Moses, Moses is depicted both as prophet and as king. Both are allied with the notion of Moses as philosopher. In this kind of thought world, the two sides of the Lukan portrayal of Jesus and the church fit together nicely. Both aspects are necessary to say all that Luke wants to say about Jesus and his disciples.

(3) What is the nature of this narrative with this plot and with this depiction of Jesus and his followers? How would it have been heard by a late-first-century Mediterranean auditor? When reading Acts as volume one of Luke-Acts, an ancient auditor would have been aware that this is a succession narrative. The concept of succession was pervasive in Mediterranean antiquity. Rulers (Diodorus Siculus 17ff.), philosophers (Diogenes Laertius, *Lives of Eminent Philosophers*), jurists (Pomponius Sextus, *Enchiridium*), magi (Lucian, *Menippus*, says he resolved to go to Babylon and address himself to one of the Magi, the disciples and successors of Zoroaster), leaders of Israel (Josephus, *Antiquities* 4.7.2 § 165, says Moses appointed Joshua to succeed him), prophets (Eusebius, *Preparation for the Gospel* 9:30 citing Eupolemos; *Church History* 5.17.4; "Letter of Peter to James," in *Kerygmata Petrou* 1:2), rabbis (*m. Pirke Aboth* 1), bishops (Irenaeus, *Against Heresies* 3.3.3), leaders of catechetical schools (Eusebius, *Church History* 6.29.4), and Gnostics (the epistle of Ptolemy to Flora speaks of the apostolic

tradition that has come down in succession to the Gnostics) all were at times depicted in terms of the line of succession of which they were a part.

The concept sometimes found expression in succession narratives, which embodied it in a concrete way. (1) A succession narrative used for rulers is found in the first century B.C. in Diodorus Siculus 17ff. In Book 17 "all the acts of Alexander" the Great up to his death are narrated (17.1.5; 18.1.6); in Books 18ff., "all the acts of those who succeeded to his kingdom" are given (17.118.4; 18.1.6). This succession narrative is rightly called a history (17.1.5) (see Appendix B). (2) Succession narratives used for philosophers were numerous in Mediterranean antiquity. Some are known only from citations and fragments; others are extant in significant parts or the whole.

Three types of succession narratives of philosophers may be mentioned. (a) The successions of multiple schools: From the first and second centuries B.C. we know of Sotion, Heraclides, Sosicrates, Alexander, Iason, Antisthenes, and Nicias who wrote such works. This type of succession narrative is found in the third century A.D. in Diogenes Laertius, *Lives of Eminent Philosophers* (Mejer, 62–63). At least in its developed form found in Diogenes Laertius, this type belongs to biography. (b) The succession of one school: From the period before Plutarch, we know of Phaenias of Erestus, *On the Socratics*; Idomeneus of Lampsacus, *On the Socratics*; Sphaerus of Borysthenes, *On the Eretrian Philosophers*; Straticles, *On Stoics* (Mejer, 74–75). From the first century B.C., Papyrus Herculaneum 1018 traces the succession of the Stoic school, pausing at four points to add anecdotes about various individuals in the line of succession (Camparetti; Traversa); Papyrus Herculaneum 1021 offers the succession of the Academics; and Herculaneum Papyri 1232, 1289, 1418, 176 give the succession of the Epicureans.[1] Plutarch produced *On the First Philosophers and Their Successors* and *On the Cyrenaics*. After Plutarch, Galen wrote *On Plato's Sect* and *On the Hedonistic Sect* (= Epicureans). These writings are rightly regarded as *bioi* ("lives," Scott). (c) The life of a founder that includes a list or a brief narrative of his successors and other disciples: From pre-Christian times we know of Aristoxenos's *Life of Pythagoras,* which contained a biography of Pythagoras and a history of the Pythagoreans in chronological order,[2] and Andronicus's *Life of Aristotle,* which contained a reference to Aristotle's successor and/or disciples.[3] From the third and fourth centuries A.D. we know of Ptolemy's *Life of Aristotle* with its notice of succession, and we possess Iamblichus's *Life of Pythagoras,* in which section 36 is a list of successors with the occasional anecdote thrown in plus a list of Pythagoreans generally, and the anonymous Christian *Life of Pachomius* with an expanded succession narrative dealing with two of Pachomius's successors following the biography of the founder of communal monasticism.

Diogenes Laertius's *Lives of Eminent Philosophers* also contains biographies of Socrates, Aristippus, Phaedo, Euclides, Zeno, and Epicurus that conform to this pattern. In the lives of Aristippus, Zeno, and Epicurus a succession list is expanded into a brief narrative with anecdotes about the successors.[4]

Certain recurring terminology is associated with the concept of succession in antiquity. (a) When speaking of one person's passing something on, the terms are normally *apoleipō* ("leave to"; e.g., Diodorus Siculus 18.1.4), *kathistēmi* ("to appoint"; e.g., Josephus, *Antiquities* 4.7.2 § 165); and *diatithēmi* ("bequeath"; e.g., Josephus, *Antiquities* 13.16.1 § 407). (b) When speaking of another person's receiving what is passed on, the terms are usually *paralambanō* ("receive"; e.g., PHerc 1018, col. 10 and col. 48) and *diadechomai* ("succeed to"; e.g., Diodorus Siculus 18.1.6; Eusebius, *Church History* 6.29.4). (c) When speaking of the status of the person in the succession, such terms as *diadochoi* ("successors"; e.g., PHerc 1018, col. 53; Josephus, *Antiquities* 4.7.2 § 165) and *mathētai* ("disciples"; e.g., PHerc 1018, col. 12 [*hypo*/"under"] and col. 17 [*tou*/"of"]) are employed. In succession of rule what is passed on is "kingdom/rule" (*basileia*); in philosophical succession it is the school (*scholia*) or way of life (*hodos*, *bios*, or *mathētēs*) that is passed on.

Luke-Acts is a document that resembles some of the succession narratives. (1) Like them it employs some of the succession terminology. (a) The followers of Jesus are called *mathētai*/"disciples" both during Jesus' earthly ministry (e.g., Luke 5:30; 6:1, 13, 17, 20; 7:11; 8:9, 22; 9:14, 16, 18, 40, 43, 54; 10:23; 11:1; 12:1, 22; 14:26, 27, 33; 16:1; 17:1, 22; 18:15; 19:29, 37, 39; 20:45; 22:11, 39, 45) when they are with Jesus (Luke 7:11; 9:18; cf. 9:49; 14:27; 22:39) and after Jesus' departure (Acts 6:1, 2, 7; 9:1, 10, 19, 25, 26, 38; 11:26, 29; 13:52; 14:20, 22, 28; 15:10; 16:1; 18:23, 27; 19:9, 30; 20:1, 30; 21:4, 16) when they walk the Way of Jesus. (2) In Luke 22:28–30 we encounter the term *diatithēmi*. The logion is usually thought to be a Q saying (//Matt 19:28). The Matthean version of the saying is clearly eschatological.

> You . . . in the new age, when the Son of Man is seated on his throne of glory, will yourselves sit on twelve thrones, judging the twelve tribes of Israel.

The reference is to the role of judgment given to the saints at the last judgment (cf. 1 Cor 6:2). This has predisposed readers to take the Lukan version in the same way.

> I bequeath (*diatithēmai*) to you, as my Father bequeathed to me, a kingdom/rule, that you may eat and drink at my table in my kingdom/rule, and sit on thrones judging the twelve tribes of Israel.

This has been taken to refer to the new world, the messianic banquet, and the role of the apostles in eschatological judgment. It should not be read in this way.

A right reading requires that three expressions be clarified. (a) In Luke-Acts, what is Jesus' rule/kingdom? Acts 2:34-36 indicates that it is his session at God's right hand (cf. Luke 22:69; 1 Cor 15:20-28). (b) What does it mean to eat at the king's table? The expression comes from the Jewish scriptures (e.g., 1 Sam 20:29b; 2 Sam 9:7, 9, 11 = "ate at the king's table like one of the king's sons"; 2 Sam 19:28; 1 Kings 2:7; 4:27; 18:19). It means to be accorded a place of honor within the king's house such as the king's sons have. (c) What does it mean to judge the tribes of Israel? Again the expression comes from the Jewish scriptures (e.g., Exod 2:14, "a prince and a judge over us"; 18:22, "let them judge the people at all times"; 2 Sam 15:4, "Absalom said: 'Oh that I were judge in the land! Then every man with a suit or cause might come to me, and I would give him justice'"; Mic 7:3, "the prince and the judge ask for a bribe"). It refers to functionaries in Israel who rendered decisions about what was right. Sometimes such judges were also princes, king's sons.

Taking these three expressions together yields a reading that sees Luke 22:29-30 as referring to the apostles' role in Jesus' reign from his exaltation to his parousia. It is one of honor. They are as sons of the king in that they eat at his table and function as decision makers among the people. The apostles are not seen as successors, as in the later apostolic succession of the Old Catholic Church (that is, late second to early third century). They rather rule, as judges did in ancient Israel, within and under the reign of Christ (Jervell, 75-112; Nolland, 3.1067).

This seems to describe the role of the apostles in Acts. Take, for example, the centrality of Jerusalem in the missionary enterprise in Acts (1:4,8; 8:14-15; 11:1-2; 11:22; 15:2). This includes the Jerusalem frame of reference for Paul's entire ministry in Acts (9:27-29; 11:25-26; 13:1-13; 15:2; 16:5; 18:22; 21:17). Jerusalem control of missions in Acts is closely tied to the fact that, for Luke, Jerusalem is the place where the twelve apostles reside (8:1; 9:28; 11:1-2; 15:2,4; 16:4). The twelve apostles in Acts function as appointed people of honor who make key decisions within the early church under the reign of Christ. If this reading is accepted, then the Lukan writings employ a second key technical term used for succession in antiquity. It is terminology that views the apostles' succession from the point of view of the one who gives it, Christ.

(2) Luke-Acts is also like certain of these succession narratives in its overall pattern and presentation. (a) Pattern—The Third Gospel gives an account of the founder of the community while Acts offers a narrative about Jesus' successors. This pattern, insofar as the Third Gospel is concerned, corresponds most closely to that of the six lives in Diogenes Laertius mentioned

above, to that of Iamblichus's *Life of Pythagoras*, to that of the anonymous *Life of Pachomius*, to that of the first-century B.C. *Life of Aristotle* and the fourth-century B.C. *Life of Pythagoras*. Insofar as Acts is concerned, the correspondences are closest to the succession narratives within lives of founders and the successions of single philosophical schools where a rather extensive list and narrative of subsequent disciples is found. The Gospel of Luke has the fullness of treatment found in the lives of founders that were followed by a brief succession note. Acts has the inclusiveness of the narratives of the succession within lives of founders and narratives of the succession of a single school. The pattern of Luke-Acts looks like a synthesis of two different types of succession narratives: lives of founders that contain a succession narrative and narratives of the succession of a single school.

(b) Presentation—The presentation of the two components, life of the founder and list or narrative of successors, is similar as well. In the non-Christian biographies mentioned, the life of the founder is presented with some fullness, even if not with the full, rounded character of a modern biography. These biographies, however, do not extend to the list or brief narrative about successors anything like the same fullness accorded to the founder. The second component can be said to be biographical only because it is part of a larger whole that is deemed biographical because of its treatment of the founder's life. Even in the successions of individual schools, the narrative of disciples does not possess the fully developed treatment of character that is found in the longer lives of founders. This presentation corresponds to what one encounters in Luke-Acts. Jesus' life is set forth in the Third Gospel with some fullness. In Acts, however, Luke "does not describe the personality, the individual features, the appearance, virtues, or even the death of his characters" (Conzelmann, xli).[5] Like the biographies of founders that are followed by a list or narrative of successors and the successions of single schools, Luke-Acts makes no attempt to provide full biographical data for Jesus' successors. The succession data is considered biographical because it falls within the life of the founder as one characteristic of his distinctiveness.

There are some differences between Luke-Acts and the philosophical biographies that seem closest to the two-volume Christian work. (1) The most noticeable difference is that of scale. Acts, the Lukan narrative about successors, is much longer than the mere lists and the brief narratives of the philosophical lives of founders and successions of single schools. It is more developed even than the extensive succession narrative in the Christian *Life of Pachomius*. (a) Scale, however, is not a determinant of genre. Among the biographical writings of antiquity one finds the briefest of accounts (e.g., the "Life of Socrates" in Diogenes Laertius; the *Lives of the Prophets*) and long, leisurely narratives (e.g., the "Life of Epicurus" in Diogenes Laertius; Philostratus, *Life of Apollonius of Tyana*) both described as *bioi* ("lives").

Likewise, Paul's writings are called "letters" even though they are usually much longer than the brief papyrus letters of antiquity to which they are often compared. Scale speaks not to the issue of genre but to that of authorial creativity. (b) If Luke is writing a succession narrative like that of the biographies mentioned above, the difference in scale in his second component argues for his remarkable creativity. We know that the author is one who can write in ways that are appropriate for whatever character and setting he is describing. In this regard he is the equal of the best of his time. The similarities between Luke-Acts and the ancient biographies of founders followed by their successors and the successions of single schools (vocabulary, pattern, presentation) would enable the auditors to recognize it as a succession narrative, and the scale of the expanded second component would bespeak the author's creativity and call for careful attention as to why the change was made.

(2) Although the pattern and presentation in Luke-Acts point to analogies with the biographies of founders of communities and their successors and the successions of single schools, the vocabulary points to a synthesis of royal and philosophical succession: a succession both of apostolic rule (*diatithēmi* + kingdom) and of a messianist way of life (*mathētai* + name of the master).

(a) The succession of a way of life is reflected in the correspondences between Jesus' career in Luke and the disciples' mission in Acts. The following examples are illustrative, not exhaustive (Talbert 1974, 15–23).

Luke		*Acts*	
3:21	Jesus is praying after his baptism.	1:14,24	The disciples are praying as they await their baptism with the Spirit.
3:22	The Spirit descends on Jesus after prayer.	2:1–13	The Spirit fills them after their prayers.
4:16–30	Jesus' ministry begins with a sermon involving fulfillment of scripture and rejection of Jesus	2:14–40	The church's ministry begins with a sermon involving fulfillment of scripture and rejection of Jesus.
4:31–8:56		2:41–12:17	
	The fulfillment is illustrated by preaching and healing. Conflicts illustrate rejection.		The fulfillment is illustrated by prophecy and wonders. Persecutions illustrate unbelief.
10:1–12	The mission of the 70, which foreshadows the	chaps. 13–20	The missionary journeys

	Gentile mission of the church.	of Paul to the Gentiles.
9:51–19:28		19:21–21:17
	Jesus makes a journey to Jerusalem, which is a passion journey under divine necessity, and is not understood by the disciples.	Paul makes a last journey to Jerusalem, which is a passion journey, under divine necessity, and is not understood by Paul's friends.
19:37	Jesus receives a good reception, and people praise God for what they have seen.	21:17–20 Paul receives a good reception, and God is glorified for the things done among the Gentiles.
19:45–48	Jesus goes into the temple with a positive attitude to it.	21:26 Paul goes into the temple with a friendly attitude toward it.
22:54	A mob seizes Jesus.	21:30 A mob seizes Paul.
22:26; 23:1; 23:8; 23:13	The four trials of Jesus (Sanhedrin, Pilate, Herod Antipas, Pilate)	chaps. 23, 24, 25, 26 The four trials of Paul (Sanhedrin, Felix, Festus, Herod Agrippa)
23:16,22	Pilate says he will release (*apolysō*) him.	26:32 Agrippa says: "This man could have been released" (*apolelysthai*).
chap. 24	Jesus' ministry ends on the note of the fulfillment of scripture.	chap. 28 Paul's ministry ends on the note of the fulfillment of scripture.

These correspondences suggest that the Way opened up by Jesus in the Third Gospel and taught to his pre-Easter disciples continues in the Way of his successors or disciples after Easter. This succession of a way of life is wider than and continues beyond the Twelve. All of Jesus' disciples participate in it.

(b) The succession of apostolic rule is reflected in the centrality of Jerusalem and the Twelve in the missionary enterprise in Acts (see above). This succession is limited to and ends with the Twelve. No succession vocabulary links the Twelve to anyone after them in Acts. That the evangelist produced a narrative that utilizes a synthesis of a succession of rule with a succession of a way of life is yet another evidence of his creativity. There are enough similarities between Luke-Acts and other Mediterranean succession narratives to furnish the auditors adequate clues about the type of literature to which they were listening. There are enough differences to cause auditors to listen carefully to discern the distinctives and to ask why they might exist.

To read Luke-Acts in its precanonical context finally involves regarding it as a narrative theology. Traditional redaction criticism took its cue from the study of the Pauline letters. Just as a Pauline letter can be properly understood only if one can specify the particular problem(s) in the church that evoked its writing, so, it was assumed, grasping a Gospel's (or Acts') meaning is contingent on one's being able to determine the specific problem(s) in the community from which it comes and to which it is written as a response. The Gospels and Acts are occasional literature best interpreted as arguments addressed to specific pressing problems in the immediate community at the time of writing.

Foundation documents like the canonical Gospels and Acts, however, seem more analogous to systematic theology, albeit in narrative form, than to occasional writings like the Pauline epistles. That is, they attempt to set forth the Christian position not only in light of problems present and pressing, but also real but past, and real but potential. Such narrative theology tells the story of the community's founder (in the Gospels) and of the early church (in Acts) in a way that expresses the values of the group in a balanced way, not just in response to one or more immediate issues that clamor for attention in the community's present. Luke-Acts offers a balanced presentation of the Christian position in narrative form. In that sense it is narrative theology (Talbert 1992, 229–30).

An ancient auditor in the precanonical period would have taken Acts to be volume two of Luke-Acts, would have heard its story against the background of the plan of God's fulfillment in the events of the narrative, would have regarded it as a succession narrative giving the biography of the founder of the Messianist movement and an account of the founder's followers, and would have read the narrative as a theological, not an occasional, document. Given all this, Acts must be read in light of Luke, and vice versa.

How would an ancient auditor have heard Acts when it was read in its canonical context—that is, separated from Luke and set between the Gospels and the Epistles. (1) How would Acts have been regarded in terms of its literary context in Mediterranean antiquity? It is unlikely that it would have been regarded as a historical monograph. "The history of an incipient religious movement is an unprecedented subject for an ancient monograph" (Palmer, 29).[6] It is moreover unlikely that it would have been regarded as a romance. The presupposition is that Acts narrates truthful history. What then? *Bios* ("biography") was written of peoples as well as individuals. Dikaiarchus in the fourth century B.C. wrote *Bios Hellados*, a life of Greek culture from the Golden Age to his own time, as well as *bioi* of individuals like Plato and other philosophers (Vogel 2.241). In the same century, Aristoxenos wrote a *bios* of the Pythagoreans (Wehrli, 2.15–17). Varro, in the first century B.C., wrote *De vita populi Romani*, a social treatment of the Roman people. A biography of a people or a group, like that of an individual, looked for the essence or individuality of the subject. Acts, taken alone, would naturally have been regarded as a *bios* of a people, the church, analogous to such *bioi* of Dikaiarchus (Burridge 246), Aristoxenos, and Varro and with similarities to the successions of individual schools such as one finds among the Herculaneum papyri (see Appendix B). Acts would have been heard to describe the character or essence of Jesus' disciples as a distinctive people after the resurrection/ascension. They are therein depicted as the people empowered by the Holy Spirit to give unstoppable, universal witness to Jesus, in spite of every conceivable obstacle, while they wait for his return. From first (Acts 1:8–11) to last (28:30–31), this would seem to describe the character of the people called Christians as they are portrayed in the Acts of the Apostles. To see Acts as a *bios* of a people, moreover, would fit neatly with the view of Christians as a third race (e.g., Tertullian, *To the Nations* 1.8; 1.20; *Scorpiace* 10; preaching of Peter [so Clement of Alexandria, *Miscellanies* 6.5.39–41]–"We are the third race of humanity"). What is the distinctive character of Jesus' community? The church is mission!

(2) How would Acts have been regarded in terms of its relation to the First Testament? The Hebrew Bible has often been thought to have formed the model for the shaping of the New Testament. We have Tertullian's statement, for example, that the Roman church "associates the Law and the Prophets with the evangelical and apostolic books" (*On the Prescription of Heretics* 36). In such a scheme, the former prophets would serve as the model for Acts. Just as Joshua, Judges, Samuel, and Kings serve as a sketch of the history of Israel during the period when much of what is found in the latter prophets is being preached, so Acts offers a sketch of much of the history of the early church during which time the preaching and teaching found in the epistolary writings of the New Testament were being promulgated. If the Law and the Gospels correspond, and if the latter prophets and the apostolic writings serve similar functions, then the former prophets and Acts perform similar functions in their respective testaments. Acts serves as a narrative setting for the apostolic writings that follow.

(3) How would Acts have been heard in terms of its relation to the Second Testament? (a) Explicitly, Acts with its portrayal of the correspondences between Peter and the Jewish Christians on the one hand and Paul

on the other would function as a theological guide for reading the apostolic writings that follow. The following chart is suggestive of the loose correspondences (Talbert 1974, 23-26).

Peter/Jewish Christians	*Paul/Pauline Christianity*
2:1-4 A special manifestation of the Spirit.	13:1-3 A special manifestation of the Spirit.
2:14-40 Apostolic preaching results from the Spirit.	13:16-40 Apostolic preaching results from the Spirit.
3:1-10 A mighty work follows. A lame man is healed.	14:8-13 A mighty work follows. A lame man is healed.
3:12-26 The healing of the lame man is followed by a speech beginning, "Men, . . . why?"	14:15-17 The healing of the lame man is followed by a speech that begins, "Men, . . . why?"
6:8-8:4 Stephen is stoned to death at the instigation of Diaspora Jews after a speech. The result is the preaching in a widening context.	14:19-23 Paul is stoned at the instigation of Jews from Antioch and Iconium after a speech so he is thought dead. The result is more preaching in a wider context.
chaps. 10-11 Peter has a mission to Gentiles. Divine guidance leads Peter in a direction other than that planned by him. In 10:9-16 the Spirit guides him through a vision. He then has to justify his actions in Jerusalem.	chaps. 13-21 Paul has a mission to Gentiles. Divine guidance leads Paul in a direction different from that planned by him. In 16:6-10 Paul is led by a vision to Macedonia. He then has to justify his actions in Jerusalem.
chap. 12 The first half of Acts ends with the imprisonment of Peter (12:4) at a Jewish feast (12:4). The jailing of Peter is associated with a Herod (12:5-6), involves	chaps. 21-28 The second half of Acts ends with the jailing of Paul at a Jewish feast (21:16). The jailing has a loose relation to a Herod (25:13, 23-24), involves

escape from the hands of the Jews (12:3-4, 6-11), and concludes with no information about the fate of Peter (12:17) but only the success of the word of God (12:24).	escape from death at the hands of Jews (23:12-35), and concludes with no information about the fate of Paul (28:30-31) but only the success of the word of God (28:30-31).

The overall impression gained from such correspondences is the unity of Jewish and Pauline Christianity.

In the context of the Marcionite attempt to dismiss Jewish-Christian apostles because only Paul was regarded as a true apostle of Christ, such a pattern would have meaning. The Muratorian Canon indicates how Acts was used in such a context. It reads as follows: "Moreover the Acts of *all* the Apostles are included in one book." At the end of the second century, Acts functioned, over against Marcion, to keep Pauline and non-Pauline epistolary components together in the New Testament canon by emphasizing *all* the apostles who were in harmony with one another.

(b) Implicitly, the narrative of Acts with its correspondences between the Jewish and Pauline Christians would function as a legitimation device for the truth of Christianity. In Mediterranean antiquity one argument for or against a particular religion or philosophy had to do with whether or not the position contained contradictions. When Josephus defended the Jews against pagan attacks in his *Against Apion*, for example, one argument he used to legitimate the Jewish religion was that Jews everywhere agreed about religion and ethics. In Judaism there were no contradictions on such matters (*Against Apion* 2.20 §§ 179-81), such as, of course, one found among pagan teachers.

Because of the precanonical unity of Luke and Acts, Acts must be read in light of Luke. Because of their separation within the New Testament canon, Acts must be read separately from the Third Gospel. It is in the interplay between these two types of reading that the richest yields are harvested.

One final question before the reading begins. Acts comes to us in two very different types of text. Which text type of Acts will be read, the B text (= the Alexandrian text epitomized by Codices Vaticanus and Sinaiticus) or the D text (= the Western text epitomized by Codex Bezae)? The options are basically four: (a) The B text is original, and the D text is a paraphrase; (b) D is original and B is an abbreviator; (c) Luke issued his work in two forms, so both are normative; (d) B was original, was translated into Aramaic by Jewish Christians, then back into Greek as D. Of these four options it is the first that has the most to commend it. In this commentary, therefore, we will be reading basically the B text. This is essentially the text found in the latest editions of Nestle and the United Bible Societies (UBS).

Notes

1. PHerc 1018 is in neither the Oxford nor the Naples facsimiles; PHerc 1021 is found in vol. 4 of the Oxford facsimiles; PHerc 1232, 1289, and 1418 are found in vol. 5 of the Oxford facsimiles; PHerc 176 is in vol. 1. The basic question about these papyri is whether or not they were first written as successions of single schools and then later joined into a connected whole or were a part of a connected whole from the first.

2. Aristoxenos, a pupil of Aristotle most famous for his works on music, also wrote a life of Pythagoras (Wehrli, 2.10-15, frags. 11-25), a life of Archytas (Wehrli, 2.22-24, frags. 47-50), a life of Socrates (Wehrli, 2.24-27, frags. 51-60; Vogel, 2.246), and a life of Plato (Wehrli, 2.27-28, frags. 61-68; Vogel, 2.247). Scholars have concluded that his biography of Pythagoras consisted of the life of Pythagoras and a narrative about his followers (Fritz, 22 n. 35). This conclusion is consistent with the evidence of the fragments.

3. Ingemar Düring collects the corpus of biographies of Aristotle from Medieval times written in Latin, Greek, and Arabic. He concludes they all derived from a fourth-century biography by Ptolemy (469-70, 475). Certain of these contain a section on the succession. Arnaldo Momigliano (86-87) contends the *Vita Marciana* of Aristotle (one of Düring's collection with a succession note) is likely to represent the substance of the biography Andronicus wrote about 70 B.C. to introduce his epoch-making edition of Aristotle.

4. One needs a context for understanding the meaning of a situation in which there are only two known pre-Christian biographies of founders of philosophical schools with succession data included and several such lives from the third and fourth centuries A.D. An analogy might be the existence of two late biographies in the form of a dialogue: Palladius's *Dialogue on the Life of Chrysostom* (A.D. 408) and Sulpicius Severus's *Dialogue on the Life of St. Martin* (A.D. 397). There is only one such pre-Christian biography: Satyrus's *Life of Euripides* from the third century B.C. (POxy 1176; Hunt, 124-82; Arrighetti, 1-168). Were the fourth- and fifth-century A.D. writers modeling their works after Satyrus, or is Satyrus merely the only extant example of a form of biography whose many examples are now lost?

5. Although Hans Conzelmann intended this comment to exclude Acts from the biographical genre, it actually proves the similarity of Acts to the succession narratives which offer the most apt analogies to Luke-Acts.

6. Palmer contradicts the evidence by then asserting that Acts is a historical monograph.

RECEIVING AND PREPARING FOR MISSION

Acts 1

Watching and Waiting (Acts 1:1–14)

This introductory section of Acts consists of two components: vv. 1–2 and vv. 3–14. The first component, 1:1–2, is a secondary preface (see Luke 1:1–4 for the primary preface). Prefaces for sequential books in the writings of Mediterranean antiquity are of three types: (1) a retrospective summary of the preceding volume(s) and a prospective summary of the current book (e.g., Philo, *Life of Moses* 2.1; Polybius 4.1.1–4; Josephus, *Against Apion* 2.1 §§ 1–2); (2) a retrospective summary only (e.g., Xenophon, *Anabasis* 2.1.1; 3.1.1; 4.1.1–4; 5.1.1; 7.1.1; Diodorus Siculus 2.1; 3.1; Josephus, *Antiquities* 8.1 § 1; 13.1 § 1; Herodian, *History of the Empire* 3.1.1; 4.1.1; 5.1.1; 6.1.1; 7.1.1; 8.1.1); and (3) a prospective summary only (e.g., Polybius 1.3.1–2). Acts 1:1–2 is a secondary preface of type 2, where books in sequence begin with summaries of what has happened before but not of what lies ahead. That it is so brief reflects its author's conformity to the aesthetic judgment, reflected by people like Lucian of Samosata, that prefaces should be short and not pretentious (*On How To Write History* 55).

Verse 1 summarizes the contents of the first book (= the Third Gospel). It dealt with what Jesus began to do and teach. Verse 2 has two functions: (1) it designates the ascension as the marker of the end of what Jesus began to do and teach (Luke 24:51), and (2) it says the ascension happened only after Jesus had given commandment to the apostles whom he had chosen (Luke 24:46–49).

Acts 1:3–8 may be read as a development of (2), Jesus' postresurrection, pre-ascension instruction of the disciples. Acts 1:9–11 as an explication of (1), Jesus' ascension. As such, Acts 1:3–11 is a recapitulation, with variation, of the events of Luke 24 referred to in the secondary preface of Acts

19

1:1-2. In Luke 24, the instruction and the ascension function to close the time of Jesus' earthly ministry; in Acts 1, they function to lay the foundation for the ministry of the church that is about to begin. These differing functions account for the different slants of Luke 24 and Acts 1.

Acts 1:3-14 may be read with either of two foci: Christology or discipleship. How? Theology done via narrative is by its very nature unable to make its multiple points simultaneously by means of systematic theology's "on the one hand, on the other." Instead, narrative subtleties are communicated by rhetorical techniques that serve as catalysts for the same narrative's being read first one way and then another. With each reading, a different slant is seen. Such techniques are found in both Greco-Roman and Jewish materials. For example, Vergil in his *Aeneid*, as well as in his *Georgics*, uses double and triple structure (e.g., Duckworth, 1-19). The same is true for Horace (e.g., Carrubba, 68-75). The same type of phenomena have also been seen in certain Israelite and Jewish practices, biblical (e.g., Porten, 93-128) and postbiblical (e.g., Thiering, 189-209). To read a text in terms of multiple patterns yields multiple points. In 1:3-14 the reader meets a first example of this practice in Acts.

One way Acts 1:3-14 can be read is from the angle of vision derived from its *Gattung* (=its conventional form of communication). When this is done, the narrative focuses on something said about Jesus (Christology). The same text can also be read from the angle of vision derived from its surface structure (=how it is organized). When this is done, the narrative focus is on what is said to Jesus' disciples (discipleship). Seen in this light, Acts 1:3-14 has both Christological and discipleship foci. The reading that follows will take account of first the one and then the other.

When the narrative of Acts 1:3-14 is read from the point of view of its *Gattung*, the focus is Christological. The central event in Acts 1:3-14 is Jesus' ascension. The ascension is narrated here not as the soul's ascent in this life either in ecstasy (e.g., the so-called Mithras liturgy) or in a vision (e.g., *1 Enoch* 14—a dream vision; *1 Enoch* 39:3-44:1—a vision due to being carried off by whirlwinds; *1 Enoch* 71—a vision when his spirit ascended into the heavens; *T. Levi* 2:5-5:7—a dream vision; *2 Baruch* 52:7-53:12—a dream vision; *Testament of Abraham* 9:6-15:2—a vision when carried off by an angelic chariot). Nor is it narrated as the soul's ascent at death (e.g., *Testament of Job* 52:10—Job; *Testament of Abraham* 7:4, 8; 20:10, 12-15 [Recension A]—Abraham; Clement of Alexandria, *Stromateis* 6.132—Moses). Nor is it told as the ascension of God's messenger at the end of an appearance (e.g., Gen 17:22; 35:13; Tob 12:20-22; *Testament of Abraham* 4:4; *Jubilees* 32:20).

Rather the ascension in Acts 1:9-11 is told in a way most like the Mediterranean stories of a whole person's being carried off/transported at the end of his earthly existence from the human world to that of God/the gods. Such stories are found in both the Greco-Roman and the Jewish worlds. In the Greco-Roman world one hears about such assumptions in the traditions about Romulus (Dionysius of Halicarnassus 2.56.2; Ovid, *Metamorphoses* 14.806-50); Hercules (Diodorus Siculus 4.38.4-5; Apollororus of Athens, *Bibliotheca* 2.7.7); Aeneas (Dionysius of Halicarnassus 1.64.4-5); and Apollonius of Tyana (Philostratus, *Life of Apollonius* 8.30). In the Jewish world one hears about such assumptions in the traditions about Enoch (Gen 5:24; Sir 44:16; 49:14; Wis 4:10-11; *1 Enoch* 70; *2 Enoch* 67; *Jubilees* 4:23); Elijah (2 Kgs 2:1-8; Sir 48:9,12; 1 Macc 2:58; *1 Enoch* 93:8); Ezra (2 Esdras 14:9); Baruch (*2 Baruch* 76:2-5); and Moses (Josephus, *Antiquities* 4.8.47-48 §§ 325-26; *Assumption of Moses* 45-50; *Acts of Pilate* 16:7; Clement of Alexandria, *Miscellanies* 1.23) (Lohfink).

Compared with these stories of transport, Acts 1:9-11 is like that of Elijah in 2 Kings in that (a) Elijah's departure was witnessed by a disciple (2:10; cf. Acts 1:9); (b) the disciple received a double portion of his Spirit afterwards (2 Kgs 2:9, 15; cf. Acts 2); (c) the terminology for the assumption in 2 Kgs 2:9-11 is *analambanein* (cf. Acts 1:11). Acts 1:9-11 is like the account of Moses in Josephus in that Moses disappeared in a cloud (*Antiquities* 4.8.48 § 326; cf. Acts 1:9). Acts' assumption story is like that of Baruch in *2 Baruch* in that Baruch was taken up after forty days of instructing the people (*2 Baruch* 76:2-5; cf. Acts 1:3). The story of Jesus' ascension in Acts 1:9-11 is like that of Enoch's assumption in *2 Enoch* in that (a) it happens as Enoch talks with the people (*2 Enoch* 67:1; cf. Acts 1:9a); (b) it is associated with angels (*2 Enoch* 67:2; cf. Acts 1:10); (c) it tells of the people's return to their homes after the event (*2 Enoch* 67:3; cf. Acts 1:12); (d) it tells of worship that follows (*2 Enoch* 68; cf. Acts 1:12-14).

When Acts 1:3-14 is compared with ancient assumption stories, it is seen to possess most of their characteristics. The following chart is illustrative.

THE SETTING

1. People are present with whom a conversation has been going on (*2 Enoch* 67:1; cf. Acts 1:3,4,6,9a).
2. Sometimes such people are disciples (2 Kgs 2:9-11; cf. Acts 1:2).
3. The assumption occurs after forty days of instruction of the people (*2 Baruch* 76:2-5; cf. Acts 1:3).

THE ASSUMPTION

4. It is witnessed/seen (2 Kgs 2:9-11; Dio Cassius 56.46; cf. Acts 1:9).
5. It is described as an *analambanein* (2 Kgs 2:9-11; cf. Acts 1:11).
6. It involves a cloud (Josephus, *Antiquities* 4.8.48 § 326; Plutarch, *Romulus* 27; cf. Acts 1:9).

7. It is on a mountain (Josephus, *Antiquities* 4.8.48 §§ 325–26; cf. Acts 1:12).
8. It is associated with the presence of heavenly beings (*2 Enoch* 67:2; Ps.-Callisthenes, *Alexander Romance*; cf. Acts 1:10).

THE SEQUEL

9. Afterwards the people return home (*2 Enoch* 69; cf. Acts 1:12).
10. It is followed by the people's worship (*2 Enoch* 68; cf. Acts 1:12–14).
11. It is followed by the choice of a successor (*2 Enoch* 69; cf. Acts 1:15–26).
12. It is followed by the reception of the Spirit by witnesses of the assumption (2 Kgs 2:9, 15; cf. Deut 34:9; Acts 2).

From these correspondences it seems obvious that the ascension of Jesus in Acts 1 is described by means of the *Gattung* of a bodily assumption into heaven at the end of the hero's life. Acts 1:3–14 corresponds closely to this *Gattung*. When Acts 1:3–14 is read in terms of the *Gattung* of an assumption, its focus is obviously on Christology. The section says something about Jesus. What exactly does it say?

In order to clarify the distinctive Lukan depiction of Jesus' ascension in Acts 1, it is necessary to look more closely at the treatments of Jesus' ascension in early Christianity generally. Several questions focus the issues.

(1) How did early Christians generally see the ascension's relation to Jesus' resurrection? (a) Primitive Christianity regarded the ascension as part of the resurrection. The earliest Christians spoke of Jesus' being raised (cf. the pre-Pauline tradition in 1 Cor 15:3–5; Rom 4:25; 1:3–4). In a Palestinian Jewish context this would have meant three things: the ultimate victory over death, transference of the one raised to a heavenly dimension of reality, and, since he was the first, a special status for Jesus (cf. Rom 1:3–4; Phil 2:9–11). This understanding continued in some streams of later Jewish Christianity (e.g., *T. Benjamin* 9:3, 5; *Gospel of Peter*) (Ramsey, 135–44).

In other forms of early Christianity, however, these three dimensions of meaning of the one event are treated as three separate events on a time line: the resurrection of Jesus is understood as the ultimate victory over death (Eph 1:20; 1 Pet 1:21; Heb 13:20; Justin, *1 Apology* 31, 42); the ascension of Jesus is seen as a separate, subsequent event (Eph 1:20; 4:10; 1 Pet 3:22; Heb 4:14; 8:1; Justin, *1 Apology* 31, 42); and the exaltation of Jesus is viewed as still another event later in the sequence (Eph 1:20; 1 Pet 3:22; Heb 8:1; 10:12; Justin, *1 Apology* 42).

Among those Christians who regarded the ascension as an event separable from the resurrection, there is considerable variety of opinion. The heretic Cerinthus, as part of his docetic Christology, contended that the ascension took place *before* Jesus' resurrection (Irenaeus, *Against Heresies*

1.26.1). Others regarded the ascension as an event *after* the resurrection. In certain writings, no specific time interval between the two events is given (e.g., Col 3:1; Eph 1:20; 1 Tim 3:16; 1 Pet 3:21-22; Heb 13:20; 4:14; 8:1; Justin, *1 Apology* 42). In other documents the ascension is depicted as an event occurring later in the day on Easter (Luke 24:50-53; John 20:17-23 [7:38-39]; Mark 16:19; *Epistle of Barnabas* 15:9; Aristides, *Apology* 2:8; 15; *Testament of Adam* 3:8-11). In still other Christian sources there is a specified interval after Easter: forty days (Acts 1:3); many days (Acts 13:31); five hundred forty-five days (*Ascension of Isaiah* 9:16); five hundred fifty days (*Apocryphon Jacobi* 2:19-20); eighteen months (Valentinians—so Irenaeus, *Against Heresies* 1.1.5; 1.3.2; Ophites—so Irenaeus, *Against Heresies* 1.30.14); twelve years (*Kerygma Petrou*); eleven to twelve years (*Pistis Sophia* 1; *Book of Jeu*) (Lake, 5.16-22).

(2) Was the ascension regarded by early Christians generally as an observable event? There are two streams of thought in the early church regarding this matter. On the one hand, most sources make no reference to its being an observable event (Mark 16:19-20; Luke 24:50-53; John 20:17-26; 1 Tim 3:16; Eph 4:8-11; 1 Pet 3:21-22; Rev 12:1-6). On the other hand, some early Christians regarded the ascension as an observable phenomenon (Acts 1:9-11; Justin, *1 Apology* 21; 50:12; *Epistle of the Apostles* 51; *Ascension of Isaiah* 11:22-33; Tertullian, *Apology*, 21:23; *Gospel of Peter*).

(3) What was the location of the ascension? Most early Christian sources do not connect the ascension with any specific location. Others do. John 20:17-26 implies Jerusalem generally. Luke 24:50-51 says Bethany. Acts 1:12 implies the Mount of Olives. Of course, Luke 19:29 links Bethany and the Mount of Olives.

From what has been said so far, it is possible to describe the distinctive view of the ascension of Jesus in Acts 1:3-14. (a) In Acts the ascension is observable. This is part of the Lukan emphasis on the corporeality of Jesus in his death, burial (Luke 23:52, 55; 24:3, 23), resurrection (Luke 24:39, 43; Acts 1:4; 10:41), and ascension (Acts 1:9, 10). Theologically, that Jesus' resurrection and ascension are regarded as corporeal means that Christians' future salvation is also believed to be corporeal.

(b) The ascension happens after forty days of Jesus' instruction of his apostles. In Jewish writings reference to forty days/years is frequent (e.g., Gen 7:17—the flood lasted forty days; Exod 24:18 and 34:28—Moses was on Sinai forty days; Exod 16:35—Israel wandered in the wilderness forty years; 1 Kgs 19:8—Elijah wandered forty days; *4 Ezra* 14:23,36,42-45—Ezra dictated the destroyed scriptures for forty days; *2 Baruch* 76:1-5—Baruch was given forty days to instruct the people before his translation to heaven). The reference in *2 Baruch* 76 is closest to that in Acts 1. The forty days of instruction functions theologically in two ways. First, it insures that the apostles are fully instructed. They have been with Jesus during his public ministry (Acts 1:21), and they have now been further instructed during forty days after the resurrection. Nothing necessary is lacking in their knowledge for ministry. Second, it puts a limit on the period of legitimate postresurrection appearances and postresurrection teaching. Later Gnostic appeals to secret revelations from the resurrected Christ are thereby outside the pale.

(c) The ascension in Acts serves as the transition to the Lord's exaltation and heavenly session. As such it makes the heavenly rule possible (Acts 2:33a), as well as the gift of the Holy Spirit (Acts 2:33b) and the dispensation of forgiveness (Acts 5:31). In this way, the ascension is a means to the soteriological benefits that, in Lukan theology, flow from the exalted Lord. When Acts 1:3-14 is read in terms of the *Gattung* of assumption story, it tells one something about Jesus.

Having read the narrative of Acts 1:3-14 Christologically from the angle of vision provided by its *Gattung* (= a story of an assumption), it is now time to attempt a reading of the same material from the perspective of its surface structure and its focus on discipleship. Acts 1:3-14, when read as instruction to disciples, consists of an introductory summary (v. 3), two promises (vv. 4-8 and vv. 9-11) and an example of behavior that seeks to appropriate the promises (vv. 12-14). The two paragraphs that contain the two promises both contain the same three components. In outline form, the section looks like this.

v. 3   = an introductory summary about Jesus' teaching
vv. 4-8   = an example of Jesus' post-Easter instruction
           (a) the risen Jesus' word (vv. 4-5)
           (b) the disciples' query (v. 6)
           (c) the risen Jesus' response in two parts:
               reproof (v. 7)
               promise (v. 8)
vv. 9-11   = an example of angelic instruction
           (a) the risen Jesus' action (v. 9)
           (b) the disciples' behavior (v. 10a)
           (c) the angelic response in two parts:
               reproof (v. 11a)
               promise (v. 11b)
vv. 12-14 = an example of behavior seeking to appropriate the promises

The various components of this surface structure need explanation.

The introductory summary (v. 3) indicates that the disciples are fully instructed (during forty days). About what? Jesus spoke to them about the kingdom of God. (1) In Luke-Acts, kingdom of God is sometimes used for the future hope. It is synonymous with the Age to Come and is associated with the messianic banquet (Luke 13:28-29; 14:15). In this regard, it is like the kingdom of God in certain Jewish sources (*Testament of Moses* 10:1; *Sibylline Oracles* 3:46-48, 767; 4Q246; 4Q521; the *Kaddish* prayer ["May he establish his kingdom in your lifetime and in your days . . . speedily and at a near time"]). In this sense it is associated with the phrase "enter the kingdom of God" (Luke 18:17, 24, 25; Acts 14:22), with "fulfilled in the kingdom of God" (Luke 22:16), with "until the kingdom of God comes" (Luke 22:18), with "supposed the kingdom of God to appear immediately" (Luke 19:11), and with "kingdom of God is near" (Luke 21:31). Luke uses the coming of the kingdom of God interchangeably with the revelation of the Son of Man (Luke 17:20-21, 22-30), with the Son of Man's coming with power (Luke 21:27), and with "your redemption" (Luke 21:28). The kingdom's coming is a cosmic event observable to all (Luke 17:24). It comes upon all who dwell on the face of the whole earth (Luke 21:35).

(2) In other places in Luke-Acts, kingdom of God refers to a present reality. It is synonymous with the divine activity that overthrows the kingdom of evil and is associated with healing/exorcism (Luke 9:2; 10:9; 11:20; 17:21) and with Jesus generally (Acts 28:23). In this sense it goes with the phrase "receive the kingdom" (Luke 18:17). (3) In many places, it is impossible to tell whether a future or a present connotation is intended. All that is possible to infer is that kingdom of God means divine vindication (Luke 4:43; 8:1,10; 9:11; 11:2; 12:31; 23:51; Acts 1:3; 19:8; 20:25; 28:31). (4) There is, in addition, sometimes a use of the concept of the "kingdom of the Messiah": in some places, Jesus' rule from exaltation to parousia (Luke 1:33; 22:29-30; Acts 1:6); in other places, Jesus' parousia (Luke 23:42).

At no point in Luke-Acts is kingdom of God used of a transformed society within history created by human moral initiative. What the risen Jesus is speaking about with his disciples is the ideal state of affairs belonging to the ultimate future (redemption), God's kingly activity to establish such an ideal state of affairs, and the connection of both the ideal state of affairs and the divine activity that brings it with Jesus.

Verses 4-8 consist of three parts, the first of which is a word of the risen Jesus (vv. 4-5): "he charged them not to depart from Jerusalem, but to wait for the promise of the Father, which, he said, 'you heard from me, for John baptized with water, but before many days you shall be baptized with the Holy Spirit'"(cf. Luke 24:49). The promise of the Father is, of course, the Holy Spirit (cf. Isa 32:15; Joel 2:28-29). Immersion in the Holy Spirit is one image used by Acts' author to speak of the profound experience of God's presence the disciples have been promised (cf. 1 Cor 12:13). It is not the only one, however. The author of Acts uses various images when speaking about the experience of the Holy Spirit. When the experience is viewed from the angle of divine initiative, it is spoken of in terms of the Spirit's being given (5:32; 8:20; 10:45; 11:17; 15:8), being poured out (2:17-18; 2:33; 10:45), coming on persons (1:8; 19:6), falling on people (8:16; 10:44; 11:15). When viewed from the point of view of the person(s) experiencing the Spirit, it is spoken of in terms of receiving the Spirit (2:38; 8:15, 17, 19; 10:47; 19:2), being filled with the Spirit (4:31; 9:17; cf. 6:5; 11:24), and being baptized with the Spirit (1:5; 11:16). These various modes of expression are referring to the same experiential reality: for example, in the story of Cornelius five of the terms are clearly used interchangeably: give the Spirit (10:45; 11:17), pour out the Spirit (10:45), Spirit fell on (10:44; 11:15), receive the Spirit (10:47), and be baptized with the Spirit (11:16); in Acts, 2:4 (filled with the Spirit) fulfills 1:5 (be baptized with the Spirit). It is this experiential reality, spoken of in a variety of ways, that will enable the disciples' ministry. Until they are so empowered, as Jesus had been (Luke 3:21-22; 4:18-21), they are to wait in Jerusalem.

The second part of this small paragraph is the disciples' query (v. 6): "Lord, will you at this time restore the kingdom to Israel?" Restoration of the kingdom (= sovereignty) to Israel is something promised in the scriptures (Jer 23:1-8; Ezekiel 17; 34; Sir 36:1-17) and for which Jews regularly prayed in the Eighteen Benedictions. *Psalms of Solomon* 17 speaks of the Son of David who will shatter unrighteous rulers and destroy godless nations, who will gather together a holy people, and who will judge the tribes of the people and the nations. Roman writers like Tacitus (*History* 5.13) and Suetonius (*Vespasian* 5.6) attributed the outbreak of the war of A.D. 66-70 to such Jewish expectations of world domination by their nation under the Messiah (cf. Josephus, *War* 4.3 §§ 121-223). It is against the background of such hopes that the disciples' question is to be understood.

The third part of the paragraph is Jesus' response in two parts (vv. 7-8). First, there is reproof: "It is not for you to know the times or seasons which the Father has fixed by his own authority" (v. 7). The risen Christ continues the emphasis of his pre-Easter instruction (cf. Luke 17:20-37). In this regard, moreover, the Lukan Jesus speaks with the same sentiments as certain rabbis: "No one knows . . . when the kingdom of the house of David will be put back in its place, and when the evil kingdom will be wiped out" (*Mekilta* on Exod 16.32 [59b]). This reproof negates any attempt to calculate the time of the End. Apocalyptic speculation is ruled out for Jesus' disciples.

Second, there is a promise: "You shall receive power when the Holy Spirit has come upon you; and you shall be my witnesses in Jerusalem, and in all Judea and Samaria and to the end of the earth" (v. 8; cf. Luke 24:47-48). This is not a demand; it is a promise or prophecy! The promise has two parts: first, the disciples will be empowered by the Spirit (remember Luke 24:49;

Acts 1:4–5), and second, they will be witnesses far and wide because of their empowering (remember Luke 4:16–21; 5:1–11). Isaiah had spoken of God's desire that His people be a light to the nations (Isa 49:6). Now Jesus' disciples will fulfill that hope in their universal outreach (Luke 2:29–32; 3:6; 4:24–26, 27; 10:1; 17:11–19; 24:47). Their witness will start in Jerusalem but it will extend to the "end of the earth."

The expression "the end of the earth" has various meanings in the literature of the time: Babylon (Deut 28:49), Rome (*Psalms of Solomon* 18:15 [16]), Spain (Strabo, *Geography* 3.1.2, 8; 3.5.5; 2.5.14; 2.4.3), everywhere (1 Macc 3:9; Jer 16:19). Dio Chrysostom, *Oration* 13.9, tells how when he decided to consult the Delphic oracle about his mission in life, Apollo told him to keep on doing with all zeal the very thing in which he was engaged "until thou comest to the uttermost parts of the earth." In 13.10 Dio Chrysostom reflects: "Should I not follow his [Odysseus's] example if God so bade?" So he says, "I proceeded to roam everywhere." This seems to be the best of the alternatives in the reading of Acts 1:8. Jesus promises that the disciples will be witnesses everywhere, but only after they have been empowered by the Holy Spirit (Ellis, 123–32, offers a survey of the options).

It is with this promise or prophecy of the risen Christ that Acts begins. Although 1:8 does not give an exact outline of the book, it does give the theme for all that follows: the empowered witness of Jesus' disciples goes everywhere. In beginning this volume with such a prophecy that controls what follows, the author of Acts conforms to Mediterranean literary practice. For example, Xenophon of Ephesus, *An Ephesian Tale*, opens with an oracle (= prophecy of Apollo) that sets the stage for all that follows. The novel's plot unfolds as the fulfillment of the prophecy. The Acts of the Apostles reflects the same practice.

The second promise comes in the subsequent paragraph, 1:9–11. Like vv. 4–8, this little paragraph consists of three parts. First, there is the risen Jesus' action: "as they were looking on, he was lifted up, and a cloud took him out of their sight" (1:9; cf. Luke 24:51). Here the ascension is described as an assumption into heaven that can be witnessed by the natural eyes of the disciples. Second, there is the disciples' behavior: "they were gazing into heaven as he went" (v. 10a). Third, there is an angelic response (their white apparel identifies them as angels—cf. 2 Macc 11:8; Mark 16:5; John 20:12; Hermas, *Vision* 2.1; 3.5; *Similitude* 8.2.3) to the disciples' behavior in two parts. In the first place, there is reproof ("Men of Galilee, why do you stand looking into heaven?"—v. 10b). Then comes the promise ("This Jesus who was taken up from you into heaven will come in the same way as you saw him go into heaven"—v. 11). The reproof means that the disciples were manifesting a wistful, defeated quietism in the face of Jesus' absence. This is as inappropriate a stance for disciples as is an apocalyptic enthusiasm that attempts to calculate the time of the End. The promise is a word of assurance and encouragement. Just as the presence of God (= the cloud) has taken Jesus away, so the presence of God will return Jesus in victory (cf. Luke 21:27—"you will see the Son of Man coming in a cloud with power and great glory"; Mark 14:62b; 1 Thess 4:17; Dan 7:13). This is the basis of Christian confidence. The promise, moreover, is made not by one but by two angels, insuring its truthfulness (Deut 19:15; John 8:17).

Verses 12-14 set forth an example of behavior that seeks to appropriate the benefits promised in vv. 4-8 and vv. 9-11. The witnesses of the ascension return to Jerusalem from the Mount of Olives, which was opposite the city about half a mile's distance (Josephus, *Antiquities* 20.8.6 § 169; *m. Sotah* 5:3) and go to the upper room where they were staying. An upper room was sometimes spoken of, in antiquity, as a place of assembling (Acts 9:37, 39; 20:8), as here; sometimes as a place of prayer (Dan 6:10-11), as here; sometimes as a place of decision making (*m. Shabbat* 1:4), as in Acts 1:15-26, if indeed that event is to be understood as taking place in the upper room.

The site was early venerated by the presence of a small church, as Epiphanius tells us. He says that when Hadrian visited Jerusalem in the 130s,

> he found the temple of God trodden down and the whole city devastated save for a few houses and the church of God, which was small, where the disciples, when they had returned after the Savior had ascended from the Mount of Olives, went to the upper room. For there it had been built, that is, in the portion of Zion which escaped destruction, together with blocks of houses in the neighborhood of Zion. . . . (*Epiphanius' Treatise on Weights and Measures, the Syriac Version*, ed. Dean, 30)

With the shifting of the site of Zion, the location is no longer known.

The witnesses, the men of Galilee (v. 11) who gathered there, are named (v. 13—cf. Luke 6:14-16 for the same names, except for Judas Iscariot, but in a different order). Then we hear that the Eleven, together with the women (Luke 23:49,55), Mary the mother of Jesus (Luke 1:26-38; 2:1-7; 2:33-35; 2:48-51), and Jesus' brothers (Mark 6:3; John 7:3), "with one accord devoted themselves to prayer" (v. 14).

The exemplary behavior of those who are fully instructed is to pray. Prayer is the way to appropriate the promises. The reference to the united prayer of the disciples must be understood in light of the context, both the immediate context of Acts 1:3-14 and the larger context of Luke-Acts as a whole. The immediate context with its focus on the two illustrations of postresurrection instruction of the apostles enables us to see two dimensions of the import of the prayer. (1) The disciples are praying for the promise of the Father (vv. 4-5), the coming of the Holy Spirit, which will empower them for their witness (v. 8). In so doing they are acting in accordance with the words of the pre-Easter Jesus in Luke 11:9-13: "Ask, and it shall be given you . . . the heavenly Father (will) give the Holy Spirit to those who ask him!" (2) They are also praying for the coming of the Son of Man, "this Jesus, who . . . will come in the same way as you saw him go into heaven" (v. 11). In so doing they are acting in accord with the pre-Easter Jesus' words in Luke 18:1-8 where in the parable of the unjust judge he told them that "they ought always to pray and not to lose heart" (Luke 18:1) because God will "vindicate his elect, who cry to him day and night" (Luke 18:7a; cf. Rev 6:9-11).

The larger context of Jesus' instruction on prayer in the Third Gospel and the prayer scene in Acts 4:24-30 make probable yet a third dimension of their prayer. (3) They are, most likely, also probably praying for protection in the time of tribulation or temptation that precedes the End. In so doing they are acting in accord with the words of the pre-Easter Jesus who taught them to pray, "lead us not into temptation" (Luke 11:4), exhorted them to "watch at all times, praying that you may have strength to escape all these things that will take place, and to stand before the Son of Man" (Luke 21:36), and specifically told them to "pray that you may not enter into temptation" (Luke 22:46b).

This exemplary section of Acts 1:3-14 shows the apostles acting in a way that reflects the evangelist's conception of how Jesus taught them to behave in just such a situation as they find themselves: the situation of waiting for God to act. If you want the empowering of the Holy Spirit, pray. If you want the parousia of the Son of Man, pray. If you want protection from temptation or preservation through the tribulation, pray. In any case, while you wait, pray!

Replacing Judas (Acts 1:15-26)

Acts 1:15-26 is a thought unit distinct from 1:1-14, yet it is related to the former section. Whereas in 1:1-14 the concern is that the witnesses be empowered and ultimately vindicated, in 1:15-26 it is that the number of the witnesses be complete. Access to the Lukan mind may be gained by first tracing the train of thought in the unit as indicated by the surface structure, and then by noting the *Gattung* to which the material belongs.

The surface structure of the unit looks something like this in outline.

1:15:   the setting
1:16-22:   a speech of Peter in two parts
            vv. 16-20—why the number "twelve" is incomplete
            vv. 21-22—who constitutes a qualified replacement
1:23-26:   the response to Peter's speech

v. 23–they put forward two
vv. 24-25– they prayed
v. 26a–they cast lots
v. 26b–he was enrolled

Each of these components will be examined in turn.

Verse 15 offers the setting for the thought unit. "During those days," taken in context, must refer to the time when the disciples with one accord are devoting themselves to prayer (v. 14). Like most decisive events in Luke-Acts, what follows arises out of prayer (e.g., Luke 1:10; 3:21-22; 6:12-16; 9:18, 28; 11:1; 22:39-46; Acts 10). Peter's initiative "in the midst of the brothers" reflects his obedience to Jesus' commission (Luke 22:32: "once you have turned back, you must strengthen your brothers"). This is the only place in Luke-Acts where, following his repentance (Luke 22:61-62), Peter acts on behalf of the other disciples. The parenthetical remark about there being about one hundred and twenty persons in the one place is important in at least two ways. First, it echoes the Jewish rule that there be a hundred and twenty men in a city in order for it to have its own council (*m. Sanhedrin* 1:6). Other Jewish parallels reflect the expectation that there would be one leader for each ten members (e.g., 1QS 6:3-4; 1QSa 2.22; CD 13:1-2). That the Messianist group includes women as well as men among the one hundred and twenty merely reflects the gender equality assumed in Lukan Christianity (see Talbert 1982, 90-94). Second, the number one hundred and twenty (10 x 12) is symbolic, probably referring to the restored tribes of Israel. To summarize: the one hundred and twenty disciples, symbolizing the restored Israel (Acts 15:16), are of sufficient size to require a council of leaders for themselves.

Verses 16-22 present the speech of Peter before the assembled Messianists. The speech falls into two parts (vv. 16-20 and vv. 21-22), each introduced by the language of divine necessity: "It was necessary (*edei*, v. 16) for scripture to be fulfilled concerning Judas"; "it is necessary (*dei*, v. 21) that one of the men . . . become with us a witness." As a backdrop for all the action in Luke-Acts there is the belief that everything that happens in salvation history occurs according to the divine plan.

The notion that a divine necessity controls human history, shaping the course of its events, was a widespread belief in Mediterranean antiquity. (a) Polybius, for example, saw early in his career that Roman power was irresistible. A Stoic, he believed that the Roman order of things was part of a divine providence that ruled the world. This belief he expounded in his *Histories*. In 1.4.1-2 he says,

> Fortune (*hē tychē*) having guided almost all the affairs of the world in one direction and having forced them to incline towards one and the same end, a histo-

rian should bring before his readers under one synoptical view the operations by which she has accomplished her general purpose.

(b) Josephus shared in this cultural belief, but as a Jew he viewed the divine necessity as deriving from the personal will of God, who is a living person and not a neutral necessity. So in his *Antiquities* 10.8.2-3 § 142, he tells of Jeremiah's prophecy of the fall of Jerusalem being fulfilled and says that these events manifest the nature of God, "which foretells all which must (*dei*) take place, duly at the appointed hour." Pagan and Hellenistic Jew alike thought of history's unfolding according to a divine necessity or compulsion that could be expressed in terms of *dei* or *deon esti*. A Jew would have heard it in terms of his belief in a personal deity, but the cultural context was in agreement that history unfolded according to a divine necessity. It was in these terms that Luke's language would have been heard.

In Luke-Acts the notion of the plan of God is expressed in a number of different ways. Sometimes the language of God's plan (*boulē*, Luke 7:29-30; Acts 2:23; 4:28; 5:38-39; 13:36; 20:27), will (*thelēma*, Luke 22:42; Acts 21:14; 22:14), or authority (*exousia*, Acts 1:7) is used. On other occasions the expression is "it is necessary" (*dei*, Luke 2:49; 4:43; 9:22; 13:33; 17:25; 21:9; 22:37; 24:7, 26, 44; Acts 1:16, 21; 3:21; 4:12; 5:29; 9:6, 16; 14:22; 16:30; 17:3; 19:21; 20:35; 23:11; 24:19; 25:10; 26:9; 27:24). On still other occasions "to fulfill scripture" is the terminology (Luke 4:21; 9:31; 21:24; 22:16; 24:44; Acts 1:16; 2:28; 3:18; 12:25; 13:25, 27). Sometimes the phrase is "it is about to" (Luke 9:31, 44; 22:23; 24:21; Acts 17:31; 26:22-23). The language "as determined" (Luke 22:22; Acts 10:42; 22:14; 26:16) is occasionally found. Whatever the language, the author of Luke-Acts refers to God's guidance of events from beginning to end (Squires).

Verses 16-20 state why the number of the Twelve is incomplete. It is because of the defection of Judas, which happened to fulfill scripture (v. 16). Verses 17-20 are arranged in a concentric pattern: ABB'A'.

> A–v. 17: Judas was allotted a share in this ministry (*diakonias*); cf. Luke 6:12-16
>> B–vv. 18-19: Judas bought a parcel of land but died tragically ("falling headlong")
>> B'–v. 20a: "Let his habitation become desolate" (Ps 69:25)
> A'–v. 20b: "May another take his office (*episkopēn*)" (Ps 109:8)

A (v. 17) and B (vv. 18-19) describe actions related to Judas. B' (v. 20a) and A' (v. 20b) state the consequences of his crime: he loses both his farm and his share in the apostolic ministry. It is because of the latter that the number of the Twelve is incomplete.

The B component of the pattern poses a problem: namely, its description of the death of Judas. In earliest Christianity there are three different accounts of the death of Judas: Matthew 27:3–10; Acts 1:18–19; and Papias. (a) According to Matthew 27, Judas was sorry he betrayed Jesus and returned the money he had been given; he then hanged himself; and the chief priests with the returned money bought the potter's field in which to bury strangers. (b) According to Acts 1, Judas bought a farm (*epaulis*, "dwelling place") with his ill-gotten gain, fell headlong (*prēnēs*), burst open (cf. Aesop, *Fables* 177b, for one's bursting open as a result of a fall; cf. Chariton, *Chaereas and Callirhoe* 1.3.1, for death by falling off a ladder on a farm), and all his insides spilled out. (c) According to Papias, in the fourth book of his *Interpretation of the Sayings of the Lord*, as quoted by Apollinarius of Laodicea, Judas died from swelling to such a size that he could not get through where a wagon could easily pass. He died after much torment in a place of his own, bursting asunder and his bowels being scattered (Goodspeed 267, gives a translation of part of the tradition).

Various attempts at harmonization have been tried from ancient times to modern; none with success. (Examples are given in Lake 5.22–30.) Rather than to try to harmonize the accounts, it is better to see them as alternative traditions with their varying versions of Judas's end reflecting their views of what was the typical death for such a sinner. (a) In Matthew where Jesus is depicted as a Davidic king (Matt 1:1; 2:2), Judas's end is depicted as that appropriate for the betrayer of a king. In 2 Sam 17:1–23, for example, Ahithopel betrays David; and when his advice is not followed by the rebels, he hangs himself. Hanging oneself is an appropriate death for one who betrays a king. (b) In Papias, Judas's betrayal is viewed as that of a traitor who makes false accusations. Consequently, his fate is to swell up, to die miserably, and to have his entrails fall out, as in *Ahikar,* where the traitor Nadin swells up and dies, and especially in Josephus, *War* 11.3–4 §§ 447–53, where Catullus, the Roman governor, having made false accusations, dies miserably, his entrails falling out of his body. Such is the appropriate death of one who makes false accusations. (c) According to Luke-Acts where Jesus is understood as the Righteous One (Luke 23:47; Acts 3:14; 7:52; 22:14), Judas's treachery is understood as twofold. On the one hand, he is the persecutor and betrayer of the Righteous One. Hence he dies from a fall to the ground. As, for example, Wis 4:16–19 says, those who have contributed to the death of the righteous man will die themselves "because he [God] will dash them speechless to the ground." On the other hand, Judas is seen as having made false accusations against Jesus. Hence, his insides spill out, as Josephus, *War* 11.3–4 §§ 447–53, has shown is appropriate for such a villain. In Acts 1:18–19, therefore, Judas's end shows how Luke-Acts views his crime. It is making false accusations against the Righteous One.

His end reflects the specifics of his deeds. His demise leaves his place in the apostolic ministry open. This is the problem that Peter addresses.

Verses 21-22 specify who constitutes a qualified replacement for Judas. Again, finding a replacement is a divine necessity (v. 21). Just the Eleven will not do; it takes the Twelve (Luke 22:28-30). Such a replacement must be one who "accompanied us the whole time the Lord Jesus came and went among us, beginning from the baptism of John (i.e., the beginning of Jesus' ministry—Luke 3:23; 16:16; Acts 1:5; 10:37; 11:16; 13:24-25; 18:25; 19:3-4) until the day he was taken up from us" (vv. 21-22a). From among such people Jesus will choose Judas's replacement (v. 24). From the point of view of Luke-Acts, an apostle is one who has been with Jesus during the whole of his public ministry and has been chosen by Jesus.

This view of apostleship has similarities and dissimilarities with the rabbinic practice at Jamnia after A.D. 70. According to *j. Sanhedrin* 1:2, "At first each one would appoint his own students, as Rabbi Johanan ben Zakkai ordained Rabbi Eliezer and Rabbi Joshua." The rabbinic practice was like that found in Luke-Acts in that those appointed or ordained were the ones who had been with the master for a long time. The rabbinic practice is unlike that in Acts 1:15-26 in that whereas a rabbi appointed his own students during his lifetime, in Acts 1 the risen Lord chooses after the community has put two persons forward. The differences, however, should not detract from the fact that in both cases a qualification is one's having been with the teacher for a lengthy period of time.

Views of apostleship vary in early Christianity. In the 50s Paul's letters reveal that apostles were of two types: apostles of Christ (like Paul—1 Cor 9:1-2; 15:8-9; Gal 1:1,11-17; 1 Thess 2:6; Rom 1:1; 2 Cor 1:1; 1 Cor 1:1; other than Paul—Andronicus and Junia, Rom 16:7; all the apostles, 1 Cor 15:7; those who were apostles before Paul, Gal 1:17, 19) and apostles of the churches (our brethren, 2 Cor 8:23; Epaphroditus, Phil 2:25). The basic difference between the two types lies in who sends the apostle. Is it Christ or a church? Apostles of Christ, like Paul, had two qualifications: they had seen the risen Christ and had received a call from him. This understanding of an apostle of Christ is akin to what Epictetus says about the true Cynic. The Cynic is called by God (*Dissertations* 3.21.18; 3.22.2). Consequently, he knows himself to be a messenger (*angelos*), a scout (*kataskopos*), and a herald (*kēryx*) of God (3.22.69) because he is divinely sent (*apostaleis*), like Diogenes (1.24.6). Indeed, the ultimate presupposition for genuine Cynicism is awareness of being divinely sent (*apo tou dios apestaltai,* 3.22.23). Of course, when late-first-century Gnostics, like Menander, the disciple of Simon Magus, claimed that they were sent (*apestalmenos*), other criteria were called for, such as the necessity of having been with Jesus all of his public ministry. But in Paul's time, there was no requirement about

having been with Jesus during his lifetime. If there had been, Paul would
not have qualified.

In the period A.D. 80–100, there remains the same distinction between
apostles of Christ and apostles of the churches. Luke-Acts speaks about
apostles of Christ in Luke 6:13; Acts 1:2, 26; 2:37, 42, 43; 4:33, 35; 5:2; 5:18;
6:6; 8:18; 15:2, 22, 23; 16:4 (cf. 13:31). Acts 14:4, 14 (cf. 13:1–3) refer to
apostles of a church, Antioch of Syria. In this dominant schema of Luke-
Acts, the Twelve are viewed as apostles of Christ; Paul and Barnabas are
viewed as apostles of the church in Antioch of Syria.

It must be said, however, that alongside this dominant schema in Acts
there are echoes of the view of Paul's being an apostle of Christ like that
found in his letters. Acts 9:15 has the risen Jesus speak about Paul in such
terms, although the technical term "apostle" is not used: "this man is a chosen instrument of mine to carry my name before Gentiles, kings, and
Israelites." Acts 22:21 continues the idea and uses the verbal form from
which "apostle" is derived: "Go, I shall send (*exapostelō*) you far away to
the Gentiles." Acts 26:16–18 also makes the same point, again using the verbal form: "I have appeared to you for this purpose, to appoint you as a . . .
witness of what you have seen [of me] and what you will be shown. I shall
deliver you from this people and from the Gentiles to whom I send (*apo-
stellō*) you." These three texts indicate that Paul has seen the risen Lord and
has received a commission from him. In two of the three, the verbal form
apostellein has been used. One might compare the situation in Acts, then,
to that of two slides being shown on a screen simultaneously, one super-
imposed on top of the other.

In Luke-Acts, the dominant view is that the Twelve are apostles of Christ
and Paul is an apostle of the church at Antioch. In so portraying Paul, Acts
makes him subject to the Twelve. The significance of this can be seen if the
various images of Paul in the ancient church are noted.

There are diverse images of Paul preserved in the ancient church's memory and imagination. These images give us leads to the character of the circles that created and preserved them. If they are divided into two camps,
orthodoxy and heresy, three different pictures of Paul emerge in each category. The following sketch makes this clear (Talbert 1974b, 442–43):

1. Orthodoxy
   a. Paul is *the* evangelist, teacher, and administrator of the orthodox
      church *par excellence*. Here the Twelve are ignored. Cf. Pastoral
      Epistles, Polycarp, *Acts of Paul.*
   b. Paul is ignored. Appeal is made exclusively to the Twelve as the
      church's teachers and administrators. Cf. *Didache, Barnabas* 5:9;
      8:3; Aristides, *Apology*, 2; Justin, *1 Apology*, 39,42,50,53.

  c. Paul is acknowledged as an apostle and teacher of the church, but
  he is subordinated to the Twelve. Cf. *Epistle of the Apostles* 31.
2. Heresy
  a. Paul is the only true apostle and *the* source of true teaching. Cf.
  Marcion, Valentinus (Clement of Alexandria, *Miscellanies* 50:7, says
  Valentinus claimed to have derived his views from Theudas, a pupil
  of Paul)
  b. The Twelve are the source of truth. Cf. *Gospel of Philip* 122:16–18.
  Paul is the apostle of Satan. Cf. the Ebionites (Epiphanius, *Medicine
  Chest* 30.16.6–9); the Cerinthians (Epiphanius, *Medicine Chest*
  28.5.1–3); the Severiani (Eusebius, *Church History* 4.29.5); the
  Elkesites (Eusebius, *Church History* 6.39)
  c. Paul and the Twelve together furnish support for Gnostic teaching
  (Ptolemy's *Letter to Flora*)

From this sketch it is clear that not everyone in the ancient church has the
same estimate of Paul and the Twelve. Within this spectrum, Luke-Acts falls
into category (c) under orthodoxy. In Acts, both the Twelve and Paul are
presented as legitimate teachers of the church. Paul, however, is subordinated to the Twelve, as in the *Epistles of the Apostles* 31.

This tells us that Acts comes from a circle that is seeking to avoid the
extremes of claiming either Paul or the Twelve as the church's sole legitimate guides. Acts represents an inclusive form of early Christianity that sees
a place for (1) Jewish (so the Twelve) and Gentile Christians (so Paul); (2)
for newcomers (so Paul) as well as charter members (so the Twelve); (3) for
educated people (so Paul) as well as the uneducated (so the Twelve). Paul
and the Twelve together function as the church's guides. What they do and
say, as Acts tells the story, is remarkably similar. That Paul is nevertheless
subordinated to the Twelve is Acts' narrative way of indicating that the
authority deriving from religious experience (so Paul) is subject to the criterion of the tradition of the earthly Jesus (with which the Twelve are
acquainted—Acts 1:21–22—and of which they are witnesses).

The person so qualified to be one of the Twelve will join the Eleven in
their "witness to his [Jesus'] resurrection" (v. 22b). Not only did the qualifications for apostles of Christ shift from the 50s to the period A.D. 80–100,
so also did the functions of apostles. Paul clearly understood his apostleship
in terms of preaching and planting churches in territory where no other
Christian witness had ever been (2 Cor 10:14,16; Rom 15:19–24). In Luke-
Acts, however, the Twelve are not portrayed as church planters in pagan territory but rather in the dual role of witnesses to Israel and of rulers over the
reconstituted Israel.

Luke 22:28–30 is the basis for viewing the Twelve as rulers over a reconstituted Israel. This is usually thought to be a Q saying (//Matt 19:28). The Matthean version of the logion is clearly eschatological.

> In the new world, when the Son of Man shall sit on his glorious throne, you who have followed me will also sit on twelve thrones, judging the twelve tribes of Israel.

This has predisposed some scholars to read the Lukan version in the same way.

> I bequeath (*diatithēmai*) to you, as my Father bequeathed to me, a kingdom/rule, that you may eat and drink at my table in my kingdom/rule, and sit on thrones judging the twelve tribes of Israel.

So Luke 22:28–29 has been taken to refer to the new world, the messianic banquet, and the role of the apostles in eschatological judgment. It should not be read in such a way.

A right reading requires that three expressions be clarified. (1) In Luke-Acts, what is Jesus' rule/kingdom? Acts 2:34–36 indicates that it is his session at God's right hand (cf. Luke 22:69; 1 Cor 15:20–28). (2) What does it mean to eat at the king's table? The expression comes from Luke's Bible (e.g., 1 Sam 20:29b; 2 Sam 9:7, 9, 11, "ate at the king's table like one of the king's sons"; 2 Sam 19:28; 1 Kgs 2:7; 4:27; 18:19). It means to be accorded within the king's house a place of honor such as the king's sons have. (3) What does it mean to judge the tribes of Israel? Again the expression comes from Luke's Bible (e.g., Exod 2:14, "a prince and a judge over us"; 18:22, "let them judge the people at all times"; 2 Sam 15:4, "Absalom said: 'Oh that I were judge in the land! Then every man with a suit or cause might come to me, and I would give him justice'"; Mic 7:3, "the prince and the judge ask for a bribe"). It refers to functionaries in Israel who rendered decisions about what was right. Sometimes such judges were also princes, king's sons.

Taking these expressions together yields a reading that sees Luke 22:29–30 as referring to the apostles' role in Jesus' reign from his exaltation to his parousia. It is one of honor. They are as sons of the king in that they eat at his table and function as decision makers among the people. The apostles are not successors as in the later apostolic succession of the Old Catholic Church. They rather rule, as judges did in ancient Israel, within and under the reign of Christ.

This seems to describe one of the roles of the apostles in Acts. Take, for example, the centrality of Jerusalem in the missionary enterprise in Acts (1:4, 8; 8:14–15; 11:1–2; 11:22; 15:2). This includes the Jerusalem frame of reference for Paul's entire ministry in Acts (9:27–29; 11:25–26; 13:1–3; 15:2; 16:5; 18:22; 21:17). Jerusalem control of missions in Acts is closely tied to the fact that, for Luke, Jerusalem is the place where the twelve apostles reside (8:1; 9:26; 11:1-2; 15:2,4; 16:4). The twelve apostles in Acts function as appointed people of honor who make key decisions within the early church under the reign of Christ.

The mindset is very much like what Plutarch says about human rulers during the period of the Roman Empire. In his *Precepts for Ruling the State* 813D-E, he says:

> When a man enters on any public office, he must not only keep in mind the considerations of which Pericles reminded himself when he assumed the general's cloak–"Be careful, Pericles; you are ruling free men, you are ruling Greeks, Athenian citizens"–but he must also say to himself: "Although you are ruling you are a subject, and the city you rule is under the control of proconsuls, and of the procurators of Caesar."

The apostles' honor and decision making in Luke-Acts is within and under the overarching reign of Christ.

This role of judges, however, has been bequeathed (*diatithēmai*) to them by Christ. This is the language of succession when it reflects the situation from the perspective of the one giving the kingdom. For example, in *Antiquities* 13.16.1 § 407, Josephus says of the Hasmonean king, Alexander, that he "left behind him two sons . . . but bequeathed the kingdom (*tēn basileian dietheto*) to Alexandra." In Luke-Acts the Twelve do not stand on the same level as Christ, but they derive from him their role of judging the twelve tribes of the reconstituted Israel. To function as judges is one of the Twelve's roles in Acts.

The other role of the Twelve in Acts is that of bearing witness (Acts 1:8, 22; 2:32; 3:15; 5:32; 10:39, 41; 13:31) to the resurrection of Jesus (= God's vindication of Jesus; cf. Acts 2:22-24; 3:15; 4:10; 5:30; 10:39-40; 13:28-30). The Lukan view is that after the resurrection of Jesus this new evidence is presented to Israel by the Twelve (Acts 5:32; 10:39-42; 13:31) in an effort to overcome the ignorance that produced Jesus' death (Acts 3:17) and to gain Jewish repentance (Acts 2:38; 3:19). This mission to Israel is foreshadowed in Luke 9:1-6 where the Twelve are sent out by Jesus. In order for their witness to be effective, they must not only be empowered (Acts 1:8, 4-5) but also their symbolic number must be complete. Prophetic symbolism demands twelve witnesses for the twelve tribes. Acts 1:15-26, therefore, just as Acts 1:1-14, is concerned with preparation for the mission that is about to begin.

In Acts 1:15-26, the dual role of the apostles is in plain view. When Peter takes the initiative in calling for a decision about Judas's replacement, he is acting as a judge of the reconstituted Israel. When he refers to the Twelve as witnesses to the resurrection of Jesus, he speaks about the second role, that of witnessing to Israel about God's vindication of Jesus by the resurrection (Acts 3:15, 26).

Verses 23–26 deal with the response to Peter's speech. A series of four verbs indicates the direction of the action. (1) In v. 23, we hear that "they *proposed* two, Joseph called Barsabbas, who was also known as Justus, and Matthias." Who proposed the names of the two qualified disciples? The "they," in context, must refer to those addressed in v. 16, "My brothers." It is the community as a whole who propose these two.

(2) In vv. 24–25, we are told that "they *prayed*." The prayer consists of (a) an address ("You, Lord"), (b) an ascription ("who know the hearts of all"), and (c) a petition ("show which one of these two you have chosen to take the place in this apostolic ministry from which Judas turned away to go to his own place").

(a) To whom do they pray? In Lukan thought it is Jesus who chooses apostles (Luke 6:12–16: "he chose Twelve, whom he also named apostles"; Acts 1:2: "to the apostles whom he had chosen"). In Luke-Acts prayer is sometimes offered to the risen Jesus (Acts 7:59–60: "Lord Jesus, receive my spirit"). So here, "Lord" most likely refers to the risen Jesus. In this Luke is one with early Christianity generally where Jesus is sometimes addressed in prayer (1 Cor 16:22b; Rev 22:20b) and where Jesus and the Father are believed to act together to answer prayer (1 Thess 3:11; 2 Thess 2:16; John 14:13–14).

(b) What is the attribute of the one to whom prayer is offered? The risen Jesus is one who knows human hearts. This is a trait of the deity in scripture (Deut 8:2; 1 Sam 16:7; LXX Pss 7:9; 43:21; 64:6; 139:23; 1 Cor 4:5; 14:25; Heb 4:12; 1 John 3:20; Rev 2:23). It is also a trait of the pre-Easter Jesus (e.g., Luke 5:20–23; 7:39–43; John 2:25).

(c) For what is petition made? The risen Jesus is asked to make known the one whom he has chosen to be the twelfth apostle, now that Judas has "turned away to go to his own place" (*Targum on Ecclesiastes* 6.6 says: "On the day of his death his soul goes down to Gehenna, the one place where all the guilty go"). In praying in this way, the disciples follow the word of the Lukan Jesus (Luke 10:2: "ask the master of the harvest to send out laborers for his harvest") and act in a way that will be characteristic of the later church in Acts (e.g., 4:31; 9:11; 10:2, 9; 12:5; 13:3).

(3) In v. 26a "they *gave* lots to them, and the lot *fell* upon Matthias." Casting lots was a widespread practice in ancient Judaism (Lev 16:8; Num 26:55; 1 Chr 25:8–31; 26:13–16; Jonah 1:7; 1QS 5:3; *m. Yoma* 3:9; 4:1; *Tamid* 1:2; 3:1). According to Jewish belief, "The lot is cast into the lap, but the decision is wholly from the Lord" (Prov 16:33) (Beardslee, 245–52). There is, however, no mention in the New Testament of any Christian use of the practice after the Spirit is given at Pentecost. Matthias is chosen by the Lord through the lot. Of Matthias we hear no more in the New Testament. Gnostics made use of his name, as they did of the other apostles. Hip-

polytus, *Refutation of Heresies* 7.20.1, says that Basilides and Isidorus, his disciple, claim that Matthias communicated to them secret discourses which he heard from the Savior.

(4) In v. 26b we hear that "he *was counted* with the eleven apostles." With this act the community confirms what the Lord decided. The number of the Twelve was once again complete. Preparations for a post-Easter witness to Israel are finished. All that remains in the way of readiness for the mission is the gift of the "promise of the Father" (Acts 1:4–5, 8). That will come in Acts 2.

Having traced the train of thought in Acts 1:15–26, there remains the task of trying to locate the focus of this section of the Lukan narrative. This may be done by means of an inquiry into the Gattung of the thought unit. In the Old Testament there is a *Gattung* used for "the choice of supplementary leadership" (e.g., Exod 18:14–25 and Num 27:12–23). This *Gattung* consists of four components: (1) the problem (Exod 18:14–18: Moses is not able to perform the duty of judging alone; Num 27:12–14); (2) the proposed solution (Exod 18:19–23: choose others to judge the people; Num 27:15–17); (3) the qualifications of the new leadership (Exod 18:21: able men who fear God, are trustworthy, and who hate a bribe; Num 27:18–21); and (4) the setting apart of the new leaders (Exod 18:25: Moses chose able men and made them heads over the people; Num 27:22–23).

In line with his usual imitation of the LXX, the Lukan evangelist shapes Acts 1:15–26 (and later Acts 6:1–6) in accord with this form: (1) the problem (Acts 1:15–20: Judas's defection); (2) the proposed solution (Acts 1:21a, 22b: a replacement for Judas must be chosen); (3) the qualifications of the new leadership (1:21b–22a: the person must have been with Jesus from the beginning of his ministry until his ascension); and (4) the setting apart of the new leader (Acts 1:23–26: they proposed two; they prayed to Jesus; they cast lots; Matthias was enrolled). The very choice of the *Gattung* used shows the passage's thrust to be on the selection of new and additional leadership for the community of disciples. Recognizing Luke's choice of a *Gattung* confirms the impressions gained from the surface structure of the thought unit. The leadership of the reconstituted Israel is now set. The Messianists wait for the promise of the Father.

FULFILLING THE MISSION: PHASE ONE

Acts 2:1–12:25

Pentecost (Acts 2:1–47)

Acts 2:1–47 is a large thought unit focusing on events that occurred on the day of Pentecost. It is composed of four *Gattungen:* (1) a typological narrative (vv. 1–11), (2) speeches giving the meaning of the events (vv. 12–36), (3) a dialogue explaining the proper response to the events and their apostolic interpretation (vv. 37–40), and (4) a summary telling of the results of the events and their apostolic interpretation (vv. 41–47). Each must be examined in turn.

Acts 2:1–11 is a typological narrative describing the events on Pentecost. It falls into three parts:

v. 1:   time and place of the events
vv. 2–4:   the events: audition, vision, action
vv. 5–11: explanation of the action of v. 4.

Verse 1 locates the events of Acts 2 on the day of Pentecost when "they" (= the disciples) were all in one place together (= the upper room, as in 1:13–14?). Tob 2:1; 2 Macc 12:32; Josephus, *War* 6.5.3 § 299; and Paul (1 Cor 16:8) call the feast Pentecost. In the Old Testament it is usually called the feast of Weeks (Exod 23:16; Lev 23:15–21; Deut 16:9–12). It was a one-day festival celebrating the wheat harvest. The distinctive feature of the festival in ancient Israel was the presentation to Yahweh of an offering of two loaves of new corn. By the second century A.D. rabbinic Judaism regarded Pentecost as the day the law was given to Israel at Sinai (*b. Pesahim* 68b: "It is the day on which the Torah was given"). The question is: was it associated with the Sinai covenant before the second century? Yes. *Jubilees,* written in the second century B.C. does so. It is true that *Jubilees* 6:17–18 connects Pentecost with the covenant with Noah. *Jubilees* 1:1, however, associates it also with the giving of the law at Sinai.

40

Jewish festivals are associated with certain months in the Jewish year. The first month of the Jewish year is in the spring. In the first month Passover is celebrated. In the seventh month there are the Day of Atonement and the feast of Tabernacles. In the third month there occurs the festival of Weeks or Pentecost (VanderKam, 1.814-20). *Jubilees* 6:1 identifies Pentecost in Noah's time with the third month. In *Jubilees* 1:1, it is also in the third month that the Mosaic law was given. In other words, multiple covenants are associated with Pentecost in the second-century B.C. book of *Jubilees*. If mental associations of Pentecost with the Sinai covenant would have been possible already at the end of the first century A.D., the typological associations in Acts 2 begin immediately.

Typological writing is the method of referring to a person, event, or thing in the present in terms of a person, event, or thing in scripture so as to make a statement about the nature of what is described in the present. Early Christians used typological writing frequently. For example, the reference in Mark 1:6 to John the Baptist's wearing a garment of haircloth and a leather girdle echoes the description in 2 Kgs 1:8 of Elijah the Tishbite's distinctive appearance. In so doing, Mark makes the point that John the Baptist is the Elijah who was to return before the Messiah (cf. Mark 9:11-13). The same phenomenon is found in Matthew's depiction of Jesus as the second Moses (echoing Deut 18:15-19) and the Epistle to the Hebrews' depiction of the Christian life as wilderness wanderings between exodus and promised land (Hebrews 3-4). In what follows in vv. 1-11, echoes of the Sinai covenant are to be heard.

Verses 2-4 relate the events that happened on Pentecost: an audition ("a noise like a strong driving wind," v. 2), a vision ("there appeared to them tongues as of fire," v. 3), and action ("they were all filled with the Holy Spirit and began to speak in different tongues, as the Spirit enabled them," v. 4). In the first place, Luke here describes a theophany. Any intrusion of the heavenly world into human affairs in Luke-Acts is likely to be accompanied by visions and auditions (Luke 1:11, 13-17; 2:9, 10-11; 3:21-22; 9:30-31; 22:43; 24:4-7; Acts 9:3, 4-6; 10:3-6, 10-15; 12:7-8; 16:9-10; 18:9-10; 23:11; 27:23-24), that is, things seen and things heard. It is certainly the case in Acts 2.

In the second place, in Luke-Acts most happenings are fulfillments of some kind of prophecy (Luke 1:1: "a narrative of the things which have been fulfilled among us"; cf. Talbert 1982, 234-40). Luke here describes the fulfillment of the prophecy of John the Baptist (Luke 3:16: "he will baptize you with the Holy Spirit and with fire") and the prophecies of Jesus (Luke 24:49: "And behold, I send the promise of my Father upon you"; Acts 1:5: "before many days you shall be baptized with the Holy Spirit"; Acts 1:8: "you shall receive power after the Holy Spirit has come upon you"). That "they were all filled with the Holy Spirit" (2:4) fulfills the promise "you shall be baptized with the Holy Spirit" (1:5) and shows that the two expressions refer to one experience.

In the third place, most significant events in Luke-Acts occur in connection with prayer (Luke 3:21–22; 6:12–16; 9:18, 28; Acts 10). So it is here. In Luke-Acts, prayer functions in three ways: (1) as a means of knowing God's will/plan/purpose (Luke 3:21–22; 9:18–22, 28–31; Acts 10:1–8, 9–23; 11:5–17; 22:17–21); (2) as a source of power to enable one to do God's will (Luke 4:18–21; 22:39–46; Acts 1:14 and 2:1–4 [cf. Luke 11:13]; 4:29–31); (3) as a catalyst for God's accomplishing the divine plan/purpose (Luke 11:2–4; 18:1–8; 22:31–32; Acts 8:15; 9:40; 12:5, 6–11, 12, 13–17). In this context, it is function (2) that is applicable. The disciples have been praying for the gift of the Holy Spirit (Acts 1:14) just as Jesus had told them to do (Luke 11:13: "how much more will the Father in heaven give the Holy Spirit to those who ask him"). Now their prayers are answered. They are filled with the Holy Spirit (v. 4), empowered to do God's will.

Beyond these general observations there are also echoes of the Sinai events as they are narrated in Exodus 19 and discussed by Philo and later Jewish teachers. (a) The people are all in one place together (Acts 2:1). This is an echo of Exod 19:17 and has similarities with the tradition in *Mekilta* on Exod 19:2, 8 and 20:2, where it is said that the Israelites at Sinai were all of one heart. (b) There were both sound and fire (Acts 2:2–3). This echoes Exod 19:16–19 and has similarities with certain passages from Philo. In *The Decalogue* 9:33, Philo says,

> God wrought on this occasion a miracle . . . by bidding an invisible *sound* to be created in the air . . . which giving shape and tension to the air and changing it to *flaming fire*, sounded forth like the breath through a trumpet. (cf. also Philo, *Special Laws* 2.31.188–89)

(c) There was also speech in different tongues (v. 4) that was understood by those who heard it in their own languages (v. 8).

Verses 5–11 give an explanation of the tongues in v. 4. In Jerusalem there lived "devout Jews from every nation under heaven" (v. 5). The reference is not to the large crowds in Jerusalem for the feast (Josephus, *Antiquities* 14.13.4 § 337; 17.10.2 § 254; *War* 1.13.3 § 253; 2.3.1 §§ 42–43) but rather to Jews who had come from all over the world to settle in Jerusalem (cf. Acts 6:9). These Jerusalemites gathered when they heard the noise and to their amazement heard the Galileans, who were notorious for poor linguistic skills (*b. Erubin* 53a,b; *b. Megilla* 24b), speaking in the language of each auditor (vv. 6–8). The homelands of those now resident in Jerusalem are mentioned in a fashion like the tables of nations of the Jewish Diaspora, found in writers like Philo (e.g., *Legation to Gaius* 281–83) and Josephus (e.g., *Antiquities* 1.6.1-4 §§ 122-47, which contains 50 percent of the names in Acts 2:9-11, including Judea, which has often been thought to be out of place in vv. 9-11). The clear-cut emphasis of this subunit is found in the threefold refrain "heard them speaking in his own language" (v. 6); "hear them in his own native language" (v. 8); and "hear them speaking in our own tongues" (v. 11).

This phenomenon of people hearing in their own languages echoes Philo's statement in *The Decalogue* 11:46: "Then from the midst of the *fire* . . . there sounded forth to their utter amazement a *voice*, for the flame became *articulate speech in the language familiar to the audience.*"

Later rabbinic statements elaborate on the same tradition. For example, *Tanhuma* 26c says,

> Although the ten commandments were promulgated with a single sound, it says, "All the people heard the voices"; it follows then that when the voice went forth it was divided into seven voices and then went into seventy tongues, and every people received the law in their own language. (Lake 5.116)

This is very much the same as the tradition ascribed to Rabbi Johanan, on the basis of Exod 20:18 (thunderings), who said that God's voice, as it was uttered, split up into seventy voices, in seventy languages, so all nations should understand (*Exodus Rabbah* 5:9 [on 4:21]). (cf. also *b. Shabbat* 88b; *Midrash Tehillim* 92:3 [on 92:1]; Fragment Targum on Deut 27:8).

In telling his story this way, the evangelist seems to be describing xenolalia, a variation of glossolalia found repeatedly in Christian history. It is similar to the cases of modern people who claim to hear their own language being spoken by persons with the gift of tongues. It may be that "tongues of men and of angels" in 1 Cor 13:1 refers first to xenolalia and then to glossolalia. In any case, a sharp distinction between what Luke describes here and what he describes elsewhere (e.g., Acts 10:46; 19:6) cannot be drawn. They are two sides of the same coin.

The echoes are unmistakable. Sound, fire, and speech understood by all people were characteristic of the Sinai theophany. The same ingredients are found in the Pentecostal events. The Sinai theophany and the establishment of the Mosaic covenant would be brought to mind as surely as would Elijah by the description of John the Baptist's dress in Mark 1:6. The typology of Acts 2:1-11, then, is that of making a covenant.

The Pentecostal events of Acts 2:1-11, however, are not just a Messianist renewal of the Sinai covenant. Luke-Acts thinks in terms of a new covenant. The Lukan Jesus said, "This cup is the new covenant in my blood, which will be shed for you" (Luke 22:20; cf. Exod 24:8). Luke's Bible speaks of a new covenant in Jer 31:31-34. In Ezek 11:17-20, God says about the new covenant: (a) "I will assemble you out of the countries where you have been scattered, and I will give you the land of Israel" (v. 17); (b) "I will give them a new heart and put a new spirit within them" (v. 19); and (c) I will "give them one heart" (v. 19). At Pentecost in Acts 2, this promise is fulfilled. A new spirit is given, the Holy Spirit! The promise of the Father has been fulfilled in the presence of those who have been assembled out of the countries to which they had been scattered. The gift of the Spirit will produce a people with one heart (vv. 41–47).

Acts 2:12–36 is a long section composed of two speeches that attempt to give the meaning of the events that have transpired in vv. 1–11. There is first a mockers' speech (v. 13) and then Peter's speech (vv. 14–36). The mockers' speech gives the incorrect interpretation of the phenomena: "They have had too much new wine." In some religions of Mediterranean antiquity states of ecstacy were accompanied by drunkenness (e.g., Bacchus, so Ovid, *Metamorphoses* 3.528–45; 4.25–30; 2 Macc 6:7 indicates observance of the feast of Dionysius in Palestine and some Jewish participation in it). Hence the conventional dismissal of religious enthusiasm.

Peter's speech gives what, for the author of Acts, is the correct interpretation of the events that have just transpired. It begins by saying what the phenomena do not mean (vv. 14–15): "these people are not drunk, as you suppose, for it is only nine o'clock in the morning." In the Mediterranean world, even the worst debauchery did not begin until nine in the morning (Cicero, *Philippics* 2.41.104: "But how many days did you most disgracefully carouse in that villa! From the third hour there was drinking, gaming, vomiting"). Then the speech says what the phenomena do mean (vv. 16–36). The argument breaks into two parts (vv. 16–21 and vv. 22–36), each beginning with a major address to the people: "You who are Jews, indeed all of you staying in Jerusalem, let this be known to you, and listen to my words" (v. 14); "You who are Israelites, hear these words" (v. 22). (a) The first part of Peter's speech says that the phenomena of the day of Pentecost are a fulfillment of prophecy (vv. 16–21). (b) The second part of the address contends that the phenomena of Pentecost are the gift of the risen and exalted Christ (vv. 22–36).

Verses 16–21 make two points. (a) The dominant emphasis is the apostle's interpretation of the Pentecostal phenomena. The gift of the Spirit on Pentecost is a fulfillment of the prediction of Joel 2:28–32 that God would one day pour out his Spirit on all flesh (vv. 17–20). This includes "your sons" and "your daughters," "my servants" and "my handmaids." There are no gender distinctions. All shall prophesy. This includes "your young men" and "your old men." There are no distinctions based on age. All shall see visions and dream dreams (cf. *Numbers Rabbah* 15.25: "In the world to come all Israel will be made prophets"). (b) The subordinate emphasis is directed to the need of the Jerusalemites to repent (v. 21): "and

it shall be that everyone shall be saved who calls on the name of the Lord."
In this context, "the Lord" can only refer to Jesus (1:24; 2:36, 38).

Verses 22–36 also make two points, one dominant and the other subordinate. (a) The dominant thrust of vv. 22–36 is their explanation of the meaning of the Pentecostal events. The Spirit is a gift of the risen and exalted Christ. "Exalted at the right hand of God, he (Jesus) received the promise of the Holy Spirit from the Father and poured it forth, as you [both] see and hear" (v. 33; cf. Luke 3:16–17; *T. Judah* 24:2–3, speaking about the rising of a star from Jacob [the Messiah]: "And the heavens will be opened upon him to pour out the Spirit as a blessing of the Holy Father. And he will pour the Spirit of grace upon you. And you shall be sons in truth"). (b) The subordinate point of the subsection takes the more space. It is that Jesus, in spite of having been commended by God through his miracles (v. 22), was killed by the Jerusalemites, who used lawless men to crucify him (v. 23). God, however, vindicated Jesus by raising him from the dead (v. 24), as the apostles bear witness (v. 32). Moreover, the risen Jesus has been exalted to God's right hand (v. 33) and has been made both Lord and Christ (v. 36). Jerusalemite rejection of Jesus flies in the face of God's vindication of him. Jerusalem, therefore, stands in need of repentance.

How should this speech of Peter be understood? Is it a précis of an actual speech by the apostle? Is it an example of the kerygma of the church, either the ancient church's or that of the church of Luke's own time? Is it a Lukan theological invention? Is it what was deemed appropriate by Luke for the particular individual in his particular time and place and circumstances? The answers given to these questions for this one speech will likely affect how all the speeches of Acts will be viewed in the reading that follows. The place to begin in attempting any answer to these questions is with how speeches were understood in Mediterranean antiquity. Two sets of data may be used: statements about speeches made by ancient authors, and examples of speeches where there are outside controls to check them. We begin with statements made by ancient authors about their practices.

Thucydides, *History of the Peloponnesian War* 1.22.1, is the place to start. He writes as follows:

> As to the speeches that were made by different men, either when they were about to begin the war or when they were already engaged therein, it has been difficult to recall with strict accuracy *the words actually spoken*, both for me as regards that which I myself heard, and for those who from various other sources have brought me reports. Therefore, *the speeches are given in the language in which, as it seemed to me, the several speakers would express, on the subjects under consideration, the sentiments most befitting the occasion*, though at the same time I have adhered as closely as possible to the general sense of what was actually said.

Two things are said here. First, the speeches attempt to be appropriate in language and content to the person and occasion. Second, the speeches attempt to adhere as closely as possible to the general sense of what was said.

Polybius, *Histories* 12.12.25, critiques one Timaeus for his abuses, one of which has to do with speeches. In speeches that "sum up events and hold the whole history together" Timaeus has

> untruthfully reported them in his work, and has done so of a set purpose. For he has not set down the words spoken nor the sense of what was really said, but having made up his mind as to what ought to have been said, he recounts all these speeches . . . like a man in a school of rhetoric attempting to speak on a given subject, and *shows off his rhetorical power*, but gives no report of what was actually spoken.

Over against Thucydides' two aims, Timaeus has added a third. The speeches are an opportunity for the author to display his rhetorical skills, even if this sacrifices the essential truth of what might have been said. This sacrifice of truthfulness on the altar of rhetoric offends Polybius.

Tacitus, *Annals* 15.63, remarks on the occasion of Seneca's death that the farewell speech of that philosopher had been published literally, so that the historian did not need to reproduce it in Seneca's own words. Can one assume, however, that Tacitus aimed to give the gist of the speech correctly?

Pliny, *Epistle* 1.16, "To Erucius," speaks about Pompeius Saturninus:

> His histories will please you . . . for the words he puts into the mouths of his characters are as vivid as his own public speeches, though condensed into a simpler and terser style.

Lucian, in his *On the Art of Writing History* 58, offers the following advice:

> If you have to introduce a character making a speech, let the content of it be, first, suitable to the speaker and the situation . . . though indeed you have license to be rhetorical here and to demonstrate your stylistic ingenuity.

Lucian combines Thucydides' desire to have the speech be appropriate to the person and situation with Timaeus's concern for rhetorical display.

There are a number of speeches in antiquity for which we have outside controls. Four may be mentioned. (a) Josephus, *Antiquities* 12.6.3 §§ 279-84, gives the farewell speech of Mattathias in a very different form from that in his source, 1 Macc 2:50-68. (b) Herod's speech to his soldiers is found in Josephus, *Antiquities* 15.5.3 §§ 127-46, and in his *War* 1.19.4 §§ 373-79 in two very different forms. (c) Plutarch (*Otho* 15) and Tacitus (*Histories* 2.47) manifest agreement in their accounts of Otho but offer entirely different versions of his last address. (d) Dio Cassius's report of

Caesar's speech to his soldiers (38.36–46) is very different from that reported by Caesar himself (*Gallic War* 1.40). These comparisons incline the reader of ancient Mediterranean speeches to doubt that they represent anything like a précis of what was said. What has been said about speeches in ancient history applies equally to speeches in ancient Greco-Roman biography (Cox, 63) and to the Babylonian Talmud (Kaplan, 154). At best, what a modern reader might have a right to expect from an ancient speech, like that of Peter in Acts 2, is that the author of Acts will have constructed it so that it conforms to what he thought was appropriate to the individual, to the time, the place, and the circumstances. What is true of Acts 2 is probably true also for the other speeches in Acts.

The primary question about such a speech is its function in the Lukan plot. How does Peter's speech in Acts 2 function? There are at least three roles that Peter's address performs in its immediate context. First, it is an illustration of what the fulfillment of Jesus' promise in Acts 1:8 means ("you will be my witnesses in Jerusalem"). Second, it is an explanation of what has transpired (the Pentecostal phenomena, vv. 1–11). Third, it is a catalyst for what is about to happen (the Jewish conversions, vv. 37–40, 41). In Acts as a whole, Peter's speech functions as a frontispiece, just as Jesus' speech in Luke 4:16–27 does in the Third Gospel.

Verses 37–40 consist of a dialogue in which Peter explains the proper response to the events of Pentecost and their apostolic explanation. "When they (= the Jewish auditors) heard this, they were cut to the heart, and they asked Peter and the other apostles, 'What are we to do?'" Given where God stands in the entire affair, the auditors need to make a response. What is it to be? Peter gives his prescription in three parts. (a) What to do—"Repent and be baptized, every one of you, in the name of Jesus Christ for the forgiveness of your sins; and you will receive the gift of the Holy Spirit" (v. 38). (b) Why do it—"for the promise (= the promise of the Father, the Holy Spirit) is made to you and to your children and to all those far off, whomever the Lord our God will call" (v. 39). (c) Exhortation to act—"Save yourselves from this corrupt generation" (v. 40).

It would be a mistake to take this passage as evidence that Luke-Acts links the reception of the Holy Spirit exclusively to baptism. There is no clear-cut theological or ecclesiastical pattern of how and when the Spirit can be expected to be given in Luke-Acts. In Acts 8:12–17 the Samaritan converts to Christianity are baptized without receiving the Spirit. Their experience of the Spirit comes after baptism with the laying on of the apostles' hands. In 10:44–48, Cornelius and his family received the gift of the Spirit before they were baptized. In 19:5–6 the Spirit comes on the disciples of John the Baptist after their baptism in the name of Jesus and in connection with Paul's laying his hands on them. If the evangelist had any preference, it would seem to be reflected in the career of Jesus where, after his baptism and while he is praying, the Spirit descends on him (Luke 3:21–22), foreshadowing the disciples' experience. No doubt the diversity evidenced in the narrative of Acts reflects the diversity of experience in the church of Luke's own day.

It would also be a mistake to take this text as evidence that in Luke-Acts there is only one function of the Spirit. At least three major and five minor functions can be noted (Trafton). Major functions: (a) In 1:8 the risen Jesus promised power to witness from the gift of the Spirit. That is certainly in evidence in Acts 2. When the disciples are filled with the Spirit they bear powerful witness to Jesus, both in tongues and in the more normal type of preaching. There can be no doubt that one function of the Holy Spirit in Acts, perhaps the dominant one, is empowering for witness in two ways: first, by granting boldness to human witnesses (4:31; 6:10), and second, by providing confirming miracles (5:32). The motif of empowering by the Spirit builds on an Old Testament/Jewish base. There the Spirit is understood as an empowering, enabling agent. A craftsman is, by the Spirit, enabled to build the Tabernacle (Exod 31:3); an administrator is, by the Spirit, equipped for leadership (Deut 34:9); judges are, by the Spirit, given physical strength (Judg 14:6) and power in war (Ps.-Philo 27:9–10); Daniel is enabled to understand mysteries (Dan 5:14); Ezra is enabled to write down the holy scriptures (*4 Ezra* 14:22); the Messiah will be empowered for his rule (Isa 11:2; 11QMelch 2:18; *1 Enoch* 49:3; 62:2; *Psalms of Solomon* 17:37; *T. Levi* 18:7). Of all the instances of a person's being empowered for a special task in ancient Judaism, the one that is closest to that of the apostles in Acts is the case of the prophet Micah. In Mic 3:8 the prophet says,

> But as for me, I am filled with power,
> with the Spirit of the Lord,
> with authority and with might;
> to declare to Jacob his crimes,
> and to Israel his sins.

Here the Spirit is associated with power, and the two are linked with preaching to Israel about his sins. This is like the Twelve, who receive power after the Holy Spirit has come upon them and who then preach to the Jerusalemites about their sin of rejecting Jesus.

(b) Acts 2:38–39, however, points to another function of the Spirit. The gift of the Spirit here incorporates people in the reconstituted Israel, the people of God. This function of the Spirit is found elsewhere in Acts in 6:3; 7:55; 8:15, 17; 10:44, 47; 11:17, 24; 15:8–9; 19:6. In this regard Acts stands with Paul (Rom 8:9; 1 Cor 12:13) in seeing a soteriological role of the Spirit (cf. Targum Ps.-Jonathan on Exod 33:8).

(c) There is yet another function of the Spirit in Acts that is also found in Acts 2. It is revealing the divine will to God's people, either through Old Testament prophecy (e.g., Acts 2:25-28, 30-31; 28:25), through Christian prophecy (Acts 11:28; 13:2; 16:7; 20:22-23; 21:11), in community decisions (15:28; 16:6-7), and in the direction of individuals (10:19-20; cf. Wis 9:17). Again, it is as though three different slides were projected onto a screen, one on top of another.

Minor functions: (a) The Spirit bears ethical fruit (6:5; 11:24; cf. *T. Joseph* 11:24; *T. Simeon* 4:4; 1QS 4:6; 1QH 15:7; Gal 5:22-23). (b) The Spirit produces praise to God (10:46; cf. Ps.-Philo 32:14; *1 Enoch* 61:11-12; 71:11). (c) The Spirit effects supernatural relocation (8:39; cf. 1 Kgs 18:12; 2 Kgs 2:16). (d) The Spirit strengthens the church (10:31; cf. Num 11:17, 25; Isa 63:14; Neh 9:20). (e) The Spirit effects miracles (5:32b; 10:38; cf. Josephus, *Antiquities* 8.15.4 § 408). It is not until the eschatological Spirit poured out by the risen Lord is understood to function in these multiple ways that one can arrive at any balanced view of the Spirit in Acts.

It would furthermore be a mistake to think that the Lukan connection of the gift of the Holy Spirit with Pentecost is the single perspective of early Christianity. It is not. (a) Acts 2 locates the gift of the Spirit on Pentecost, fifty days after Passover, after the period of the resurrection appearances is over. (b) John 20:22 locates the gift of the Spirit on Easter day, as part of a resurrection appearance, apparently after the ascension (John 7:39 taken with 20:17). (c) Ephesians 4:8 locates the gift of the Spirit after the ascension but with no specification of exactly when. (d) Mark 15:38 understands the gift of the presence of God to occur at the rending of the veil of the temple before Easter (Moyter, 155-57). There is no way to harmonize these diverse traditions. It is better to see them as different ways of speaking about the origins of the one experiential reality (the gift of the Holy Spirit) that fit the individual theological agendas of their respective sources. In Acts, the gift of the Spirit is located at Pentecost, the time that various covenants—including the Sinai covenant—were made, because in Lukan theology this was the culmination of the establishment of the new covenant.

It would likewise be a mistake to take this passage as proof that tongues were, for Luke, not only a normal but also a necessary evidence of the baptism in the Holy Spirit. Although glossolalia or xenolalia is often a part of the experience of the Holy Spirit in Acts, it is not always so (e.g., 4:31; 8:17; 9:17-18). In fact, in Acts the public manifestations of the gift of the Spirit are sometimes tongues (2:4; 10:46; 19:6), sometimes prophecy (19:6), sometimes praise (10:46), sometimes bold preaching (4:31), sometimes healing (9:17-18). Sometimes the reception of the Holy Spirit is mentioned without any accompanying signs being specified (8:17).

It would finally be a mistake to think of Pentecost as a once-for-all event for the evangelist. In Acts the outpouring of the Holy Spirit is depicted as repeatable in the life of the church (e.g., 4:31; 8:17; 10:1-11:18; 19:1-6).

Verses 41-47 are a summary (cf. 4:32-35) telling of the results of the Pentecostal events and their apostolic interpretation. The summary is organized in a chiastic pattern:

> v. 41—evangelization
>> v. 42—common life
>>> v. 43—signs and wonders
>> vv. 44-47a—common life
> v. 47b—evangelization.

The results of the Pentecostal events as described in Acts 2 are primarily two. (a) Evangelistic outreach results from the empowered witness of the apostles (v. 41: three thousand converts; v. 47b). (b) The establishment of a new kind of community results from the empowering and the outreach. It includes the nurture of the new converts (vv. 42, 46), corporate worship (vv. 42, 46), and a unity manifested in a sharing of possessions (vv. 44-45). Underlying both results is the empowered witness of the apostles (v. 43; cf. 5:32 where such manifestations of the Spirit are regarded as a second witness testifying to the veracity of the apostles' words). In the narrative plot of Acts so far, the emphasis is that as empowering follows petition so evangelism and church unity follow Pentecost.

The Dual Witness (Acts 3:1–4:23)

In Acts 2:17-21 Peter interprets the Pentecostal phenomena as a fulfillment of Joel 2:28-32. Part of the prophecy that is fulfilled reads, "And I will show . . . *signs* on the earth beneath" (Joel 2:19). Acts 2:43, a summary statement, says, "many . . . *signs* were done through the apostles." Acts 3:1-10 offers a concrete example of the signs done by the apostles. A man lame from birth is healed. What immediately follows is an attempt by the apostles to interpret the sign (3:12-26; 4:8-12) and an effort by the authorities to come to terms with it (4:7, 14, 16, 22).

Why break the narrative at 4:23? The Lukan architecture demands it. In Acts 1-5 there is a series of correspondences both in content and in sequence between 1:12-4:23 and 4:24-5:42. The following list makes this clear.

1. 1:12-14, 15-26 Gathered together, the church is at prayer.

   4:24-31a Gathered together, the church is at prayer.

2. 2:1-11 They were all filled with the Holy Spirit.

   4:31b They were all filled with the Holy Spirit.

3. 2:14-36 Peter preaches.

   4:31c They spoke the word of God with boldness.

4. 2:41-47 The communal life of the church is portrayed.

   4:32-35 The communal life of the church is portrayed. It is illustrated by examples in 4:36-37 and 5:1-10.

5. 2:43a Fear comes upon every soul.

   5:5b, 11 Fear comes upon the whole church and all who heard.

6. 2:43b Wonders and signs are done by the apostles.

   5:12a Signs and wonders are performed by the apostles.

7. 3:1-11 A lame man is healed by Peter and John.

   5:13-16 Healings are done by Peter.

8. 3:12-26 Peter delivers a speech in Solomon's Portico.

   5:12b They are all together in Solomon's Portico.

9. 4:1-7 The apostles are arrested by the Sadducees. They are kept in custody until the morrow. Then they are before the Council.

   5:17-28 The apostles are arrested by the Sadducees. They are kept in custody overnight. Then they are brought before the Council.

10. 4:8-12, 19-20 Peter's defense

    5:30-32 Peter's defense

11. 4:13-17 The Council deliberates.

    5:33-39 The Council deliberates.

12. 4:18, 21-23 The apostles are released.

    5:40-42 The apostles are released.

It is preferable to see these correspondences not as signs of Luke's use of different sources nor as a reflection of a two-stage judicial procedure but rather as due to the conscious art of the evangelist (Talbert 1974, 35-39). In any case, they indicate that the break in the narrative comes at 4:23. Moreover, Acts 4:22 functions together with 3:2 as an inclusion holding the unit together.

The thought unit, 3:1-4:23, is composed of a miracle story, two speeches, and the various responses to the speeches. The "sign + speech" pattern provides the testimony of the two witnesses necessary under Jewish law to guarantee truthfulness (Deut 19:15; John 8:17): apostles and Holy Spirit (Acts 5:32). The responses indicate who belongs and who is cut off from the people of God (Acts 3:22-23). The surface structure of the unit looks like this.

The Sign (3:1-11)
    vv. 1-3: the problem
    vv. 4-8: the miracle
    vv. 9-11: the reactions

Peter's Speech (3:12-26)
    vv. 12-16: *how* the healing happened
    vv. 17-26: *what* the healing demands and why

Responses (4:1-4)
    vv. 1-3: by the rulers: arrest of the apostles
    v. 4: by the people: many believe

Peter's speech (3:5-12)
    vv. 5-7: the setting of the speech
    vv. 8-12: the speech
        vv. 9b-10: *how* the healing happened
        vv. 11-12: *what* the healing means

Responses (4:13-23)
    vv. 13-18: of the authorities
    vv. 19-20: of the apostles
    vv. 21-22: of the authorities
    v. 23: of the apostles.

Each of these components must be examined in turn.

The miracle story of 3:1-11 is comprised of the customary three components: (1) a statement of the problem ("lame from birth," v. 2), (2) a description of the cure ("in the name of Jesus of Nazareth, walk," v. 6), and (3) a reference to the responses to the sign ("they were filled with amazement and astonishment," v. 10; "all the people hurried in amazement toward them," v. 11).

(1) Verses 1-3 provide a statement of the problem: where, when, what. The event takes place in the temple area (cf. Josephus, *War* 5.5 §§ 184-247, for a description of the temple) near the three o'clock hour of prayer. The afternoon temple service had its roots in Exod 29:38-42 and Num 28:1-8. Josephus, *Antiquities* 14.4.3 § 65, says it took place at about the ninth hour

(3 P.M.). The time of the evening sacrifice was also regarded as an appropriate time of prayer (Dan 9:21). A man lame from birth (v. 2; who was over
forty years old, 4:22) was carried every day to the Beautiful Gate, where he
would beg for alms (v. 3). The identity of the Beautiful Gate is uncertain, but
it may be the Nicanor Gate, which Josephus says excelled the gates that
were covered in gold and silver because it was of Corinthian brass (*War*
5.5.3 § 201; cf. *m. Middoth* 2:3).

(2) Verses 4–8 recount the miracle. When the lame man asks for alms,
Peter says something: "I have neither silver nor gold, but what I do have I
give you: in the name of Jesus Christ the Nazorean, [rise and] walk" (v. 6).
That he has no money is not owing to legal regulations. Although *m. Berakoth* 9:5 says one cannot enter the temple with a wallet, *t. Berakoth* 7:19
explains that what is meant is to carry one's money unostentatiously, that is,
not exposed to view. Peter and John have no money of their own because,
as members of the Messianist community, their wealth is held in common
(Acts 2:44–45). What they offer is far better. Peter then does something: he
takes the lame man by the hand and raises him up "and immediately his feet
and ankles grew strong" (v. 7). The man's behavior proves he is healed. He
leaps up, stands, walks around, jumps, and praises God (v. 8). He acts as the
lame were expected to do in the messianic times (Isa 35:6; cf. Luke 7:22).
The man's response ("praising God") is a Lukan equivalent to faith (Luke
17:11–19, esp. vv. 18–19).

(3) Verses 9–11 provide the responses to the miracle. When the people
recognized the beggar and realized that he was healed, they "were filled
with amazement" (v. 10) and hurried toward him "in amazement" (v. 11).

The meaning of the miracle story as a whole is derived from its Lukan context. In the first place, it is a Lukan belief that a valid testimony to Christ
requires two witnesses: here, the witness of the apostles and the witness of
the Holy Spirit. Acts 5:32 makes this explicit: "we [apostles] are witnesses
to these things, and so is the Holy Spirit whom God has given to those who
obey him." The same viewpoint is found in Heb 2:3b–4: "it was attested to
us by those who heard the Lord, while God also bore witness by signs and
wonders and various miracles and by gifts of the Holy Spirit distributed
according to his will." Paul echoes the same idea in 1 Thess 1:5; 1 Cor 2:3–5;
and Rom 15:18–19. The signs are the Holy Spirit's witness to the resurrection of Jesus (Acts 2:33: "Being therefore exalted at the right hand of God,
and having received from the Father the promise of the Holy Spirit, he has
poured out this which you see and hear"). The Holy Spirit not only empowers the apostles to give a bold witness, but also, through them, bears a witness of His own. By the mouths of two witnesses is the authority of Jesus

established. The healing of the lame man, then, is the Holy Spirit's testimony to the status of Jesus as Lord.

In the second place, in Luke-Acts salvation encompasses the whole person (e.g., Luke 4:18-19; 4:43 against the background of 4:31-37, 38-39, 40-41; 5:17-26; 7:18-23; 8:43-48; 13:10-17; 18:35-43; 19:1-10; Acts 10:36-38). The physical healings of the bodies of the afflicted are foretastes of the resurrection of the dead, just as one's conversion is a foretaste of the ultimate redemption from all sin. There is in Luke-Acts no reduction of salvation to a purely spiritual transaction any more than there is a reduction of it to a purely physical or political reality. The whole person is affected.

In the third place, the sign is not a magical event. It involves faith (3:8, 16). Any prior faith in the story, however, is not that of the man healed; there is no evidence of that until after the event (3:8). This, then, is not a faith healing! From Luke's point of view, to be healed is not the equivalent to being saved (Luke 17:11-19), but healing may evoke faith and result in salvation, as obviously the evangelist believed here (Acts 4:12). If there was any faith prior to the healing, it belonged to someone other than the cripple. Verse 16 is a notoriously difficult text. One way to translate it is as follows:

> And by [the apostles'] faith in his [Jesus'] name
> this one whom you see and know [the beggar] his [Jesus']
>   name has made strong,
> and the faith [of the apostles] which is through it [Jesus'
>   name] has given him this wholeness. . . .

In this reading, the healing is owing to Jesus and is enabled by the apostles' faith, which has, in turn, been created by Jesus. If faith (human response to the divine initiative) is involved, then this sign cannot be designated as magic (human control of the divine powers to make them work for humans). Luke-Acts wants to distance the Christian movement from magic (e.g., Acts 8:9-11, 19-24; 13:6-12; 16:16-18; 19:18-19). The sign of 3:1-11 is the result of the Holy Spirit's witness, not of human attempts to control the numinous world.

If Acts 3:1-11 gives the divine witness, 3:12-4:23 gives the apostolic witness to Jesus. This witness involves first an interpretation of the healing before the people (3:12-26) and then before the rulers (4:1-23, especially 4:8-12). The first attempt at apostolic interpretation comes at 3:12-26, the speech of Peter before the people. This witness is held together by an inclusion: "the people" in 3:11 and 4:1a. Its setting is specified in 3:11: "all the people hurried toward them in amazement."

The speech falls into two parts (vv. 12-16 and vv. 17-26), each of which is organized in a concentric pattern (Krodel, 18-19). The first part, vv. 12-16, looks like this.

A–v. 12: The healing is not by the apostles' power.
  B–v. 13a: God glorified his servant.
    C–v. 13b: You handed him over and denied him.
    C'–vv. 14-15a: You denied him and put him to death.
  B'–v. 15b: God raised him from the dead.
A'–v. 16: Jesus' name made the man strong.

The dominant point of this first part of the speech is *how* the healing happened. It did not happen by the power of the apostles (cf. Acts 14:15; *Acts of John* 24; cf. Acts 10:26; Rev 19:10) but by the name of Jesus. How? The very Jesus whom the Jerusalemites denied and killed God raised from the dead, vindicating him and enabling his power. The subordinate point in the speech is, therefore, that the Jerusalemites acted wrongly in rejecting Jesus.

The second part of the speech looks like this.

A–vv. 17-18: The Jerusalemites' evil ways
  B–v. 19a: Repent
    C–vv. 19b-21: that the Lord may send you the Messiah
      D–vv. 22-23: Scripture says
        E–v. 24: the prophets
        E'–v. 25a: the prophets
      D'–v. 25b: Scripture says
    C'–v. 26a: God sent his servant to you
  B'–v. 26b: to turn you
A'–v. 26c: from your evil ways.

This segment of Peter's speech does not concern itself with how the healing occurred (= Jesus' postresurrection power). It focuses solely on *what* the healing demands: the repentance of the Jerusalemites.

Why is repentance needed now? The speech offers a series of reasons. (1) Your former actions, denying and killing Jesus, were done in ignorance (v. 17). That excuse no longer applies. Repent. (2) Repent so that your sins can be blotted out and the parousia can occur (vv. 19-21). There existed a Jewish belief that the End was contingent on Israel's behavior: (a) *Testaments of the Twelve Patriarchs* (*T. Dan* 6:4: "the enemy is eager to trip up all who call on the name of the Lord because he knows that on the day in which Israel trusts, the enemy's kingdom will be brought to an end"; *T. Simeon* 6:2-7; *T. Judah* 23:5); (b) *Testament of Moses* 18:1 ("until the day of repentance with regard to which the Lord will regard them in the consummation of the end of days"); (c) *4 Ezra* 4:39 ("the End is delayed because of sin," a view of the author that is rejected by God); (d) R. Eliezer b. Hyrcanus (A.D. 80-120) said, "If Israel repent, they will be redeemed; if not, they will not be redeemed" (*b. Sanhedrin* 97b); (e) R. Simeon b. Yohai

(A.D. 140– 160) said, "If Israel were to keep two Sabbaths according to the laws thereof, they would be redeemed immediately" (*b. Shabbat* 118b); (f) R. Judah (A.D. 170–200) said, "Great is charity, in that it brings the redemption nearer" (*b. Baba Bathra* 10a); (g) R. Jonathan said, "Great is repentance for it brings about redemption" (*b. Yoma* 86b). The third evangelist apparently subscribed to this conviction: "Behold, your house will be abandoned. [But] I tell you, you will not see me until [the time comes when] you say, 'Blessed is he who comes in the name of the Lord'" (Luke 13:35). It is assumed in Acts 3:19 (cf. Rom 2:4; 2 Pet 3:9).

(3) Repent so that you will not be cut off from the people (vv. 22–23). At this point the author of Acts quotes from Deut 18:15: "A prophet like me will the Lord, your God raise up for you . . . to him you shall listen" (v. 22). The Jewish hope for a prophet like Moses at the Endtime (e.g., 1QS 9:11; 4QTest 5–8; John 1:2) is here applied to Jesus. Then, instead of the climactic verse of Deut 18:19 ("If any man will not listen to my words which he speaks in my name, I myself will make him answer for it"), Luke substitutes "Everyone who does not listen to that prophet will be cut off from the people" (v. 23), perhaps echoing Old Testament passages like Exod 12:19; Lev 20:3–5; and Num 15:30. The notion of being cut off from the people is widely used in postbiblical Judaism (e.g., *Jubilees* 6:12, 14; 1QS 2:16; *m. Kerithoth* 1:1–2). Being cut off from the people means being excommunicated so that one will not share in the Age to Come (cf. *m. Sanhedrin* 10:1). What Peter is saying is that unless the Jerusalemites repent of their prior attitude toward Jesus, they will fall under the condemnation of the Lord, who speaks in scripture. They will be excluded from God's people. Therefore, repent.

(4) Repent so that you will be able to fulfill the intent of the covenant with Abraham, namely, that you be a blessing to the Gentiles (v. 25). (5) Repent in order to take advantage of the privileged position granted to you by God: "For you first, God raised up his servant and sent him to bless you by turning each of you from your evil ways" (v. 26; cf. Rom 1:16). The entire second part of Peter's speech to the people is focused on the need for the Jerusalemites to repent.

Not until all has been said that needs to be said is the speech interrupted: "while they were still speaking to the people, the priests, the captain of the temple guard, and the Sadducees confronted them" (4:1). At this point, Luke moves into the responses to Peter's speech. In Acts 3:1–4 two responses are given: that by the rulers (vv. 1–3) and that by the people (v. 4). On the one hand, the rulers' response is negative. They were disturbed that the apostles were proclaiming in Jesus the resurrection of the dead (v. 2). According to Acts 23:8, the Sadducees say there is no resurrection of the dead. The rulers, then, "laid their hands on them and put them in custody until the next day" (v. 3). On the other hand, the response of many of the people is positive: "many of those who heard the word came to believe and [the] number of men grew to [about] five thousand" (v. 4; 2:41). The Jerusalemites are divided over Jesus (Luke 2:34; 12:51-53).

Acts 4:5-12 offers a second speech by Peter set in the context of a hearing before the Council. Verses 5-7 provide the setting for Peter's second speech. The next day the religious authorities assembled in Jerusalem. Among them were Annas the high priest (who had been high priest from A.D. 6-15 [Josephus, *Antiquities* 18.2.1-2 §§ 26-35]) and Caiaphas (the son-in-law of Annas who served as high priest from A.D. 18-36 [Josephus, *Antiquities* 18.2.2 § 35]). Perhaps Annas is spoken of as high priest still because he was, from a Jewish point of view, wrongly deposed; perhaps because he remained the power behind the throne since he was succeeded by his son-in-law and five of his sons (Josephus, *Antiquities* 20.9.1 § 198). The authorities put the apostles in their midst (the Sanhedrin was arranged like the half of a round threshing floor so that they all might see one another, *m. Sanhedrin* 4:3) and asked them, "By what power or by what name have you done this?" (v. 7).

Then Peter, filled with the Spirit (Luke 12:11-12: "the Holy Spirit will teach you in that very hour what you ought to say"; 21:12-15), gives his second speech, this time not to the people but to the rulers. The speech falls into two parts: (1) the first focusing on *how* the healing happened (vv. 8b-10); (2) the second dealing with *what* the healing means (vv. 11-12).

(1) The address ("Leaders of the people and elders," v. 8b) is followed by their question ("If we are being examined today about a good deed done to a cripple, namely, by what means he was healed," v. 9) and the apostles' answer to the question ("it was in the name of Jesus Christ the Nazorean whom you crucified, whom God raised from the dead; in his name this man stands before you healed," v. 10). The leaders receive the same answer as the people had earlier. The healing is by the power of the risen Jesus.

Although in the plot of Luke-Acts Jesus has ascended into heaven (1:9-11), he is not regarded as absent. The risen Jesus is present in the world through his Spirit (cf. Acts 16:7, the Spirit of Jesus), through his name (3:6; 16:18, cures through the name; 10:43, forgiveness mediated through the name), through the tradition of his words and deeds (10:34-43; 13:16-41), in the lives of his followers who have incorporated his model life (remember the correspondences between the events of Jesus' career in Luke and the events in the careers of his followers in Acts), and in various visions (9:3-6, 10-12, 15-16; 22:17-21; 23:11) (MacRae, 151-65; O'Toole, 471-98). Here the activity of the risen Jesus is through his name.

(2) Verses 11-12 shift the focus from how the healing happened to what the miracle means. Peter begins with a citation from Ps 118:22: Jesus is "the stone rejected by you, the builders, which has become the cornerstone"

(v. 11). Psalm 118:22 was widely used in early Christianity (Matt 21:42//Mark 12:10//Luke 20:17; 1 Pet 2:7; *Barnabas* 6:4). Its gist here is that although Jesus has been rejected by the Jerusalemites, God has given him an exalted status. How exalted is it? Verse 12 says, "There is no salvation through anyone else, nor is there any other name under heaven given to the human race by which we must (*dei*) be saved."

Peter's climactic statement demands attention. What does it mean in its Lukan context? First, this is a Messianist's response to Jewish leaders. One Jew is addressing other Jews. In middle Judaism (third century B.C. to second century A.D.), numerous groups struggled with the question of who was heir to the scriptures of Israel and the promises made by God to ancient Israel. Essenes, Pharisees, Sadducees, Messianists, and others all offered their own claims. In Acts 4:12 Peter's claim is that the Messianists' stance is the right understanding of Israel's heritage.

Second, this claim by a Messianic Jew must be set within the context of Acts as a whole. How does the author of Acts understand the relation of Jesus to other religious claims? Acts distinguishes between cultural pluralism, which provides the missionary context for the Christian witness on the one hand, and religious pluralism on the other. It is the latter with which we are concerned. Consider the spectrum of religious options found in the narrative of Acts. (a) Magic is one option noted several times by Acts' author (8:9-24, Samaritan; 13:6-12, Jewish; 16:16-18, pagan; 19:13-20, Jewish and pagan). The attitude of Acts toward magic is uniformly negative. The remedy prescribed is to renounce magic and believe in Jesus' name. (b) Popular paganism is another option noted by Luke (14:8-18; 17:16-34; 19:23-41). This polytheistic system blurs the distinction between God and humans (14:8-18), contributes to rank superstition (17:16-34), and is motivated by contemptible greed (19:23-41). The Lukan attitude toward polytheistic paganism is also negative. The prescription offered by Acts is repentance, together with belief in the one true and living God and recognition of Jesus as the coming judge. This is very much the stance of the early Hellenistic Christian kerygma in Paul's time (cf. 1 Thess 1:9-10).

(c) God-fearers in the Jewish synagogues represent yet a third option in Luke's religious world (8:26-39; 10:1-48; 13:16,43; 14:1; 16:13-15; 17:12; 18:4). These pagans had already made the transition from polytheism to monotheism and had already imbibed much of the Jewish ethical value system. To these folks Acts says the scriptures point to Jesus, who will be the Endtime judge. Jesus is the one who offers forgiveness of sins. What is required is attachment to Jesus.

(d) Nonmessianic Jews constitute the final option in Luke's religious world (2:14, 22, 29-41; 3:17-26; 4:8-12; 5:29-32; 13:16-43; 14:1; 15:7-

11; 17:11; 18:4-5). Fellow Jews are, of course, monotheistic and committed to a certain ethical stance approved by the Messianists. To these nonmessianic Jews, however, Acts offers two clearcut words: Acts 4:8-12 ("There is no other name") and 15:7-11 (Peter says: "we believe we are saved through the grace of the Lord Jesus, in the same way as they [the Gentiles] are").

Acts does not consider all religious positions as equal. Some, like magic, receive only condemnation; others, like popular paganism, receive only correction; still others, like the god-fearers and nonmessianic Jews, are offered completion as well as correction. Acts, however, does not consider any of the other religious options as equal to the Messianists' stance. Conversion (repentance/faith/baptism) is necessary in every case, even in the case of nonmessianic Judaism (cf. 2:38; 15:7-11). Acts 4:12 is a specific instance of such a demand for nonmessianic Jews.

How does the stance of Acts compare with that found in the Third Gospel? Comparison of Luke 5:1-11 and 7:1-10 shows that Peter, a Jew, and the devout Gentile with sympathies for Judaism come to Jesus in the same way: (a) confession of sin or unworthiness (5:8; 7:6) and (b) trust in Jesus' authority (5:5, 11; 7:7-8).

> Whether it is a Jew whose tradition is fulfilled or a pagan whose appropriate response to the light available is completed, the way to Jesus involves some discontinuity with the past (hence the sense of unworthiness or sin) and a submission to a new authority (the lordship of Jesus). (Talbert 1982, 83)

The Third Gospel agrees with Acts about the relative merits of other religious traditions.

In this stance with regard to other religious traditions, Luke-Acts does not stand alone in early Christianity. Q (Matt 10:32-33//Luke 12:8-9), Paul (Rom 3:30; 9:30-33), Mark (8:38), Hebrews (10:9-10), the Deutero-Pauline tradition (1 Tim 2:5), the Fourth Gospel (John 14:6), and 1 John (2:23) take the very same position, as do Ignatius, *Philadelphians* 9:1 ("he is himself the door to the Father, through which Abraham and Isaac and Jacob and the prophets and the apostles and the church enter") and Hermas, *Vision* 4.2.4, and *Parable* 9.12.5 ("a man cannot enter the kingdom of God in any other way than through the name of his Son").

This type of exclusivist stance would have been a serious offense to a Mediterranean pagan. About A.D. 200, a Christian lawyer, Minucius Felix, wrote a dialogue consisting of an exchange between a pagan (Q. Caecilius Natalis) and a Christian (Octavius Jannarius). The pagan grants the Christians the freedom to decide most things for themselves, but one thing he finds impossible. He calls the Christians' claim to possess "the truth" arrogant and irresponsible.

The Romans believed that when Christians claimed exclusive possession of divine knowledge, they were capable of anything. . . . An irreconcilable difference existed between pagans and Christians on this issue. The pagan took the position that matters pertaining to the divine mystery were obscure and so should be left open to debate. The Christian, however, was convinced that he was in possession of the truth, because Jesus Christ embodied the ultimate revelation about God. (Benko, 59)

Nothing could better describe the character Peter in the plot of Acts. The Peter of Acts 4:8–12 is neither a pluralist nor an inclusivist; he is an exclusivist. This is what the healing of the lame man means: Jesus is the only Savior.

If Jesus is the only Savior, from what does he save? The narrative of Acts gives its clues. In Acts 2:40 Peter says to the Jerusalemites at Pentecost, "Save yourselves from this corrupt generation." Assumed is the belief that the present generation is disobedient to God's will and that it will not fare well at the last judgment (cf. Luke 3:7–9 for John the Baptist's estimate of this generation). What is needed is forgiveness of one's sins. This, the Messianists say, comes through Jesus (Acts 10:43; 13:38–39; 26:18). Only thereby can one expect to be included among the people of God who will have a place in the Age to Come (3:23; 26:18). In the meantime, the power of Jesus protects and delivers from the powers of evil in this present evil age (e.g., illness, Acts 3:1–11; 5:15–16; demons, Acts 16:16–18; 19:12; enemies, Acts 18:10; 23:11); and the presence of the Holy Spirit, poured out by Jesus (2:33), empowers Jesus' followers (2:38; 4:31).

The second speech of Peter evokes its responses. In 4:13–18, the authorities try to come to terms with what has happened. (a) They first of all observe the boldness (*parrēsia*, a trait of Cynic philosophers also [Dio Chrysostom, *Oration* 32:11; 77/78:37, 45]) of Peter and John. They are amazed that *am-haaretz* ("people of the land"), who are unschooled in rabbinic lore (*m. Demai* 2:2–3), would be so bold. They also recognize them as companions of Jesus (v. 13), that is, Galileans. In the general mindset, there was a significant difference between Judean and Galilean Judaism in the first century. Galilean sages like Haninah b. Dosa were marked by "miracles," while Judean sages like Johanan b. Zakkai were known for their "learning." How then could these unlettered Galileans be so bold? Of course, the reader has already been told. Unlike the characters in the story, the reader knows that Peter spoke when he was "filled with the Holy Spirit" (v. 8a). (b) The rulers are also perplexed because the evidence stands before them. "When they saw the man who had been cured standing there with them [the apostles], they [the authorities] could say nothing in reply" (v. 14; cf. Luke 21:15).

After sending the apostles out, the Sanhedrin confer among themselves and reach a conclusion: "so that it may not be spread any further among the people, let us give them a stern warning never again to speak to anyone in this name" (v. 17). So they call the apostles back "and ordered them not to speak or teach at all in the name of Jesus" (v. 18).

Peter and John reply, "Whether it is right in the sight of God for us to obey you rather than God, you be the judges. It is impossible for us not to speak about what we have seen and heard." The apostles' response is akin to that echoed in Josephus, *Antiquities* 17.6.3 § 159, where Jews respond to Herod with the same "either-or" fervor, and in *Antiquities* 18.8.2 § 268, where Jews make the same determined stand before Petronius ("we will not disobey the laws of God who is superior to Gaius"). It also is akin to that of Socrates, who, when offered the possibility of release if he would stop teaching, said, "Men of Athens . . . I shall obey God rather than you. . . . God commands me to do this" (Plato, *Apology* 29D-E; cf. *1 Clement* 14:1; *2 Clement* 4:4).

The authorities are left no recourse. "After threatening them further, they released them, finding no way to punish them, on account of the people who were all praising God for what had happened" (v. 21). After their release, the apostles go back to "their own people" and report what had happened (v. 23). At this point, the rulers who have rejected Jesus yet once more are cut off from the people (3:23). They are no longer the rulers of the reconstituted Israel (Luke 20:9-16, 17-19). The apostles are (Luke 22:29-30; Acts 1:15-26).

Hostility Grows (Acts 4:24-5:42)

The risen Jesus in Acts 1:8 promised an empowered witness that would begin in Jerusalem. The narrative that follows contains three cycles of material in which such a mission is carried out: 1:12-4:23; 4:24-5:42; and 6:1-8:3. The first two cycles, with the apostles as the focus, correspond closely in contents and sequence; the third, whose focus is on Stephen, more loosely. Repetition with variation characterizes the cycles. What distinguishes these three cycles of witness in Jerusalem is the ascending degree of hostility directed against the Messianists: (1) warning (4:17-18, 21); (2) beating (5:40); and (3) martyrdom and persecution (7:54-60; 8:1, 3). In this regard, these three cycles are like the collection of five conflict stories in Mark 2:1-3:6, where opposition begins with grumbling and ends with a plot to kill Jesus. Acts 4:24-5:42 is the middle cycle of empowered witness in Jerusalem. It consists of a prayer scene (4:24-31), two summaries (4:32-35; 5:12-16), two examples (4:36-37; 5:1-11), and a trial (5:17-42). Each needs attention.

Acts 4:24–31 is a prayer scene consisting of (1) the occasion (4:24a); (2) the prayer (4:24b–30); and (3) the answer to the prayer (4:31). When Peter and John told "their own people" (v. 23) what the chief priests and elders had said to them, the threats served as a catalyst for the community's prayer (vv. 24b–30). The prayer, which has some loose similarities to that in Isa 37:16–20, begins with (a) an address ("Sovereign Lord", v. 24b) characteristic of Jewish (Neh 9:6; Tob 8:17; Wis 11:26; Josephus, *Antiquities* 4.3.2 §§ 40, 46) and early Christian practice (Rev 6:10; *Didache* 10:3; *1 Clement* 59:4; 60:3; 61:1–2).

The address is followed by (b) a dual ascription: "you who made heaven and earth" (v. 24c; cf. Isa 37:16) and "you who said by the Holy Spirit through the mouth of our father David" (v. 25a). The God who is addressed is the creator and revealer. The second ascription contains a quotation from Ps 2:1–2 (vv. 25b–26), which is then interpreted in v. 27 as applicable to Jesus' passion. "Gathered together" (vv. 26,27) against the Lord's "anointed" (vv. 26, 27) were "kings" (vv. 26, 27 [Herod = a king]) and "rulers" (vv. 26, 27 [Pilate = a ruler]), "Gentiles" (vv. 25b, 27), and "peoples" (vv. 25b, 27). Psalm 2:1–2 is here interpreted not only eschatologically (as in 4QFlor 1:18–19) but also messianically (as in *Psalms of Solomon* 17:23–24; cf. Rev 19:19). After the address and ascription come (c) the dual petitions for boldness (v. 29b) and for signs and wonders (v. 30).

The first petition is answered immediately (as was Moses' prayer, Josephus, *Antiquities* 4.3.2–3 §§ 40–51; as was Izates' petition, Josephus, *Antiquities* 20.4.2 §§ 90–91). "As they prayed, the place where they were gathered shook (a sign of a theophany; cf. Exod 19:18; Isa 6:4; *4 Ezra* 6:15, 29; Vergil, *Aeneid* 3.88–91), and they were all filled with the Holy Spirit and continued to speak the word of God with boldness" (v. 31). Further evidence of apostolic boldness will be in evidence in v. 33 and in 5:12b. The second petition will be answered in 5:12, 15–16.

In this unit the witness to Jesus is understood to consist both of deeds (signs) and words. The word without the deed is insufficient because there is little interest in the abstractions of another's system of belief. It takes the deeds to pique the interest and raise the questions. Likewise, the deed without the word is incomplete. Only if the true meaning of the event is known can one discern the proper response to make to it. In Luke-Acts, the deed and the word are held together as the necessary dual testimony to the truth about Jesus.

The prayer (4:24b–31) is followed by a summary (4:32–35) that has similarities to one in Acts 2:41–47. It falls into an ABA' pattern.

A—v. 32: the common life of the church
  B—v. 33: an answer to the petition in v. 29b
A'—vv. 34–35: the common life of the church

The B component (v. 33) picks up the theme of 4:31b and reaffirms it. The community empowered by the Spirit engages in a bold and powerful witness. The A (v. 32) and A' (vv. 34–35) components advance the discussion by focusing on the inner life of the church. Verse 32 says "the community of believers was of one heart and mind, and no one claimed that any of his possessions was his own." Verses 34–35 say "there was no needy person among them, for those who owned property or houses would sell them, bring the proceeds of the sale and put them at the feet of the apostles, and they were distributed to each according to need."

Acts 4:32, 34–35 describes the fellowship of the Christian community empowered by the Spirit as the realization of both pagan and Jewish ideals about possessions. In Mediterranean antiquity the notion of an ideal period in history, an ideal state, an ideal friendship, an ideal religious or philosophical group, the ideal Israel, the ideal future, all shared ideas echoed in vv. 32 and 34. It is difficult to reduce the background of Acts 4:32, 34 to any one of these idealizations. All seem to play a role as backdrop for the Lukan presentation. We may examine the Lukan statements one by one.

(1) The community was of one heart and soul (v. 32a). This is similar to the ideals of friendship in antiquity. Aristotle said a friend was "one soul dwelling in two bodies" (Diogenes Laertius 5.20). Cicero said that the essence of friendship was in the formation of a single soul, as it were, from several (*On Friendship* 25.92). Plutarch speaks of friends "who, though existing in separate bodies, actually unite and fuse their souls together" (*Dialogue on Love* 21:9 [967E]).

(2) They had their possessions in common (v. 32b). Seneca claims that in the golden age of ultimate human origins common ownership of property was practiced (*Epistle* 90.38). Sharing of possessions was a feature of Plato's ideal state (*Republic* 420C–422B; 462B–464A; *Laws* 679B–C; 684C–D; 744B–746C; 757A). Plato's *Critias* 110C–D pictures the early days of Athens as a time when "none of its members possessed any private property, but rather they regarded all they had as the common property of all." Various religious or philosophical communities practiced such sharing of goods. The founding of the Pythagorean community at Croton involved the sharing of possessions (Porphyry, *Life of Pythagoras* 20). The Cynic epistles mention such repeatedly: "Diogenes the Cynic used to say that . . . friends have things in common" (Crates 27. "To the Same"); "the property of friends is held in common" (Diogenes 10. "To Metrocles"); "And if you need anything that is yours, write us, for my possessions, Plato, are by all rights yours, even as they were Socrates'" (Socratics 26. "To Plato"). The Essenes are spoken of in such terms by Philo (*Every Good Man Is Free* 77, 79, 84–85; *Hypothetica* 11.4–9, 10–11) and Josephus (*War* 2.8.3 § 122; cf. 1QS 6:18–20, 21–23 for community of property at Qumran). The friendship tradition also

contained the ideal. Aristotle said, "Among friends everything in common is quite correct, for friendship consists in sharing" (*Ethics* 8.11 [1159B]; 9:8 [1168B]. Euripides said, "True friends cling not to private property; their wealth is shared in close community" (*Andromache* 376-77). When the ideal future is envisioned, it is prophesied: "Lives will be in common and wealth will have no division" (*Sibylline Oracles* 2.321).

(3) There was no needy person among them (v. 34a). When Seneca referred to the ideal state of affairs during the primitive period when property was shared, he says that "you could not find a single pauper" (*Epistle* 90.38). When Isocrates spoke of the old Athenian constitution that decreed private property which was to be shared by all, he claims "no one had any need" (*Areopagiticus* 83) and calls on his listeners to imitate their ancestors to cure society's ills (84). When Deut 15:4 looks forward to the ideal future for Israel it says, "Since the Lord, your God, will bless you abundantly . . . there should be no one of you in need."

(4) Those who owned property would sell it and bring the proceeds to be shared (v. 34b). Aristotle said, "It is clear that it is far better for possessions to be privately owned, but to make them common property in use" (*Politics* 2.2.4 [1263A]). Isocrates, in describing the old Athenian constitution, notes that people owned property privately but brought it to be shared by all (*Areopagiticus* 35).

The summary, Acts 4:32-35, depicts the primitive Christian community in Jerusalem as having realized the ideals about property held by Jews and pagans alike in Mediterranean antiquity. The reason these ideals are actualized is the disciples' empowering by the Spirit (4:31; chap. 2) (Dupont 1979, 85-102; Mitchell, 262-64). If Lucian's *Peregrinus* is any indication, the values espoused by Acts continued in the church. Lucian tells of the rogue Peregrinus, who became a Christian. When he did and was imprisoned as a result, the other Christians met his every need and money came pouring in. Lucian comments, "All this they take quite on trust, with the result that they despise all worldly goods alike, regarding them merely as common property" (13).

It is interesting to note that here the apostles are responsible both for the preaching of the word (v. 34) and for the administration of funds (v. 35). This will soon be changed (6:1-6). The results of the Spirit's empowering are both evangelism and the creation of deep fellowship. It will soon be necessary to recognize that the same persons cannot implement both. A division of labor will be called for.

Acts 4:36-5:11 narrates both a concrete example of this fellowship among the Messianists (4:36-37) and a perversion of it (5:1-11). Such contrasts are characteristic of Mediterranean literature. For example, contrasting pairs of characters who serve as foils for one another appear with great frequency in the comedies of Plautus and Terence (e.g., two young men, two sweethearts, two slaves). Such would be no surprise to Luke's auditors.

Barnabas (9:27; 11:22, 30; 12:25; chap. 13; chap. 14; 15:12, 22, 30, 35; 15:36–41), a Levite (according to Num 18:20 and Deut 10:9 a Levite should not have owned an estate, but Josephus [*Life* 76] indicates that by his time this was done), sells a field and brings the money and lays it at the feet of the apostles (vv. 36–37; cf. v. 35a where "and laid it at the apostles' feet" concludes the summary). His behavior is a concrete example of the community's realization of the Mediterranean ideal regarding property. It is a transcending of cultural roles (Cicero, *De Officiis* 1.150–51, ranks occupations, placing owners of cultivated land at the top and fishermen at the bottom). In Lukan thought, the Holy Spirit indwells the community ("they were filled with the Spirit," v. 31). The Spirit's inner leading is not only to mission (1:8; 4:31b, 33) but also to community (2:44–45; 4:32, 34–35). This community fellowship is first of all spiritual ("of one heart and soul," v. 32a). This spiritual unity, however, spills over into the physical, financial world of believers (vv. 32b, 34–35). This is part of the Lukan belief that wealth is used properly when it builds relationships and community (Luke 12:33–34; 16:9; Acts 2:44–45; 11:27–30; 24:17). What concerns the evangelist are the social benefits of wealth rightly used. What he wants to avoid is the use of wealth in the service of private indulgence. Wealth is properly used, he thinks, when disciples live out of their being filled with the Holy Spirit. Only if they do not follow the guidance of the Spirit will they use wealth for private indulgence instead of to express and build community. Barnabas is depicted here as one who follows the Spirit's leading (cf. 11:24).

Ananias and Sapphira constitute the negative example (5:1–11). Their behavior represents a contrast to the ideal behavior of the summary (4:32–35). In form, this difficult text falls into two parts, vv. 1–6 and vv. 7–11. The first focuses on Ananias, the second on Sapphira. Each half has the same basic components.

Verses 1–6	*Verses 7–11*
Ananais–v. 1	Sapphira–v. 7
Peter said–vv. 3–4	Peter said–vv. 8–9
Ananias fell down and died–v. 5a	Sapphira fell down and died–v. 10a
Young men/carried/buried–v. 6	Young men/carried/buried–v. 10b
Great fear upon all–v. 5b	Great fear upon all–v. 11

What is the sin of the couple? It is twofold. On the one hand, it is retaining some for themselves when they said it was all devoted to God (v. 2) and thereby lying to God (vv. 3–4). That is, they have failed to fulfill a vow (Num 30:2: "When a man makes a vow to the Lord . . . , he shall not violate his word, but must fulfill exactly the promise he has uttered"; Deut 23:22–24:

"When you make a vow to the Lord, your God, you shall not delay in fulfilling it; otherwise you will be held guilty . . . you must keep your solemn word and fulfill the votive offering you have freely promised to the Lord"). On the other hand, Ananias and Sapphira have entered into a conspiracy over property (vv. 2a, 9). Taken together, they have conspired not to fulfill a vow.

What is the cause of their sin? Peter says to Ananias, "Why has Satan filled your heart?" (v. 3). In Luke 22:3 we are told that Satan entered into Judas; vv. 5-6 associate this with accepting money for betraying Jesus (cf. John 13:27: Satan entered into Judas; *Martyrdom of Isaiah* 3:11: Beliar dwelt in the heart of Manasseh; 1QS 3:13-4:25). There is a satanic root to the couple's lying to God (cf. John 8:44, where Satan is a liar).

This is a typological story, told in terms of the two sins and their appropriate end. On the one hand, the phrase "kept back some" echoes Josh 7:1-26. There Achan keeps back some of the property devoted to God, and it results in his death. Lying to God (= failure to fulfill one's vow) has as its appropriate end, death. On the other hand, the notion of a couple's conspiracy regarding property echoes 1 Kings 21 where there is a story of a man and his wife (Ahab and Jezebel) involved in a conspiracy over land (Naboth's vineyard) that issues in their deaths. This story involves a prophet's word and its fulfillment: indictment (21:19a, 20), prophecy of punishment (vv. 19b, 21-24, 28-29), followed by fulfillment (1 Kgs 22:37-38; 2 Kgs 9:30-37). The appropriate end of those involved in such a conspiracy is death. Just as Judas's end in Acts 1:18-19 is described in terms of what is appropriate to his particular crime, so here with Ananias and Sapphira.

What is the story's function in Acts? It serves to illustrate a threat to the church's unity, and it illustrates one way such a threat is resolved. There is divine intervention against the persons posing the threat. As such, the story is a narrative illustration of the Pauline warning found in 1 Cor 3:16-17.

> Do you not know that you are the temple of God, and that the Spirit of God dwells in you? If anyone destroys God's temple, God will destroy that person; for the temple of God, which you are, is holy.

Ancient temples were often protected by a curse against anyone who violated the sanctuary of the deity (Polybius 31.9.3; Diodorus Siculus 14.63, 70; 22.5; 28.3; 31.189; Livy 29.18). It is not uncommon to hear stories of the tragic end of those upon whom such a curse came (Talbert 1987, 7-8). Against this background Paul issues his warning; against this backdrop the story of Ananias and Sapphira is told. God does not take lightly threats to the integrity of the community that is filled with the Spirit. Like Judas (Acts 1:18-19), Ananias and Sapphira do not live to enjoy their gain.

The two examples of contrasting attitudes toward wealth are followed by another summary (5:12–16). It falls into a concentric pattern.

A–v. 12–13a: answer to the petitions in 4:29–30
B–v. 13b: response of people to the apostles
B'–v. 14: response of people to the apostles
A'–vv. 15–16: answer to the petition in 4:30

If the first petition of the prayer of 4:24–30 (for boldness) had been answered initially in 4:31, 33, it is answered again in 5:12b–13a. The apostles, with boldness, dare to return to Solomon's Portico in spite of the danger even if other Messianists do not. The second petition (for signs and wonders) is answered here in vv. 12a and 15–16. The sick and the demon possessed are healed. So powerful is the healing ministry of the apostles that people even carry the sick out into the streets and lay them on cots and mats "so that when Peter came by, at least his shadow might fall on one or another of them" (v. 15; cf. 19:11–12; Luke 8:44–48). This obviously reflects a Mediterranean belief that being touched by a person's shadow means being in contact with his soul or essence. Such contact may be for good or ill depending on the character of the person whose shadow touches one. For example, Cicero gives a negative example. Quoting Ennius, he has Thyestes say,

> Strangers, draw you not near to me! Back there, back! Lest a tainted touch from me, lest my very shadow harm you . . . . Oh, such a deadly violence of sin clings to my body." (*Tusculan Disputations* 3.12.26)

In the case of Peter, the example is positive. As a Spirit-filled apostle, his very essence is a medium of power to aid those in distress (Horst 1977, 204–12). The people hold the apostles in high esteem (v. 13), and many converts are made (v. 14; 2:41; 4:4). The successes of the Messianists here have the same result that the healing of the lame man had in 3:1–4:23. The apostles are arrested.

The large thought unit 4:24–5:42 ends with a trial story in five scenes: (1) 5:17–21a; (2) 5:21b–27a; (3) 5:27b–32; (4) 5:33–39; and (5) 5:40–42. Each of the scenes consists first of the establishment's initiative against the Messianists to halt their innovations and then of the various responses to those initiatives. The trial story gives us a picture of a religious establishment's attempt to deal with religious innovation within its ranks. The scenes may be taken up in order.

(1) In the first scene, 5:17–21a, the apostles are put in the public jail. Their opponents are the high priest and the party of the Sadducees. The Sadducees are called *hairesis* ("a party"), a term used for the Pharisees in 15:5 and 26:5 and for the Messianists in 24:5, 14, and 28:22. Middle Judaism

had various parties each of which claimed to represent the true reading of the scriptures of Israel. One such party was the Sadducean group, associated with the high priest and the temple cult. The Sadducees are described by Josephus as being "very rigid in judging offenders, above all the rest of the Jews" (*Antiquities* 20.9.1 § 199). These persons are filled with *zēlou* (= not jealousy but zeal). Elsewhere in Acts one hears that the Jews were filled with zeal (13:45); that the Jews were zealous (17:5); that thousands among the Jews have believed and they are all zealous for the law (21:20); that Paul was brought up strictly, being zealous for God as Jews are (22:3; cf. Gal 1:14–the pre-Christian Paul was extremely zealous for the traditions of his fathers; Rom 10:2–the Jews have a zeal for God but it is not enlightened).

What does this mean? (a) In Num 25:11 LXX, God commends Phinehas for killing the Israelite man and Midianite woman, saying that the act causes his wrath against Israel to cease. God's stance prior to Phinehas's act is said to have been "being zealous with zeal among them." God then gives Phinehas a covenant so that he and his seed after him shall be priests, "because he was zealous for his God" (Num 25:13 LXX). (b) 1 Macc 2:24 says that Mattathias burned with zeal and killed the Jew who was offering pagan sacrifice. (c) 1QH 14:13–15 has the psalmist say, "The nearer I draw to you, the more I am filled with zeal against all that do wickedness and against all men of deceit." (d) *m. Sanhedrin* 9:6 says that those, like Phinehas, who are zealous and set upon religious criminals to kill them are granted exemption from punishment. (e) *Numbers Rabbah* 21, in a context related to Phinehas, says, "Everyone who sheds the blood of the godless is like one who offers a sacrifice." The zeal spoken of is zeal for the purity of the Jewish faith, as it is understood by whoever is zealous. In Acts 5:17, it is the priestly group that, like Phinehas the priest, is zealous for the Lord. Out of such zeal, they arrest the apostles and put them in prison.

The divine response to Sadducean initiative takes the form of an angel's (in whose existence the Sadducees did not believe, Acts 23:8) opening the doors, bringing them out, and commissioning them to speak to the people (vv. 19–20). This is the first of three divine deliverances from prison in Acts (cf. 12:6–19; 16:25–34). It belongs to a specific *Gattung* in antiquity. Perhaps the closest analogy is found in Euripides, *Bacchae*. There followers of Bacchus are persecuted by a leader who seeks to stop the movement by imprisoning its followers (346–57) and one of its leaders (510–19). The cult followers, however, are freed from prison by Bacchus himself (615–40). Such stories have as their function to say that nothing is able to stop the progress of the god and his movement. So it is here as well. "They went to the temple early in the morning (because the temple was closed at night

[Josephus, *Apion* 2.119; *m. Shekalim* 5:1]) and taught" (v. 21b). In spite of the zeal of the priests, the Messianists' word spreads.

(2) In the second scene (vv. 21b–27a) the Council gathers together and sends for the prisoners. The narrative that follows says first that the apostles are not found in the jail (vv. 22–24). The court officials state, "We found the jail securely locked and the guards stationed outside the doors, but when we opened them, we found no one inside" (v. 23a). It then says that the apostles are found in the temple (v. 25), obeying the angelic command of v. 20. Thereupon the captain and his officers bring them, but without violence (vv. 26–27a). The effect of scene two is to create the impression that the mystified establishment is up against a mightier opponent.

(3) In scene three (vv. 27b–32), the Council questions the apostles about their disobedience to an earlier command (4:17–18) not to teach in Jesus' name (vv. 27b–28). Here a motive other than their zeal is evident. "You . . . want to bring this man's blood upon us" (v. 28b; Judg 9:24 LXX says God is avenger of blood spilled innocently). The apostles' response is a bold one: "We must obey God rather than men" (v. 29). This type of response is typical of Lukan heroes (4:19–20; 26:19). Jewish heroes as well spoke this way (e.g., Dan 3:16–18; 2 Macc 7:2; Josephus, *Antiquities* 17.6.3 § 159). It, moreover, echoes the words of Socrates in Plato's *Apology* 29D: "I should, then, obey God rather than you." It would have been regarded as the right thing to do in Mediterranean antiquity. For example, in Plutarch's biography of Caius Marcius Coriolanus we hear of one Titus Latinus, quiet and modest, free from superstitious fears and vain pretentions, who had a vision of Jupiter bidding him to tell the Senate a certain message. Titus neglected to do as bidden, even after having the vision a second and third time. Whereupon he suffered the loss of an excellent son by death and himself became suddenly palsied. He was then brought to the Senate on a litter. No sooner had he delivered the message than at once he felt the strength return to his body. He rose up and walked away without aid, much to the amazement of all. In antiquity it was believed necessary to obey heavenly commissions. If the apostles obey the angel's command to go preach in the temple, their behavior is to be regarded as exemplary.

Peter then delivers a brief sermon (vv. 30–32). Although the Jerusalem establishment had Jesus killed (v. 30b), God raised Jesus (v. 30a) and exalted him at his right hand as leader (*archēgos* = pioneer; cf. 3:15; Heb 12:2) and savior (v. 31a). In this role the risen-exalted Jesus grants Israel repentance and forgiveness of sins (v. 31b). In Lukan soteriology, saving benefits flow from the exalted Jesus. Two witnesses verify these claims: the apostles and the Holy Spirit (v. 32; cf. John 15:26–27). The effect of this scene is once again to identity the Messianist movement with the divine will.

(4) In scene four (vv. 33–39), the Council wants to kill the apostles

(v. 33), emulating Phinehas. This initiative is aborted by the intervention of one of their own number, Gamaliel the Pharisee (vv. 34-39). Acts 22:3 has Paul claim this Gamaliel as his teacher. Gamaliel was the grandson of Hillel. He is to be distinguished from his son, R. Simeon ben Gamaliel I, who was contemporaneous with the war against Rome, A.D. 66-70 (Josephus, *Life* 189-98), and from his grandson, R. Gamaliel II, the successor of R. Johanan ben Zakkai at Jamnia (ca. A.D. 90-110). If Gamaliel I was a member of the Council, he had been one of those to condemn Jesus (Luke 22:66-73). His speech is preceded by a statement of his virtues: "a teacher of the law, respected by all the people" (v. 34). With this Lukan judgment, the Mishnah agrees (*m. Sota* 9:15 says of him, "When R. Gamaliel the Elder died, the glory of the Law ceased and purity and abstinence died"). He was a great teacher.

Gamaliel's speech falls into an ABB'A' pattern.

A—v. 35: Be careful
    B—v. 36: Remember Theudas
    B'—v. 37: Remember Judas
A'—vv. 38-39: Be cautious

In A (v. 35), Gamaliel utters a warning, "Be careful what you are about to do to these men." This is followed in B and B' by two examples. B (v. 36) recalls a movement associated with Theudas (Josephus, *Antiquities* 20.5.1 §§ 97-99, dates Theudas to A.D. 45-46! Origen, *Against Celsus* 1.57, places Theudas before the birth of Christ and places Judas after him, in the days of the census). It went nowhere because after its leader was killed, all those loyal to him disbanded so that his movement came to naught. B' (v. 37) recalls a movement associated with Judas (Josephus, *Antiquities* 18.1.1 §§ 1-10; *War* 2.8.1 §§ 117-18; 7.8.1 §§ 252-58, puts Judas about A.D. 6). It too went nowhere because its leader perished and "all who were loyal to him were scattered."

Judas and Theudas are examples of a continuing series of individuals who appeared from the end of the first century B.C. to the end of the first century A.D., gaining a following but ultimately failing. (a) During the time of Herod, Ezekias, the leader of a band of bandits in Galilee, was slain, and his movement came to naught (Josephus, *Antiquities* 14.9.2 §§ 158-60; *War* 1.10.5 §§ 204-5). (b) After Herod's death, Judas (the son of Ezekias), Simon, and Athrongeus led movements that were put down (Josephus, *Antiquities*, 17.10,5-7 §§ 271-284: *War* 2.5.4 §§ 55-65). (c) In A.D. 6-7, Judas led an uprising over Quirinius's census (Josephus, *Antiquities* 18.1.1 §§ 4-10; *War* 2.8.1 § 118). (d) During the days of Fadus (A.D. 44-48), the prophet Theudas appeared (Josephus, *Antiquities* 20.5.1 §§ 97-99). (e) In A.D. 49, a group of Galileans led by Eleazar rose up (Josephus, *Antiquities* 20.6.1 §§ 118-24).

(f) In the days of Felix (A.D. 52-60) an Egyptian prophet (Acts 21:38) appeared and attracted followers with his promises of the Endtime (Josephus, *Antiquities* 20.8.6 §§ 169-72; *War* 2.13.5 §§ 261-63). (g) In the time of Festus (A.D. 60-62) an unnamed imposter appeared and attempted to lead people into the wilderness as a prelude to the End (Josephus, *Antiquities* 20.8.10 § 188). (h) In the days of the emergency government (A.D. 66-70), a false prophet called for the people to go to the temple where they would receive signs of the coming deliverance (Josephus, *War* 6.5.1 § 285). (i) In A.D. 73 in Cyrene, a weaver, Jonathan, led people into the desert with vain promises (Josephus, *War* 7.11.1 §§ 438-42).

Both examples cited by Gamaliel are of Jewish movements led by individuals who were killed or driven off and whose followers then disbanded. The implication is that it would be so with the Messianists whose leader, Jesus, had been crucified. Now all the Council has to do is to wait for his followers to scatter. Of course, there is the remote possibility that they might be right. So A' (vv. 38-39) advises caution. "If this endeavor . . . is of human origin, it will destroy itself. But if it comes from God, you will not be able to destroy them; you may even find yourselves fighting against God." Jewish sentiment paled at the thought of fighting God. That was something ignorant Gentiles did (2 Macc 7:19). Anyone who did such a thing had God as his enemy. In 3 Macc 7:9, an enlightened pagan king says of the Jews:

> If we devise any evil scheme against them or cause them any trouble, we shall have not man but the most high God, who is ruler of all power, as our adversary to exact vengeance for what is done.

God forbid that it should be so. Hence Gamaliel advises caution instead of execution. To wait and see is the better option (*m. Pirke Aboth* 4:11 attributes to R. Johanan the Sandalmaker a similar saying: "Any assembling that is for the sake of Heaven shall in the end be established, but any that is not for the sake of Heaven shall not in the end be established").

(5) In scene five (vv. 40-42), the Council takes Gamaliel's advice and does not kill the apostles (Gamaliel's student Saul did not take his advice [Acts 22:4; 26:9-11]). In so doing, the Sadducees submit to what a Pharisee says, as Josephus says they normally did in order to survive with the masses (Josephus, *Antiquities* 18.1.4 §§ 16-17). The body does, however, beat them (Deut 25:3; *m. Makkoth* 3:10-14; 2 Cor 11:24) and charge them again not to speak in the name of Jesus (v. 40).

(a) The beating does not subdue them. They rejoiced that they had been "found worthy to suffer dishonor for the sake of the name" (v. 41). Rejoicing in suffering can be found in nonmessianic Judaism (2 Macc 6:30; *b. Shabbat* 88b). It is found also among certain pagans (Epictetus 1.29.49; 2.1.38-39). Among Christians, it is a distinguishing motif (Rom 5:3-4; Phil

1:29; Heb 10:34; James 1:2, 12; 1 Pet 4:13). The Lukan Jesus had already laid the foundation:

> Blessed are you when people hate you,
> and when they exclude and insult you,
> and denounce your name as evil
> on account of the name of the Son of Man.
> Rejoice and leap for joy on that day! (Luke 6:22-23)

(b) The command to cease and desist is as ineffective as the earlier one (4:17-18). "And all day long, both at the temple and in their homes, they did not stop teaching and proclaiming the Messiah, Jesus" (v. 42). The total effect on the hearer of section 5:17-42 is that the established order is being overwhelmed by the new currents in the unfolding plan of God.

If prayer leads to empowering and empowering to witness, the mission is not deterred by opposition, even imprisonment and flogging.

Martyrdom (Acts 6:1-8:4)

Acts 6:1-8:4 is the third cycle of empowered witness to Jerusalem. Acts 1:12-4:23 and 4:24-5:42 reflect remarkable correspondences in contents and sequence that indicate the boundaries of the first two cycles (cf. the unit on Acts 3:1-4:23 for details). In these thought units the apostles present the people and their rulers with a second offer of salvation. Now, in light of the resurrection of Jesus, there can be no appeal to ignorance by the Jerusalemites (3:17; 13:27). The third cycle is like the first two in several respects: (a) all three have Messianist witnesses brought before the Council (4:3; 5:17-18; 6:12); (b) all three have Messianists give a defense before the Council (4:5-12; 5:27-32; 7:1-54); (c) all three give the reactions of the Council: they deliberate (4:16-17) and release the apostles with a warning (4:21); they check their impulse to put them to death after listening to Gamaliel's advice of caution (5:33-39) and release the apostles after a beating (5:40); they are infuriated, rush upon Stephen together, throw him out of the city, and stone him (7:54, 57, 58). It is in the reactions of the Council to the Messianists that the differences lie. There is an ascending degree of hostility toward the empowered witnesses: from warning to beating to martyrdom.

Luke's use of three cycles of witness to Jerusalem involves redundancy, a necessary aspect of communication. Repetition is a means of emphasis; it combats the tendency to forget; it has a persuasive effect; it preserves narrative unity in spite of developments. Repetition without growth, however, soon becomes monotonous. So Luke not only uses repetition in his three cycles but also employs variation in order to avoid monotony (Tannehill, 2.74–77).

Will the Jerusalemites accept Jesus as Messiah the second time around? Many do (2:41; 4:4; 5:14; 6:7); many do not. So the Jerusalemites are divided. At the end of the Stephen episode, the witness to Jerusalem in Acts is complete. Thereafter the gospel moves on, in fulfillment of the risen Jesus' promise (1:8).

This large thought unit (6:1–8:4), the third of the three cycles of empowered witness to Jerusalem, consists of two main components: (1) a *Gattung* dealing with the choice of supplementary leadership (6:1–7) and (2) a martyrdom (6:8–8:4). Each must be examined in turn.

Acts 6:1–7 is a paragraph held together by an inclusion: "the number of disciples continued to grow" (*plēthynontōn*, v. 1) and "the number of disciples . . . increased greatly (*eplēthyneto*, v. 7). The core of the unit, vv. 1–6, reflects an Old Testament form used for the choice of supplementary leadership (e.g., Exod 18:14–25; Num 27:12–23). This *Gattung* consists of four components: (a) the problem (Exod 18:14–18; Num 27:12–14); (b) the proposed solution (Exod 18:19–23; Num 27:15–17); (c) the qualifications of the new leadership (Exod 18:21; Num 27:18–21); (d) the setting apart of the new leaders (Exod 18:25; Num 27:22–23). Following his usual imitation of the LXX, the Lukan evangelist shapes both Acts 1:15–26 and 6:1–6 in terms of this form. Thereby both cycle one (1:12–4:23) and cycle three (6:1–8:4) of the empowered witness to Jerusalem begin with the same *Gattung*, a further signal of the author's plan for his narrative.

The individual components of the *Gattung* of 6:1–6 repay careful attention. (a) The problem: Acts 2:45 ("they would sell their property and possessions and divide them among all according to each one's need") and 4:34–35 ("There was no needy person among them . . . they were distributed to each according to need") speak of the overflow of the spiritual unity of the earliest disciples. The needs of any and all are met. Success takes its toll, however. "As the number of disciples continued to grow, the Hellenists (= Greek-speaking Jewish Christians) complained against the Hebrews (= Aramaic-speaking Jewish Christians) because their widows were being neglected in the daily distribution" (v. 1).

In Jewish society widows were viewed as particularly needy and dependent. The Old Testament singles them out, along with orphans, as primary objects of charity (Exod 22:22; Deut 10:18; Ps 146:9; Sir 35:14–15), a practice continued in Messianist (James 1:27) and non-Messianist Judaism (*Testament of Job* 9–10, 13, 14; *m. Ketuboth* 4:12; 11:1–6; 12:3–4; *m. Gittin* 5:3). Apparently the Messianists had already set up some type of structure for caring for their needy. Non-Messianist Judaism had two types of poor relief. In the one, on Fridays three relief officers would give enough money from that collected from local residents to cover fourteen meals for the resident poor. In the other, three officers would go to various houses to collect food and drink to have available on a daily basis for poor strangers. The daily distribution in Acts does not correspond to either model. It combines parts of both in a daily distribution to permanent residents as a general practice. It is implied that it is made out of the common funds provided by the voluntary contributions mentioned in 2:44–45 and 4:34–35.

Half of the problem, then, is that a diverse membership presents structural problems. The other half of the problem comes in v. 2: the Twelve say, "It is not right for us to neglect the word of God to serve at table." There was a practical need to have the structures of the community reflect the spiritual oneness of the disciples. There was also the problem that the Twelve's self-concept or calling did not match the need. Here are the two sides of the problem.

(b) The proposed solution: In vv. 3–4, the Twelve offer the following solution: "Select from among you seven reputable men, filled with the Spirit and wisdom, whom we shall appoint to this task, whereas we shall devote ourselves to prayer and to the ministry of the word" (= preaching). A division of labor is proposed within the leadership. This is something that would have been a part of Luke's readers' way of thinking at the end of the first century, not only because of Moses' example (Exod 18:19–20, 23) but also because of Christian practice from as early as the 50s (1 Cor 12:4–7, 28–30: "apostles . . . administrators"). Town councils of seven men were, moreover, common administrative entities in first-century Judaism (Josephus, *Antiquities* 4.8.14 § 214: "Let there be seven men to judge in every city"; 4.8.38 § 287; *War* 5.20.5 §§ 569–71: "seven judges in every city to hear the lesser quarrels").

(c) Qualifications for the new leadership: The necessary qualifications are both stated explicitly (v. 3b) and hinted at (v. 5; cf. v. 9). It is explicitly stated that they should be "reputable men, filled with the Spirit and wisdom" (cf. 1 Tim 3:8–13, although it is not until Irenaeus that the Seven are regarded as deacons [*Against Heresies* 1.26.3; 3.12.10; 4.15.1]). Those entrusted with setting up and implementing the social structures of the community's life, just as the apostles, were to be "full of the Spirit." This was exactly the kind of people they did, in fact, choose: for example, "they chose Stephen, a man filled with faith and the Holy Spirit" (v. 5). Only thereby could the structures reflect the spiritual basis of the community's life. The choice of these seven indicates an implicit criterion as well. At least some of them, maybe all judging from their Greek names, come from the segment of the church that feels discriminated against. Not only did they need to have a good reputation (being wise and spiritual), they also needed to represent the interests of the neglected (the Hellenists).

(d) The setting apart of the new leaders: The choice of the Seven is apparently made by the congregation (vv. 3), which presents them to the apostles for confirmation (v. 6a) and then, after praying, lays their hands on them (v. 6b; cf. 13:3, where again the laying on of hands is used in connection with a commissioning to a task). This indicates the broad-based decision-making of the Messianists. It also reflects the theological perspective of the evangelist in yet another way. That all make the choice reflects the Lukan belief that all have the Spirit living in and guiding them. That the Twelve confirm the community's decision is in line with the Lukan theme that they are Jesus' appointed judges of the reconstituted Israel (Luke 22:29-30). Effecting the appropriate structural changes in the community leads to further growth (v. 7: "the word of God continued to spread"; cf. Luke 8:4-15). Just structures further evangelization.

Acts 6:1-7 functions in two different ways in the plot of Acts. On the one hand, looking back, it describes yet another threat to the unity of the community. This threat is resolved not by direct divine intervention (as in 5:1-11) but by structural changes effected by the community. The idealization of the community in Acts' narrative does not eliminate the narrative's realism about ongoing problems faced by the reconstituted Israel. An ideal apostolic age does not mean an absence of problems but to every problem a solution that conforms to apostolic norms. On the other hand, looking ahead, this paragraph introduces two characters who will be active witnesses in chaps. 7 and 8, Stephen and Philip. It is a Lukan trait to introduce a character early on and then develop that person's role later (e.g., Saul in 7:58; 8:1, 3; 9:1-30). In particular, in this thought unit (6:1-8:4), 6:1-6 serves to introduce Stephen, who will dominate the rest of the section as its chief empowered witness.

The martyrdom that follows (6:8-8:4) falls into an ABB'A' pattern.

A—Narrative leading up to Stephen's speech (6:8-15)
  B—The high priest's question (7:1)
  B'—Stephen's answer (7:2-53)
A'—Narrative about events after Stephen's speech (7:54-8:4)

Each of the components needs investigation.

Acts 6:8-15, "A" in the pattern, tells of events leading up to Stephen's speech. The unit is held together by an inclusion: evidences of Stephen's spirituality in vv. 8 and 15. Its components are four. (a) Stephen's performance of wonders and signs (v. 8) is a partial answer, along with 5:12, to the petition of 4:30. The Holy Spirit is bearing witness to Jesus' resurrection (5:32). This witness is born through one who is himself "filled with the Spirit" (v. 5).

(b) This empowered witness provokes disputes with Hellenistic Jews (v. 9; cf. 21:27, where Paul's opponents are also Hellenistic Jews). With how many groups does Stephen debate? One? Two? Three? Four? The repetition of the definite article (*tōn*) leads one to expect two groups. So one might translate as follows: "Certain *of those* from the synagogue called Freedmen, even Cyrenians and Alexandrians, and *of those* from Cilicia and Asia debated with Stephen." Jewish freedmen are known from antiquity (Philo, *Embassy to Gaius* 155), as are Jewish proselytes who are freedmen (Tacitus, *Annals* 2.85). A synagogue of Alexandrians is known to have existed in Jerusalem (*t. Megillah* 3.6 [224]; *j. Megillah* 3.1 [73d.35]). At least one reference to a synagogue of Tarsians exists (*b. Megillah* 26a). A synagogue for Jews from abroad, that of Theodotos, is known from what may be a first-century inscription in Jerusalem (Deissmann 1922, 440, gives the text and translation; reservations about the first-century dating are expressed by Kee; Kee's argument is overturned by Riesner). The point: Hellenistic Jews had their own synagogues in the holy city. It is from these people from abroad that Stephen's opposition comes.

Stephen, like Jesus before him (Luke 19:47–21:4), is triumphant in these disputations: "but they could not withstand the wisdom and the spirit with which he spoke" (v. 10). This is as Jesus had said it would be: "When they take you before synagogues . . . do not worry about how or what your defense will be or about what you are to say. For the Holy Spirit will teach you at that moment what you should say" (Luke 12:11–12); "I myself will give you a wisdom in speaking that all your adversaries will be powerless to resist or refute" (Luke 21:15).

(c) The defeated opposition then secures enough false charges against him to have him seized and brought before the Council (vv. 11–12). The false witnesses claim Stephen has been saying "blasphemous words against Moses and God." Defeated in debate, they resort to false witness (violating the commandment against false witness [Exod 20:16]).

(d) Before the Council the false witnesses testify as follows: "This man never stops saying things against [this] holy place and the law. For we have heard him claim that this Jesus the Nazorean will destroy this place (= the temple) and change the customs that Moses handed down to us" (vv. 13b–14). These charges are similar to the ones that will be made later against Paul (Acts 21:20–21, 28; 24:6; 25:8), and with the same degree of truthfulness. "All who sat in the Sanhedrin looked intently at him and saw that his face was like the face of an angel" (v. 15; cf. *Acts of Paul* 3; cf. Palestinian Targum of Gen 33:10, where the phrase "face of God" is replaced with "I have seen thy face as though I had seen the face of an angel"; *Martyrdom of Polycarp* 12:1, for the radiant face of a soon-to-be martyr).

Such charges made before the Council lead the high priest to ask Stephen point blank, "Is this so?" (7:1). The high priest's question constitutes "B" in the pattern. "B'" in the pattern is Stephen's answer. It comes in 7:2-53. It is given from the perspective "as your fathers did, so do you." Stephen's response accuses his accusers. They are the ones who act against the authority of Moses and have changed what he delivered. The accusers' devotion to the temple is part of their disobedience to Moses. The speech has two main parts: (1) a selective history of Israel (vv. 2-50), and (2) a comparison of past behavior with present conduct (vv. 51-53).

(1) In vv. 2-50, a selective history of Israel, the train of thought runs from Abraham to Moses (for similar reviews of Israel's history, cf. Ps 106:6-46; Ezek 20; Neh 9:6-38). The speech begins with God's promise to Abraham (vv. 3, 4, 5, 7). When the time came for God to fulfill the promise, Moses was sent as God's servant. This part of Moses' role involves two stages: vv. 23-29 and 30-43. In the first, vv. 23-29, Moses comes to offer deliverance in Egypt. The people do not understand (v. 25: "they did not understand"; cf. Acts 3:17; 13:27) and so reject him as ruler and judge (v. 27). As a result, Moses departs. In the second stage, vv. 30-43, God comes down to rescue his people (v. 34). He sends Moses, who had been rejected as ruler and judge, as ruler and deliverer (v. 35). Once again, this time in the wilderness, the people "were unwilling to obey him" (v. 39) and turned back to idolatry, making and worshiping the golden calf (v. 41; violating the commandment against graven images [Exod 20:4]), behavior that ultimately led to the exile (v. 43). Moses, then, was rejected not once but twice by Stephen's hearers' ancestors. Nevertheless, it was the rejected one whom God made ruler and deliverer for them. The Moses who was rejected, moreover, was also the one who said to the Israelites, "God will raise up for you, from among your own kinsfolk, a prophet like me" (v. 37; cf. Acts 3:22-23).

Another part of Moses' role involved making a place of worship as God directed: "Our ancestors had the tent of testimony (Exod 25-27; 33:7-11) in the desert just as the One who spoke to Moses directed him to make it according to the pattern he had seen" (v. 44; cf. Hebrews 8-9, where the Tabernacle is the true type of worship). This was brought to Canaan at the time of the conquest (v. 45). This was in obedience to God who had told Abraham that he was to be worshiped "in this place" (the land of promise, not the Temple). It was Solomon who built the first temple (v. 47). "Yet the Most High does not dwell in houses made by human hands" (v. 48). The people, then, deviated from the Mosaic pattern of worship when the Temple was built.

This view of the Temple has some similarities with that found in the *Sibylline Oracles* 4:8-11 (a Jewish source from the late first century A.D.):

> For [the great God] does not have a house,
> > a stone set up as a temple,
> dumb and toothless, a bane which brings many woes to men,
> but one which it is not possible to see from earth
> > nor to measure with mortal eyes,
> > since it was not fashioned by mortal hand.

It would have sounded reasonable to a pagan like Plutarch, who said, "Further, it is a doctrine of Zeno not to build sanctuaries of the gods" (*Moralia* 1034b). The only other place, however, where the proposed alternative to the Temple is the wilderness Tabernacle is Hebrews 8–9.

Stephen is not attacking merely an idolatrous understanding of the Temple, a practice that Solomon's prayer of dedication also disdained (1 Kgs 8:27–30) and that Jeremiah condemned (Jeremiah 7). Rather, Stephen's speech says that the very existence of the Temple involves faithlessness to Moses and the pattern of worship he received from God. Temple worship, for Stephen, is yet another example of their Jewish ancestors' disobedience of the law. Not only was Moses himself rejected twice but also his Tabernacle type of worship was forsaken by a faithless people. The entire survey of Israelite history is told as one of a dual rejection of Moses and of a changing of the customs he handed down (cf. 7:11, 14). That Stephen's evaluation of the Temple is different from that of the author of Luke-Acts (whose attitude is positive about the Temple as long as it stands) argues that here Luke is depicting what he regarded as appropriate for Stephen in his time and place.

(2) A comparison of past behavior with present conduct comes in 7:51–53. "You are just like your ancestors. Which of the prophets did not your ancestors persecute? They put to death those who foretold the coming of the righteous one, whose betrayers and murderers you have now become." On the one hand, the rejection of Moses' authority was typical of the fathers' treatment of God's messengers generally (cf. Luke 13:34; 6:22–23). The refusal of God's people to heed the prophets is proverbial in Jewish writings (e.g., 2 Kgs 17:13–14; 2 Chr 24:21; Jer 2:30; 26:20–23; Josephus, *Antiquities* 9.13.2 §§ 265–66; 9.14.1 § 281). Persecution and killing of the prophets is also a typical motif in Jewish literature (e.g., 1 Kgs 19:10; Neh 9:26; 2 Chr 36:16; *Martyrdom of Isaiah; Lives of the Prophets*). Stephen is saying nothing more about this matter than has been said already by others.

On the other hand, the sting of Stephen's speech comes in the words, "You are just like your ancestors" (v. 51b). (a) In betraying and murdering the righteous one (v. 52b), they have not listened to Moses, who prophesied, "God will raise up for you . . . a prophet like me" (v. 37; see 3:22–23;

Deut 18:15-18; John 5:46-47). (b) In bearing false witness against Stephen (6:13-14), they violate the commandment in Exod 20:16. (c) When they kill Stephen, they will violate yet another commandment (Exod 20:13), just as they did with Jesus' death. They are correctly described as those "who received the law . . . but did not observe it" (v. 53). In conclusion, one would have to say that Stephen's response to the charges is that his accusers and their ancestors, not he, are those who act against the authority of Moses and have changed what he delivered. The accusers stand accused.

Acts 7:54-8:4, "A'" in the pattern, deals with events after Stephen's speech. There are five components in the narrative. (1) The first is the reaction to Stephen's speech: "when they heard this, they were infuriated, and they ground their teeth at him" (v. 54; grinding the teeth is a sign of rage, especially of the wicked against the righteous; cf. Job 16:9; Ps 35:16; 37:12; Lam 2:16). Indictment produces fury.

(2) The second component is an account of Stephen's vision and speech about it. "But he, filled with the Holy Spirit, looked up intently to heaven and saw the glory of God and Jesus standing at the right hand of God, and he said, 'Behold I see the heavens opened and the Son of Man standing at the right hand of God'" (vv. 55-56). It is part and parcel of the literature of martyrdom that martyrs see visions (e.g., *Martyrdom of Isaiah* 5:7; *Passion of Saints Perpetua and Felicitas* 10-13). Stephen sees the Son of Man (the only occurrence of this title outside the Gospels and on any lips other than those of Jesus) standing at God's right hand. The references are normally to "sitting at God's right hand" (e.g., Acts 2:34-35; Luke 22:69), echoing Psalm 110:1. What is the significance of the "standing"?

The reference to the Son of Man standing at God's right hand has been the subject of endless debate. Many of the possibilities have inherent plausibility: (a) the standing one is the vindicated righteous man, after death, in the presence of God who protects him with His right hand (Wis 5:1 in the context of 4:16-5:16); (b) the standing one is the living one, the one who will not die (Rev 5:6; Ps-Clementine, *Homilies* 2.22; *Recognitions* 3.47); (c) the standing one is part of the heavenly court, an angel not God (1 Kgs 22:19; Rev 8:2; *3 Enoch* 16:3-5); (d) the standing one is the heavenly judge (Isa 3:13; 2:19, 21; Amos 9:1; *Assumption of Moses* 10:3); (e) the standing one is he who offers assistance to martyrs (*Martyrdom of Polycarp* 2:2-3). Any preference must mesh with the Lukan narrative. The early chapters of Acts have contrasted the Jerusalemite rejection of the "righteous one" (3:14; 7:52; Luke 23:47) with God's vindication of him to his right hand (2:34-35; 5:31). It is difficult not to hear the echo of Wis 4:16-5:16. This one who has been vindicated has now experienced the ultimate victory over death and will not die. He is, moreover, the one who is faithful to his word: "Everyone who acknowledges me before others, the Son of Man will acknowledge before the angels of God" (Luke 12:8). As Stephen prays later, "Lord Jesus, receive my spirit" (v. 59), so the Son of Man stands to do (Luke 23:43). A collage of connotations seems probable in this context.

(3) The reaction to Stephen's vision speech comes in 7:57-59a. "They cried out in a loud voice, covered their ears, and rushed upon him together. They threw him out of the city, and began to stone him. The witnesses laid down their cloaks at the feet of a young man named Saul." To whom does "they" refer? In context, "they" must be those in the Council together with the false witnesses. What started off as a trial ends up as something other than what is described in the Mishnah as proper procedure for stoning (*m. Sanhedrin* 6:1-4). It comes close to a spontaneous lynching. Stoning was often made use of in lynch law (Philo, *Special Laws* 1.54-57; Josephus, *Antiquities* 14.2.1 §§ 22-24; 2 Chr 24:20-22) (Blinzer, 147-61).

(4) Verses 59b-60 give Stephen's final two words. (a) "As they were stoning Stephen, he called out, 'Lord Jesus, receive my spirit.'" This echoes Jesus' prayer in Luke 23:46, which is an adaptation of Ps 31:6. It is a Messianist adaptation of an even wider cultural form of prayer (e.g., Lucian, *Peregrinus* 36, "Spirits of my mother and my father, receive me with favor"). Here is another example of prayer to Jesus (remember Acts 1:24-25). The reader knows that Stephen's prayer is answered because of what the earthly Jesus taught ("By your endurance you will gain your lives," Luke 21:19). The martyr has his reward (see *Martyrdom of Apollonius*: The Christian Apollonius says, "Proconsul Perenius, I thank my God for this sentence of yours which will bring me salvation").

(b) "Then he fell to his knees and cried out in a loud voice, 'Lord, do not hold this sin against them,' and when he had said this, he fell asleep." According to *m. Sanhedrin* 6:2, the condemned man is urged to cry out a prayer for his own forgiveness on the way to being stoned ("May my death be an atonement for my sins"), a recognition and confession of guilt. Stephen the martyr echoes the prayer of the martyr Jesus in Luke 23:34 ("Father, forgive them, they know not what they do"). Such a prayer became the model for later Christian martyrs (e.g., James the Just, as he is being stoned, prays, "I beseech thee, O Lord, God and Father, forgive them, for they know not what they do" [Eusebius, *Church History* 2.23.16]; the martyrs of Lyons and Vienne prayed for those who had inflicted torture even as did Stephen, the perfect martyr, "Lord, lay not this sin to their charge" [Eusebius, *Church History* 5.2.5]). This is no confession of guilt but a righteous man's intercession for his tormenters.

(5) The reaction to Stephen's martyrdom is given in 8:1-4. (a) "Now Saul was consenting to his execution" (v. 1a). The religious zealot did not follow his teacher's (22:3) advice of wait and see (5:34-39). Nor did the others any longer abide by Gamaliel's counsel. "On that day, there broke out a severe

persecution of the church in Jerusalem" (v. 1b). Saul's part in the persecution was to attempt to "destroy the church; entering house after house (= the meeting places of the Messianists, cf. 2:46, "breaking bread in their homes") and dragging out men and women, he handed them over for imprisonment" (v. 3). With the martyrdom of Stephen and the persecution against the Messianists, Jerusalem has uttered its second and final No to Jesus. (b) *m. Sanhedrin* forbids public lamentation for one who has been executed. No matter; "devout men buried Stephen and made a loud lament over him" (v. 2; cf. Cynic epistles, Socratics 14, "Aeschines to Xenophon": After Socrates drank the poison and died, his friends who were present "after weeping . . . carried him out and buried him"). (c) The persecution drove the Messianists from the city: "all were scattered throughout the countryside of Judea and Samaria, except the apostles" (v. 1c). The apostles remain in Jerusalem because in the plot of Luke-Acts, they are the judges of the reconstituted Israel and must be identified with the holy city. The rest are scattered. "Now those who had been scattered went about preaching the word" (v. 4). In trying to beat out the flames of the Messianist movement, its opponents scatter the sparks far and wide and only increase the scope of the fire (see Luke 12:49).

The martyrdom of Stephen functions in at least two ways in the plot of Luke-Acts. On the one hand, it grounds Stephen's martyrdom in that of Jesus and so serves as a model for Luke's readers. The story of Stephen's death in Acts parallels that of Jesus in the Third Gospel. (a) Both are tried before the Council (Luke 22:66–71; Acts 6:12–7:1). (b) Both die a martyr's death. (c) Acts 7:59, "Lord Jesus, receive my spirit," echoes Luke 23:46, "Father, into thy hands I commit my spirit." (d) Acts 7:60, "Lord, do not hold this sin against them," echoes Luke 23:34, "Father, forgive them, for they do not know what they are doing." (e) Both stories contain a Son of Man saying: Luke 22:69 ("But from this time on the Son of Man will be seated at the right hand of the power of God") and Acts 7:56 ("Behold, I see the heavens opened and the Son of Man standing at the right hand of God"). This is remarkable because Acts 7:56 is the only occurrence of the title outside the Gospels and on any lips except those of Jesus. (f) Both men's deaths issue in evangelistic results (Luke 23:39–43; Acts 8:1, 4). Moreover, the story of Stephen's martyrdom fulfills Jesus' words in Luke 21:12–19, especially v. 16 ("some of you they will put to death"). The deaths of Jesus and Stephen are portrayed as martyrdoms in Luke-Acts, the former being the model for the latter. Together they serve as models for Luke's readers. (For a survey of attitudes toward martyrdom in antiquity, see Talbert 1982, 212–18.)

On the other hand, the martyrdom of Stephen functions in the service of the common Christian notion that persecution only serves to spread the gospel. Three early Christian sources illustrate this. (a) The *Epistle of Diognetus* says,

> Christians when they are punished increase the more in number every day. (6:9)

> Can you not see them thrown to wild beasts, to make them deny their Lord, and yet not overcome? Do you not see that the more of them are punished, the more numerous the others become? (7:7-8)

(b) Justin Martyr, *Dialogue* 110, says,

> Now it is evident that no one can terrify or subdue us who have believed in Jesus over all the world. For it is plain that, though beheaded, and crucified, and thrown to the wild beasts, and chains, and fire, and all other kinds of torture, we do not give up our confession; but the more such things happen, the more do others and in larger numbers become faithful and worshipers of God through the name of Jesus. For just as if one should cut away the fruit-bearing parts of a vine, it grows up again, and yields other branches flourishing and fruitful; even so the same thing happens with us.

(c) Tertullian, *Apology* 50, says,

> We conquer in dying; we go forth victorious at the very time we are subdued. . . . The oftener we are mown down by you, the more in number we grow; the blood of Christians is seed.

The Stephen episode in Acts is the bridge over which the gospel marches unhindered out of Jerusalem.

Philip's Mission (Acts 8:4-40)

Acts 8:4-40 is a thought unit held together by its chief character, Philip (not the apostle of Acts 1:13 but one of the Seven [6:5]). It consists of two stories: 8:5-25, in which Philip evangelizes Samaria, and 8:26-40, in which Philip evangelizes the Ethiopian eunuch. It functions to give two concrete examples of the summary in 8:4: "Now those who had been scattered (by the persecution of 8:1b) went about preaching the word" (see 11:19-26 for the third example of such preaching). Each of the two stories needs attention.

In Acts 8:5-25 Philip evangelizes the Samaritans (cf. 1:8). The Samaritans shared a common heritage with Judaism (descendants of Abraham, adherents of the Torah). They were descendants of those who had intermarried with the mixed population that settled in Israel after the Assyrian conquest of the northern kingdom (2 Kgs 17:24-41) and were regarded as idolatrous by the Jews (Amos 3:9, 12; 8:14; Hos 8:5-6; Isa 8:4; Mic 1:5-6). In the fourth century B.C., Manasseh, the brother of the Jewish high priest, married the daughter of the Samaritan Sanballat and was consequently expelled from Jerusalem. He responded by building a temple on Mount Gerizim (Josephus, *Antiquities* 11.8.2 §§ 306-12; John 4:20). In 128 B.C. the Hasmonean ruler John Hyrcanus destroyed the Samaritan temple, causing deep and lasting resentment (Josephus, *Antiquities* 13.10.2-3 §§ 275-83). Sometime in the period 6-9 B.C., certain Samaritans desecrated the Jerusalem Temple with human bones, an act that led to their exclusion from the Temple in Jerusalem (Josephus, *Antiquities*, 18.2.2 §§ 29-30). Since the route through Samaria was the quickest route from Galilee to Jerusalem (Josephus, *Life* 52 § 269), pilgrims often tried to go that way. This was sometimes met by Samaritan hostility (Luke 9:52-53). In the time of Claudius, for example, there was a notorious event of Samaritan mistreatment of Galileans on their way to Jerusalem. One pilgrim was actually murdered (Josephus, *Antiquities* 20.6.1 § 118; *War* 2.12.3 § 232). By New Testament times, Samaritans were considered by Jews to be apostates from Judaism (Josephus, *Antiquities* 11.8.6 § 340), the equivalent of Gentiles. Jewish hostility toward them was very great (John 4:9; Luke 9:54; Matt 10:5; *m. Shebiith* 8:10, "He that eats the bread of the Samaritans is like to one that eats the flesh of swine"). One of the things associated in the Jewish mindset with Samaritans was magic (*b. Sota* 22a).

In the plot of Acts, the first place the scattered Messianists go when they are driven out of Jerusalem by persecution is to Samaria. They receive a warm welcome. There may have been a cultural reason for both the flight to Samaria and the warm welcome. Josephus tells us that when

> Alexander died, his empire was partitioned among his successors (the Diadochoi); as for the temple on Mount Gerizim, it remained. And, whenever anyone was accused by the people of Jerusalem of eating unclean food or violating the Sabbath or committing any other such sin, he would flee to the Shechemites, saying he had been unjustly expelled. (*Antiquities* 11.8.7 §§ 346-47)

Whatever the cultural reasons, the Messianists used them for evangelization.

The section 8:5-25 is held together by an inclusion (v. 4, preaching the word; v. 25, preaching the gospel, speaking the word). It consists of two scenes: vv. 5-13, in which Philip is center stage, and vv. 14-25, in which Peter is central. In both scenes, Simon of Samaria plays a key role. Taken as a whole, 8:5-25 speaks about the defeat of a magical view of the gospel and the Holy Spirit.

Scene one, vv. 5-13, has as its major point that the power of Jesus' name is greater than that of magic. The scene has three paragraphs: vv. 5-8, 9-11, and 12-13. The first two depict the similarities between Philip and Simon.

(a) In vv. 5–8 the focus is on Philip and the Samaritans. "Philip went down to *the* (P[74], Sinaiticus, and Vaticanus have an article here) city of Samaria (= Sebaste, *the* city of the district of Samaria—Josephus, *War* 2.6.3 §§ 96–97) and proclaimed the Messiah to them" (v. 5). The crowds "paid attention to him" when they saw the signs he was doing, "for unclean spirits . . . came out of many . . . and many paralyzed and crippled people were cured" (vv. 6b–7). (b) In vv. 9–11 the focus is on Simon and the Samaritans. The thought moves in a concentric pattern:

> A—Simon astounds the people with his magic (v. 9)
>> B—Therefore, they all "paid attention to him" (v. 10)
>> B'—They "paid attention to him" (v. 11a)
> A'—Because he astounded them with his magic (v. 11b).

In the ancient world, Simon was depicted in two very different ways: (a) sometimes he was portrayed as a magician (Justin, *1 Apology* 26:2; 56:1–2; *Dialogue* 120:6; *Acts of Peter* 2:4, 6; 4:8; 6:16–17; 8:25, 28; 9:31–32; Pseudo-Clementine *Homilies* 2.22.3; 2.24.1; Origen, *Contra Celsus* 1.57); (b) sometimes as a Gnostic (Justin, *1 Apology* 26:3; *Dialogue* 120:6; *Acts of Paul, Third Corinthians; Epistle of the Apostles* 7; Irenaeus, *Against Heresies* 1.12.1-4; 1.16.2; 1.23; 3.preface; Hippolytus, *Refutation* 6.9–20; Tertullian, *Against All Heresies* 1; Clement of Alexandria, *Stromateis* 2.52.2; 7.107.1; Epiphanius, *Panarion* 21). Of course, in Acts 8 Simon is depicted as a magician.

"Magician" was a term of defamation in antiquity. It was what one called one's opponent to discredit him. Nonmessianic Jews used the term of Jesus (Luke 11:15: "he casts out demons by Beelzebul, the prince of demons"; Justin, *Dialogue* 69: "They dared to call him a magician"; *b. Sanhedrin* 43a: "he practiced sorcery and beguiled and led Israel astray") and of Samaritans (*b. Sota* 22a: "as a Samaritan or as a magician"). Pagans used the term of maverick philosophers (e.g., Philostratus, *Life of Apollonius of Tyana*, where Apollonius's opponents call him a magician, and the biography, which, in part, is written to defend him against the charges; cf. also Apollonius of Tyana, *Letters* 1, 2, 5, 8, 16, 17); of Jews (Juvenal, *Satires* 6.542-47), especially Moses (Pliny, *Natural History* 30.2.11; Eusebius, *Preparation for the Gospel* 9.8.1–2); and of Jesus (Origen, *Contra Celsus* 1.6, 28, 38). Messianic Jews used the term of their opponents as well (e.g., Acts 13:6, a magician named Bar-Jesus who was a Jewish false prophet; 8:9, 11, Simon).

Among the charges levelled against magicians generally is the one focused on later in the story: the use of miracle to gain money for oneself. (a) Aesop, *Fables* 65, tells of a witch who made great gain from her magic.

(b) Tacitus, *Annals* 16.30–32, tells how Servilea spent her dowry to learn the future from a magus. (c) Apuleius, *Apology* 67,102, is accused of having used magic to marry a widow for her wealth. (d) Philostratus, *Life of Apollonius of Tyana* 6.39 and 8.7, distances the philosopher from magicians by emphasizing that the philosopher is not money-grubbing. In 8.7.3, in his defense before Domitian, Apollonius critiques magicians:

> The practitioners of the art are all avaricious; all their clever devices they have invented for the sake of profit; and they chase after enormous sums of money by deceiving people who have any kind of craving and by pretending that they have unlimited powers.

(e) The *Acts of Thomas* 20 offers the people's view of the apostle: "we think because of his miracles he is a magician. Yet his compassions and his cures, which are done by him freely . . . declare that he is a righteous man." (f) Origen, *Contra Celsus* 1.68, compares the gospel miracles

> with works of sorcerers who profess to do wonderful miracles, and the accomplishments of those who are taught by the Egyptians, who for a few obols make known their sacred lore in the middle of the marketplace.

According to Mediterranean belief, magicians looked for customers not converts. Such a one is Simon.

In the first two paragraphs the similarities between Philip, the Messianist, and Simon, the Magus, are set forth. Because of their mighty deeds, both get the attention of the Samaritans. The similarities are followed by remarkable differences in paragraph three, vv. 12–13. (c) In vv. 12–13 the focus is on Philip, the Samaritans, and Simon. "They began to believe Philip as he preached the good news about the kingdom of God and the name of Jesus Christ" and "men and women alike (cf. 8:3; 2:17–18; 1:14) were baptized" (v. 12). Even the one who had practiced magic, Simon himself, believes and is baptized (v. 13). What better testimony can there be to the superiority of the power of Jesus over magic?

The narrative began by describing a power encounter: that is, an encounter between the spiritual power of the Messianists' God and that of another in which it is demonstrated that the power of the Messianists' God is greater than that of the other deity (cf. Exodus 7–12, Moses versus Pharoah; 1 Kings 18, Elijah versus the prophets of Baal; Acts 13:6–12, Paul versus Bar-Jesus). In such encounters, often the leaders of the other faith align themselves with the new deity, as here. In a power-oriented society, as Samaria is portrayed in this story, a demonstration of power serves as a catalyst for people's becoming open to the gospel. Philip's evangelization does not stop there, however. He then preaches, a truth encounter leading to correct understanding and calls for commitment, symbolized by baptism, as necessary for conversion. The thrust of scene one is the superiority of Jesus' name to magic.

In scene two, vv. 14–25, Peter is center stage. This subsection is held together by an inclusion: v. 14, they sent; v. 25, they returned. The point of this section is that the power of the Holy Spirit is not a commodity to be bought. The material falls into two paragraphs (vv. 14–17; vv. 18–24) and a concluding summary (v. 25).

Verses 14–17 are a narrative about the apostles and the Samaritans. When the apostles in Jerusalem (8:1, "all were scattered . . . except the apostles") hear that Samaria has accepted the word of God, they send Peter and John to pray for them that they may receive the Holy Spirit "for it had not yet fallen upon any of them; they had only been baptized in the name of the Lord Jesus" (v. 16). When the apostles lay their hands on the Samaritan converts, "they received the Holy Spirit" (v. 17).

In Acts, the Twelve in Jerusalem represent the judges for a reconstituted Israel (Luke 22:29–30). As such they perform a supervisory role with reference to new developments in the Messianist mission. People either come to Jerusalem to report and receive approval (9:27; 11:2; 15; 18:22) or Jerusalem sends representatives to check on and supervise new enterprises (8:14; 11:22–24). It is a way of saying that the expanding religious experience of messianic Judaism is under the control of the true tradition about Jesus, embodied in the apostles.

There is in Acts no set procedure for reception of the Holy Spirit. (a) In 2:38 (repent, be baptized, and receive the Holy Spirit), the gift of the Spirit seems to be linked with baptism. (b) Here in 8:15–17 the bestowal of the Spirit comes after baptism through the laying on of hands (so also probably 19:5–6). (c) In 10:44–48 the Spirit is poured out in connection with Peter's preaching prior to baptism (cf. 1 Cor 2:1–4; Gal 3:1–5; 1 Thess 1:5, which seem to indicate this was the procedure in Pauline churches). (d) In 9:17–18 the reception of the Holy Spirit appears to be in connection with the laying on of hands before baptism. The narrative of Acts seems to say that the gift of the Holy Spirit cannot be captured in any set procedure (Luke 11:13—God gives the Holy Spirit).

> The important thing for Luke seems to be the *total experience* of respondents to the gospel, including such typical components as repentance, faith, water-baptism and forgiveness of sins, along with possession of the Spirit—but not ordered according to any rigidly determined pattern. Accordingly, the fact that the Samaritans *eventually* receive the promised gift of the Spirit may be viewed as adequate fulfillment of Acts 2:38. (Spencer, 213–14)

It would be a mistake to take Acts 8 as a paradigm of Messianist experience, just as much as it would be to take Acts 2:38 or 10:44–45. God is free; experience varies.

Verses 18-24 offer a dialogue between Simon and the apostles. It falls into an ABA' pattern:

A–Simon (vv. 18-19)
  B–Peter (vv. 20-23)
A–Simon (v. 24).

"A," vv. 18-19, reveals the fact that Simon, although baptized, has not transcended his magical past. He offers the apostles money, saying, "Give me this power too, so that anyone upon whom I lay my hands may receive the Holy Spirit" (v. 19). Magic is mechanical. It views the Spirit as a commodity that can be bought and sold. Such knowledge and techniques are, of course, expensive (19:19). Simon, however, is willing to pay. "Magic seeks a craft that can rationally control the divine powers; it has no place for 'gift' as the free disposition of the divine apart from human manipulation" (Johnson 1992, 149). Simon is depicted, in this place, as a baptized magician.

"B," vv. 20-23, gives Peter's response. "May your money perish with you, because you thought you could buy the gift of God with money" (v. 20). There is only one thing Simon can do in his circumstances. Peter says, "Repent of this wickedness of yours and pray to the Lord that, if possible, your intention may be forgiven" (v. 22).

"A'," v. 24, narrates Simon's response to Peter's call for repentance. "Pray for me to the Lord, that nothing of what you have said ('may your money perish with you') may come upon me." Even Simon's response to the call for repentance remains within the bounds of his magical worldview. Another dimension of ancient magic was its use for malevolent ends. It could be used as a curse on an opponent. Simon takes Peter's word in v. 20 as such a curse. He makes no change in his orientation. Instead he asks to be spared from what he takes as a curse of a more powerful magician against another, weaker one. The story ends with Simon, the magician, depicted as one who is baptized but not changed and as one with whom God is not pleased (cf. 1 Cor 10:1-12; Luke 12:10?).

The concluding summary ends the story with continuing evangelization by the apostles in many Samaritan villages (v. 25). In so doing, they fulfill the promise of Jesus in Acts 1:8 ("you will be my witnesses . . . throughout . . . Samaria").

In Acts 8:26-40 Philip evangelizes the Ethiopian eunuch. This is a fulfillment of Acts 1:8 but not "to the ends of the earth." The phrase, "to the ends of the earth," is a geographical statement. Here Philip's witness is geographically within Judea. This story consists of three scenes: vv. 26-30b, 30c-35, and 36-40. In the story, scene two, the dialogue between Philip and the eunuch, is central. The unit is held together by an inclusion (v. 26, an angel said; v. 39, the Spirit caught up).

Scene one, vv. 26-30b, depicts events leading up to the dialogue between Philip and the eunuch. It is comprised of two balanced panels: vv. 26-28 and 29-30.

Panel One: vv. 26–28	*Panel Two: vv. 29–30*
An angel said, Go (v. 26)	The Spirit said, Go (v. 29)
he went (v. 27a)	he ran to him (v. 30a)
what he sees (vv. 27b–28)	what he hears (v. 30b)

In panel one, when an angel of the Lord tells Philip to head south on the road that runs from Jerusalem to Gaza (v. 26), he obeys (v. 27a). He sees "an Ethiopian eunuch, a court official of the Candace, that is, the queen of the Ethiopians, in charge of her entire treasury, who had come to Jerusalem to worship, and was returning home. Seated in his chariot, he was reading the prophet Isaiah" (vv. 27b–28).

Ethiopia in antiquity was not modern Ethiopia but what is now called Sudan. The biblical tradition gives a certain picture of the place. Ethiopia was a remote and distant land (Ezek 29:10; Esth 1:1; 8:9), renowned for its wealth (Job 28:19; Isa 45:14) and its military prowess (2 Kgs 19:9; 2 Chr 14:9-13; Isa 37:9; Jer 46:9). The Ethiopians were a dark-complexioned people (Jer 13:23; cf. Herodotus 3.20; Philostratus, *Life of Apollonius* 6.1), one of the wicked nations of the world (Isa 20:3-5; 43:3; Ezek 30:1-9; Nah 3:9; Zeph 2:11-12), who were to be among those foreigners who would be converted and acknowledge the true God of Israel (Ps 68:31-32; Zeph 3:9-10). The curiosity of the educated classes of the Mediterranean world in Ethiopia was aroused by two Roman expeditions into the region, one military in 23 B.C., and one scientific in A.D. 62 (Dio Cassius 54.5; Pliny, *Natural History* 6.35; Seneca, *Natural Questions* 6.8.3). The stereotyped image of Ethiopia and its people from antiquity is reflected in Heliodorus's romance *An Ethiopian Story*.

Eunuchs in antiquity were viewed in two very different ways. On the one hand, they were regarded positively. Herodotus 8.105 says that among barbarians eunuchs were especially prized as servants because of their trustworthiness. Heliodorus, *An Ethiopian Story*, connects eunuchs with Ethiopian royalty. On the other hand, there was also a negative view of eunuchs among some in antiquity. Lucian, *The Eunuch* 6, tells a tale of a eunuch who applies for a chair of philosophy at Athens. His chief competitor says such people ought to be excluded not only from philosophy but also from temples and holy-water bowls and all places of public assembly. The Jewish scriptures were hostile to such people (Lev 21:20; 22:24: an emasculated man is physically blemished and in a permanent state of ritual impurity; Deut 23:1: they are not to be admitted to the assembly of the Lord). This attitude was continued in postbiblical Judaism (Philo, *Special*

Laws 1.324–25; 3.41–42: they belong to the unworthy barred from entering the sacred congregation; Josephus, *Antiquities* 4.8.40 §§ 290–91: total separation from eunuchs is enjoined; *m. Megillah* 2:7; 1QSa excludes those with physical defects from the assembly of God; 1QM 7.3–6 also excludes the maimed).

The eunuch in Acts 8:27 holds a high position in the Ethiopian government. He is in charge of the entire treasury of the Candace (not a personal name but a title; Pliny, *Natural History* 6.186: "They said that it is ruled by a woman, Candace, a name that has passed on through a succession of queens for many years"). This, then, reflects the positive attitude toward eunuchs among barbarians.

The Ethiopian eunuch had come to Jerusalem to worship (v. 27). He is neither Jew nor proselyte. He may have been a god-fearer (a Gentile marginally attached to Judaism). Yet it would not have been possible for him to participate in the worship in the Temple because of his physical blemish. In this regard, his status was like that of other foreigners who came to the Temple in spite of being excluded from it. Josephus, *Antiquities* 3.15.3 §§ 318–19, mentions foreigners who made the arduous journey to the Temple only to find themselves barred from full participation in the cultic ceremonies. In *War* 6.9.3 §§ 426–27, Josephus again mentions the exclusion of foreigners and other polluted who have come to the Temple to worship. The Ethiopian eunuch was among those foreigners who had come to worship but found themselves excluded from the Temple.

Now he is returning home (v. 28) by the road that runs down to Gaza, "the desert route" (v. 26). From Gaza a caravan route led to Egypt. (Arrian, *Anabasis* 2.26, says, "This [Gaza] is the last place on the road from Phoenicia to Egypt. After it the desert begins.") While seated in his chariot, he is reading the prophet Isaiah (v. 28). This is what Philip sees.

In panel two (vv. 29–30b), when the Spirit tells Philip to go and join up with the chariot, he obeys. As he comes near, he hears the eunuch reading Isaiah. Most reading in antiquity was out loud. The eunuch follows the common practice. The art of reading silently, however, was also practiced. (a) Euripides, *Hippolytus*, lines 856–74, has Theseus read a letter silently. (b) Antiphanes, *Sappho*, in a fragment, says a letter when read is inaudible to anyone standing near the reader. (c) Plutarch, *On the Fortune of Alexander* 340A, says Alexander the Great could read silently. (d) Plutarch, *Brutus* 5, indicates Julius Caesar could read silently. (e) Suetonius, *Augustus* 39, mentions some unnamed senators under Augustus who could do the same. (f) Cyril of Jerusalem, *Procatechesis* 14, refers to women reading in silence ("their lips move but the ears of others do not hear"). (g) Augustine, *Confessions* 6.3, says Ambrose read silently (Gillard, 689–96). Perhaps the reason the eunuch follows the dominant practice of reading aloud is because this was the way the study of Torah was done: audibly (*m. Pirke Aboth* 6:6). That he studied Torah on a journey corresponds to occasional rabbinic practice (*b. Hagigah* 12a, 14a; *b. Erubin* 54b). This audible reading is what Philip hears.

Scene two (vv. 30c–35), the dialogue between Philip and the eunuch, is the central part of the story. It falls into a concentric pattern.

> Philip said (v. 30c)
>> Eunuch said (v. 31a)
>>> Eunuch's invitation (v. 31b)
>>> Eunuch's passage (v. 32–33)
>> Eunuch said (v. 34)
> Philip said (v. 35).

Philip asks the eunuch, "Do you understand what you are reading?" (v. 30c). The eunuch replies, "How can I, unless someone instructs me?" (v. 31a). The scriptures are not self-explanatory. They need an interpreter. So the eunuch invites Philip to get in and sit with him (v. 31b). The passage the eunuch is reading is from Isaiah 53:7–8 LXX (vv. 32–33). The eunuch asks, "About whom is the prophet saying this, himself or someone else" (v. 34)? Then Philip, beginning with this scripture passage, "proclaimed Jesus to him" (v. 35).

Exactly how Philip interpreted the text from Isaiah 53 is not stated, other than that it is a christological interpretation. The larger context of Luke-Acts offers a clue. The interpretation of scripture made by Jesus in Luke and that by the church in Acts are paralleled (Talbert 1966, 33–34).

Luke: Jesus as Interpreter	*Acts: The Church as Interpreter*
1. John is the one who prepared the way as Malachi 3:1 says (7:27).	The accurate interpretation of scripture sees John as forerunner (18:24–28).
2. My person is the fulfillment of scripture's hopes (4:16–20:17).	Jesus is the fulfillment of scripture's hopes (3:22–26; 30; 4:11; 10:43; 13:23; 17:2–3; 28:23).
3. My sufferings, death, resurrection, and exaltation are a fulfillment of scripture (9:22, 44; 17:25; 13:33; 24:7; 18:31–34; 22:37; 24:25–27, 32; 24:44–49).	Jesus' sufferings, death, resurrection, and ascension are a fulfillment of scripture (2:25–28, 31; 3:24–25, 17–18; 8:30–35; 13:27–39; 17:2–3, 11; 26:22–23).
4. Scripture promises the Spirit (24:49; Acts 1:4).	The coming of the Spirit fulfills scripture (2:16–21).

5. Scripture points to rejection of the Christ by the Jews (20:17-18).

The rejection of Jesus by the Jews is a fulfillment of scripture (13:40-41, 27; 28:25-27).

6. Scripture foretells a mission to the Gentiles (24:47; 4:25-27).

Scripture is fulfilled in the church's mission to Gentiles (13:47; perhaps 14:26; 15:15-18; 26:22-23).

7. Scripture teaches a general resurrection from the dead (20:37).

Scripture teaches a general resurrection of the dead (24:14-15; 26:6-8).

These seven points of Lukan exegesis present seven aspects of salvation history running from the Baptist to the general resurrection. This salvation history was foretold by scripture. It is the predetermined plan of God that has been largely fulfilled in these last times. Luke is saying that the church's interpretation of scripture is an extension of Jesus' interpretation of the same.

In fact, from Luke's point of view, the risen Jesus taught his disciples the correct way to read scripture. In Luke 24:13-35 the risen Jesus teaches the two on the road to Emmaus how to understand the scriptures.

> "Oh, how foolish you are! How slow of heart to believe all that the prophets spoke! Was it not necessary that the Messiah should suffer these things and enter into his glory?" Then beginning with Moses and all the prophets, he interpreted to them what referred to him in all the scriptures. (Luke 24:25-27)

The same claim is made in Luke 24:44-47. The key part of the text is v. 46: "Thus it is written that the Messiah would suffer and rise from the dead on the third day." A christological reading of scripture focuses on the humiliation and exaltation of the Messiah. It is in this light that one should hear Acts 8:32-33. The Isaiah text refers to Jesus generally and to his humiliation (vv. 32-33a) and exaltation (v. 33b, "his life is taken from the earth") in particular.

Middle Judaism manifested remarkable diversity as different groups made their claims to be the true heirs of ancient Israel, to have the true interpretation of the scriptures of Israel, and to be the fulfillment of the promises of God to ancient Israel. (a) For example, take the case of 1 Maccabees. 1 Maccabees 1:41-64 tells what Antiochus Epiphanes did to attempt to eliminate Judaism. He forbade observance of the sabbath, the practice of circumcision, the reading of the law, the sacrificial cult of the Temple, and observance of the laws of cleanness and uncleanness. For 1 Maccabees these prohibited practices are regarded as the marks of Jewish identity. Anyone who participated in such an orientation would read the scriptures of Israel with this slant. If so, then the scriptures would be seen as an etiological narrative explaining the origins of and justification for these marks of Jewish identity. That is one way to read the Jewish scriptures. (b) A Messianist Jew, however, would read the same scriptures very differently. Such a Jew, preoccupied with the salvation from sin offered through Jesus, would read the scriptures as belonging to those so saved. If so, then the scriptures of Israel would be a foundation myth (telling about creation, fall, redemption, and judgment) and would contain essential prophecies of the End Times, especially of the Messiah. Here the clue to understanding the scriptures is Jesus, the Messiah. Philip, a Messianist Jew, offers to the eunuch a christological interpretation of the prophet Isaiah (for Qumran's reading of Isaiah, see 4Q161–164; the Teacher of Righteousness claimed to have the hermeneutical key to a correct reading of scripture, 1QpHab 2; in such a reading prophecy is fulfilled in the Qumran community.).

Scene three (vv. 36–40) gives the results of the dialogue between Philip and the eunuch. There are two panels: vv. 36–38, 39b and 39a, 40. Panel one begins with the eunuch's question: "Look, there is water. What is to prevent my being baptized?" (v. 36). A similar query is found in the story about Cornelius in Acts 10:47 and 11:17 ("Can anyone withhold water for baptizing these people?"). A similar query is also found in the mouth of Mattidia in the Pseudo-Clementine *Homilies* 13.5.1 (She asks, "What then prevents me from being baptized this day?" i.e., seeing that she has repented already. Peter says, "There is nothing, therefore, to prevent her being baptized," i.e., since she has already fasted the required time). In the context of Acts 8, the eunuch's concern would be about his acceptability, given his disfigurement. Implicit in the condensed narrative is the eunuch's positive response to Philip's proclamation. Will, however, the same thing that prevented him from full participation in the Temple worship in Jerusalem prevent his being baptized into the Messianic community?

The ancients were far from being open about including others in their religious activities. Only Greeks were supposed to be initiated into the Eleusinian mysteries. Foreigners were barred access to the temple of Hera at Agros. In some temples, slaves were not permitted to take part in worship. In other cults men were excluded; in still others, women. Jews prohibited Gentiles from access to the inner courts of the Temple. Jewish law prohibited a eunuch's participation in the assembly of Israel. The eunuch's concern is well placed. (Verse 37 is not part of the original text of Acts. It is absent from the earliest and best manuscripts, although attested as early as Irenaeus, *Against Heresies* 3.22.8.)

There being no reason for his exclusion from full inclusion in the reconstituted Israel, "he ordered the chariot to stop, and Philip and the eunuch both went down into the water, and he baptized him" (v. 38b). The eunuch continues on his way rejoicing (v. 39b, an appropriate response to salvation; cf. Luke 10:20; 19:37; Acts 2:46; 8:8; 13:48, 52; 16:34). In this episode,

Ps 68:32 is being fulfilled ("let Ethiopia extend its hands to God") as are Isa 56:4–5 ("to the eunuchs . . . I will give an eternal, imperishable name") and Wis 3:14 ("Blessed also is the eunuch . . . for special favor will be shown him for his faithfulness, and a place of great delight in the temple of the Lord"). His inclusion continues a Lukan motif (e.g., Luke 7:36–50, a sinful woman; 14:12–14, 21, the poor, maimed, lame, blind; 6:27–30 and 15:1–2, tax collectors and sinners).

Panel two (vv. 39a, 40) focuses on Philip. When Philip and the eunuch came up out of the water of baptism, "the Spirit of the Lord snatched Philip away" and "Philip came to Azotus" (twenty miles up the coast from Gaza). This type of supernatural transference of a person from one place to another is mentioned elsewhere in antiquity (1 Kgs 18:12; 2 Kgs 2:16; Bel and the Dragon 36; Fragment Targum on Pentateuch, Gen 28:10: "as soon as our father Jacob lifted up his feet from Beersheba to go to Haran, the earth shrank before him and he found himself in Haran"; Philostratus, *Life of Apollonius of Tyana* 8.10; *Gospel of the Hebrews* [so Origen, *On Jeremiah* 15:4, and Jerome, *On Micah* 7:6]). Whatever his transport, Philip's mission remains the same. "He went about proclaiming the good news to all the towns until he reached Caesarea" (v. 40).

Taken together, the two episodes in Acts 8 point to the inclusiveness of the gospel as God's doing (vv. 26, 29, 39). All sorts of people are included in the messianic community: Ethiopians, Samaritans, eunuchs, women as well as men, magicians as well as those impressed by magic. All can believe in Jesus, all can be baptized, all can receive the gift of the Holy Spirit, all can be fully included in the church. In Luke-Acts, however, inclusiveness is not an absolute value. It is a contingent value. Such inclusion demands radical repentance. A member of the messianic community is not a magician who has gotten control of God through Jesus' name to make him do his or her bidding. Jesus' disciples are rather those over whom God has gotten control so they will do his bidding. These two stories in Acts 8 say, Be included but be changed. The former is contingent on the latter.

Paul's Conversion (Acts 9:1–31)

In Acts there are two main missionary thrusts in the post-Easter period: Acts 2–12 and 13–28. This is highlighted by the correspondences in contents and sequence between Acts 2–12 and 13–28. The following list is illustrative (Talbert 1974, 23–24).

1. 2:1–4– A special manifestation   13:1–3–A special revelation
    of the Spirit   of the Spirit

2. 2:14–40–Apostolic preaching is the result.

   13:16–40–Apostolic preaching results.

3. 3:1–10–A mighty work follows. A man, lame from birth, is healed.

   14:8–13–There follows a mighty work. A man, lame from birth, from birth, is healed.

4. 3:12–26–The healing is followed by a speech, beginning with the words, "Men . . . why?"

   14:15–17–The healing is followed followed by a speech, beginning, "Men . . . why?"

5. 6:8–8:4–Stephen is stoned at the instigation of Jews from Asia after a speech. Persecution spreads the gospel in a widening circle.

   14:9–23–Paul is stoned at the instigation of Jews from Antioch and Iconium after a speech. This results in further preaching in a wider context.

6. chaps. 10–11–Peter has a mission to the Gentiles (cf. 15:7–11). Divine guidance leads him in a direction other than that planned by him. In 10:9–16 Peter objects but is guided by a vision. Peter justifies his actions in Jerusalem in chaps. 11 and 15.

   chaps. 13–21–Paul has a mission to the Gentiles. Divine guidance leads him in a direction other than that planned by him. In 16:6–10 Paul is guided by a vision to Macedonia. In chaps. 15 and 21 Paul's actions are justified.

7. chap. 12–The first half of Acts ends with Peter's imprisonment (12:4) at a Jewish feast (12:4). It is linked with a Herod (12:5–6); also escape from the hands of the Jews (12:3–4, 6–11). It ends with no information about the fate of Peter (12:17) but with a statement about the success of the Word of God (12:24).

   chaps. 21–28–The second half of Acts ends with Paul's imprisonment at a Jewish feast (21:16). A Herod is involved (25:13, 23–24); also escape from death at the hands of Jews (23:12–34). It ends with no information about the fate of Paul (28:30–31) but with a statement about the success of the Word of God (28:30–31).

Prior to each missionary thrust, three prerequisites for the mission are put in place: (1) a choosing of witnesses (Luke 6:13 and Acts 1:24; Acts 9:15a); (2) a commissioning of the witnesses (Luke 24:46–49 and Acts 1:8; Acts 9:15b–16; cf. also 22:14–15, 21; and 26:16–18); and (3) an indication that the time to move out has arrived (Acts 1:4–5, 8 together with Acts 2; Acts 13:1–3). Acts 9:1–31 tells of the choice, conversion, and commissioning of Paul for the missionary outreach of chaps. 13–28 and all that entails.

That the conversion, call, and commissioning of Paul come in the context of chaps. 2–12, not chaps. 13–28, is a reflection of how good writing is done in ancient narrative. Lucian, *How to Write History* 55, says of the historian, "When he has finished the first topic he will introduce the second, fastened to it and linked with it like a chain . . . ; always the first and second topics must not merely be neighbors but must have common matter and overlap." Luke uses the chainlink principle in this instance, having chaps. 13–28 connected to chaps. 1–12 by the link in chap. 9.

In Acts 9, the choice, conversion, and commissioning come in connection with a Christophany. In Mediterranean culture generally, religious vocation was often based on a divine manifestation to the person. For example, in Euripides, *Bacchae* 467–70, Dionysius defends his mission to bring a new religion to Greece by claiming it was grounded in a theophany of Zeus. In like manner, Acts says that when God gets ready to move out to the Gentiles, He chooses and commissions His servant through a Christophany.

Acts 9:1–31 is regarded by the author of Acts as a crucial part of the narrative's plot. This is proven by the threefold repetition of the story (here in chap. 9 as presented by the narrator, later in speeches of the character, Paul, in chaps. 22 and 26). Because the narrator of Acts 9 enjoys an omniscience that the character, Paul, does not enjoy in chaps. 22 and 26, it is the Acts 9 narrative that is authoritative for the perspective of Acts. The narrator's omniscient point of view enables him to see what is unavailable to the limited point of view of Paul (Kurz, 126, 131).

The narrative of Acts 9:1–31, using multiple patterns and *Gattungen,* depicts Saul's Damascus experience in three complementary ways: (1) as a conversion, in which Christ changes an opponent into an ally; (2) as a conquest, in which Christ overpowers his enemy; and (3) as a commissioning, in which Christ chooses an emissary. In so doing, the author of Acts merely follows a standard practice of his time: the phenomenon of double and triple structure, as it is found, for example, in Horace, Vergil, the Dead Sea scrolls. It was in this way that ancient narrative could be made to yield multiple, complementary points. Depending on the angle of vision (the pattern or *Gattung*), a narrative's sequence could yield different readings (Talbert 1970, 362–63). In what follows, the large thought unit will be read first in terms of the one and then in terms of the other patterns and *Gattungen* and their respective points.

First, Acts 9:1-30 can be read as a narrative of Saul's conversion. Both *Gattung* and pattern feed into this way of reading. On the one hand, Acts 9:1-30 belongs to the *Gattung* of an ancient conversion story. Given the competition among a wide variety of viewpoints, value systems, religions, and philosophies in Mediterranean antiquity, conversions were inevitable. They involved not just an adding on of yet another center of value to one or more already held to (= adhesion), but also a breaking from something upon entering into a new alliance. This is often true even within a pagan, polytheistic context. They might, for example, involve a move from skepticism, magic, or religious provincialism to cultic paganism; from ignorance, self-indulgence, or meaninglessness to philosophy; from one philosophical school to another; from paganism to Jewish monotheism; or from one form of Judaism to another.

Stories of such conversions are to be found in ancient Mediterranean literature. (1) Cultic paganism: For example, (a) Plutarch, *The Obsolescence of Oracles* [*Moralia* 434.45D-F], tells of a ruler of Cilicia who turns from skepticism to belief in an oracle; (b) Horace, *Odes* 1.34, speaks of his own renunciation of skeptical philosophy and new adherence to the traditional gods; (c) Ovid, *Metamorphoses* 3.574-698, relates the captain of a ship's renunciation of improper behavior (i.e., kidnapping) and devout adherence to Bacchus; (d) Apuleius, *Metamorphoses* 11.1-30, gives Lucius's renunciation of magic and unchaste behavior as part of his new devotion to Isis; (e) 1 Macc 1:10-15, 41-50; 2:15-22 speaks about Jews renouncing their provincial religious past as part of their commitment to Greek gods which in turn is part of their adherence to a common culture.

(2) Philosophic paganism: For example, (a) Diogenes Laertius, *Lives of Eminent Philosophers* 2.6.48, relates the response of Xenophon to the call by Socrates in which he forsakes ignorance for a search for knowledge; (b) Diogenes Laertius, *Lives* 4.3.16-18, and Lucian, *Double Indictment* 17, both tell of Polemo's conversion from a life of intemperance to the self-control of the philosophic way; (c) Lucian, *Nigrinus* 1-5, speaks of a man's conversion from the quest of luxury and status to the philosophical way; (d) Aulus Gellius, *Attic Nights* 5.3.1-7, relates Protagoras's conversion from ignorance to philosophy; (e) Aulus Gellius, *Attic Nights* 3.13.1-5, gives an account of Demosthenes' conversion from Plato and the Academy to another philosophic way.

(3) Nonmessianic Judaism: For example, (a) Jdt 5:17-21; 6:2-8; 14:6-10, relates the conversion of Achior, an officer in the Assyrian army, who breaks with his pagan past and is circumcised; (b) *Joseph and Aseneth* is an account of the conversion of the pagan Aseneth from her idols to the God of Joseph; (c) the *Testament of Job* 2-5 offers the conversion of the pagan Job from idol worship to the worship of the Creator; (d) Josephus, *Antiq-*

uities 20.2.1 §§ 17-22; 20.2.3-4 §§ 34-48, presents the conversion of the pagan ruler Izates from idolatry to full inclusion in the Jewish community; (e) the *Apocalypse of Abraham* 1-7 gives the conversion of Abraham from idol worship to devotion to the creator; (f) Josephus, *Antiquities* 13.9.1 §§ 54-58; and 13.11.3 §§ 318-19, tells of the conversions (circumcision) of the Idumeans and Itureans because of their desire for cultural inclusion among the Jews.

(4) In the Apocryphal Acts there are countless stories of pagans being converted to Christ: for example, (a) *Acts of Paul* 1-2, 6, Patroclus, a boy raised by Paul is converted; (b) *Acts of Peter* 4, 23-29, a lad raised by Peter is converted; (c) *Acts of John* 63-81, Callimachus is converted because of his resuscitation; (d) *Acts of Thomas* 51-59, many people are converted because of a resuscitation. In each case, the convert leaves behind an old way of life to take up a new one.

(5) In the Acts of the Apostles there are as many as ten conversion stories: 2:1-47; 3:1-4:4, 32-37; 8:4-25; 8:26-40; 9:1-31; 10:1-48; 13:6-12; 13:13-52; 16:11-15; 16:25-34. One of these, it is noted, is found in chap. 9.

From the evidence derived from conversion accounts found in pagan sources, Jewish materials, and the Christian apocryphal Acts, it is possible to isolate five stable components in these ancient conversion stories: (a) the context; (b) the catalysts leading to conversion; (c) the counterforces that pose an obstacle or opposition; (d) the conversion itself; (e) the confirmation of the genuineness of the conversion by postconversion evidence. Acts 9 fits the *Gattung* perfectly. (a) The context is given—Acts 9:1-2. (b) Catalysts for conversion are specified—Acts 9:3-6, a power encounter; 9:8-9, a period of preparation. (c) Counterforces are mentioned—Acts 9:10-16, Ananias's reluctance. (d) The conversion is given—Acts 9:17-19. (e) Postconversion evidence of the genuineness of the conversion is presented—Acts 9:20-22, 29a, preaching; 9:23-25, 29b-30, persecution; 9:19b, 26-28, participation in the Messianist community (so Craig Joseph, building on Black). Examination of the details is in order.

(1) Acts 9:1-2 provides the context: "Now Saul, still breathing murderous threats against the disciples of the Lord, went to the high priest and asked him for letters to the synagogues in Damascus, that, if he should find any men or women who belonged to the Way, he might bring them back to Jerusalem in chains." (a) Damascus, about 135 miles north of Jerusalem, was not only a member of the Decapolis (Pliny, *Natural History* 5.74) but also had a large Jewish population (Josephus, *War* 2.20.2 §§ 559-61). (b) The conditional sentence in Greek allows the possibility that there may be Messianists in Damascus, although the narrative of Acts has given no hint of such to this point. (c) The Messianists are called "disciples" (6:1) and "those who belonged to the Way" (19:9, 23; 22:4; 24:14, 22; cf. 16:17;

18:25, 26; John 14:6; *Barnabas* 18-21; the Way was also used by Qumran as a designation of itself, CD 1.13; 2.6; 20.18; 1QS 9.17, 18; 10.21). (d) Saul's intensity directed against the Messianists comes out of a long tradition in his community. In Num 25:1-5, Moses slays immoral Israelites at Baal-peor. In Num 25:6-15, Phinehas slays a disobedient Israelite man and a Midianite woman in the plains of Moab. In 1 Macc 2:23-28, 42-48, Mattathias, burning with zeal for the law, slays a Jew who is about to sacrifice to a pagan deity. 1QH 14.13-15 has the psalmist say, "The nearer I draw to you, the more I am filled with zeal against all that do wickedness and all men of deceit." Saul stands in a respected tradition. (e) 1 Macc 15:15-24 contains a letter asking that dissidents be turned over to the high priest for punishment.

(2) Acts 9:3-6, 8-9, speaks about catalysts leading to Saul's conversion. There are two of them. First, there is the power encounter in which the risen Jesus confronts his opponent, Saul (vv. 3-6). There are both a vision and an audition. (a) Vision: "A light from the sky (a standard feature of theophanies—Exod 19:16; 2 Sam 22:15; Ps 27:1; 78:14; Isa 9:2; 42:16; 60:1, 20; Mic 7:8; Dan 10:6) suddenly flashed around him. He fell to the ground" (another feature of theophanies—Ezek 1:28; Dan 8:17; Rev 1:17). That Paul's traveling companions saw no one (v. 7) is no surprise. Supernatural beings become visible only to those to whom they choose to disclose themselves (Homer, *Odyssey* 16.154-63, tells how Athena is seen only by Odysseus and the dogs). (b) Audition: He "heard a voice saying to him, 'Saul, Saul, why are you persecuting me?'" and again "I am Jesus whom you are persecuting." Generally Mediterranean peoples believed that any leader is injured if his followers are attacked (Euripides, *Bacchae* 784-95). Christians, in particular, held that Jesus is so closely identified with his disciples that what is done to them is done to him (Luke 10:16—"Whoever listens to you listens to me. Whoever rejects you rejects me"; 1 Cor 8:11-12; Matt 25:35-40, 42-45; 10:40-42). The power encounter involving vision and audition are one catalyst for Saul's conversion.

Second, there is in 9:8-9 mention of a period of preparation. The risen Jesus had told Saul to go into the city and wait to be told what to do (v. 6). "Saul got up from the ground, but when he opened his eyes he could see nothing; so they led him by the hand and brought him to Damascus. For three days he was unable to see, and he neither ate nor drank" (cf. 13:11). It is unlikely that a prebaptismal fast existed in the time of Acts, but this reference may have been taken as a warrant by later Christians for such a period (as in *Didache* 7:4; Justin, *1 Apology* 61; Tertullian, *On Baptism* 20), just as the episode of the Seven (6:1-6) may have served to justify deacons as functionaries in the later church. Saul's fast seems more likely to have reflected the standard Jewish practice of fasting as a sign of repentance (Jer

14:12; Neh 1:4; Jonah 3:7-8). Thereby Saul places himself in a position to be able to receive what the Lord has in store for him.

(3) There are counterforces of resistance to Saul's conversion. In Acts 9:10-16 Ananias resists his commission. He says, "Lord, I have heard from many sources about this man, what evil things he has done to your holy ones in Jerusalem. And here he has authority from the chief priests to imprison all who call upon your name." His reluctance is understandable. He eventually is obedient and goes as directed.

(4) The conversion as such comes at 9:17-19. "Laying his hands on him, Ananias said: 'Saul, my brother, the Lord Jesus, who appeared to you on the way by which you came, has sent me, that you may regain your sight and be filled with the Holy Spirit.'" Then scales fall from his eyes, and he regains his sight. He is then baptized, eats, and recovers his strength. (a) Laying on of hands for healing is common in Luke-Acts (Luke 4:40; 13:13; Acts 28:8). (b) That Saul is addressed as "brother" indicates that Ananias now accepts him as part of the community. (c) The conjunction of regaining sight and being filled with the Spirit seem to be two sides of one coin here. Hence, when v. 18 says he sees, it can be inferred that he has been filled. The visible sign of his filling is his healing (cf. Gal 3:5). If so, there is once again considerable variety in the arrangements associated with the reception of the Holy Spirit in Acts.

(5) Acts 9:19b-30 offers postconversion evidence of the genuineness of Saul's conversion. (a) In 9:20-22 and 28b-29a, Saul preaches Jesus and debates with the Hellenists. The persecutor has become the preacher. This is one sign of the genuineness of his conversion. It fulfills one part of his commission spoken by the risen Jesus in v. 15 ("carry my name before . . . Israelites"; cf. 28:23-28). (b) In 9:23-25 and 29b-30 Saul suffers persecution (at Damascus, "the Jews conspired to kill him"—v. 23; at Jerusalem, the Hellenists "tried to kill him"—v. 29b). Saul is now an opponent of the very group with whom he sided against Stephen. This fulfills another part of the risen Jesus' commission ("I will show him what he will have to suffer for my name"; cf. 2 Cor 11:24). (c) In 9:19b, 26-28, Saul participates in the community of the Way. "He stayed some days with the disciples in Damascus" (v. 19b). In Jerusalem, after Barnabas vouches for him before the apostles, he is able to move freely among the disciples (v. 28a). All three of these items speak with the same voice. Saul's conversion is legitimate and genuine (Matt 7:15). Christ has changed an opponent into an ally. When the risen Jesus encounters a person, he produces radical transformation.

On the one hand, consider the pattern. This section can be read in terms of two components that overlap (9:1-19 and 9:13-30). In the first place, the initial component (9:1-19) contains two parallel panels, one about Saul and the other about Ananias, each with the same basic ingredients (Krodel, 173–74).

Panel One: 9:1–9	*Panel Two: 9:10–19*
Saul (vv. 1–2)	Ananias (v. 10a)
Vision (v. 3)	Vision (v. 10b)
Response: fell down (v. 4a)	Response: Here I am (v. 10c)
Christ's first word: Why are you persecuting me? (v. 4b)	Christ's first word: Go find Saul (vv. 11–12)
Saul's reply: Who are you? (v. 5a)	Ananias' reply: He is an enemy (vv. 13–14)
Christ's second word: Rise and enter the city (vv. 5b–6)	Christ's second word: Go (vv. 15–16)
Saul obeys (v. 8a,c)	Ananias obeys (v. 17a)
Saul's condition: three days without sight, no food or drink (v. 9)	Saul's new condition: sees, is baptized, eats (vv. 17b–19)

These two panels offer the two stages leading up to Paul's conversion: the power encounter with the risen Jesus (panel one) and the assistance of Ananias (panel two).

In the second place, 9:13–30 also consists of two panels, each with the same ingredients (Gill, 46–48).

Panel One: 9:13–25	*Panel Two: 9:26–30*
Ananias hesitates to believe Saul is truly converted (vv. 13–14)	Jerusalem disciples fear Saul (v. 26)
The Lord reassures Ananias (vv. 15–16)	Barnabas reassures Jerusalem Christians (v. 27)
Paul is with the disciples (v. 19b)	Paul is with them (v. 28a)
Paul preaches (vv. 20–22)	Paul preaches (vv. 28–29)
Jews plot to kill him (vv. 23–24)	Jews plot to kill him (v. 29b)
Paul escapes (v. 25)	Paul escapes (v. 30)

The very pattern that makes the narrative repetitious indicates the issue is whether or not Saul's experience is genuine. Ananias and the disciples in Jerusalem doubt it. The narrative functions, however, as a confirmation of Saul's conversion in a number of ways: (a) the vision to Ananias (vv. 15–16); (b) Paul's preaching (vv. 20, 22; 28–29) in obedience to the commission of

v. 15; (c) Barnabas's vouching for him (v. 27); and (d) Paul's sufferings (vv. 23–25; 29–30) in fulfillment of the Lord's prophecy in v. 16. If the two panels of 9:1–19 set out to describe Saul's conversion, the two panels of 9:13–30 function to confirm the authenticity of that Damascus event for Saul of Tarsus.

Paul's conversion is treated in three different strands of early Christian tradition: the genuine letters of Paul, the deutero–Paulines, and Acts. How do these sources understand the nature and function of Paul's conversion? On the one hand, the nature of Paul's conversion is seen the same way by all the sources. It is conversion from one form of Judaism to another. Paul went from being a highly committed Pharisee to being a highly committed Messianist. The Gentiles whom he later won to Jesus, however, converted from paganism to a new religion (messianic Judaism). On the other hand, the function of Paul's conversion differs depending on the source consulted. In Paul's letters, the apostle's conversion-call has sometimes an apologetic function to legitimate his apostleship (Gal 1:13–17; 1 Cor 15:8–10), sometimes an exemplary function to provide a model of true conversion for his churches (Phil 3:4–17). In the deutero-Paulines the same two functions are found: the conversion-call as the basis for his apostleship (Eph 3:1–13) and Paul's conversion as a prototype for the conversion of all people (1 Tim 1:12–16). In Acts Paul's conversion signals a new departure in the unfolding of God's plan and serves to legitimate the Gentile mission that will follow.

Second, in Acts 9:1–30 Paul's conversion is of a special type. Here Christ overpowers his enemy, making the point that nothing can withstand the progress of the gospel. This point is tied to the *Gattung* employed. The narrative belongs to the *Gattung* of a deity's overpowering an enemy. There are four components in this *Gattung:* (a) an enemy engages in an act against God's house or God's people (2 Macc 3:7–23a; 4 Macc 4:1–8; *Acts of Peter* 132 [NHL]; 1QapGen 20; Acts 9:1–2); (b) there is divine intervention resulting in the enemy's distress, like falling to the ground or being in darkness (2 Macc 3:24–30; 4 Macc 4:10–11; *Acts of Peter* 136; 1QapGen 20; Acts 9:3–9); (c) a devout person intervenes on the enemy's behalf and God's opponent is relieved of his afflictions (2 Macc 3:31–34c; 4 Macc 4:13; *Acts of Peter* 138; 1QapGen 20; Acts 9:10–19); and (d) the enemy then believes in God and demonstrates it by his deeds (2 Macc 3:35–40; 4 Macc 4:14; *Acts of Peter* 138; 1QapGen 20; Acts 9:20–22). This is the form of a story about a god overpowering an enemy.

Paul's Damascus-road experience is depicted in Acts 9 as a Christophany in which the risen Jesus overpowers Saul, the persecutor of the church (9:1; cf. 8:3). Given the narrative plot so far (7:58; 8:1, 3; 9:1–2), this would likely have been one of the first things to impact the ancient auditor of Acts. It would not have been the last, however.

Third, Acts 9:1–25 can also be read in terms of a chiastic pattern: ABCDC'B'A' (Bligh, 95).

A—Saul plots against the Christians in Damascus (vv. 1–2)
    B—Saul sees the vision, is blinded, and fasts (vv. 3–9)
        C—Ananias sees a vision, is commissioned to go to Saul (vv. 10–14)
            D—Saul's mission is foretold by Christ (vv. 15–16)
        C'—Ananias goes to Paul and reports his vision (v. 17)
    B'—Saul's sight is restored, he is baptized, and eats (vv. 18–19a)
A'—Saul preaches Christ in Damascus; the Jews plot to kill him
    (vv. 19b–25).

The significance of this surface structure is that its centerpiece focuses the item of central significance for the auditor of the Acts: Paul's commission. "This man is a chosen instrument of mine to carry my name before Gentiles, kings, and Israelites, and I will show him what he will have to suffer for my name." When the risen Christ overpowers Saul and the persecutor of the church is converted, it is in the interests of the mission described here. If so, then in Acts 9 Christ not only overpowers his enemy in the process of converting him; he also chooses him as an emissary.

From Luke's point of view, the Lord has in Saul a witness fundamentally different from the Twelve. In Luke-Acts there are two kinds of disciples: those "with him" and those not with him. In Luke 8:38–39 the Gerasene demoniac, when healed, begs Jesus that "he might be with him." But Jesus sends him away, saying, "Return to your home and declare how much God has done for you." In Luke 9:49–50 John asks about a man casting out demons in Jesus' name who was not following "with us." These disciples who are not with Jesus are those who have been touched by Jesus in some way but do not accompany him throughout his ministry. By contrast, Luke 8:1; 22:28; 24:44; Acts 1:21–22; 13:31 speak of those who were with Jesus from the baptism of John until the ascension. The Twelve fit into this category; Paul into the camp of those not with Jesus during his ministry. In Luke–Acts these two types of disciples function symbolically. The Twelve who were with him function as the symbol of the authentic tradition about Jesus. Those who were not with him, like Paul, bear witness on the basis of their religious experience (see Acts 26:16). The Twelve who symbolize the tradition were not ready to be Jesus' witnesses until they were empowered by an experience (Acts 2). Paul, who symbolizes those bearing witness out of vivid experience, was not ready to be used by Christ until he was vouched for by the Jerusalem apostles (i.e., his experience was deemed legitimate by the tradition). For Luke-Acts it is not either tradition or experience but rather both tradition and experience. Both are necessary to enable one to be an adequate witness for the Lord.

Peter's Witness in Judea (Acts 9:32–11:18)

Acts 9:32–11:18 is a large thought unit containing three stories about Peter: (1) 9:32–35; (2) 9:36–43; and (3) 10:1–11:18, a two-part episode–10:1–49, the events, and 11:1–18, the justification of the events. The first two units focus on the evangelization of Jews; the third on the conversion of a Gentile. All three are set in Judea. (Caesarea was the capital of the procurators of Judea and so would have been regarded as part of that province.) All fulfill Jesus' promise in 1:8 ("you will be my witnesses . . . throughout Judea"). These three stories about Peter's witness follow three stories about the Hellenists' witness in 6:8–8:40, which also fulfill Jesus' promise in 1:8 ("witnesses in Jerusalem, throughout all Judea and Samaria"). The first two stories about Peter (9:32–35 and 9:36–43) are answers to the church's prayer in 4:30 ("stretch forth your hand to heal"). The third is a reflection of the apostle's deepest conviction: "we must obey God rather than men" (4:19–20; 5:29).

These three stories have links with the Old Testament, the Third Gospel, and with the Pauline section of Acts. First, each of the three Petrine narratives echoes an event in the career of the earthly Jesus (Acts 9:32–35//Luke 5:18–26; Acts 9:36–43//Luke 8:40–56; Acts 10//Luke 7:2–10). This indicates that what the risen Lord commands is in continuity with what the earthly Jesus did (cf. John 14:12). Second, two of the events echo the Elijah-Elisha cycles of the Old Testament (Acts 9:36–43//1 Kings 17; 2 Kings 4; Acts 10//2 Kings 5). This typological writing points to Peter's vocation's being in the line of prophetic succession (cf. Acts 2:17–18). Third, each of the three stories about Peter has a parallel in the narrative about Paul later in Acts (9:32–35//14:8–12; 9:36–43//20:7–12; 10:1–11:18//chaps. 13–28). This says that Paul's mission does not deviate from that of his Jewish-Christian predecessor. There is a unity in Christian practice.

The first two stories (9:32–35; 9:36–43) may be examined together. Both are miracle stories with the usual form: problem (v. 33; v. 37), cure (v. 34; vv. 40–41), reactions (v. 35; v. 42). (a) The first is set in Lydda, a Judean town (1 Macc 11:34) between Jerusalem and Joppa. A paralytic is healed with the result that "all the inhabitants of Lydda and Sharon (the coastal plain between Joppa and Caesarea; Isa 33:9) saw him and they turned to the Lord" (v. 35). (b) The second miracle story is set in Joppa, on the coast. A disciple named Tabitha, who did many meritorious works and who got sick and died, is resuscitated by the prayers of Peter (cf. 28:8). (For examples of other resuscitation stories in antiquity, see 1 Kgs 17:17-24; 2 Kgs 4:8-37; 13:20-21; *b. Abodah Zarah* 10b; *b. Megillah* 7b; Pliny, *Natural History* 7.37; Lucan, *Civil War* 6.750; Philostratus, *Life of Apollonius* 4.45; Apuleius, *Metamorphoses* 2:28-30; Lucian, *Philopseudes* 25; Matt 9:18-26//Mark 5:21-43//Luke 8:40-56; Luke 7:11-17). "This became known all over Joppa, and many came to believe in the Lord" (v. 42).

The stories function both literarily and theologically in the narrative of Acts. Literarily, the two stories serve to get Peter from Jerusalem, where the apostles reside (8:1), to Joppa (9:43), where he will be accessible to Cornelius. Theologically, the two miracle stories make a couple of points. On the one hand, they continue the Lukan emphasis that miracles may serve as a catalyst for faith (e.g., Luke 4:31-5:11; cf. Talbert 1982, 241-46). For the evangelist miracle does not always produce faith; it is not compelling proof (Luke 17:11-17). When it does evoke faith, however, that faith is as genuine as that evoked by any other means.

On the other hand, that Peter resides "a long time in Joppa with Simon, a tanner" (v. 43), is very significant. Because Lev 11:39-40 pronounces unclean anyone who touches the carcass of even a clean animal, a tanner (even a Jewish one) would be perpetually unclean. Being a tanner, therefore, was one of the trades a father should not teach his son (*m. Ketubim* 7:10; *b. Kiddushin* 82a Bar.). The rabbis said that tanneries could not be within fifty cubits of a town (*m. Baba Bathra* 2:9); that even if a tanner's wife agreed before marriage to live with him, he must put her away if she could not stand her circumstances after marriage (*m. Ketuboth* 7:10); that a synagogue building could not be sold for use as a tannery (*m. Megillah* 3:2). If Peter lives with a Jewish tanner over a period of time, it means that he has already come to the position that the cleanliness laws do not apply to Jews and to those who associate with them. Although Luke does not contain Mark 7:15, some such value judgment must underlie Peter's behavior in Joppa. What is left for Peter to see is that such rules do not apply to contact with Gentiles as well (so chap. 10).

The third story is the crucial one for Luke. The fact of its repetition makes this obvious. First the events are narrated (10:1-49); then they are recounted (11:1-18); later they are recalled (15:7-11, 14). Like the threefold repetition of Saul's conversion (Acts 9; 22; 26), this reiteration is for emphasis. Here the evangelist legitimates the principle of the move to the Gentiles (11:18; 15:7-9). Two separate problems have to be dealt with in establishing the Gentile mission's legitimacy. On the one hand, there is the question of the cleanliness laws (10:28; 11:3; see Leviticus 11). One obstacle to a mission to Gentiles is that it brings Jews who follow the laws of purity into contact with people whose person and food are reckoned unclean. At least some strains of ancient Judaism expected the purity laws regarding food to be suspended in the days of the Messiah ("All the animals which in this world are declared unclean, God will in the future [i.e., the days of the Messiah] declare clean"—*Midrash on the Psalms* 146 § 4 [268]). Has that time come? On the other hand, there is the matter of whether or not God wants the Gentiles included at this point in time (10:44-48; 11:1,18). Isaiah 2:1-4 and Tob 14:5-7, for example, look to a time when the Gentiles will be included. It will not be until the time of the End, however. Has that time come? Acts 10:1-11:18 focuses on both of these issues.

In order to see clearly what the author is doing in Acts 10:1-11:18, one needs to understand the surface structure. Acts 10:1-49 is a narrative of the events; 11:1-18 offers the justification of the events. The first section, 10:1-49, moves back and forth between Cornelius and Peter in an ABA'B' pattern. The emphasis is on God's initiative and human obedience to it.

A–10:1-8: Cornelius's vision (vv. 3-6) and obedience (vv. 7-8)
  B–10:2-29: Peter's vision (vv. 10-16), the Spirit's command (vv. 19-20), the recounting of Cornelius's vision (v. 22), and Peter's obedience (vv. 23-29)
A'–10:30-33: Cornelius recounts his vision (vv. 30-32) and his obedience (v. 33)
  B'–10:34-48: Peter's obedience to the command of the risen Lord to preach [vv. 33c; 39; 41; 42] (vv. 34-43) and his obedience to God's initiative in baptizing (vv. 44-48)

"A," 10:1-8, offers Cornelius's vision and obedience. This narrative is told in terms of the *Gattung* of an angelophany with a command (e.g., Gen 19:1-22; Josh 5:13-15; 1 Chr 21:15-30). Verses 1-8 fit this *Gattung*'s five components: (1) introduction (vv 1-2); (2) an angel is seen (v. 3); (3) the one who sees reacts in fear (v. 4a); (4) the angel speaks God's command (vv. 4b-6); and (5) the person obeys (vv. 7-8).

(1) Introduction (vv. 1-2)– The location of the events is Caesarea, whose population was largely Gentile. It was the center of Roman administration and the location of the army, as well as the site of some of Herod the Great's grandest building projects (Josephus, *Antiquities* 15.9.6 §§ 331-41). It is, therefore, no surprise to find there a centurion named Cornelius (v. 1). This Gentile centurion was "devout and God fearing," that is, he prays to God constantly and gives alms generously to the Jewish people (vv. 2, 22, 35). That is, he was neither born a Jew nor is a proselyte; he is one of those Gentiles who followed Jewish practices without going all the way to becoming a proselyte (cf. Acts 13:26, 43, 50; 16:14; 17:4, 17; 18:7).

There was no technical term always used for Gentiles attracted to Judaism in antiquity but the reality existed. (a) Literary sources attest it: for example, Philo, *Moses* 2.20–24; Josephus, *Antiquities* 3.8.9 § 217; 14.7.2 §§ 110, 116; 20.8.11 § 195; *War* 2.18.1 § 463; *Against Apion* 2.11 § 123; 2.40 §§ 282–86; Juvenal, *Satires* 14.96–106; Suetonius, *Domitian* 12:2; Epictetus, *Dissertations* 2.9.19–20). (b) Archaeological evidence supports it. An inscription from Aphrodisias in Caria and dated third century A.D. published by Joyce Reynolds and Robert Tannenbaum supports the case. This stele has inscriptions on two of its four faces. On face A, three people are called proselytes (*prosēlytos*); two are called worshippers of God (*theosebēs*). On face B, the first heading of a list is "Jews"; the second heading of the list is "worshippers of God" (*theosebis*). There was in antiquity a distinction between those born Jews, those who were not born Jews who had become proselytes, and those who were not born Jews but who because of reverence for Jewish monotheism and its high moral code had accepted some of the Jewish way of life without becoming full-fledged converts (Murphy-O'Connor 1992, 418–24). It is to this third group that Cornelius belongs. Such people are depicted in Acts as a major source of converts to the Messianist cause.

(2) An angel is seen (v. 3): "One afternoon about three o'clock (cf. 3:1), he saw plainly in a vision an angel of God come in to him and say to him, 'Cornelius.'"

(3) The one who sees reacts in fear (v. 4a): "He looked intently at him and, seized with fear. . . ." Fear is a normal reaction to a manifestation of the supernatural world (Gen 15:12; 2 Sam 6:9; Luke 1:30; Rev 1:17).

(4) The angel speaks the command (vv. 4b–6): The angel tells Cornelius that his prayers and almsgiving have ascended as "for a remembrance before God" (v. 4b). Because of his piety God has remembered him (Sir 35:7: "the sacrifice of a righteous man is acceptable, and the memory of it will not be forgotten"; prayer is a spiritual sacrifice [cf. Tob 12:12; Heb 13:15; 1 Pet 2:5]). God is now acting to answer his prayer and assist him. "Send some men to Joppa and summon one Simon who is called Peter" (v. 5).

(5) The person obeys (vv. 7–8): Cornelius calls two of his servants and a "devout soldier" from his staff, explains everything to them, and sends them to Joppa to get Peter. In Luke-Acts, angelophanies signal events of great import (Luke 1:5–23; 1:26–38; 2:8–20; 24:1–11; Acts 1:6–11); so here. Angelophanies with commands are one way Luke shows that God directs the course of salvation history.

"B," 10:9–29, focuses on Peter. At the very time the men are coming to get Peter, the apostle has a vision as well (vv. 10–16). The use of double revelations is widespread in antiquity (e.g., Livy 8.6.8–16; Dionysius of Halicarnasus, *Roman Antiquities* 1.55–59; Strabo, *Geography* 4.1.4—a group is told to use for their voyage a guide received from the goddess Artemis, while a woman devotee of Artemis is told in a dream to sail with the group as their guide; Achilles Tatius, *Clitophon and Leucippe* 4.1.4-8; Apuleius, *Golden Ass* 11.6.13; 11.22; *Joseph and Aseneth* 14-15–an angel communicates different things to both parties in order to get them together; Eusebius, *Church History* 6.11.1-3–a bishop elsewhere has a vision that indicates he will be bishop in Jerusalem, a similar vision is also given to the Jerusalem Christians; remember Acts 9:10-12). This is a variation on the theme of the validity of two witnesses. A double revelation legitmates the matter at hand.

Both Cornelius and Peter have their revelations while they are praying. This is in line with the Lukan belief that prayer is the means by which God makes the divine will known for new departures in the unfolding of His plan for history (cf. Luke 3:21-22; 6:12-16; 9:18-22; 9:28-31; 22:39-46; Acts 1:14; 13:1-3).

Peter's trance (vv. 10-16) contains a vision and an audition (Luke 3:21-22; Acts 9:3-6). The vision is of a threefold lowering and raising of something like a large sheet that contained in it all the earth's four-legged animals and reptiles and the birds of the sky (vv. 11-12). The audition consists of a voice, "Get up, Peter, slaughter and eat" (v. 13). Peter takes this instruction to mean he should eat from the unclean creatures in his vision. He protests as though it were a test (cf. Luke 4:3, 6, 9-11): "Never have I eaten anything profane and unclean" (v. 14; cf. Ezek 4:14). The voice speaks a second time: "What God has made clean, you are not to call profane" (v. 15; cf. Rom 14:14; Mark 7:15; 1 Tim 4:1-4). Peter ponders the vision (vv. 17, 19), in doubt about its meaning.

At this point the three men arrive from Cornelius (v. 17). The Spirit then says to Peter, "There are three men here looking for you. So get up, go downstairs, and accompany them without hesitation, because I have sent them" (v. 20). The men then tell Peter about Cornelius's vision (v. 22). What has been communicated to Peter through his vision, the audition, the Spirit's word, and the account of Cornelius's vision is that the cleanliness laws of Judaism do not apply so as to block associations with Gentiles who are seeking God.

Peter is obedient to what he has been given. So he invites them (Gentiles) in and shows them hospitality (v. 23). Then the next day he and some Jewish-Christian brethren go with them to Cornelius's (a Gentile's) house (vv. 23-25). When Peter enters Cornelius's house, the centurion "falling at his feet, paid him homage" (v. 25). The apostle will not tolerate this any more than will Paul later on (14:11-15). He says to Cornelius, "Get up, I myself am also a human being" (v. 26). Although the cleanliness laws are transcended, the scriptural prohibition against idolatry is not (Exod 20:3).

Jesus' witnesses do not draw attention to themselves but to the Lord they represent (cf. 2 Cor 4:5).

At the same time Peter indicates what a stretch it is for him to be there in the house of a Gentile.

> You know that it is unlawful for a Jewish man to associate with, or visit, a Gentile, but God has shown me that I should not call any person profane or unclean. And that is why I came without objection when sent for. (vv. 28–29)

No specific law forbade Jews to associate with Gentiles. It was the result of purity regulations. Jews refused to eat the food of Gentiles (Dan 1:8–16; Tob 1:10–13; Jdt 10:5; 12:1–20; additions to Esther LXX 14:17; *Joseph and Aseneth* 7:1; 8:5; *m. Hullin* 1:1—what is slaughtered by a Gentile is deemed like the flesh of a beast that died of itself, i.e., unclean; Tacitus, *History* 5.5—"they sit apart [from non-Jews] at meals"). This was, however, the very purpose of purity rules according to the *Epistle of Aristeas* 139, 142, which speaks of various rules of purity as "impregnable ramparts and walls of iron" to protect Israel from mingling with the other nations. These deeply ingrained mores have been transcended by Peter because of what God has shown him (v. 28).

In his disregard for laws of purity in the interests of making disciples, Peter acts in a way that is not only obedient to post-Easter religious experience but also in continuity with what the earthly Jesus had foreshadowed (Luke 5:12–15; 5:29–32; 7:36–50; 10:29–37; 11:37–41; 15:1–2; 19:1–10). Again, religious experience and tradition agree in determining the conduct of Jesus' disciples.

"A'," 10:30–33, shifts the focus back to Cornelius. Here the centurion recounts his vision (vv. 30–32) and his obedience (v. 33). (a) This is the third time in the chapter this vision has been presented (vv. 3–6, the narrator's account offered to the reader; vv. 22, Cornelius's servants' account given to Peter; vv. 30–32, Cornelius's account spoken to Peter). From v. 31 ("your prayer has been heard"), it seems that Cornelius understands his prayers to God to have consisted of a petition. What might it have been? In the Eighteen Benedictions there were petitions for a redeemer (Benediction 1), for forgiveness (Benediction 6), and for redemption (Benediction 7). Given the speech that follows with its focus on Jesus as the one by whom forgiveness is gained, this may very well have been the gist of Cornelius's petition. (b) Cornelius speaks pointedly about his obedience to the heavenly vision: "So I sent for you immediately" (v. 33a). He then lays the burden on Peter: "Now therefore we are all here in the presence of God to listen to all that you have been commanded by the Lord" (v. 33b). The point is, I have done what God told me to do; now it is your turn to be obedient. Speak.

"B'," 10:34–49, shifts the focus back to Peter. It also shifts to the matter of the admission of the Gentiles into the people of God. This section falls into two parts: (1) the speech of Peter (vv. 34–43) and (2) the gift of the Holy Spirit (vv. 44–49). (1) The speech (vv. 34–43) falls into an ABCB'C'A' pattern, something like this:

A–vv. 34b–35: universalism
    B–vv. 36–38: Jesus: what he did
        C–v. 39a: witnesses
    B'–vv. 39b–40: Jesus; what was done to him
        C'–vv. 41–42: witnesses
A'–v. 43: universalism.

Verses 34b–35 begin with a universalistic emphasis. "God shows no partiality (*Testament of Job* 4:8; Rom 2:11; Gal 2:6; Col 3:25; Eph 6:9; 1 Pet 1:17; James 2:1, 9; *1 Clement* 1:3; *Barnabas* 4:12; Polycarp, *To the Philippians* 6:1). Rather, in every nation whoever fears him and acts uprightly is acceptable to him" (cf. *Eliahu Rabbah* [13] 14–"Do I show partiality? Whether Gentile or Israelite, whether man or woman, whether male slave or female slave obeys a commandment, the reward for it is immediate"). One stream of ancient Judaism held that there were righteous Gentiles. For example, *t. Sanhedrin* 13:2 records an anonymous saying: "The children of the wicked among the heathen will not live [in the world to come]." Anonymous statements are generally earlier than the comments on them. So this may be from the pre-A.D. 70 period. It implies that there are *righteous* Gentiles who will live in the world to come.

This saying is opposed by Rabbi Eliezer and supported by Rabbi Joshua (both leading rabbis of the period A.D. 70–90). Eliezer, who usually speaks for the House of Shammai, says,

> None of the Gentiles has a portion in the world to come, as it says, "the wicked shall return to Sheol, all the Gentiles who forget God" (Ps 9:17). "The wicked who shall return to Sheol" are the wicked Israelites.

Rabbi Joshua, who usually speaks for the House of Hillel, says,

> If it had been written, "The wicked shall return to Sheol, all the Gentiles," and then said nothing further, I should have maintained as you do. But in fact it is written, "All the Gentiles who forget God," thus indicating that there are also righteous people among the nations of the world, who do have a portion in the world to come. (Sanders, 466–67)

Peter's speech begins with a statement showing affinities with the anonymous saying and Rabbi Joshua's comment about it (cf. also *b. Sanhedrin* 105a; *b. Baba Kamma* 38a). Cornelius, it is implied, is a righteous Gentile.

As such, his prayers are answered by God. Peter is now present to tell him about the prayed-for redeemer and the forgiveness of sins.

Verses 36-38 speak about what Jesus did. He did two things. (a) He preached. After John the Baptist's preaching, Jesus started preaching in Galilee. (b) He healed. Anointed by God with the Holy Spirit, Jesus engaged in a healing ministry. This is certainly Luke's view of what Jesus did in the pre-Easter period (Acts 1:1, "began to do and to teach"). Verse 39a brings in the witnesses: "We are witnesses of all that he did both in the country of the Jews and in Jerusalem." Again, the Lukan perspective about the apostles is evident. They had been with Jesus from the beginning to the end of his ministry (1:21-22).

Verses 39b-40 focus on what was done to Jesus first by the people ("they put him to death by hanging him on a tree") and then by God ("This man God raised on the third day and granted that he be visible"). Human rejection is countered by divine vindication. Once again the witnesses enter, this time in vv. 41-42. The risen Jesus did not appear to everyone but only to "us, the witnesses chosen by God in advance, who ate and drank with him after he rose from the dead" (Luke 24:36-42; Acts 1:4; cf. Ignatius, *Smyrneans* 3:3). God commissioned these Twelve to "testify that he is the one appointed by God as judge (17:31) of the living and the dead."

The speech ends on the same note of universalism with which it began. In v. 43 we hear, "*Everyone* who believes in him will receive forgiveness of sins through his name." The same emphasis characterized Peter's speech at Pentecost when he spoke only to Jews. In 2:38-39 he says to Jews in Jerusalem, "Repent and be baptized *every one* of you, in the name of Jesus Christ for the forgiveness of your sins. . . . For the promise is made to you and to *all* those far off, whomever the Lord our God will call." The emphasis so far in the preaching of Peter has been on the connection of forgiveness of sins with Jesus (e.g., 5:31, "to grant Israel repentance and forgiveness of sins"). Now the one who offers forgiveness of sins to Israel also makes an offer to Gentiles, for God shows no partiality! Furthermore, the prophets support this very point (v. 43a). This language of "all" and "everyone" picks up the theme of universal outreach which runs throughout Luke-Acts (e.g., Luke 2:29-32; 3:6; 4:25-27; 24:47—"that repentance and forgiveness of sins should be preached in his name to all nations"; Acts 1:8).

(2) While Peter is still speaking the Holy Spirit falls "upon all who were listening to the word" (v. 44). The device of interrupting a speech (cf. 11:15) is widespread in antiquity (e.g., Acts 17:32; 22:22; 23:7; 26:24; Josephus, *Antiquities* 16.11.5 §§ 379-86; Xenophon, *Hellenica* 6.5.37). Never mind. What needed to be said has been said. The device merely reinforces the suddenness of the events, a characteristic of supernatural occurrences.

Peter's speech asserting the universal applicability of the name of Jesus is proved true by the events that transpire. The risen Jesus has poured out (v. 45; cf. 2:17, 33) the Spirit even on Gentiles.

The Jewish Christians ("those from the circumcised," v. 45) accompanying Peter (v. 23) are amazed that the gift of the Holy Spirit should have been poured out on the Gentiles also (v. 45), for they could hear them speaking in tongues and glorifying God (v. 46). Note that the accompanying sign of the gift of the Spirit here is not only tongues but also praise (as in Ps-Philo 32:14; *1 Enoch* 61:11–12; 71:11). In Acts such accompanying signs are sometimes tongues (2:4; 10:46; 19:6), sometimes healing (9:17–18), sometimes praise (10:46), and sometimes powerful preaching (4:31) and prophecy (19:6). Just as there is no set scheme of when the Spirit is given in relation to baptism, so there is no one public evidence of the gift of the Spirit. Variety reigns.

Why the Jewish Christians' surprise? Perhaps the Targum Pseudo-Jonathan on Exod 33:16, can offer an answer. Note the contrast between the MT and the targum. On the one hand, Exod 33:16 MT has Moses say to God, "How shall it be known that I have found favor in thy sight, I and this people? Is it not in Thy going with us, so that we are distinct . . . from all other people that are upon the face of the earth." On the other hand, the targum reads,

> In what will it be known that I have found mercy before Thee but in the converse of Thy Shekinah with us, that distinguishing signs may be wrought for us, *in the withholdment of the Spirit of prophecy from the nations, and by Thy speaking by the Holy Spirit to me and to Thy people, that we may be distinguished from all the peoples upon the face of the earth.* (Ethridge, 556)

The gift of the Spirit is here understood as a distinguishing mark of Israel. If such a perspective were assumed by Luke's characters, they could only ask, How could the Gentiles receive the gift? Could there be other than amazement among the Jewish Christians?

Peter's response is that if God has so obviously included the Gentiles, the church's reception of them must follow. "Can anyone withhold water for baptizing these people who have received the Holy Spirit even as we have" (v. 47; 2:4)? He then commands them to be baptized (1 Cor 1:14–17–Did apostles normally abstain from baptizing?; cf. John 4:2) in the name of Jesus Christ (v. 48; 1 Cor 1:13; 6:11). By the initiating act of the Lord and the responsive act of the apostle, the Gentiles are included in the people of God. As a demonstration of the genuineness of what has transpired, "they invited him to stay for a few days" (v. 49; cf. Acts 16:15–"If you consider me a believer in the Lord, come and stay at my home"; John 4:40). The implication is that Peter did as they asked.

Acts 11:1–18, the second section of 10:1–11:18, tells of an evaluation by the church in Jerusalem of what had transpired in Caesarea. Acts 11:1–18 offers the justification for Peter's behavior in 10:1–49. The emphasis throughout is on the divine initiative and human obedience to it. This section consists of three parts: (1) vv. 1–3 (the Jewish Christians' question); (2) vv. 5–17 (Peter's defense of his actions); and (3) v. 18 (the resolution).

(1) "Now the apostles and the brothers who were in Judea heard that the Gentiles too had accepted the word of God" (v. 1; cf. 8:14: "Now when the apostles in Jerusalem heard that Samaria had accepted the word of God"; 11:21–22: "a great number . . . turned to the Lord. The news about them reached the ears of the church in Jerusalem"). The Jerusalem apostles and others are depicted in Acts as keeping a watchful eye out for new developments in the Messianist mission. So when Peter went up to Jerusalem "the circumcised believers confronted him, saying, 'You entered the house of uncircumcised people and ate with them'" (v. 3). For these Jewish Christians the purity laws still apply to Messianists' dealings with Gentiles.

(2) Peter's response consists of four examples of divine initiative told from the apostle's perspective, together with two additional appeals to communal discernment and a word of Jesus. The four examples of divine initiative come first in this discussion. (a) Verses 5–10 recount Peter's vision and audition. It is merely a retelling of the basic facts of 10:9–16. God declared all people clean. (b) Verses 11–12a repeat Peter's experience of the Spirit's telling him to accompany the three men without discrimination. Again, it is a repetition of the facts of 10:19. What Peter did, he did in response to God. (c) Verses 13–14 relate Cornelius's story about the angel who had appeared to him, as told to Peter after the apostle had entered the Gentile's house. Once again, it repeats 10:30–32. Once again, what transpired was God's doing. (d) Verses 15–17 describe the Holy Spirit's falling on the Gentiles, just as it had on the Jerusalem disciples at Pentecost, even as Peter was speaking. Verse 16 not only repeats the essential facts of 10:44–46 but also expands it, as the next paragraph will make clear.

This brings us to the two other types of argument. First, there is an appeal to a saying attributed to the risen Jesus. Verse 16 remembers the word of the Lord: "John baptized with water but you will be baptized with the Holy Spirit" (cf. 1:5). What happened to Cornelius fulfills the prophecy of the risen Lord. To this is to be added an instance of communal discernment. In v. 12b Peter says: "These six brothers also went with me." Going to a Gentile's house was not just Peter's doing. Christian brethren concurred in his discernment. There are then in this section justifying Peter's action four instances of divine initiative, an appeal to a saying of the risen Jesus, and an instance of communal discernment.

On the basis of these six arguments, the apostle's defense culminates in his own question in response to that of the Jewish Christians in Jerusalem.

The translation should run as follows: "If then God gave to them, to those believing in the Lord Jesus Christ (Cornelius and his company), the same gift he gave to us (at Pentecost), who was I to be able to hinder God?" (v. 17). Translated in this way, it avoids the notion that here the gift of the Spirit at Pentecost is linked, as with the story of Cornelius and the other Gentiles, with coming to believe in Jesus (rather than empowerment of those who already believed).

(3) There follows the climax to the entire unit. In v. 18 the resolution of the controversy is given. "When they heard this (Peter's arguments), they (the circumcised believers) stopped objecting and glorified God, saying, 'God has then granted life-giving repentance to the Gentiles too.'" The church deems right what God's acts so indicate.

Looked at in terms of its *Gattung,* the story of Cornelius fits into the ancient form of a conversion story, just as Acts 9:1-30 does. It consists of the usual five components: (a) the context (10:1-2, 22, 30-32; 10:9b-10a); (b) the catalysts (10:3-6 and 10:10b-16—double vision and audition; 10:34-43—preaching); (c) the counterforces (10:14, 17; 10:28; 11:3); (d) the conversion (10:44-48a); (e) the postconversion evidence of genuineness (10:48b; 11:18). Acts 10:1-11:18 may be accurately called the conversion of Cornelius.

Nothing Can Stop the Gospel
(Acts 11:19-12:25)

Acts 11:19-12:25 is a large thought unit consisting of two main parts: (1) a narrative cast in the pattern of the extension of the gospel to non-Jews (11:19-30; 12:25), and (2) a sandwiched section containing two stories about Herod and a summary (12:1-24).

The technique of intercalation/sandwiching is widespread in Mark and is also reflected in Luke. Two examples suffice. First, in Mark 6:7-13 the Twelve are sent out; in 6:30 they return. In between (vv. 14-29) is the story of John the Baptist's beheading by Herod Antipas. Here the intercalated material functions to give a sense of duration to the apostles' journey. This material is also found in Luke although in an abbreviated form. In Luke 9:6 the apostles depart; in 9:10 they return. In between, in 9:7-9 the Baptist material is condensed and adjusted but is present nonetheless. Second, in Mark 5:21-24a, 35-43, there is the story of the resuscitation of Jairus's daughter. In between the two parts of the story comes 5:24b-34, the miracle story of the healing of the woman with the issue of blood. Luke 8:40-42a, 49-56 also gives the raising of the twelve-year-old girl; 8:42b-48, the story of the healing of the hemorrhaging woman. In both Mark and

Luke, the sandwiched material functions to give the sense of a lapse of time, from the beginning of the process of dying to the point of the child's already having died. The use of the technique in Acts 11:27–12:25 functions in the same way as in the two examples cited from the Gospels: to give a sense of elapsed time between a journey's beginning (11:30) and its completion (12:25). Recognition of the use of this technique in 11:27–12:25 allows one to see that the dominant thrust of the unit is to be found in 11:19–30 and 12:25. With that dominant section we begin.

Acts 11:19–30 and 12:25 constitute a narrative cast in the pattern of the extension of the gospel to non-Jews. Like Acts 8:5–25 and 10:1–11:18, 11:19–26 is composed of four components: (1) non-Jews are evangelized (11:20; cf. 8:5; 10:34–43); (2) non-Jews believe (11:21; cf. 8:6–8; 10:44–48); (3) Jerusalem conducts an investigation (11:22; cf. 8:14; 11:1–17); and (4) Jerusalem confirms the new work (11:23–26; cf. 8:15–17, 25; 11:18). To this recurring pattern, Luke adds a fifth component, one to be found again later in Acts (cf. 16:1–5; 21:20–26). (5) After the principle of Gentile inclusion has been established, the victors in the debate perform an act of conciliation to reinforce Christian unity (11:27–30; 12:25). Each component must be examined in turn.

(1) Acts 11:19–20 tells of the attempted evangelization of non-Jews. "Now those who had been scattered by the persecution that arose because of Stephen" (v. 19a) resumes the thread of 8:1–4: "All were scattered. . . . Now those who had been scattered went about preaching the word." It is a Lukan theme that persecution spreads the gospel. The fact that the preachers go first to Jews (v. 19b) fits Acts' theme of "to the Jew first, then to the Greeks" (1:8; 13:46; 18:5–7; cf. Rom 1:16). The preachers speak about Jesus to the Greeks also in Antioch of Syria (v. 20). Antioch was the third among the cities of the Roman world at this time (Josephus, *War* 3.2.4 § 29). Although it contained a large Jewish population (Josephus, *War* 7.3.2–4 §§ 41–62; *Apion* 2.4 § 39), it was a Gentile city. Any church that would be there would contain a mixture of converted Jews and Gentiles (cf. Gal 2:11–14).

(2) Acts 11:21 speaks about the conversion of the Greeks. "The hand of the Lord was with them, and a great number who believed turned to the Lord." Here is further evidence of a Gentile mission prior to Paul's journeys. This mission depends on a dual witness: that of the preachers (v. 20b) and that of the Lord (remember 4:30; 5:32; cf. 14:3). From the Lukan perspective, without the dual witness there would not have been a great number who turn to the Lord.

(3) Acts 11:22 offers another instance of the Jerusalem supervision of the missionary outreach in Acts. "The news about them reached the ears of the church in Jerusalem, and they sent Barnabas [to go] to Antioch." In

8:14–17, after Philip had evangelized the Samaritans, Jerusalem sent Peter and John to complete the process. In 9:26–30 Paul's conversion is legitimated by the Jerusalem Christians. Acts 11:1–18 tells how even Peter was accountable to the Jerusalem church after his visit to the house of Cornelius. In 15:1–35 the various dimensions of Paul's missionary work in chaps. 13–14 are debated and approved by Jerusalem. On Paul's missionary travels he is accompanied by Jerusalem Christians: Barnabas and Silas. After each journey Paul returns to Jerusalem. The significance of this pattern is that for Luke Jerusalem is the center where the Twelve reside. Remember that even in the midst of the persecution after Stephen's martyrdom the apostles did not leave the city (8:1b). Furthermore, the Twelve are those who were with Jesus from his baptism by John to his ascension (1:21–22). They know the true facts of the gospel history. As such, they are witnesses to the people (1:22; 5:32; 10:41; 13:31). In Acts, then, the Twelve stand for the true tradition about Jesus. Their witness is the norm for what is authentically messianic. Jerusalem control means the control of the spreading Messianist experience by the tradition of the earthly Jesus. That a Jerusalem delegate is dispatched to Antioch is Luke's way of saying that this Gentile religious experience needs to be checked to make sure it stands within the boundaries of what is truly Messianist.

(4) In Acts 11:23–26 a delegate from Jerusalem approves the new work. When Barnabas arrives in Antioch "he rejoiced and encouraged them all to remain faithful to the Lord" (v. 23). The Jerusalem stamp of approval is a continuation of 10:1–11:18. After the examination of Peter in 11:1–17, the Jerusalem Christians had approved, in principle, his evangelization of Cornelius: "God has then granted life-giving repentance to the Gentiles too" (v. 18). Once this principle is established in the Lukan plot, the narrative tells of its implementation on a grand scale by others (11:19–24). That Barnabas would be positive is to be expected by Luke's readers given the Jerusalem church's earlier decision in 11:18.

That he would be positive is also to be expected given Luke's description of him as "a good man, filled with the Holy Spirit and faith" (v. 24; cf. *T. Simeon* 4:4, where Joseph is described in similar terms). In Acts 1:8 the risen Jesus had said that his disciples would be witnesses to the ends of the earth after they had experienced the Holy Spirit (cf. Luke 24:47–49). According to Lukan theology, the gift of the Spirit is the experiential base from which the mission to all nations takes off. Without the Spirit there is no mission.

The Jerusalem connections to the new mission cannot be reduced to approval only; they also include what is necessary to nurture it (as in 8:14–17). Verses 25–26 tell how Barnabas went to Tarsus to find Saul so that he could aid in the development of the new believers. "For a whole year they met with the church and taught a large number of people" (v. 26a). In Acts evangelization is followed by nurture. Acts 2:42 says that after the Pentecostal ingathering, "they devoted themselves to the teaching of the apostles and to the communal life, to the breaking of the bread and to the prayers." Acts 4:23–35 also tells of their corporate worship and sharing. So here Barnabas and Saul meet with the church and teach. This nurturing task requires additional leadership so that the tasks at hand can be performed (remember 1:15–26; 6:1–6). Having confidence in Saul's conversion (9:27), Barnabas enlists him to help. In so doing, the narrative of Acts has Barnabas vouch not only for the authenticity of Paul's conversion (9:26–30) but also for the legitimacy of his ministry (11:25–26). As a result, not only is the mission to the Gentiles in Antioch approved by Jerusalem's representative, the future missionary to the Gentiles is also.

One comment made in v. 26b needs attention. "It was in Antioch that the disciples were for the first time called Christians" (*christianous*). Up to this point the followers of Jesus have been called "saints" (9:13, 32, 41), "disciples" (6:2, 7; 9:1, 10, 26, 36), "believers" (4:32; 5:14; 10:45), "the church/assembly" (2:47; 5:11; 8:1, 3; 9:31; 11:22, 26), "the brothers" (1:15; 10:23; 11:1). Now outsiders give the disciples a new name: *Christianoi*. The suffix *-ianoi* (*-iani*) frequently denotes the followers of the named person, especially partisans of a political leader (e.g., *Pompeiiani*—Appian, *Civil War* 3.11.82; *Caesariani*—*Civil War* 3.13.91; *Herodianoi*—Mark 3:6; 12:13) or a teacher (e.g., Valentinians; Simonians). If so, then Christians would mean "followers of Christ" (assuming "Christ" is taken in a Gentile context as a proper name). The name continues to be a label used by outsiders (Acts 26:28; 1 Pet 4:16; Josephus, *Antiquities* 18.3.3 § 64—"the tribe of Christians, so named from him, are not extinct at this day"; Tacitus, *Annals* 15.44—"Christus from whom their name is derived"; see also Pliny, *Epistles* 10.96–97; Lucian, *Alexander the False Prophet* 25.38). It is first used by a Christian as a self-designation in Ignatius (*Ephesians* 11:2; *Romans* 3:2; *Magnesians* 4; *Polycarp* 7:3) and in the *Didache* 12:4.

(5) Acts 11:27–30 and 12:25 function as a demonstration of the unity of Gentile and Jewish Messianists in the one people of God as evidenced by the sharing of material possessions. The backdrop of this expression of fellowship is the prophecy of Agabus. "At that time some prophets came down from Jerusalem to Antioch, and one of them named Agabus stood up and predicted by the Spirit that there would be a severe famine all over the world" (vv. 27–28a). Luke adds, "and it happened under Claudius" (v. 28b). Wandering prophets were part and parcel of early Christianity in Syria (Acts 21:10; *Didache* 12:1–5), just as were settled prophets (Acts 13:1–3; 21:8–9; *Didache* 11:1–2). Here the itinerant Agabus prophesies a future famine, which the narrator says happened in the days of Claudius.

Grain shortages were frequent in the Roman world of the first century A.D. Seneca, writing about problems in Rome in A.D. 40-41 under Caligula, says, "We were threatened with . . . lack of provisions . . . very nearly at the cost of the city's destruction and famine and the general revolution that follows famine" (*Brevity of Life* 18.5). During much of the reign of Claudius, evidence suggests that there were serious shortages in general (Suetonius, *Claudius* 18.2; Tacitus, *Annals* 12.43; Dio Cassius 60.11) and in the East in particular. In A.D. 46 or 47, under the procurator Tiberius Julius Alexander, there was famine in Judea. Helena, Queen of Adiabene, visited Jerusalem to find the inhabitants dying. She sent to Cyprus for dried figs and to Egypt for grain (Josephus, *Antiquities* 3.15.3 §§ 320-21; 20.2.5 §§ 51-52). When her son was informed of the famine, he sent great sums of money to the principal men of Jerusalem (*Antiquities* 20.2.5 § 53). "All over the world" in Agabus's prophecy is poetic hyperbole (v. 28b; cf. 17:6; 24:5). The famine was extensive but not empire-wide. That Agabus correctly foretells the coming famine lays the foundation for the readers' confidence in his words later in Acts (21:10-11).

"So the disciples determined that, according to ability (1 Cor 16:2), each should send relief to the brothers who lived in Judea" (v. 29). These Gentile Christians in Antioch are shown acting in the same way that the new converts in Jerusalem had acted earlier. They share their material goods, however, not with one another but with the Jewish Christians in Jerusalem. In this way they demonstrate their full participation in the church of the apostles and testify to the unity of Jews and Gentiles within the Messianist fellowship (cf. Eph 2:11-22). It is significant, moreover, that when the Antiochian disciples act in this way, they are behaving like their teacher Barnabas (4:36-37): "like teacher, like disciple" (Luke 6:40).

The church in Antioch sends its gifts to the Jerusalem elders by Barnabas and Saul (v. 30). These elders, the recipients, are the church leaders in Jerusalem (cf. 14:23; 15:2, 4, 6, 22, 23; 16:4; 20:17; 21:18). Barnabas and Saul are here functioning as apostles of the church of Antioch (cf. Phil 2:25; 2 Cor 8:23). "After Barnabas and Saul completed their relief mission, they returned from Jerusalem, taking with them John, who is called Mark" (12:25; 13:13; 15:37; 1 Pet 5:13; Col 4:10; Phlm 24; 2 Tim 4:11).

The portrayal of wealth in this unit reflects one half of the larger picture found elsewhere in Luke-Acts. The evangelist gives a two-sided portrayal. On the one hand, Luke sometimes depicts wealth in negative terms. Acts 1:18 says Judas's betrayal of Jesus was for money (Luke 22:5-6). In 5:1-11, Ananias and Sapphira lie to the Holy Spirit because of money. Simon the magician seeks the ability to impart the Holy Spirit by the laying on of hands in exchange for money (8:18). In 16:16-24, the Philippian owners of a divining slave girl cause Paul and Silas to be thrown into prison over their loss of gain. Acts 19:23–41 tells how the silversmiths in Ephesus riot over the threat to their income. Felix, in 24:26, keeps Paul in prison in hopes that he will be given a bribe. Throughout Acts the author says in effect that a concern for money to the point of valuing it above all else is a primary trait of a godless individual and a fallen world (cf. Luke 12:13–15, 16–21, 22–34; 16:13, 19–31; 18:18–23, 24–25; 1 Tim 6:10; Polycarp, *To the Philippians* 4:1).

On the other hand, Luke sometimes depicts wealth in positive terms. Private property is assumed (Acts 2:45; 4:37; 5:4; 11:29). Nevertheless, property ownership and rights are subordinated to human need within the community of disciples. Since property is an extension of one's personality, to commit oneself to others in a community involves sharing of wealth. That this happened in Jerusalem (Acts 2:44–45; 4:32, 34, 35, 36–37; 6:1–6; 11:27–30), Luke believes, fulfills the highest hopes of the Jews and ideals of the Greeks and Romans. It is this aspect of the Lukan portrayal of wealth that one finds in vv. 27–30. The purpose of the sharing in 11:27–30 is the furtherance of unity in the Messianist community (cf. Isa 58:7).

The movement of the narrative in Acts 8–11 has been like waves of an incoming tide, each story pushing ahead toward the ultimate limit. So in chap. 8 the word goes first to the Samaritans and then to the Ethiopian eunuch. In chap. 10 Cornelius is included. Now in Acts 11 many Greeks are incorporated, along with converted Jews in Antioch of Syria. The principle is firmly established: (a) Gentiles are included in the fellowship, and (b) Jews and Gentiles can associate with one another in the church. The stage is set. It only remains for God to say when the time to move out in an even wider circle has come. For that, the reader awaits Acts 13:1–3. In the meantime, there is an intercalated interlude to investigate.

Acts 12:1–24 is sandwiched in between the departure of Barnabas and Saul for Jerusalem (11:30) and their return (12:25). If the famine earlier predicted by Agabus (11:28) occurred in A.D. 46–47, the events of chap. 12 take place prior to (so 12:1–19) and during A.D. 44 (so 12:20–23), the year Herod died. There are three components to chap. 12: (1) Herod's hostility toward the Jerusalem disciples (vv. 1–19); (2) Herod's hostility toward the people of Tyre and Sidon (vv. 20–23); and (3) a summary (v. 24). Each must be examined in turn.

(1) The first story about Herod (12:1–19) has as its point that unrighteous rulers cannot stop the progress of the gospel. Acts 12:1–19 speaks about Herod's hostility toward the church in two stages: (a) first, he kills James, the son of Zebedee (v. 2; cf. Luke 6:12–16; Acts 1:13); (b) second, he arrests and imprisons Peter (vv. 3–5a).

This Herod is Herod Agrippa I, the grandson of Herod the Great (Luke 1:5); the son of Aristobulus; the father of Herod Agrippa II (Acts

25:13–26:32), Drusilla (Acts 24:24), and Bernice (Acts 25:13). Agrippa had been brought up in Rome where he made many influential friends, among whom were Caligula and Claudius. When Caligula became emperor (A.D. 37–41), he granted Herod Agrippa I the tetrarchy of Philip (Luke 3:1) and the tetrarchy of Lysanius (Luke 3:1). Later he added the tetrarchy of Herod Antipas (Luke 3:1; 9:7–9; 13:31; 23:6–12) to Agrippa's possessions. After Caligula's assassination, Agrippa helped Claudius receive confirmation from the Roman senate as emperor. The new emperor added Judea and Samaria to Agrippa's kingdom. So, from A.D. 41 to 44 when he died, Herod Agrippa I ruled over a reassembled kingdom of the same size as his grandfather, Herod the Great. He was as loved by the Jewish establishment as his grandfather was hated.

The execution of James, the brother of John and one of the Twelve, by the sword (*m. Sanhedrin* 7:3: "They used to cut off his head with a sword as the government does") for an unnamed reason (v. 2) serves to indicate the seriousness of the threat to Peter in what follows. (The fifth-century Philip of Side in his *Church History* says that Papias relates in his second book that James, the brother of John, was killed by Jews.)

The narrative about Peter is told as a miracle story: (a) the problem: imprisonment (vv. 3–5a); (b) the solution: prayer (v. 5b) and its answer (vv. 6–12); and (c) the reactions to the miracle: first by the church (vv. 13–17), and then by the soldiers and Herod (vv. 18–19). (a) The problem: Herod, when he sees that his execution of James has received a positive response from the Jewish establishment, imprisons Peter at Passover season (v. 3), intending to bring him before the Jewish people after the feast (v. 4b). In prison the apostle is kept under the guard of four soldiers around the clock (v. 4b; cf. Philostratus, *Life of Apollonius* 7.31, where the philosopher is accompanied by four guards). The situation seems hopeless.

(b) The solution: While Peter is chained between two guards with two other soldiers guarding the two gates, the church is at prayer for the apostle (v. 5b–6). Throughout Acts, the church is a praying community (1:14, 24; 2:42; 3:1; 4:24–30; 6:6; 8:15; 9:11, 40–41; 10:4, 9; 13:3; 16:25; 20:36; 21:5; 22:17; 28:8). Their prayer is answered. "Suddenly an angel of the Lord stood by him and a light (an accompaniment of a supernatural manifestation, 9:3; 22:6; 26:13; Luke 2:9) shone in the cell. He tapped Peter on the side and said, 'Get up quickly.' The chains fell from his wrists. . . . Then he said, 'Put on your cloak and follow me.' . . . They came to the iron gate leading out to the city, which opened for them by itself" (vv. 7–10). When Peter recovers his senses, he engages in an interior monologue: "Now I know for certain that [the] Lord sent his angel and rescued me (Dan 3:95) from the hand of Herod and from all that the Jewish people had been expecting" (v. 11). Interior monologues are found in the Old Testament (e.g., 1 Sam

18:17b, 21a), in Greek and Roman sources (e.g., Apollonius, *Argonautica* 3.772-801; Vergil, *Aeneid* 4.534-52; Ovid, *Metamorphoses* 10.319-33; Xenophon of Ephesus, *Ephesian Tale* 1.4.1-7; Longus, *Daphnis* 1.14.18), and in the Third Gospel (e.g., Luke 7:39; 12:17-19; 12:45; 15:18-20; 16:3-4; 18:4-5; 20:13). He then goes to the house of Mary, the mother of John Mark, where the church is assembled for prayer.

(c) The reactions: In the first place, the Christian reactions are semi-humorous. When Peter knocks on the door of the gate, a maid named Rhoda comes to answer it. She is so overjoyed to see it is Peter that, instead of letting him in, she runs to tell those at prayer. They will not believe her. "It is his angel," they say (v. 15b). The notion of a guardian angel was held by nonmessianic Jews (e.g., LXX Gen 48:16; Tob 5:4-16, 22; Pseudo-Philo 59:4; *Testament of Jacob* 1:10) and Messianists (e.g., Matt 18:10; Hermas, *Mandate* 6.2.2-3; *Apocalypse of Paul* 49) alike. It is only because he continues to pound on the door that they finally let him in (v. 16). The church is unable to believe in an answered prayer. In the second place, the soldiers are in a commotion over Peter's absence. They have every right to be because they must pay for his escape with their lives (cf. Acts 16:27; Matt 28:13-14; Code of Justinian 9.4.4). Herod meanwhile leaves the city (vv. 18-19).

This particular type of miracle story is found elsewhere in Acts: for example, 5:17-21, where the apostles are freed from the common prison ("the angel of the Lord opened the doors of the prison, led them out, and said: 'Go . . . tell'"), and 16:25-28, where Paul and Silas experience the opening of the prison doors and the unfastening of their fetters. It belongs to a *Gattung* of escape legends known both in Greco-Roman and in Jewish circles in antiquity. Several examples will suffice to clarify the type.

An example of a Greek story is found in Euripides' *The Bacchae* 443-48. It tells of the escape of some maidens who had succumbed to Dionysian madness.

> The captured Bacchanals you put in ward,
> And in the common prison bound with chains;
> Fled to the meadows are they, loosed from bonds,
> And dance and call on Bromius the god.
> The fetters from their feet self-sundered fell;
> Doors, without mortal hand, unbarred themselves.

The parallel to the release of Peter provided by this passage was already noted by Origen, *Against Celsus* 2.34.

From the Roman world one may mention Ovid's *Metamorphoses*

3.690–710. It tells of a convert of Bacchus, the Lydian Acoetes, who is imprisoned by Pentheus and sentenced to death. The story goes that

> while the cruel instruments, the fire, and the sword were being gotten ready to kill him, as the king had ordered, the doors flew open of their own accord and, of their own accord, though no one loosened them, the fetters fell from his arms.

The Jewish world has its own version as well. Artapanus in his book *Concerning the Jews* (as reported by Eusebius, *Preparation for the Gospel* 9.27; cf. also Clement of Alexandria, *Miscellanies* 1.23) says that the Egyptian pharaoh shut Moses up in prison.

> But when it was night, all the doors of the prison-house opened of their own accord, and of the guards some died, and some were sunk in sleep, and their weapons broken in pieces. So Moses passed out and came to the palace.

Later apocryphal Acts contain the same type of story. (a) In the *Acts of Paul,* in Ephesus Paul is shut up in prison. But by God's power, Paul, loosed from his iron fetters, goes to the seashore to baptize converts. (b) In the *Acts of Thomas,* Thomas is put in prison (142). The whole prison becomes as light as day (153); Jesus opens the doors (154); and Judas Thomas goes out to Iuzanes' house (155).

Such stories of liberation were told to say that there is nothing, certainly not a hostile ruler, that can prevent the deity and his followers from conquering the world. The author of Luke-Acts has appropriated this form to tell of several deliverances of the early Messianist missionaries with the same aim. Here in Acts 12 the point is clear. The power of the state is impotent to stop the gospel.

(2) The second story about Herod (12:20–23) has as its point that rulers who try to usurp the place of God will be judged. This passage in Acts is a variant of a similar tradition found in Josephus, *Antiquities* 19.8.2 §§ 349–50. As Josephus tells it, at a festival in Caesarea, Herod Agrippa I put on a garment made entirely of silver and came into the theater in the morning. When the sun hit it, it shone marvelously. Flatterers cried out that he was a god: "Although we had formerly reverenced you only as a man, yet we shall henceforth regard you as superior to mortal nature." The king did not rebuke them or reject their flattery. He then saw a bird of ill omen. A severe pain arose in his stomach. He then said: "I, whom you call a god, am commanded presently to depart this life; while Providence reproves the lying words you just now said to me. And I, who was called by you immortal, am immediately to be hurried away by death." After five days he died.

Josephus's account differs from that in Acts 12:20–23 in several ways. (a) In Acts, the occasion is a delegation from Tyre and Sidon; in Josephus, it is a festival in honor of Caesar. (b) In Acts, Herod's oration brings acclamation; in Josephus, it is his silver suit. (c) In Acts, Herod is eaten by worms; in Josephus, he dies of a pain in his belly. The two accounts are similar in that they both attribute Herod's death to his not rejecting the acclamation of divinity.

The story in Josephus belongs to the *Gattung* of the humiliation of a self-deifying ruler. The account in Acts 12:20-23 is a synthesis of two genres: (a) the humiliation of a self-deifying ruler (cf. vv. 22, 23a) and (b) the ignominious death of a persecutor of God's people (cf. v. 23b). The two genres need explanation.

(a) The *Gattung* of the humiliation of a self-deifying ruler has a long history in Judaism. The Old Testament prototype is found in Ezek 28:1-10 and Isa 14:12-20. In Isaiah 14 there is a taunt against the king of Babylon:

> You have said in your heart, "I will ascend to heaven" (v. 13).
> "I will make myself like the Most High" (v. 14).
> But you are brought down to Sheol, to the depths of the Pit (v. 15).

In Ezekiel 28 we hear the following of the king of Tyre:

> Because your heart is proud, and you have said, "I am a god" (v. 2)
> Because you consider yourself as wise as a god (v. 6)
> Therefore (v. 7),
> You will die (v. 8).
> Will you still say, "I am a god," in the presence of those who will slay you (v. 9)?

Daniel 4:26-34 develops the motif further.

> King Nebuchadnezzer says, "Babylon the great! Was it not I, with my great strength, who built it as a royal residence for my splendor and majesty?" (v. 27).

> A voice spoke to the king: "You shall be cast out from among men, and shall dwell with wild beasts . . . until you learn that the Most High rules over the kingdom of men and gives it to whom he will" (v. 29).

> Nebuchadnezzar then acknowledges the king of heaven and says: "Those who walk in pride he is able to humble" (v. 34).

Josephus, *Antiquities* 19.8.2 §§ 349-50, the story about Herod Agrippa I, fits into the development of this motif in ancient Judaism. So also does Josephus, *Antiquities* 18.8.9 § 306, which speaks about Caligula's demise after his attempted self-deification with the accompanying statue of himself to be put in the Jewish Temple. "But when He (God) had taken Gaius away, out of His indignation of what he had so insolently attempted, in assuming to himself divine worship. . . ."

The theme is not limited to Jewish sources, however. For example, Herodotus 7.10 has Artabanus, the king's uncle, speak to Xerxes as follows:

You see how the god smites with his thunderbolt creatures of greatness . . . ,
nor suffers them to display their pride . . . for it is heaven's way to bring low all
things of surpassing bigness . . . for the god suffers pride in none but himself.

The warning is against self-deification.

Part of the story about Herod in Acts 12:20–23 clearly fits into this *Gattung*. In vv. 22–23a we read, "The assembled crowd cried out, 'This is the voice of a god, not of a man.' At once the angel of the Lord struck him down because he did not ascribe the honor to God." The point of this *Gattung* is that God will not allow anyone, even the greatest ruler, to usurp His place. God humbles the exalted (cf. Luke 14:11; Prov 3:34; James 4:6; 1 Pet 5:5).

There is yet another *Gattung* with which Acts 12:20–23 also has affinities. It is that of the death of the persecutor of God's people: he is eaten by worms. A number of sources reflect this motif. (a) Jdt 16:17 gives part of the heroine's song:

Woe to the nations that rise against my people!
the Lord Almighty will requite them;
in the day of judgment He will punish them:
He will send fire and worms into their flesh,
and they shall burn and suffer forever.

(b) Josephus, *Antiquities* 17.6.5 §§ 168–70, speaks of the death of Herod the Great, who was viewed as a persecutor of God's people, in this way. (c) Tertullian, *To Scapula* 3, tells of the death of the persecutor Claudius Lucius Herminianus in this way. (d) Eusebius, *Church History* 8.16, describes the death of the persecutor, the emperor Galerius, in this very way. Persecutors of God's people die, eaten by worms. Acts 12:23b reads, "And he was eaten by worms and breathed his last." This part of the story in Acts reflects the end of a persecutor of God's people. Herod was certainly that, as 12:2 and 12:3–4 have shown.

In the case of Antiochus Epiphanes, as described in 2 Maccabees 9, the two forms come together. Antiochus, who was both a persecutor of God's people (9:4, "When I get there I will make Jerusalem a cemetery of Jews") and one who presumed to think himself equal to God (9:10, "the man who . . . thought he could touch the stars of heaven"; v. 12, "no mortal should think he is equal to God"), meets a terrible end. He is not only struck down but "the ungodly man's body swarmed with worms" (v. 9). Acts 12:20–23 reflects the same combination of the two forms: (a) the humiliation of a self-deifying ruler and (b) the death of a persecutor of God's people by worms.

Acts 12 needs to be considered in light of the larger Lukan attitude toward the state. Overall Luke-Acts is generally positive towards the state (e.g., Luke 7:1–10; Acts 13:4–12; 18:12–17; 19:23–41; 23:10; 23:12–33; 26:32; 27:42–43). Even when Roman officials fall below acceptable standards of behavior, the system of Roman justice is viewed favorably (e.g., Acts 16:19-39; 17:1-9; 22:22-29; 24:26-25:2; remember Pilate's recognition of Jesus' innocence before succumbing to Jewish pressure in Luke 23). Most often the Roman judicial system protects the apostles from chaos and from caprice of an unruly mob. In this mostly positive attitude toward the state, the evangelist agrees with a major stream of early Messianist thinkers (e.g., Rom 13:1-7; 1 Tim 2:1-6; 1 Pet 2:13-14; *1 Clement* 60:4-61:1; Polycarp, *To the Philippians* 12:3). This stance echoes the sentiments of the early rabbis: "Pray for the welfare of the government, for were it not for the fear of it, men would swallow one another alive" (*m. Pirke Aboth* 3:2).

Acts 12, however, is critical of rulers who exalt themselves to the place of God and who act hostilely toward the church. In this critical attitude, Luke agrees with yet another stream of early Messianist thought (e.g., Revelation; *Barnabas* 4:2-4; *Sibylline Oracles* 4.117-18). Both of these attitudes, positive and negative, have their roots in the logion of the Lukan Jesus (Luke 20:25): "Render to Caesar the things that are Caesar's, and to God the things that are God's." Luke-Acts has the most balanced and nuanced view of the state in the New Testament. It contains both poles of early Messianist thought, positive and negative. In Acts 12, the evangelist says, Neither the state's hostility toward the church nor its ruler's exaltation of himself to a godlike position can stay the triumph of the gospel.

(3) The intercalated material about Herod Agrippa I ends with a summary of the type echoing Luke 8:8 (cf. Acts 6:7; 19:20). Verse 24 says, "But the word of God continued to spread and grow" (Col 1:5-6). Nothing can stop the gospel: neither race (11:20), nor famine (11:27-30), nor persecutors (12:1-19), nor self-deifying rulers (12:20-23).

FULFILLING THE MISSION: PHASE TWO

Acts 13:1–28:31

Paul's First Missionary Journey
Acts 13:1–14:28

Acts 13:1–14:28 is a large thought unit held together by an inclusion (13:1-3, from Antioch, where they had been set apart for the work to which they had been called; 14:25-27, to Antioch, where they had been commended to God for the work they had now accomplished). It constitutes the first missionary journey of Paul. It functions as a fulfillment of three of the components of Paul's commission stated in Acts 9:15-16. "This man is a chosen instrument of mine to carry my name (1) before Gentiles, kings, and (2) Israelites, and (3) I will show him what he will have to suffer for my name." (1) In 13:7-12; 13:46-48; 14:8-18; and 14:27, Paul fulfills his commission to witness before Gentiles, one of whom is a ruler. (2) In 13:5; 13:14-41; and 14:1, Paul fulfills his commission to witness to sons of Israel. (3) In 13:50; 14:2, 5; and 14:19, Paul's sufferings for Jesus' name are highlighted.

The narrative of Acts 13-14 moves out from Antioch of Syria (13:1-3), to Seleucia, the port of Antioch (13:4), to two cities on Cyprus, Salamis (13:5) and Paphos (13:6-13a), then to Perga, the metropolis of Pamphylia (13:13b), to Antioch of Pisidia by the paved highway, the Via Sebaste (13:14-51a), to Iconium by the same road (14:1-5), to Lystra by the same road (14:6-20a), and finally to Derbe, perhaps by an unpaved road (14:20b-21a). There is then a brief retracing of steps to Lystra, Iconium, Antioch of Pisidia, Perga (14:21b-25), then to Attalia, the entry port of Pamphylia (14:25b), and from there a return to Antioch of Syria (14:26-28).

Within the inclusion (13:1-3; 14:24-28), the material falls into an ABA'B'A"B" pattern (A = to Jews, B = to Gentiles), reflecting the motif "to the Jew first and also to the Greek" (3:26; 13:46; Rom 1:16; 2:10).

[13:1-3: From Antioch
  A—13:4-5: To Jews
    B—13:6-12: To Gentiles
  A'—13:13-43: To Jews
    B'—13:44-52: To Gentiles
  A"—14:1-7: To Jews
    B"—14:8-18, 19-23: To Gentiles
[14:24-28: To Antioch

Each component needs attention.

Acts 13:1-3 is a commissioning story consisting of four components: (1) introduction (vv. 1-2a; cf. Gen 11:31-32); (2) confrontation (v. 2b; cf. Gen 12:1a); (3) commission (13:2c; cf. Gen 12:1b-3); and (4) conclusion (13:3; cf. Gen 12:4-5a) (Hubbard 1977, 103-26; and Hubbard 1978, 187-98)

(1) "In the church at Antioch there were prophets and teachers. . . . While they were worshipping the Lord and fasting" (vv. 1-2a). Like the Syrian churches reflected in *Didache* 15:1, it appears the church at Antioch has prophets and teachers as its leaders. Five are named: Barnabas (11:22), Symeon who was called Niger (Plutarch, "Life of Caius Marcius Coriolanus" 11, tells how Greeks and Romans used to give surnames on the basis of an exploit, a special excellence, from some good fortune, or from a bodily feature: e.g., Niger [=black], Rufus [=red]), Lucius of Cyrene (11:20), Manaen, who was a close friend of Herod the tetrarch (Luke 3:1), and Saul (11:25). The context of the commissioning is the worship of these prophets and teachers.

(2) "The Holy Spirit said" (v. 2b) constitutes the confrontation. This is likely a reference to a prophetic word. (3) The commission itself comes in v. 2c: "Set apart for me Barnabas and Saul for the work to which I have called them."

The Spirit leads the church to confirm the call the two had already received. Oracles often served as the basis for a mission. Dionysius, for example, defended his mission to bring a new religion to Greece by claiming that it was based on a theophany of Zeus (Euripides, *Bacchae* 469; cf. Gal 1:6; 2:2–travel in response to a revelation). Socrates' mission began with an oracle from Delphi (Plato, *Apology* 20E-22A, 28E), as did that of Dio Chrysostom (422R; 243.1-12). This was but a specific application of a more general practice: for example, "And, indeed, what colony did Greece ever send into Aeolia, Ionia, Asia, Sicily, or Italy without consulting the Pythian or Dodonian oracle, or that of Jupiter Ammon?" (Cicero, *De Divinatione* 1.1.2-3).

(4) "Then . . . they laid their hands on them (6:6; cf. Num 8:10-11; Deut 34:9) and sent them off" (v. 3). With this act, Barnabas and Saul once again

become apostles of the church in Antioch (14:4, 14; remember 11:30; 12:25). With this stereotyped commissioning account, the narrative makes clear that God's hand is behind this new step in the missionary expansion of Acts (cf. 14:27). It is, therefore, possible for the evangelist to say both that the church "sent them off" (v. 3) and that they were "sent out by the Holy Spirit" (v. 4).

Acts 13:4–5, "A" in the pattern, is a brief summary statement about the two missionaries going to Salamis on Cyprus where they preach in the Jewish synagogues. There was a large Jewish population on Cyprus (1 Macc 15:23; Philo, *Embassy to Gaius* 282; Josephus, *Antiquities* 13.10.4 § 284). The point is this: the mission follows the principle, to the Jew first.

"B" in the pattern, 13:6–12, tells of an encounter between the missionaries and a Roman proconsul in Paphos that involves a Jewish magician and false prophet, Elymas or Bar-Jesus. Court astrologers or magicians who allegedly predicted the future and attempted to alter the fates with their magic were not uncommon in the Mediterranean world. Tiberius followed the guidance of the astrologer Thrasyllus (Suetonius, *Tiberius* 14.4) and various Chaldean soothsayers (Juvenal, *Satires* 10.93–94). Nero accepted the divinations of the astrologer Babillus (Suetonius, *Nero* 36.1). Otho used the services of the astrologer Seleucus (Suetonius, *Otho* 4.1; 6.1). Vespasian had great faith in his horoscope (Suetonius, *Vespasian* 25). Domitian had in his employ the astrologer Ascletarion (Suetonius, *Domitian* 15.3). Marcus Aurelius kept Arnuphis, an Egyptian magician, with him on the Danube (Dio Cassius 71.8.4). Valerian's persecutions of Christians were encouraged by the advice of Macrianus, an Egyptian magician (Eusebius, *Church History* 7.10.4–6). Lesser rulers as well were not immune to the practice. For example, Felix, the procurator (Acts 24), used a Jew named Simon, who was a Cyprian magician (Josephus, *Antiquities* 20.7.2 §§ 141–44). A magician is also a part of the household of Senator Marcellus (*Acts of Peter* 8). It is, therefore, no surprise to find the proconsul of Cyprus advised by a magician. Nor is it a surprise to have him connected to Cyprus. Pliny, *Natural History* 30.11, says that Cyprus had in his times supplanted previous famed centers of magic. Nor is it surprising that the magician is depicted as Jewish. In the Greco-Roman mind, Jews and magic were closely linked (Strabo, *Geography* 16.2.43; Pliny, *Natural History* 30.11; Apuleius, *Apology* 90; Celsus [in Origen, *Against Celsus* 1.26; 4.33]). Nor is it surprising that the proconsul's adviser tries to interfere with the official's religious quest. For example, Plutarch (*On the Obsolescence of Oracles* 45 D-F) tells how Epicurean advisers to a ruler in Cilicia attempted to keep him from belief in oracles.

The story is told in the form of a prophetic response to a resister of God. There are five components: (1) the resistance to God's word (13:8; cf. Jer 36:27a); (2) the prophetic indictment (13:10; cf. Jer 36:29); (3) the prophecy (13:11a; cf. Jer 36:30-31); (4) the fulfillment of the prophetic word (13:11b; cf. Jer 37:1); and (5) the result (13:12; cf. Jer 37:2). The purpose of such a story (cf. also 1 Kgs 18:19-40, Elijah and the prophets of Baal; *Acts of Peter* 23-28, a contest between Peter and Simon the magician in the forum before Roman officials) is to indicate that there is one true and living God and that all other claims are counterfeit. This is certainly how this story functions in Acts 13.

(1) When the proconsul, Sergius Paulus, summons Barnabas and Saul because he wants to hear the word of God (v. 7), the magician opposes them in an attempt to turn the Roman official away from the faith (v. 8). (2) "But Saul, also known as Paul, filled with the Holy Spirit (2:4; 4:31), . . . said: 'You son of the devil, you enemy of all that is right, full of every sort of deceit and fraud. Will you not stop twisting the straight paths (Luke 3:4) of [the] Lord?'" (v. 10). Luke's hostility to magic surfaces again (8:18-24; 19:19). At this point the narrator shifts from the name Saul to Paul. The latter is appropriate in a Gentile context. (3) Paul's prophecy comes in v. 11a: "Even now the hand of the Lord is upon you. You will be blind, and unable to see the sun for a time." Blindness was a traditional punishment for wickedness (Gen 19:11; Deut 28:28-29; 2 Kgs 6:18; *Acts of Paul* 4). (4) Paul's prophetic word is fulfilled at once. "Immediately a dark mist fell upon him, and he went about seeking people to lead him by the hand" (v. 11b). (5) The result is the proconsul's belief (v. 12). Miracle is once again a catalyst for faith (9:32-35, 36-42). This is another power encounter (i.e., an encounter between the spiritual power of the Messianists' God and that of another in which it is demonstrated that the might of God is greater than that of the other). When people witness such a power encounter, they become open to the gospel. In a power-oriented society, change of faith has to be power-demonstrated. So here.

This story is yet another example of Luke's interest in the high social status of the converts to the Way. Here it is a proconsul; in 13:1 it was a friend of Herod the tetrarch; in 10:1, 48 it was a centurion; in 8:27-39 it was a court official who was in charge of the Ethiopian queen's entire treasury; in 16:14-15 it will be a wealthy woman merchant; in 17:34 it will be a member of the Athenian court. Why would such a concern be present in Acts? Origen, *Against Celsus* 3.44, quotes Celsus: "Christians must admit that they can only persuade people destitute of sense, position, or intelligence, only slaves, women, and children, to accept their faith." If, however, the Lukan narrative shows the contrary, it is a buttress for Messianist claims. This is, then, a legitimation technique.

"A'" in the pattern, 13:13-43, moves us back to a Jewish setting: on the sabbath in the synagogue. The section is held together by an inclusion (v. 14, they went into the synagogue; v. 42, they went out). For "synagogue" used as a term for a Jewish place of worship in the first century, see Philo, *Every Good Man Is Free* 81; Josephus, *Antiquities* 19.6.3 §§ 300-305; *War* 2.14.5 § 289; 7.3.3 § 44; and Luke 7:5. After the power encounter in Paphos, Paul is designated the leader of the missionaries. "From Paphos, Paul and his companions set sail" (v. 13a; contrast 11:30; 12:25; 13:2, 7). God decides who will be the leader just as He decides on the mission and the missionaries. At Perga, John Mark returns to Jerusalem (v. 13b; cf. 15:36-40). Paul and Barnabas continue to Antioch of Pisidia where they enter the synagogue on the sabbath and take their seats (v. 14).

It is usually thought that the ancient synagogue service consisted of six parts. In *m. Megillah* 4.3 we hear of five actions that cannot be performed communally without the presence of a quorum of ten adult Jewish males: recitation of the Shema, recitation of the Tefillah [prayers], the priestly blessing, reading from the Torah, and reading from the prophets. Luke 4:16-19 indicates that reading from the prophets was established by the first century A.D. Acts 13:15 shows that readings from both the Law and the Prophets were part of the service in the first century. Philo, *Special Laws* 2.62, adds a sixth component. He says that after the readings in the synagogue, "one of special experience rises and sets forth what is the best and sure to be profitable and will make the whole of life grow to something better." That such a word of exhortation was part and parcel of synagogue experience in the first century is confirmed by Luke 4:20-27 (although in Palestine the speaker sat down) and Acts 13:15-16 (where the speaker stands, as in Philo's account of Hellenistic synagogue practice, doubtless following rhetorical precedent).

Paul's sermon in vv. 16b-41 falls into three parts, designated by three direct addresses (v. 16b, "Fellow Israelites and you others who are God-fearing"; v. 26, "My brothers, children of the family of Abraham, and those others among you who are God-fearing"; v. 38, "my brothers"). The first two addresses indicate the composition of those in the synagogue: Jews and God-fearers. In the era under consideration, Jews were known as proselytizers. On the one hand, where they were in the minority, they worked by persuasion. (1) Pagan examples: (a) Valerius Maximus, *Facta et Dicta Memorabilia* 1.3.3, says the Jews were banished from Rome by Cornelius Hispalus for proselytizing; (b) Horace, *Sermones* 1.4.139-43, says, "We, like the Jews, will compel you to make you one of us"; (c) Epictetus, *Dissertations* 2.9.19-20; (d) Tacitus, *Histories* 5.5; (e) Juvenal, *Satires* 6.541-48; (f) Herennius Philo of Byblos [Origen, *Against Celsus* 1.15]; (g) Celsus [Origen, *Against Celsus* 5.41]; (h) Lucian, *Tragodopodagra* 171-73; (i) Dio Cassius 57.18.5a.

(2) Jewish evidence: (a) Philo, *Moses* 2.19-20, says that in contrast to other nations' practices, Jewish customs attract and win the attention of all,

of barbarians, of Greeks, of dwellers on the mainland and islands, of nations of the east and the west, of Europe and Asia, of the whole inhabited world from end to end. Philo mentions observance of the sabbath especially (*Moses* 2.21). (b) Josephus, *Antiquities* 18.3.5 §§ 81–84; 20.2.3–4 §§ 34–48; *War* 7.3.3 § 45–at Antioch of Syria "the Jews made converts of a great number of Greeks perpetually"; *Against Apion* 2.11 § 123–"many of them have come over to our laws"; 2.29 § 210; 2.40 § 282–"the multitude of mankind itself have had a great inclination for a long time to follow our religious observances"; (c) *Aboth de Rabbi Nathan* A.15–a Gentile comes to Shammai and Hillel; (d) *b. Shabbath* 31a–a Gentile comes to Shammai and Hillel to become a proselyte.

(3) Christian material: (a) Romans 2:17–23; (b) Matthew 23:15–"Woe to you, scribes and hypocrites. You traverse sea and land to make one convert, and when that happens you make him a child of Gehenna twice as much as yourselves." On the other hand, when they were in the majority, they sometimes made converts by compulsion: for example, 1 Macc 2:46; Josephus, *Antiquities* 13.9.1 §§ 257–58; 13.11.3 §§ 318–19. In the synagogue at Antioch of Pisidia, Paul addresses both Jews and Gentiles drawn to the synagogue.

(1) The first section of the speech comes in vv. 16b–25. It makes two points. (a) In vv. 17–23 the focus is on Jesus as the one in whom salvation history culminates. The précis of Israel's history runs from the exodus through the wilderness wanderings to Canaan and the periods of the judges and kings. Of the kings mentioned, it is David who is God's delight. "I have found David, son of Jesse, a man after my own heart; he will carry out my every wish" (v. 22). The punch line comes in v. 23: "From this man's (David's) descendants God . . . has brought to Israel a savior, Jesus." (b) In vv. 24–25 the focus is on Jesus as the one of whom John the Baptist spoke. John said, "I am not he. Behold one is coming after me; I am not worthy to unfasten the sandals of his feet."

(2) The second section of the sermon comes in vv. 26–37. It also has two points. (a) Verses 27–29 focus on the death of Jesus as the fulfillment of what was written of him. Even though the Jerusalemites failed to recognize Jesus as the savior of David's line and had him killed, they still fulfilled what the scriptures prophesied about him (cf. Luke 24:25–27). The motif that the Jews did not understand their own scriptures is not uncommon in the early church (e.g., *Barnabas* 10:2–9; Justin, *1 Apology* 31–"But these Jews, though they read the books, fail to grasp their meaning"). (b) Verses 30–37 focus on the resurrection of Jesus as the fulfillment of God's promise to the fathers in Ps 2:7 ("You are my son; this day have I begotten you"), Isa 55:3 ("I shall give you the benefits assured to David"), and Ps 16:10 ("You will not suffer your holy one to see corruption"). In the resurrection of Jesus (Ps

16:10), the promises to David (Isa 55:3) are realized in the enthronement of Jesus as messianic king (Ps 2:7; cf. Acts 2:36; Rom 1:4).

(3) The third section of the speech comes in vv. 38-41. It also has two points. (a) Verses 38-39 offer a summary of the benefits available through Jesus. "Through this one forgiveness of sins is announced to you, and from all that you were unable to be justified from by the instrumentality of the law of Moses, everyone believing in him is justified." (so Kilgallen, 480-506) The point is twofold. On the one hand, forgiveness of sins and justification are juxtaposed as synonyms (cf. Rom 4:1-8). On the other hand, whereas the law is totally unable to mediate forgiveness, Jesus can do precisely that. Luke includes justification language in a Pauline speech because he knows it was characteristic of the apostle. Lukan speeches reflect what is appropriate to the character and his context. (b) Verses 40-41 offer a warning about one's response to the preaching. "Be careful, then, that what was said in the prophets (Hab 1:5) does not come about." Make a positive response to Jesus.

The results of the sermon are given in vv. 42-43. First, Paul receives an invitation to return the next sabbath to say more. Second, there are many converts to the Messianist gospel among both Jews and Gentile worshippers of God. Paul and Barnabas speak further to them, urging them to remain faithful.

"B'" in the pattern, 13:44-52, is a narrative about Jewish rejection and Gentile inclusion presented in an ABCDA'B'C'D' pattern (Talbert 1984, 59).

A—The whole city gathered to hear the word (v. 44)
   B—The Jews reject it (v. 45)
      C—Paul turns to the Gentiles (vv. 46-47)
         D—The Gentiles are glad (v. 48)
A'—The word spread throughout all the region (v. 49)
   B'—The Jews stir up persecution (v. 50)
      C'—Paul shakes off the dust from his feet (v. 51)
         D'—The disciples are filled with joy (v. 52).

On the following sabbath "almost the whole city gathered to hear the word of the Lord" (v. 44). Such mass responses of excitement are a feature of Hellenistic novels (e.g., Chariton, *Chaereas and Callirhoe* 3.4.4-18) and apocryphal Acts (e.g., *Acts of Peter* 3; *Acts of John* 31). But "when the Jews saw the crowds, they were filled with zeal (Acts 5:17; 17:5; 21:20; 22:3) and with violent abuse contradicted what Paul said" (v. 45). The term "Jews" used here is a problem. What does it mean? Both Messianists like Paul and Barnabas and their non-Messianist opponents are Jewish. The contest here is between two forms of ancient Judaism. The term "the Jews" in this context must mean "establishment Judaism" as opposed to what it would have regarded as deviant Judaism. Faced with establishment opposition, Paul and Barnabas say, "It was necessary that the word of God be spoken to you first, but since you reject it and condemn yourselves as unworthy of eternal life, we now turn to the Gentiles" (v. 46). Isaiah 49:6 is cited as scriptural justification for their stance (v. 47). The Gentiles are delighted (v. 48), their joy signaling their incorporation in the people of God.

The word of God continues to spread through the entire region (v. 49). The establishment Jews then "incited the women of prominence who were worshippers and the leading men of the city, stirred up a persecution against Paul and Barnabas, and expelled them from their territory" (v. 50). Women were especially drawn to Judaism in antiquity (e.g., Josephus, *War* 2.20.2 § 561—at Damascus "yet did the Damascenes distrust their wives, which were almost all addicted to the Jewish religion"), many from elite families (e.g., Josephus, *Antiquities* 20.2.3–4 §§ 34–35, 38—women in the house of the king, including the queen mother). Expulsion from a city was normal punishment for being undesirable (16:39; 18:2). The missionaries' response is that recommended by Jesus: they shake the dust from their feet in protest (v. 51; cf. Luke 9:5; 10:11). The bottom line: "The disciples were filled with joy and the Holy Spirit" (v. 52; cf. 11:23; 8:8, 39; 5:41; 2:46). The effect of 13:44–52 as a whole is to cast the Jews who do not believe into the camp with Bar-Jesus and the Gentiles who do believe into a grouping with the proconsul of Paphos.

In "A''," Acts 14:1–7, the missionaries travel to Iconium, where the focus moves back to the Jews. The paragraph is organized in an ABCDC'B'A' pattern (Nelson, 60).

A—They entered . . . spoke (v. 1a)
  B—Jews and Gentiles believe (v. 1b)
    C—Jews stir up the Gentiles (v. 2)
      D—Long-term preaching and miracles (v. 3)
    C'—People of the city are divided (v. 4)
  B'—Gentiles and Jews attempt to stone them (v. 5)
A'—They fled . . . preached (vv. 6–7).

As a result of the preaching of Paul and Barnabas in the synagogue in Iconium, a great number of both Jews and Greeks come to believe (v. 1). The two remain for a considerable time in the city, preaching and working miracles (v. 3). The unbelieving Jews "poisoned the minds of the Gentiles against the brothers" (v. 2). As a result of an attempt by both Jews and Gentiles to attack the apostles (v. 4), they flee to Lystra.

"B''," Acts 14:8–18, 19–23, shifts the focus once again to the Gentiles. The events in Lystra are told in terms of an expanded miracle story: (1) the ailment (v. 8), (2) the cure (vv. 9–10), and (3) the reactions to the healing

(vv. 11–13, 14–18, 19, 20–23). The third ingredient is considerably expanded to enable the inclusion of the apostolic speech (vv. 14–18). Thereby Luke can emphasize the Messianist rejection of pagan idolatry and the promotion of monotheism. Each component of the miracle story demands explanation.

(1) "At Lystra there was a crippled man, lame from birth, who had never walked" (v. 1). This echoes Luke 5:18–26 (Jesus' healing of a lame man), Acts 3:1–10 and 9:32–35 (Peter's healings of lame men). This means that Paul is doing the same type of thing that Jesus and Peter did. Why? They are all empowered by the same Spirit.

(2) "He listened to Paul speaking, who . . . saw that he had faith to be healed, and called out . . . 'Stand up straight on your feet.' He jumped up and began to walk" (vv. 9–10). The faith that Paul discerned in the man is the faith evoked by Paul's preaching (cf. vv. 7, 9a).

(3) The reactions to the miracle are four: two by the Lystrans and two by the apostles. (a) The initial reaction of the Lystrans is to mistake Paul for Hermes (the messenger of the gods—Homer, *Odyssey* 5.29; Horace, *Odes* 1.10.1–6; Philo, *Embassy to Gaius* 99) and Barnabas for Zeus (v. 12). They cry out, "The gods have come down to us in human form" (v. 11). The priest of Zeus brings oxen and garlands to the gates to offer sacrifice (v. 13). Mistaking impressive humans for deities was common in antiquity (Chariton, *Chaereas and Callirhoe* 1.1.16; 1.14.1; 3.12.15–17; Xenophon, *Ephesian Tale* 1.12.1; Josephus, *Antiquities* 10.10.5 §§ 211–12). This could be because the ancients held that "holy gods, in the form of wandering foreigners, taking on various forms, often go through countries and cities, that they may see mortals' foolish misdeeds as well as piety" (Homer, *Odyssey* 17.485–87; cited by Chariton, 2.3, as part of just such a mistake of a human for a deity). When mortals fail to recognize the deity and act improperly, they are subject to divine wrath (e.g., when the god Bacchus, in the form of a small boy, is kidnapped by sailors and mistreated, he turns them into dolphins [Ovid, *Metamorphoses* 3.574–698]).

In the Lystrans' case, there is a more specific background. Ovid, *Metamorphoses* 8:611–725, tells of Zeus and Hermes visiting this region, being entertained by an aged couple, Philemon and Baucis, while the rest of the people were wiped out for their lack of hospitality. Archaeological evidence for a cult of these two gods, dating from about A.D. 250, has been found near Lystra. If the locals had failed to honor the gods on their previous visit, they would not repeat their mistake. The priest brought oxen (expensive sacrifices) and garlands (decorations for sacrifices) so as to offer sacrifice at his temple, which was at the entrance to the city (v. 13). A temple in the front of the city, outside the gates, was common in Asia Minor: for example, Dionysius at Thera, Hecate at Aphrodisias, Artemis at Ephesus, Demeter and

Dionysius at Smyrna, Dionysius and Tyrimnus at Thyatira, and Apollo at Thyatira.

(b) The initial reaction of the Lystrans evokes the missionaries' first response (vv. 14-18). On the one hand, they do something. They "tore their garments when they heard this" (v. 14). To worship another human is blasphemy. Their reaction is very Jewish (*m. Sanhedrin* 7:5—when blasphemy is heard "the judges stand on their feet and rend their garments"). On the other hand, they say something. The speech of vv. 15-18 consists of an address (v. 15a, "Men"), the identity of the disciples (v. 15b, "We are . . . human beings"; cf. *Acts of Peter* 28—Peter says after a resuscitation, "Men of Rome, I, too, am one of you! I have human flesh and I am a sinner. . . . Do not imagine that what I do, I do in my own power; I do it in the power of my Lord, Jesus Christ"), and the work and ways of the living God (vv. 15c-18). God is the living God, the creator (v. 15c); who has related to Gentiles in the past with permissiveness (v. 16); yet who has given them a witness through nature of divine goodness (v. 17).

When the apostles react thusly, they are echoing the universal Jewish critique of idolatry ([a] non-Messianist Judaism: for example, Isa 44:9-20; Hab 2:18-19; Wis 13-15; *Epistle of Aristeas* 134-38; *Joseph and Aseneth;* Philo, *Decalogue* 66-81; Josephus, *Against Apion* 2.6 §§ 65-67; *Antiquities* 19.5.3 § 290; [b] Messianist Judaism: for example, 1 Thess 1:9-10; 1 Cor 8:4-6; 2 Cor 6:16; Rom 1:23; Acts 17:29; Aristides, *Apology* 81, 101; *Epistle of Diognetus* 2:1-2; 3:4; Preaching of Peter [in Clement of Alexandria, *Stromata* 6.40-41]). They are, moreover, setting forth the first component of the kerygma of the Hellenistic church: monotheism (1 Thess 1:9-10; 1 Cor 8:6; Acts 17:22-31). In the reactions of Paul and Barnabas to the attempted worship, Luke emphasizes his rejection of pagan idolatry and affirmation of monotheism.

(c) The second reaction of the Lystrans comes after "some Jews from Antioch and Iconium arrived and won over the crowds" (v. 19a; cf. 13:45, 50; 14:5). They stoned Paul and dragged him out of the city (v. 19b; cf. 2 Cor 11:25). The persistence and intensity of the establishment Jewish hostility toward the deviant Messianists permeates the first missionary journey. How would an ancient auditor have heard the narrative of Acts 13-14?

Selected sources from antiquity offer assistance. (a) Dio Cassius 49.22.4 says of the Jews, "The race is very bitter when aroused to anger." (b) Josephus paints a similar portrait: for example, *War* 1.7.5 § 150—"The greatest part of them were slain by their own countrymen of the adverse faction"; 2.18.3 § 466—Jew against Jew in Galilee; 4.3.12 §§ 196-207—Jew against Jew; 4.5.1 §§ 305-18—Jew against Jew; 4.6.3 § 378—Jew against Jew; 7.10.1 § 411—Jew against Jew in Alexandria; 7.11.1 § 442—Jew against Jew; *Life* 40 §§ 197-203—Pharisees associated with the Sanhedrin are sent to arrest or kill Josephus in Galilee. (c) Paul says that he had been a persecutor of the church (Gal 1:13–14, 22–23; 1 Cor 15:9; Phil 3:6; cf. Acts 9:1). The early church perceived themselves as objects of establishment Judaism's hatred (2 Cor 11:24, 26; Rom 15:31; Luke 12:11; 21:12; John 16:2; Rev 2:9; *Martyrdom of Polycarp* 12:2; 13:1; 17:2; 18:1; *Epistle of Diognetus* 5:17–"by the Jews they are warred on as aliens"; Justin, *1 Apology* 49–slander; *Dialogue* 16, 47, 96–cursing; *Dialogue* 17–prejudice against; *Dialogue* 108– "you have sent chosen and ordained men throughout all the world to proclaim that a godless and lawless heresy had sprung up from one Jesus, a Galilean deceiver"; Tertullian, *Ad Nationes* 1.14–"the seed-plot of all the calumny against us"; *Scorpiace* 10–"synagogues of the Jews–fountains of persecution"; Origen, *Homily I on Psalm 36*–"The Jews even now are not angry at the heathen who worship idols and blaspheme God; they do not hate them, but they attack Messianists with insatiable hatred" (Setzer). The ancient reader would have sensed no discontinuity between the narrative in Acts and what was generally believed by many pagans, establishment Jews, and Messianists of the time.

Why the hostility between establishment Judaism and the Messianists? The grounds for such hostility are numerous. (a) Their missions were overlapping. Competition existed for the allegiance of the same group of interested Gentiles. (b) There were territorial disputes. The groups had competing claims to the scriptures of Israel, to their correct interpretation, and to the promises of God in the scriptures. (c) Christology. The Messianists claimed that the Messiah had already come, that he had been killed by the Jerusalem Jewish establishment, and that he had been raised by God and was now the only savior. Non-Messianist Judaism resisted this claim, which became the crucial dividing line within ancient Judaism (Wilson 3.834–39).

The matter can be taken even further. At the time of Acts, there existed an imperial sociology that reflected the Roman sense of order. There were volatile crowds everywhere in the empire; there were a few firebrands always ready to stir up the crowds (Tacitus, *Annals* 1.16–18; Sallust, *Cataline* 38.1; Josephus, *War* 2.13.4 §§ 258–59). In Acts, non-Messianist Jews normally function as those who incite the crowds (6:8–15; 13:50; 14:2; 14:19; 17:5–9; 17:13; 18:12–17; 21:27–30; 22:22–23), although there are two instances of pagans who do so (16:19–39; 19:23–41). Messianists, however, are portrayed as orderly, model citizens who are protected by the Roman authorities. Luke's view of non-Messianist Jews, therefore, is that of the ruling Roman perspective: they are disturbers of the peace and a threat to public order. It is, moreover, a point of view shared by many pagans and Jews, both Messianist and non-Messianist, at the time (Wills, 631–54).

(d) The reactions of the missionaries after Paul's stoning come in vv. 20–23. Paul gets up and returns to the city with the disciples (v. 20a).

Converts have already been made in Lystra. The next day the apostles leave to evangelize Derbe (vv. 20b–21a). Then they return to Lystra, Iconium, and Antioch of Pisidia (v. 21b). "They appointed presbyters for them in each church and, with prayer and fasting, commended them (the churches) to the Lord in whom they had put their faith" (v. 23). As part of their strengthening of the churches they told them, "It is necessary for us to undergo many hardships to enter the kingdom of God" (v. 22b; cf. Luke 24:26; Acts 17:3; *b. Berakoth* 5a–Rabbi Simeon ben Yohai said: "The Holy One . . . gave Israel three precious gifts, and all of them were given only through sufferings. These are the Torah, the land of Israel, and the world to come"). Two Lukan themes recur here. First, persecution leads to the further spread of the gospel (8:1–4). Second, evangelization involves the nurture of converts (11:26).

The first missionary journey ends in 14:24–28 with the apostles' return to Antioch. They sail to Antioch, "where they had been commended to the grace of God for the work they had now accomplished" (v. 26; 13:1–3). When they arrive they report to the church "what God had done with them and how He had opened the door of faith to the Gentiles" (v. 27). An agent who is sent on a mission must return and report to his sender (*j. Haggigah* 76d). This the apostles of the church at Antioch, Paul and Barnabas, do.

The Jerusalem Council
Acts 15:1–16:5

There are four major moves to the Gentiles in Acts: (1) by Peter–Acts 10; (2) by anonymous men of Cyprus and Cyrene–Acts 11:19–21; (3) by Paul and Barnabas–Acts 13–14; and (4) by Paul and Silas–Acts 16–20. In each of these cases, the extension of the gospel to the Gentiles is followed by an episode of Jerusalem approval: (1) after Peter's efforts on behalf of Cornelius–Acts 11:1–18; (2) after the evangelization of Greeks in Antioch of Syria by men of Cyprus and Cyrene–Acts 11:22–24; (3) after the first missionary journey of Paul and Barnabas–Acts 15:1–29; and (4) after the second missionary journey of Paul–Acts 18:22 and 21:17–25. In each of the last three instances, after the principle of Gentile inclusion has been established, there is a gesture on the part of the missionaries and/or the Gentile Messianists of solidarity with the other side: (1) the church in Antioch–11:27–30; 12:25; (2) Paul–15:30–34; 16:1–5; (3) Paul–21:20–24, 26. It is within this context that 15:1–16:5 must be understood. Acts 15:1–29 represents the Jerusalem approval of the extension of the gospel to the Gentiles in chaps. 13–14. Acts 15:30–34 and 16:1–5 indicate the Pauline concern for what is necessary to insure the unity of the community.

The entire unit consists of three components: (1) 15:1-5, the occasion for the council; (2) 15:6-29, the council's deliberations and decision; and (3) 15:30-35; 15:36-16:5, implementation of the decisions of the council in two stages. Each of these components needs individualized attention.

Acts 15:1-5 falls into a chiastic pattern: ABCB'A' (Talbert 1984, 62).

A—Men from Judea teach that circumcision is necessary for salvation (v. 1)
  B—Paul and Barnabas are appointed to go up to Jerusalem about the question (v. 2)
    C—On their way, they report the conversion of the Gentiles, bringing joy to the brethren (v. 3)
  B'—When they come to Jerusalem, they are welcomed by the church (v. 4)
A'—Some of the Messianist Pharisees say that circumcision and keeping the law is necessary for Gentiles (v. 5)

This paragraph indicates that there are two issues for the council: (1) Can Gentiles be part of the covenant community (i.e., be saved) without circumcision? and (2) Can Gentiles live among Jews without becoming proselytes?

(1) "A" in the pattern tells how some from Judea had come to Antioch of Syria and were instructing the church: "Unless you are circumcised according to the Mosaic practice, you cannot be saved" (v. 1). According to majority Jewish belief, "All Israelites have a share in the world to come" (*m. Sanhedrin* 10:1; it is this assumption that John the Baptist challenges, Luke 3:7-9). The Judean Messianists are contending that the only way to be a member of the community that will share in the world to come (i.e., be saved) is to accept the distinguishing mark of ethnic Israel, circumcision. There was strong scriptural support for such a position: (a) Gen 17:10-14, 23-27—circumcision is a sign of the covenant for Abraham, the Gentile; (b) Gen 34:15-24—circumcision is a condition for aliens' being one people with Israel; (c) Exod 12:44, 48—strangers sojourning with Israel who want to keep the Passover must be circumcised. Yet diversity of opinion existed in the first century. Josephus, *Antiquities* 20.2.3-4 §§ 34-48, tells of one Jew, Ananias, who instructed a potential convert to Judaism that monotheistic worship of God was of a superior nature to circumcision, while another Jew, Eleazar, claimed circumcision was necessary for a Gentile proselyte to Judaism. Can Gentiles be a part of the covenant community without circumcision? Opinions in ancient Judaism varied. Among the Judean Messianists who were teaching at Antioch, the answer is clearly No. "Unless you are circumcised . . . you cannot be saved" (v. 1).

(2) "A'" in the pattern relates how Pharisaic Messianists in Jerusalem rein-

forced the Judeans' teaching in Antioch: "It is necessary to circumcise them and direct them to observe the Mosaic law" (v. 5). From the context of the chapter as well as from the language of the verse, it is clear that a second issue is at stake. Can Gentiles live among Jews without becoming proselytes? (a) Some Jewish circles said No. Circumcision and observance of the law were demanded. From the earliest days of the Jewish revolt against Antiochus Epiphanes, Jewish leaders compelled those who lived in areas under their control to be circumcised (1 Macc 2:46). After political independence had been achieved, the policy of forced circumcision of and required observance of the law by people within Israel's borders continued under the Hasmoneans (Josephus, *Antiquities* 13.9.1 § 257–Idumeans; 13.11.3 § 318–Itureans). During the war against Rome (A.D. 66–70), Jewish forces required circumcision of all who lived in areas under their control, regardless of whether or not they were Jews (Josephus, *War* 2.17.10 § 454; *Life* 23 §§ 112–113–forced circumcision is opposed by Josephus). (b) At the same time, the scriptures said Yes and offered in Leviticus 17–18 guidelines for sojourners. They could remain Gentiles but should observe certain things that would make social interchange with ethnic Jews possible. The Messianist Pharisees in v. 5 take the hard line. Gentiles must be circumcised and observe the law of Moses if they are to associate with ethnic Jews who have become Messianists.

Since the positions taken on these two issues by Judean Messianists run counter to the experience of Paul, Barnabas, and the church at Antioch (11:19–30), the matter needs to be settled in Jerusalem. The assumption is that Jerusalem has the authority to decide the issue. Why Jerusalem? Whereas for ancient Greeks Delphi was the center of the world, for Jews Jerusalem was (Ezek 5:5; 38:12; *Jubilees* 8:19; *1 Enoch* 26:1; Rev 20:8–9; *b. Sanhedrin* 37a). To it Jews came on pilgrimage; to it they sent offerings. From it letters went out to the Diaspora to give guidance (2 Macc 1:1–10a; 1:10b–2:18). Acts notes the links between Jerusalem and the developing mission (8:14–15; 9:27; 9:32–11:18; 11:22–29; 12:25; 15:4). The Twelve are tied to Jerusalem (8:1). It is, therefore, the center of the true tradition of the Messianists. The church at Antioch decides that Paul, Barnabas, and some others should go up to Jerusalem about this question (v. 2). The stage is set for the council.

Acts 15:6–29 is a narrative about the proceedings of the council in Jerusalem. It has two parts: (1) the discussions (vv. 6–21), and (2) the decisions (vv. 22–29). (1) The section on the discussions of the council (vv. 6–21) falls into an ABA'B' pattern.

A–The assembly debates (vv. 6–7a)
　　B– Peter's speech (vv. 7b–11)

A'–The assembly is silent and listens (v. 12)
   B'–James's speech (vv. 13-21)

"A," vv. 6-7a, tells that the apostles and elders met together over the matter and engaged in much debate.

"B," vv. 7b-11, presents Peter's speech. It is an argument from experience. First, he gives a summary of the Cornelius episode (vv. 7b-9). This is the third time in Acts it has been mentioned (chap. 10; 11:1-18). The climax comes in vv. 8-9: "God, who knows the heart (1:24; Jer 16:17-18; 17:9-10; Ps 139; Sir 42:18; Josephus, *War* 6.32.3 § 630; 1 John 3:20; *2 Clement* 9:9; Hermas, *Command* 4.3.4), bore witness by granting them the Holy Spirit (a sign of eschatological inclusion) just as He did us. He made no distinction between us and them, for by faith he purified their hearts." Second, Peter draws two inferences. (a) The first is, Do not stand against God (cf. 11:17). "Why, then, are you now putting God to the test by placing on the shoulders of the disciples a yoke (Sir 51:23-26; *m. Pirke Aboth* 3:5; Gal 5:1) that neither our ancestors nor we have been able to bear?" (v. 10; 7:53; 13:39). (b) The second is, Go with what God is doing. "On the contrary, we believe *we* shall be saved through the grace of the Lord Jesus, in the same way as *they*" (v. 11; cf. Gal 2:15-16 for the Pauline statement of the same principle). The implication is that Peter has learned from the Cornelius episode the true basis for his own salvation. "If those who did not keep the Law were saved by grace, then that must be the basis of his being saved, who had only with difficulty borne the Law" (Johnson 1983, 82).

"A'," 15:12, focuses attention once again on the assembly. "The whole assembly fell silent, and they listened while Paul and Barnabas described the signs and wonders God had worked among the Gentiles through them." The witness of the two missionaries is also, like Peter's speech, an argument from experience.

"B'," 15:13-21, is a speech of James. This James is obviously not James the brother of John, a son of Zebedee (1:13; Luke 6:14), whose martyrdom was recorded in 12:2. This is, rather, James the brother of Jesus (1:14; Mark 6:3; Gal 1:19). Before Easter, James is depicted as one who does not believe in Jesus (John 7:5). After Easter, as a result of a resurrection experience (1 Cor 15:7; *Gospel according to the Hebrews,* in Jerome, *On Illustrious Men* 2), James is portrayed as a believer (Gal 2:9; Acts 12:17; 21:18). In Galatians (2:12) and Acts (15:13-21; 21:18) he functions as the leader of the Jerusalem church. He was known for his deep, ascetic piety and bore the name "the Just One" (so Hegesippus, in Eusebius, *Church History* 2.23.4-7). Two accounts of his martyrdom at the instigation of the high priest exist: Josephus, *Antiquities* 20.9.1 § 200, and Eusebius, *Church History* 2.23. He was idealized by certain Gnostic circles (*First Apocalypse of James; Second*

Apocalypse of James; Coptic *Gospel of Thomas,* logion 12—"The disciples said to Jesus: 'We know that you will depart from us. Who is it who will be great over us?' Jesus said to them, 'Wherever you are, you are to go to James the Just, for whose sake heaven and earth came into being'") (Ward, 174–90; Bauckham, 415–80).

James's speech has two parts: (1) scripture agrees with Peter's experience (vv. 14–19), and (2) a prescription (vv. 20–21). (1) James begins with a reference to Peter's experience: "Symeon (2 Pet 1:1) has described how God first concerned Himself with acquiring from among the Gentiles a people for His name" (v. 15). He then says, "The words of the prophets agree with this" (v. 15). This does not mean scriptural authority is transcended by current experience. It means rather that current experience is confirmed by scriptural authority in that current experience fulfills scriptural prophecy. The text quoted by James comes from LXX Amos 9:11–12. The MT is anti-universalistic.

> After this I shall return and rebuild the fallen hut of David;
> from its ruins I shall again rebuild it and raise it up again,
> so that the rest of humanity may seek out the Lord,
> even all the Gentiles on whom my name is invoked.
> Thus says the Lord who accomplishes these things, known from of old.

This text, in this context, speaks about two things. (a) The first two lines refer to the resurrection of Jesus as the fulfillment of the promise of God to restore the house of David (2:30–31, 34–36). A messianic interpretation of these lines from Amos exists also at Qumran (CD 7:16; 4QFlor 1:12–13 = 4Q174). (b) The next two lines speak about the conversion of the Gentiles as the fulfillment of the promise that the nations will seek the Lord. The last line serves as a confirmation statement: God says this is so.

(2) James's speech then moves from a citation of scripture to a prescription for behavior. "It is my judgment, therefore, that we ought to stop troubling the Gentiles who turn to God, but tell them by letter to avoid pollution from idols, pollution from *porneia* (sexual immorality), pollution from the meat of strangled animals, and pollution from blood" (vv. 19–20). The reason given for these prescriptions is that "Moses, for generations now, has had those who proclaim him in every town, as he has been read in the synagogues every sabbath" (v. 21). James's prescription demands careful attention.

First, there is the problem of a textual variant. Verse 20 appears in two very different forms in the Western and Alexandrian families of manuscripts. Here, and also in 15:29 and 21:25, codex D of the Western family omits "strangled" (*pniktou*), and here, and also in 15:29, inserts instead the negative form of the Golden Rule ("and not to do to others whatever they do not wish to be done to themselves"). These changes have the effect of making the list an ethical one.

> Abstain from idolatry,
> > from sexual immorality,
> > from bloodshed,
> and do not do to others what you do not want done to yourself.

The uncials B and *aleph* include "things strangled" and omit the Golden Rule. This leaves a list with a very different slant to it.

> Abstain from food sacrificed to idols,
> > from sexual immorality,
> > from the meat of strangled animals,
> > and from eating blood.

Of the two textual traditions, it is the latter that has the better claim to be what Luke wrote. It is this text that must be interpreted in the context of Acts.

How should Acts 15:20 be understood? The usual reading takes the four polluting items to be from the laws that apply both to Israel and to the foreigner/sojourner living in the midst of Israel. These laws are largely found in Leviticus 17–18 (Callan, 284–97). A brief look at these laws is helpful.

Leviticus 17–18 is addressed to both the house of Israel and the strangers (Gentiles) who sojourn among them (17:8, 10, 15; 18:26). There are ten prohibitions mentioned: (a) no idol sacrifice (17:7–9); (b) no eating of blood (17:10–12); (c) no eating of strangled animals (17:13–14); (d) no eating of animals that have died or have been killed by beasts (17:15–16); (e) no incest (18:6–18); (f) no sex during menstruation (18:19); (g) no adultery (18:20); (h) no sacrifice of children to Molech (18:21); (i) no homosexual practice (18:22); (j) no bestiality (18:23). These regulations were given in order to facilitate social interaction between Jews and non-Jews when the latter lived in the midst of the former, a thing Lev 19:33–34 promotes. If James's prescription is to be understood against the backdrop of Leviticus 17–18, it means the Lukan James viewed the converted Gentiles as analogous to the foreigners of Leviticus 17–18.

What, then, do the various prescriptions mean? (a) Meat sacrificed to idols refers to the meat, often sold in the marketplace, that had come from a public sacrifice to a pagan deity. (b) *Porneia*, sexual immorality, is a broad term that may include incest (Lev 18:6–18; the term was used of incest in postbiblical Judaism—e.g., *T. Reuben* 1:6; *T. Judah* 13:3—and in Paul–1 Cor 5:1), adultery (Lev 18:20; the term was used of adultery in postbiblical Judaism—e.g., Sir 23:23; *T. Joseph* 3:8—and Paul–1 Thess 4:3–6), and homosexuality (Lev 18:22; the term was so used in postbiblical Judaism—*T. Ben-*

jamin 9:1; *Jubilees* 20:5). (c) Eating the meat of strangled animals was a problem for ancient Jews. Philo, *Special Laws* 4.122, talks about men who "prepare meat unfit for the altar by strangling . . . the animals." (d) Eating blood was a serious pollution for an ancient Jew (Lev 17:10–11). These prohibitions, then, are seen as the necessary restraints upon Gentile Messianists who want to associate with ethnic Jewish Messianists without offending them. So although Gentiles are free from the law in the sense of ethnic identity markers like circumcision, they are expected to refrain from selected things required of resident aliens in Leviticus 17–18.

Why the necessity to advise Gentiles to behave in this way? Luke says it is because Moses is read and preached in the synagogues all over the world. Philo agrees: "So each seventh day there stand wide open in every city thousands of schools" (*Special Laws* 2.62). So does Josephus: "And the seventh day we set apart from labor; it is dedicated to the learning of our customs and laws" (*Antiquities* 16.2.3 § 43); Moses permitted "the people to leave off their other employments, and to assemble together for the hearing of the Law, and learning it exactly, and this not once or twice, or oftener, but every week" (*Against Apion* 2.28 § 175). The Gentile Messianists are to behave in this way not because the law says so but because it is the minimum that will allow Jews who observe the law to associate with Gentiles who do not. With the speech of James at an end, the discussions (vv. 6–21) are over. Now the narrative moves to the decisions the council makes (vv. 22–29).

The section on the decisions of the Jerusalem council falls into two parts: (1) the messengers (v. 22) and (2) the message (vv. 23–29). (1) "Then the apostles and elders, in agreement with the whole church, decided to choose representatives and to send them to Antioch with Paul and Barnabas." Those chosen are Judas Barsabbas and Silas, leading men among the Messianists in the city. (For the practice elsewhere of sending four men on a mission, two from the council and two from the people, see Chariton, *Chaereas and Callirhoe* 3.4.17; for the practice of sending letters from Jerusalem to the Diaspora, see 2 Macc 1:1–10a; 1.10b–2:18.)

(2) These four messengers deliver the message sent in the form of a letter (v. 23a). There was no official mail delivery in Mediterranean antiquity, except for royal mail. Others had to find someone to deliver their correspondence. In Acts 15:22, the church at Jerusalem sends its letter via these four people, two from Antioch and two from Jerusalem. Bearers of letters could supplement the contents with verbal information or by answering questions (e.g., PLond42–"Horus who delivered the letter has brought news of your being released"; PColZen 1.6–"The rest please learn from the man who brings you the letter, for he is not a stranger to us"; cf. 1 Macc 12:23–"We write to you that your cattle and property belong to us, and ours

belong to you. We therefore command that our envoys report to you accordingly"; Eph 6:21–22; Col 4:7–8). In many circles of Mediterranean antiquity, the living voice was preferred to the written word (Seneca, *Epistle* 6.5–6– "Of course . . . the living voice . . . will help you more than the written word"; Papias, in Eusebius, *Church History* 3.39.4) (Murphy-O'Connor 1995, 37–39, 40, 57). In both the selection of messengers and the availability of the living voice to interpret the written word, the church acts with wisdom.

The letter consists of five components. (a) There is first a salutation (v. 23): A to B, greeting (cf. 1 Macc 14:20; 2 Macc 1:1; 1:10; Acts 23:26; James 1:1). (b) Next comes a statement of the occasion (v. 24): "We have heard that some of our number [who went out] without any mandate from us have upset you with their teachings and disturbed your peace of mind." The key part is that the Jerusalem church did not send those who disturbed the disciples in Antioch. (c) Then there comes a word about the messengers (vv. 25–27): the church at Jerusalem sends along with "our beloved Barnabas and Paul, who have dedicated their lives to the name of our Lord Jesus Christ," Judas and Silas who "will also convey this same message by word of mouth." Note the emphasis on Jerusalem's high estimate of Barnabas and Paul. (d) Next comes the most important part, the message (vv. 28–29a): "It is the decision of the Holy Spirit and of us not to place on you any burden beyond these necessities, namely, to abstain from meat sacrificed to idols, from blood, from meats of strangled animals, and from sexual immorality. If you keep free of these, you will be doing what is right." The decree is the same as in v. 20, except for its order. The authority for the guidelines is twofold: the Holy Spirit and the church. (e) Finally, there is the letter closing (v. 29b): "Farewell" (2 Macc 9:20; 11:21, 33; 3 Macc 3:12; 7:1, 9).

The Jerusalem decree raises questions about Luke's view of the law. Two observations focus the issues: (1) no specific appeal is made to the law as the basis for the four prohibitions of 15:20, 29; (2) not all, but only selected portions, of Leviticus 17–18 are used. Why? The larger context within which an answer must be sought is decisive. Multiple groups in middle Judaism were all laying claim to the scriptures of ancient Israel. Each group read the same scriptures in a different way. Two examples suffice. (a) Rabbinic Judaism's prioritizing of the covenants was very different from that of Paul. Whereas for the Pharisaic tradition the Mosaic covenant is central and the Abrahamic covenant is understood eschatologically, for Paul the new covenant is central and is appealed to in connection with the covenant with Abraham. The Mosaic covenant is transcended. These two stances would give radically different readings of the same scriptures. (b) At Qumran, scripture is understood both as legal prescriptions and as prophetic promise. It is this community's belief that the prophetic promises are being fulfilled in the life of their group. The Pharisaic tradition regarded scripture primarily legally and as only incidentally prophetic. Prophetic fulfillment is a future hope. Messianists saw the scriptures primarily as prophetic oracles that were being fulfilled in the salvation history that runs from John the Baptist through Jesus to the church. These differing perspectives would inevitably yield widely disparate readings of the common scriptures at the same time that all groups would hold to the formal authority of the same scriptures. The question is, How does the author of Acts read them?

It is clear that Luke reads the scriptures as prophecies that are being fulfilled in Jesus and his followers. There is a new covenant in place (Luke 22:20; Acts 2). Soteriological benefits flow from the exalted Christ, not from the law (Luke 24:46-47; Acts 5:31; 10:43; 13:38-39). As a result, the repentance that is demanded of Israel and of Gentiles alike has to do with one's response to Jesus as Messiah (Luke 12:8-9; Acts 3:22-23). The ethnic dimensions of the law are still appropriate (Acts 21:20), though not demanded (Acts 10:28, 48), for ethnic Jews. They, moreover, have no soteriological benefits even for Jews (Acts 15:11). The only ethnic aspects of the law applicable to Gentiles are certain of those designed to facilitate social interchange between ethnic Jews and Gentiles who live among them (Leviticus 17-18; Acts 15:20, 29). These have no soteriological benefits for the Gentiles who observe them (Acts 15:11). Their observance by Gentile Messianists is not because of the authority of the law. It is rather because these customs are the minimalist concession that communal spirit demands to enable ethnic Jews and Gentiles, all of whom have become believers in Jesus the Messiah, to live together in unity. They are chosen not because they are a direct obligation of the law but because they are what is likely to be a source of controversy between Jewish and Gentile Messianists living together (Blomberg, 53-80; Seifrid, 39-57).

What follows in the large thought unit Acts 15:1-16:5 is the implementation in two stages of the Jerusalem church's decision: (1) in Antioch (15:30-35), and (2) beyond Antioch (15:36-16:5). (1) The implementation process in Antioch comes in a paragraph arranged in a concentric pattern: ABB'A' (Krodel, 272).

A—to Antioch (v. 30a)
   B—letter read to Antiochians (vv. 30b-31)
   B'—exhortation given to Antiochians (v. 35)
A'—to Jerusalem (v. 33), in Antioch (v. 35).

It indicates the church at Antioch's warm reception of the decision made in Jerusalem.

When the four messengers arrive in Antioch, they call the church together. Then the letter is read and the prophets Judas and Silas exhort the church. The reaction of the Antiochians is positive: "they were delighted with the exhortation" (v. 31). When Judas and Silas return to Jerusalem they are sent off "with greetings of peace . . . to those who had commissioned them" (v. 33b). Verse 34 ("But it seemed good to Silas to remain there") is not part of the original text of Acts. Paul and Barnabas remain in Antioch, teaching and preaching. James's prescription, adopted by the church in Jerusalem, meets acceptance in Antioch. Gentile Christians are glad to make an accommodation to enable them to live together in the one community with their ethnic Jewish Messianist fellow believers.

(2) The implementation of the Jerusalem decision beyond Antioch is described in Acts 15:36-16:5. This section consists of two paragraphs (15:36-41 and 16:1-4) plus a summary (16:5). The first paragraph is held together by an inclusion (v. 36, let us return; v. 41, and he went). Within the inclusion, the organization follows an ABCA'B' pattern (Johnson 1992, 282).

```
┌ [v. 36—let us make a return visit
│    A—Barnabas's desire (v. 37)
│       B—Paul's perception (v. 38)
│          C—the split (v. 39a)
│    A'—Barnabas's action (v. 39b)
│       B'—Paul's action (v. 40)
└ [v. 41—and he traveled
```

This paragraph functions as the introduction to what follows in 16:6-18:22. It constitutes Antioch's commissioning of Paul for his second missionary journey (analogous to 13:1-3 for the first journey of chaps. 13-14). It comes before the final phase of implementation (16:1-5) in accordance with the chain-link principle enunciated by Lucian, "How To Write History" 55: "When he has finished the first topic he will introduce the second, fastened to it and linked with it like a chain . . . ; always the first and second topics must not merely be neighbors but have common matter and overlap." The paragraph's point is that disagreement over John Mark divides Paul and Barnabas. The result is two missions. Barnabas and Mark go to Cyprus. Paul, after choosing Silas, travels "through Syria and Cilicia bringing strength to the churches" (v. 41). Nothing can stop the gospel, not even divisions among missionaries.

The second paragraph (16:1-4) functions as the conclusion to 15:1-35. Its purpose is to show Paul's acts to maintain church unity after the council (analogous to 11:27-30; 12:25). There are two such acts: (a) the circumcision of Timothy (vv. 1-3) and (b) the delivery of the decisions (v. 4). (a) Paul reaches Derbe and Lystra (14:6-20), where there is "a disciple named Timothy" (17:14-15; 18:5; 19:22; 20:4; Rom 16:21; 1 Cor 4:17; 16:10; 2 Cor 1:1; Phil 1:1; 2:19; Col 1:1; 1 Thess 1:1; 3:2, 6; 2 Thess 1:1; Phlm 1:1). He is "the son of a Jewish woman who was a believer (2 Tim 1:5; 2 Tim 3:15), but his father was a Greek" (v. 1). Since he is well spoken of by believers in Lystra and Iconium (14:1-5), Paul wants Timothy to accompany him in his work. "On account of the Jews of that region, Paul had him circumcised, for they all knew that his father was a Greek" (v. 3). How should this act be understood? It does not represent agreement with the Judean Messianists of 15:1, 5. Timothy is already a believer. The act of circumcision has nothing to do with his being part of God's messianic people. Rather it is part of Paul's attempt to accommodate Jewish sensitivities after the principle of salvation by grace through faith has been established (15:11). Rabbinic law usually defined the status of a child by the father, but in mixed marriages by the mother (*m. Kiddushin* 3:12; *m. Bikkurim* 1:4). Although the principle of matrilineal descent does not appear in rabbinic tradition before the period of the Mishnah, Acts 16:1-3 seems to assume it. Luke considers it to be the case. This, then, is an act of accommodation, part of Paul's missionary strategy (cf. 1 Cor 9:20). It shows, moreover, the faithfulness of Paul to his Jewish heritage (refuting the charges in 21:21; cf. 18:18; 21:24b; 22:3-4, 12-16, 17, 21; 23:1-5; 26:4-5; cf. Rom 3:1-4).

(b) In 16:4 the narrative says, "As they traveled from city to city, they handed on to the people for observance the decisions reached by the apostles and elders in Jerusalem." Paul delivers the Jerusalem decisions not only to Antioch of Syria but also to the regions of his first missionary journey (e.g., south Galatia). The scope of the Jerusalem church's decision was originally limited to Gentile Messianists in Antioch, Syria, and Cilicia (15:23). Paul expands the scope. In this way Luke shows him to be zealously pursuing the unity of the church.

The entire thought unit is brought to a conclusion by a summary in 16:5: "Day after day the churches grew stronger in faith and increased in number" (cf. 2:41, 47; 4:4; 5:14; 6:1, 7; 8:25, 40; 9:31; 11:24-25; 12:24; 14:21-23). The progress of the Messianist mission is enhanced by the church's unity.

Paul in Philippi
Acts 16:6–40

In Acts there are two missionary journeys of Paul: 13:1-16:5 and 16:6-19:41. Both have the same four components:

13:1-3	Commission	16:6-10
13:4-14:28	Outreach	16:6-18:21
15:1-35	To Jerusalem	18:22
15:36-16:5	Return	18:23-19:41

Acts 16:6-19:41, the second of Paul's missionary journeys, looks like this:

Commission (16:6-10)
Visits to Philippi (16:11-40)
       Thessalonica (17:1-9)
       Beroea (17:10-14)
       Athens (17:15-34)
       Corinth (18:1-18)
       Ephesus (18:19-21)
To Jerusalem (18:22)
Return visits to
       Galatia and Phrygia (18:23)
       Ephesus (18:24-19:41)

Of these, only the visits to Philippi, Athens, Corinth, and the return visit to Ephesus are more than stylized summaries.

The first large thought unit in the second missionary journey is 16:6-40. This section consists of two parts: (1) a commissioning account (16:6-10), and (2) a narrative about the mission to Philippi (16:11-40). Each must be examined in order.

Acts 16:6-10 constitutes Paul's call to a Macedonian mission. This is a commissioning story analogous to that in 13:1-3. It functions as Paul's divine commission for a European mission just as 13:1-3 did for the mission in Asia Minor (Acts 13-14). It consists of four components: (a) introduction (vv. 6-8; cf. 13:1-2a); (b) confrontation (v. 9a; cf. 13:2b); (c) commission (v. 9b; cf. 13:2c); and (d) conclusion (v. 10; cf. 13:3).

(a) Frustrated by two divinely closed doors ("prevented by the Holy Spirit from preaching . . . in the province of Asia"; "tried to go on into Bithynia, but the Spirit of Jesus did not allow them"), Paul and his companions come to Troas (vv. 6-8). (b) "During [the] night Paul had a vision" (v. 9a). The vision comes in a dream (cf. Num 12:6–vision equals a dream; Dan 4:5, 9-10; 8:18, 27–dream and vision are identified; *1 Enoch* 14 identifies a vision with what is seen in sleep; *T. Levi* 2:5-5:7–the hero falls asleep and sees a vision; *2 Baruch* 52:7-53:12–the seer falls asleep and sees a vision; *2 Enoch* 69:5-6–the seer falls asleep and sees a vision).

(c) "A Macedonian stood before him and implored him with these words, 'Come over into Macedonia and help us'"(v. 9b). In antiquity important decisions frequently follow a vision or revelation (e.g., Herodotus 7.12–It seems to Xerxes that a tall and godly man stood over him and said . . . ; Plato, *Apology* 33C–Socrates feels commanded by God through an oracle; Chariton, *Chaereas and Callirhoe* 1.12–Theron's plan to throw Callirhoe into the sea the next day to get rid of her is stopped when, in sleep, he has a dream in which he sees a closed door; Suetonius, *Julius Caesar* 32—Caesar has a dream before leaving Spain for Rome that he will have sovereignty over the whole world; Suetonius, *Claudius* 1—Drusus, the father of Claudius, sees an apparition of a barbarian woman, speaking in Latin, forbidding him to pursue the defeated Germanic tribes further; Philostratus, *Life of Apollonius* 4.34—Apollonius detours on a trip to Rome because he has a dream that compels him to go to Crete; Gen 31:10-13, 24—a journey is dictated to Jacob in a dream; Josephus, *Antiquities* 11.8.5 § 334—a journey is dictated in a dream to Alexander the Great; *Life* 42 §§ 208-10—a course of action is dictated to Josephus by a dream in which a certain person stood by him and said . . .). Gentile (Cicero, *On Divination* 1.30.64; Artemidorus, *Dream Book*) and Jew (Josephus, *Antiquities* 1.12.1 § 208; 2.9.4 § 217; 5.4.2 § 193; 6.14.2 § 334; 7.7.3 § 147; 8.4.6 § 125; 11.8.4 § 327; 13.12. 1 § 322) alike regarded dreams as vehicles for divine communication. (d) From this vision, the group concludes that God has called them to proclaim the good news in Macedonia (v. 10). By means of this commissioning story, Luke makes clear that the outreach to Europe is owing not to human desire but solely to God's intervention. In what follows, Paul is not so much the apostle of the church of Antioch as he is of Christ himself (26:16-18—"a witness of what you have seen [of me] and what you will be shown").

In 16:10 the reader encounters for the first time what are called the "we-sections" of Acts. These are five sections (16:10-17; 20:5-15; 21:1-18; 27:1-29; 28:1-16) in which the normal third-person (they, he) narration of the author gives way to first-person-plural (we) narration. So in 16:10, the first occurrence, the sentence runs as follows: "When *he* had seen the vision, *we* sought passage to Macedonia at once, concluding that God had called *us* to proclaim the good news to them." Three different explanations of this phenomenon have been offered: (a) the we-sections indicate the author's presence as an eyewitness at these points (as in Polybius 3.4.13 or Josephus, *Against Apion* 1.55); (b) they point to a diary or source used by the author of Acts (like Xenophon, *Anabasis,* or Lucian, *How to Write History* 16); or they are a literary creation of the author (as in Homer, *Odyssey* 14.244-58; Vergil, *Aeneid* 3.5; Lucian, *True Story*; Ezra 8:23-9:15; *Antiochene Acts of Ignatius*). No one of these hypotheses has been able to convince a majority of scholars. The question is moot at the moment. For the purposes of this commentary, it is inconsequential.

Acts 16:11-40 presents the mission in Philippi. This unit is bracketed by references to Philippi (vv. 11-12 and v. 40b) and to Lydia and the other believers/brethren (vv. 13-15 and v. 40a). Within the inclusion, vv. 16-39 are built out of two miracle stories (vv. 16-24, 35-39 and vv. 24-34), one within the other (cf. Luke 8:40-56 for one miracle sandwiched within another; cf. Acts 11:27-30 and 12:25, with 12:1-24 sandwiched within).

Verses 11-15 set the stage. From Troas Paul and his company sail to the island of Samothrace in a day. The next day they sail to the port of Philippi, Neapolis. Then they make their way overland to Philippi, a Roman colony and a city of the first district of Macedonia (v. 12—following Nestle, 26th edition). The city was named for Alexander the Great's father. It was settled by Roman veterans after Anthony and Octavian defeated Brutus and Cassius in a battle nearby in 42 B.C. As a Roman colony it had a constitution modeled after Rome's; it was governed by praetors (magistrates, vv. 20, 38) and lictors (police, v. 38). Macedonia was a senatorial province divided into four districts. Its capital was Thessalonica (17:1). Philippi belonged to the first district, whose capital was Amphipolis (17:1).

As good Jews, on the sabbath Paul and his company look for a place of prayer (synagogue or its equivalent; cf. 3 Macc 7:20; Josephus, *Life* 54 §§ 277, 280; 56 § 293). The sabbath was for Jews a day of worship (Philo, *Decalogue* 97-98; Josephus, *Antiquities* 16.2.3 § 43). It was closely connected to their sense of identity (1 Macc 1:39-43, 45; 2 Macc 6:6; *Jubilees* 2:19-20). It was the source of criticism by pagan opponents. Jews were lazy for resting on the sabbath, so the charge ran (Tacitus, *Histories* 5.4.3; Juvenal, *Satires* 14.105-06; Seneca, so Augustine, *City of God* 6.11). That Paul looks for the place of prayer outside the city and by the river (v. 13) may reflect a Jewish custom of so locating places of prayer (Josephus, *Antiquities* 14.10.23 § 258—"may make their places of prayer at the seaside, according to the customs of their fathers"). Two episodes are related to this search for the place of prayer. The first is the conversion of Lydia (vv. 13-15), the other, an exorcism (vv. 16-18).

The first, the conversion of Lydia, comes in vv. 13-15. Where Paul expects to find a place of prayer, he finds some women gathered, one of whom is named Lydia, a dealer in purple cloth (Luke 16:19; 1 Macc 10:62), from the city of Thyatira (Rev 2:18-29), and a worshipper of God (13:43, 50). Through Paul's words and the Lord's intervention, she becomes a believer (v. 14). There is in Acts a strong emphasis on the divine initiative: (a) in salvation history (2:22, 23, 24, 33, 36; 4:28; 28:25-27); (b) in mission (1:8; 1:17, 22, 24, 26; 4:29, 31; 5:19-20; 9:15, 31; 10:9-16, 19, 28, 33; 13:2; 15:4, 7, 28; 16:6, 7, 9, 10; 18:9-10:21; 19:21; 20:22-23, 24, 32; 22:14-15, 17-18; 26:16-18; 27:23-24); (c) in conversion (2:21—will be saved; 2:39—whom the Lord summons; 2:40—be saved; 4:12; 9:3-6; 10:3-6, 44; 11:15-18—God gave them the gift; 13:48—all who were destined for eternal life came to believe; 14:27; 15:8-11—we are saved through the grace of the Lord Jesus; 16:14; 18:27—those who had come to believe through grace; 19:6; 20:24—the gospel of God's grace; 21:19; 22:6-10; 26:13-15). As a result of such divine initiative, she and her household are baptized.

Then she says to Paul and his company, "If you consider me a believer in the Lord, come and stay at my home" (v. 15). Lydia's behavior reflects the disciples' traits of being hospitable (Rom 12:13; 1 Tim 3:2; Heb 13:2; 1 Pet 4:9; 3 John 5–8) and sharing material goods with those who teach the word (Luke 10:7; Gal 6:6; 1 Cor 9:14). That Paul stays in the house of a Gentile believer indicates that Lydia is acceptable as a disciple of equal standing (see 10:15, 20, 28–29, 34; 11:2; cf. John 4:40). The narrative of Acts implies that such social inequality as existed between Jews and God-fearers in the synagogue does not exist within the Messianist movement. It also says that Paul is not a disreputable philosopher. Dio Chrysostom, *Oration* 32.11, speaks negatively about certain philosophers who

> merely utter a phrase or two, and then, after railing at you rather than teaching you, . . . make a hurried exit, anxious lest before they have finished you may raise an outcry and send them packing.

Lydia becomes the second woman in Acts who has a church in her house (cf. 12:12–the house of Mary where many gathered to pray for Peter; cf. also Col 4:15 for Nympha and the church in her house). Mention of her high social status accords with a Lukan concern (6:7; 8:27; 10:1; 13:12; 17:4; 18:8).

The second episode that happened on the way to find the house of prayer begins at v. 16. There are two miracle stories offered here, one inside the other. The first, vv. 16–24, 35–39, like other such tales, has three parts. They are (1) the problem (vv. 16–18a), (2) the cure (v. 18b), and (3) the reactions (vv. 19–24, 35–39), which are three: (a) charges are made (vv. 19–22a); (b) punishments are administered (vv. 22b–24), and (c) apologies are offered (vv. 35–40).

(1) Paul and his company meet a slave girl who had a Pythonic spirit (*pneuma pythona*). She brought her owners a large profit through her mantic prophesying (*manteuomenē*). This was not an uncommon phenomenon in Mediterranean antiquity. Plutarch describes the technique (*Obsolescence of Oracles* 414E–"the god himself after the manner of ventriloquists, . . . called . . . now Pythoness, enters the bodies of his prophets and prompts their utterances"), the Mishnah condemns the practice (*m. Sanhedrin* 7:7), and Lucian (*Alexander the False Prophet*) and Apuleius (*Golden Ass* 8.26–30) satirize profit-taking from such behavior. Later Christian thinkers regarded such divination as owing to demons (Origen, *Against Celsus* 4.90–98; 3.25–27.3; Eusebius, *Preparation for the Gospel* 4.23), as Paul will do here.

Following Paul and his group, the girl shouts, "These people are slaves of the Most High God, who proclaim to you a way of salvation" (v. 17; cf. a similar practice of demons recognizing and proclaiming Jesus' identity; see

Luke 4:34; 8:28). Although the Most High is a Lukan title for God (Luke 1:32, 35, 76; 6:35; 8:28–in the mouth of a demoniac; Acts 7:48) and Jews used it for the God of Israel (*T. Asher* 5:4; *Joseph and Aseneth* 8:2; Philo, *Legation* 278), pagans also employed the honorific term: for example, for Zeus, for the local Baal, for a mother goddess, for Isis. In a pagan context like Philippi, the slave girl's words would have been ambiguous, just as would her words about "*a* (not *the*) way of salvation" (Trebilco, 51–73).

(2) After many days, Paul turns and says to the spirit, "I command you in the name of Jesus Christ to come out of her." And it came out at that moment (v. 18). This is a conventional story of an exorcism. Such stories are found all over the Mediterranean world: for example, (a) pagan–Philostratus, *Life of Apollonius* 3.38; 4.20; Lucian, *Lover of Lies* 16.30–31; cf. Origen, *Against Celsus* 1.22, who says pagan exorcists appropriated the names of the patriarchs, Solomon, and even Jesus in their formulas, and Eusebius, *Church History* 7.10.4, who says pagan and Christian exorcists opposed one another; (b) nonmessianic Judaism–1QapGen 20:18–30; 4QPrNab; Pseudo-Philo, *Biblical Antiquities* 60:1–3; Josephus, *Antiquities* 6.8.2 §§ 166–69; 8.2.5 §§ 46–49; *b. Pesahim* 112b; *b. Meilah* 17a, b; *Numbers Rabbah* 19.8; cf. Ps-Cyprian, *On Rebaptism* 7, who says that Jews were frequently able to drive out demons using the name of Christ; (c) messianic Judaism–Jesus as exorcist (Mark 1:21–28; 5:1–20; 7:24–30; 9:14–29; Luke 11:19//Matt 12:27); Jesus' disciples as exorcists (Mark 9:38–40; Luke 13:10–17; Acts 16:18; 19:13–17). Exorcism was a practice that continued in the early church: Justin Martyr, *Dialogue* 30, 85; *2 Apology* 6; Pseudo-Clementine *Recognitions* 4.7; Tertullian, *The Shows* 26; *The Soul's Testimony* 3; Origen, *Against Celsus* 1.46; Lactantius, *Divine Institutes* 2.16; *Apostolic Constitutions* 8.1; Eusebius, *Church History* 5.7.4; 6.43.11; 8.6.9; Cyril of Jerusalem, *Catechesis* 16:15–16; Athanasius, *On the Incarnation* 48; *On the Life of Anthony* 63; Gregory of Nyssa, *Life of St. Gregory the Wonderworker* [PLG 46, col 916A]; Jerome, *Life of St. Hilarion* 22. Here the name of Jesus has authority over a demonic spirit. The girl is set free (Luke 4:18).

(3) The reactions are three. The first two are hostile. The first comes in vv. 19–22a. "When her owners saw that their hope of profit was gone, they seized Paul and Silas and dragged them to the public square before the local authorities" (v. 19). As in Luke 8:37 where the Gerasenes ask Jesus to leave their country because the healing of the demoniac has cost them financially, so here. The same emphasis will crop up again in Acts 19:23–41 when, in Ephesus, the business of those who make silver shrines of Artemis is threatened by the gospel. Tertullian continues the Lukan emphasis when he says, "you . . . insolently made a profit of your gods" (*Ad Nationes* 1.10). The eco-

nomic motivation of those opposed to the missionaries is masked behind various other appeals.

The charges leveled against the missionaries are three (v. 20). First, they are Jews (18:14–17; 19:33–34). This is both an appeal to nationalism and to racial prejudice. There was strong anti-Jewish sentiment among many Mediterranean pagans: for example, (a) Diodorus Siculus 34–35.1.1, says the Jews "alone of all nations avoided dealings with any other people and looked on all men as their enemies"; (b) Apion argues that the Jews are not only a nation giving to "fomenting sedition," but also that they "swear . . . to show no good will to a single alien, above all to Greeks" (Josephus, *Against Apion* 2.11 § 121); (c) Tacitus, *History* 5.4.1, levels the accusation that "the Jews regard as profane all that we hold sacred; on the other hand, they permit all that we abhor"; (d) Philostratus, *Apollonius* 5.33, says that "the Jews have long been in revolt not only against the Romans but against humanity." Such prejudice is appealed to in the attack on Paul and Silas.

Second, they are charged with disturbing the peace (24:5). This is an appeal to the Roman obsession with public order. Suetonius, *Life of Claudius* 25.4, reflects the Roman view of Jews as disturbers of the peace: "Since the Jews were continually making disturbances at the instigation of Chrestus, he [Claudius] expelled them from Rome" (18:2). Throughout Acts as well, Jews are depicted as inciters of the crowds (13:50; 14:2, 5; 14:19; 17:5, 8; 17:13). Clearly Luke saw them this way and expected his readers to do so also.

Third, they are charged with advocating customs that are not lawful for Romans to adopt or practice (17:18–20). This is an appeal both to traditionalism and patriotism. In Mediterranean pagan culture, novelty in religion was a bad thing. (a) Euripides, *Bacchae* 200, says: "Tis not for us to reason touching gods. Traditions of our fathers, old as time, we hold. No reasoning shall cast them down." (b) Socrates followed the advice of the Delphic oracle: "Follow the custom of the state. That is the way to act piously" (Xenophon, *Memorabilia* 1.3.1–3). (c) The *Rhetorica ad Alexandrum* 2.1423.33–34, says: "in all countries it is deemed wrong to depart from the ancestral customs" (= in religion). (d) Livy 39.8–19 tells of the ban on the Dionysian cult in 186 B.C. The consul says,

> How often, in the times of our fathers . . . has the task been assigned to the magistrates of forbidding the introduction of foreign cults . . . and of annulling every system of sacrifice except that performed in the Roman way.

(e) Cicero, who did not care much for Judaism, in his *On Behalf of Flaccus* 69, says about it, "each state has its own religion; we have ours." (f) Dio Cassius 50.23.3–50.30.5 tells how, before the battle of Actium, Octavian made a speech to his soldiers that criticized Anthony. Anthony, he said, has now abandoned his ancestors' habits of life, has emulated all alien and barbaric customs . . . pays no honor . . . to his father's gods. . . . (50.25.3–4)

His piety toward our gods? But he is at war with them as well as with his country. (50.27.7)

(g) Claudius's edict about Jews included this exhortation to the Jews: "not to set at nought the beliefs about the gods held by other people" (Josephus, *Antiquities* 19.5.3 §§ 290–91).

It was assumed that a change of gods would lead to a disruption of the fabric of society. (a) If the gods are not properly reverenced, they may pour out their wrath on the public sector at large (Horace, *Odes* 3.6.5–8). (b) If they change their gods, citizens may not obey the emperor (Tertullian, *Apology* 4, 10, 42; *Scapula* 2). (c) If they change their gods, wives, children, and slaves may not be obedient in the household to their husbands, parents, and masters. (d) Those involved in other religions will be separated from rather than integrated into the general fabric of society. They become despisers of other peoples. Given these fears, the larger society would not look with favor on purveyors of new religions. As might be expected, "the crowd joined in the attack" on Paul and Silas (v. 22a). Philo's description of how the crowds in Alexandria were quick to show hostility against the Jews there (*Embassy* 18, 19, 20, 25, 26; *Against Flaccus* 5) indicates that Luke is describing customary behavior.

The second hostile reaction to the exorcism comes in vv. 22b–24. "The magistrates had them stripped and ordered them to be beaten with rods. After inflicting many blows on them (cf. 2 Cor 11:25), they threw them into prison . . . the jailer . . . put them in the innermost cell and secured their feet to a stake." The picture of the Roman officials here is not good. Like Pilate (Luke 23), they succumb to the pressure of the crowd (1 Thess 2:2).

The third reaction to the exorcism comes in vv. 35–40. In these vv. apologies are made on the next day. The magistrates sent the lictors to release Paul and Silas. Paul said to them, "They have beaten us publicly, even though we are Roman citizens and have not been tried, and have thrown us into prison. . . . Let them come themselves and lead us out" (v. 37). This brings fear to the officials who have acted out of line. Roman citizens had the right to be free from such arbitrary treatment (Livy 10.9.3–6; Cicero, *Against Verres* 2.5.66–"To bind a Roman citizen is a crime, to flog him an abomination, to slay him almost an act of parricide"). The magistrates come and attempt to placate Paul and Silas and lead them out of prison (v. 39).

There are a number of points this section makes regarding the relation of believers to the state. First, it shows the legitimacy of disciples' appealing to their legal rights as protection against unjust treatment by nonbelievers (see 22:25; 25:11 for the same theme). Second, it says that believers must be prepared to suffer unjustly because Roman officials are sometimes swayed by mob hysteria (16:22), by greed (24:26), by favoritism (24:27), and by cowardice (Luke 23:24–25). When this happens, disciples are to see themselves replicating the sufferings of Jesus, who was arrested, subjected to false accusation, and beaten. Third, it claims that the state is usually reasonable and will correct its mistakes when these are made clear. Roman justice is basically reliable, even if individual administrators fall short of the ideal at times. Fourth, it makes very clear that the disciples are not the troublemakers but are the victims of those with questionable motives. Fifth, such unjust suffering at the hands of the state lends credence to one's claims. Juvenal, *Satires* 6.560–64, laments,

> Fellows like these are believed if they've been in some far-off prison, shackled hand and foot; if he hasn't a prison record, then he has no renown, but a sentence to one of the islands, a narrow escape from death, procures him a reputation.

The second miracle story associated with Philippi comes in vv. 24–34. It is sandwiched in the middle of the first miracle story, the exorcism (vv. 16–24, 35–39). As with all miracle stories, this one also has its three parts: (1) problem (v. 24); (2) miracle (vv. 25–26); and (3) reactions (vv. 27–34). (1) The problem is that Paul and Silas are imprisoned in the innermost part of the jail, with their feet fastened to a stake. Prison was the most severe form of custody. Jailers were notorious for their cruelty. "Everyone knows how full of inhumanity and cruelty gaolers are; pitiless by nature and care-hardened by practice, they are brutalized day by day towards savagery" (Philo, *Joseph* 81–84). The inner prison was the worst possible site (Lucian, *Toxaris* 30). Many would be confined in a small area; the air would be bad; the darkness would be profound; the stench would be almost unbearable (Lucian, *Toxaris* 29; Diodorus Siculus 31.9.2). To be put in stocks (Lucian, *Toxaris* 150–51) or chains (Philostratus, *Life of Apollonius* 7:36, 40) was a typical overnight restraint that added even greater discomfort.

(2) The miracle is like those already narrated in Acts 5:19 and 12:6–11. It is a story of a miraculous release from prison. About midnight the two missionaries are praying and singing hymns to God. This was viewed as noble behavior in antiquity. Epictetus, *Dissertations* 2.6.26–27, says, "Then we shall be emulating Socrates when we are able to write paeans in prison" (cf. Plato, *Phaedrus* 60D, 61A, B; Diogenes Laertius 2.42). The *T. Joseph* 8:5 says about the patriarch that when he was put in fetters in pharoah's prison, he "sang praise in the house of darkness and . . . rejoiced with cheerful voice, glorifying . . . God." In the *Martyrdom of Pionius* 18.12, the prisoners strengthen one another with psalms and prayers; in 11.5-6, they praise God (cf. Rom 5:3; 1 Pet 1:6; 4:13). There is a severe earthquake

(a sign of a theophany; 4:31), which shakes the foundations of the jail. The doors fly open (5:19), and everyone's chains are pulled loose (v. 26; 12:17).

(3) When the jailer awakens, he prepares to kill himself because he thinks the prisoners have escaped (remember what happened to the jailers who could not account for their prisoners in 12:19). Implied is that the jailer, having locked the prisoners in the inner prison with their feet fastened in stocks, had gone to sleep (Lucian, *Toxaris* 30, speaks about a man's rushing to the prison to see a friend only to find that "it was evening and the keeper had long ago locked the door and gone to sleep, after directing his servants to keep watch"). Paul shouts with a loud voice, "Do no harm to yourself; we are all here" (v. 28; in Philostratus, *Apollonius* 8.30, the philosopher is freed but does not try to escape).

The jailer rushes in, brings Paul and Silas out, and asks, "Sirs, what must I do to be saved?" (v. 30). Although his question relates to his physical safety, the answer he receives concerns his eternal destiny. "Believe on the Lord Jesus and you and your household will be saved" (v. 31; cf. 4:12; 13:47; 15:11; 16:17; Rom 10:9; 1 Cor 12:3; Phil 2:11). The miracle of the freeing of the prisoners is not so much for the safety of Paul and Silas as for the salvation of the jailer. "So they spoke the word of the Lord to him and to everyone in his house" (v. 32).

As in the case of Lydia, his conversion is followed by baptism and by acts of hospitality in which he shares his material goods with the missionaries (v. 34—he set food before them; see 2:44-46; 4:32-35; 11:27-30; 16:15). The jailer's actions, moreover, depict the disciples' trait of compassion for prisoners (see Heb 10:34; 13:3; Matt 25:36; Lucian, *Peregrinus* 12–13). To feed the prisoners involved some risk for the jailer. For example, during Agrippa's imprisonment, when news came that Tiberius was dead, the centurion guarding him treated him to dinner. When further news came during the meal that Tiberius was not dead, the centurion was distressed "since the penalty set for such things as he had done was death" (Josephus, *Antiquities* 18.6.10 § 231). Assumed throughout his deeds is the conviction of the solidarity of Jesus with his people (Acts 9:4; 22:7; 26:15; Matt 10:40-42; Ignatius, *Ephesians* 6:1b; *2 Baruch* 72:1-6—the nations will be judged according to how they have treated Israel). Just as in the case of the great persecutor, Saul, in Acts 9, the jailer here gives immediate evidence of the genuineness of his conversion.

The jailer is delighted when the magistrates order the release of Paul and Silas (v. 36). But only after an official apology from the officials will the missionaries depart and then only after they go to Lydia's house where they can see and encourage the disciples (v. 40). Nurture of the disciples comes before personal safety.

Paul in Thessalonica, Beroea, and Athens
Acts 17:1–34

Acts 17 consists of three parts: vv. 1–9, the mission in Thessalonica; vv. 10–15, the mission in Beroea; and vv. 16–34, the mission in Athens. The first two are stylized summaries similar in pattern to 13:16–52 and 14:1–7. The initial preaching in the synagogue is followed by resistance from the Jewish establishment. Echoes of 14:19 (Jews from another city come to stir up the populace) and 16:20–21 (charges of a political nature are made against the missionaries) can also be heard. The third part of chap. 17 is an account of a specific incident in Athens. We may begin with an examination of the two summaries (vv. 1–9 and vv. 10–15).

Acts 17:1–9 offers a summary of events in Thessalonica in two parts: (a) the initial success of the mission (vv. 1–4), and (b) the subsequent persecution of the missionaries (vv. 5–9). (a) Following the Egnatian Way westward, Paul and Silas go through Amphipolis (the capital of the first district) and Apollonia on their way to Thessalonica (the capital of the second district). Thessalonica was the chief city of the Roman province of Macedonia, the center of Roman administration. It was governed by a group of five or six politarchs which was presided over by a chief politarch (cf. 17:6). They were responsible for the maintenance of order in the city. The city had within it a synagogue (v. 1).

Following his usual custom, Paul goes first to the Jews (13:46). On three sabbaths he "entered into discussions with them from the scriptures, expounding and demonstrating that the Messiah had to suffer and rise from the dead (Luke 24:26, 46; 9:22; 17:25; Acts 3:18), and that 'this is the Messiah, Jesus, whom I proclaim to you'" (v. 3; 1 Cor 15:3–5). Converts are made from ethnic Jews and from the Gentile God-fearers (cf. 1 Thess 1:5–2:16 for Paul's account of the church's founding). The latter group included "not a few of the prominent women" (v. 4; 13:50; 16:14; 17:12).

Judaism seemed to hold a special attraction for Gentile women, especially prominent ones. Josephus mentions several instances of this phenomenon. In *War* 2.20.2 § 561, he says that at Damascus "yet did the Damascenes distrust their wives, who were almost all addicted to the Jewish religion." In *Antiquities* 18.3.5 § 81, he mentions a prominent woman in Rome, Fulvia, who became a devotee to Judaism and was promptly taken advantage of by unscrupulous Jewish rogues. In *Antiquities* 20.2.3 §§ 34–35, he tells how a pagan king's wives in Adiabene came to worship God in the Jewish manner. Indeed, one of the disciples of Jesus who provided for him was Joanna, the wife of Chuza, Herod's steward (Luke 8:3). Acts reflects this cultural fact (13:50—women of prominence who are worshippers; 17:4, 12). Acts, generally, pays especial attention to the involvement of women in the church (1:14; 5:14; 8:3, 12; 9:2; 12:12; 16:15, 40; 17:4, 12; 17:34; 18:2, 18, 26; 21:9).

(b) If Paul's mission in Thessalonica had initial success, it soon has to face hostility (vv. 5–9). The Jews, out of zeal (5:17; 7:9; 13:45), "recruited some worthless men loitering in the public square, formed a mob, and set the city in turmoil" (v. 5a). Once again, Acts emphasizes the Jewish involvement in public disorder (13:50; 14:2, 5; 14:19). Depicting the Jews as instigators of others in acts of hostility against Messianists occurs elsewhere in the writings of the early church (Luke 12:11; 21:12; 23; Rev 2:9; *Martyrdom of Polycarp* 13:1; Eusebius, *Church History* 3.32.2–3, 6). When Paul and Silas are not at the house of Jason where they have been staying, the crowd drags Jason and some other believers before the city politarchs (v. 6a; 1 Thess 2:14–16).

The charges against the Messianists are two. First, they are disturbers of public order: "These people who have been creating a disturbance all over the world have now come here" (v. 6b; cf. 16:20). The irony of a mob accusing the disciples of public disorder is striking. Second, they are guilty of seditious incitement: "They all act in opposition to the decrees of Caesar and claim instead that there is another king, Jesus" (v. 7; cf.16:21; Luke 1:33; 19:11, 12, 15, 38; 22:29–30; 23:2–3, 37). The Gospel of John also reflects such a charge in 18:33, 36. When Pilate asks, "Are you the King of the Jews?" Jesus answers, "My kingdom is not of this world." Eusebius, *Church History* 3.20, relates a story from the time of Domitian with the same concerns. The emperor examined two descendants of Jesus' family. He asked them about the Christ and his kingdom. They explained that "it was neither of the world nor earthly, but heavenly and angelic." Whereupon he dismissed them. Justin Martyr struggles with such accusations in his time: "When you hear that we look forward to a kingdom, you rashly assume that we speak of a human kingdom, whereas we mean a kingdom which is with God" (*1 Apology* 11). The plot of Luke-Acts as a whole has prepared the auditors to hear this as false witness (cf. Talbert 1982, 190–94).

The politarchs, when they hear such charges, take a surety payment from Jason and the others before releasing them (v. 9). In contrast to the authorities in Philippi, these in Thessalonica follow prescribed procedure. The charge against Jason is that he has received and lodged seditious people in his house. The security payment makes Jason responsible for Paul and Silas. The bond will be forfeited and Jason hauled into court anew if any trouble recurs involving the two missionaries. Consequently, the disciples at Thessalonica immediately send Paul and Silas to Beroea during the night (v. 10; cf. 9:23–25; 9:30; 13:50–51; 14:20 for Paul's rapid exits because of trouble he has generated).

Acts 17:10–15 offers a summary of events in Beroea. As in 17:1–9, there are the usual two parts: (a) the initial success of the mission (vv. 10–12), and (b) the later persecution of the chief missionary (vv. 13–15). (a) "Upon arrival they went to the synagogue of the Jews" (v. 10b). The pattern continues: to the Jew first (13:46; 17:2). "These Jews were more fair minded than those in Thessalonica, for they received the word with all willingness and examined the scriptures daily to determine whether these things were so" (v. 11). Many ethnic Jews and many influential Greek women and men (God-fearers) become believers (v. 12).

(b) The initial success did not continue because "when the Jews of Thessalonica learned that the word of God had now been proclaimed by Paul in Beroea also, they came there to cause a commotion and to stir up the crowds" (v. 13). The motif of Jewish incitement of the unstable crowds continues. As in 14:19, Jews from another city pursue the missionaries to the next town. Rather than risk a repeat of what had happened in Thessalonica, the disciples in Beroea (yes, a church had been formed already) send Paul on his way to the seacoast, while Silas and Timothy remain behind (v. 14). Paul's escorts take him to Athens (by boat?) and return to tell Silas and Timothy to join him as soon as possible (v. 15).

The major focus of Acts 17 comes in the story of Paul's visit to Athens, the epitome of Greek philosophy, religion, and culture (vv. 16–34). This is no summary but a fully developed incident. The narrative is held together by a frame (v. 15—to Athens; 18:1—left Athens). It falls into three sections: (1) the context (vv. 16–21), (2) the proclamation (vv. 22–31), and (3) the conclusion (vv. 32–34). Each deserves attention.

(1) In the first of these parts, vv. 16–21, the auditor learns the intent of the section. It will be an attack on pagan idolatry. (a) The usual Lukan pattern for Paul's missionary work is to have him go into the synagogue and argue with Jews and God-fearers (e.g., 13:5, 14, 43; 14:1; 16:13; 17:1, 10, 17; 18:4, 19; 19:8). This is also found here (v. 17—"so he dialogued in the synagogue with the Jews and with the worshippers"). By the inclusion of v. 16, however, Luke changes the direction of the readers' attention: "While Paul was waiting . . . in Athens, he grew exasperated at the sight of the city full of idols." Ancient authors noted the abundance of such statues in the city (Livy 45.27; Pausanias 1.14.1; 1.15.7). A university city like Athens blends enlightened philosophy and superstitious idolatry. Learning does not eliminate idolatry. The Lukan Paul is not so much impressed by Athens' culture as he is irritated by its idolatry. This is the springboard from which the passage moves. Pagan idolatry is a standard complaint voiced by non-messianic (Isa 46:1–7; Wis 14:12, 23, 27; Philo, *Decalogue* 66; Josephus, *Against Apion* 2.34 §§ 239–41; 2.36 §§ 250–54) and messianic Jews alike

(Rom 1:18, 23, 29–31; Diognetus 2:1–2; Tertullian, *On Idolatry* 1; Clement of Alexandria, *Exhortation to the Greeks* 4).

(b) In addition to his dialoguing (*dielegeto*) in the synagogue, Paul dialogues "daily in the public square with whoever happened to be there" (v. 17b). There may very well be two allusions to Socrates here. One relates to how Paul taught. If the verb *dialegomai* is correctly translated "dialoguing" here, it likely echoes Socrates' method of teaching. Xenophon in his *Memorabilia* says,

> By this process of leading back the argument even his adversary came to see the truth clearly. Whenever he himself argued out a question, he advanced by steps that gained assent, holding this to be the only method. (1.2.2–3)

> Accordingly, whenever he argued, he gained a greater measure of assent from his hearers than any man I have known. (4.4.15)

The other possible Socratic echo relates to where Paul spoke. Dio Chrysostom, *Orations* 12.14; 54.3; 80.2, appeals to the precedent of Socrates, who talked everywhere and to everyone: in the gymnasium, in the Lyceum, in workshops, and in the marketplace. (Of course, so did Diogenes the Cynic. Cf. Cynic epistles, Diogenes 38—After the games, Diogenes stayed behind. "I was passing time in the marketplace, where the rest of the crowd was. . . . I turned for a time toward those selling things, and then to those reciting, or philosophizing, or prophesying.")

Paul even engaged in discussion with Epicurean and Stoic philosophers, some of whom still had subsidized posts in Athens (so Lucian, *The Eunuch* 3). Some of them ask, "What is this babbler (*spermologos*) trying to say?" (v. 18). The charge of babbling ranks Paul with the disreputable street preachers of the time. Dio Chrysostom, *Oration* 32.9, castigates the Cynics for such behavior.

> There are, as well, quite a few Cynic philosophers, so-called, in your city . . . people whose ideals are genuine enough, but whose bellies need filling. . . . They gather at street-corners and in alley-ways and at temple gates and con youngsters and sailors and crowds made up of that sort, stringing together rough jokes and much babbling (*spermologian*) and that rubbish of the marketplace.

Lucian, *Peregrinus* 3–4, also speaks of Cynics "bawling out . . . the standard street-corner stuff" (cf. Horace, *Satires* 2.3; Epictetus, *Discourses* 3.22.26–30; Dio Chrysostom 8.9, 36; Apuleius, *Golden Ass* 8.24; 11.8). Of course, a Cynic would have valued the practice differently (Cynic epistles, Diogenes 38—After the games Diogenes argues with a philosopher, then a diviner. His victories in debate cause the bystanders to follow and listen to him teach about patient endurance. In response, people give him money, barley-meal, or invite him to dinner).

Celsus had much the same negative attitude toward the later church's preachers. He says,

Moreover, we see that those who display their secret lore in the marketplaces and go about begging would never enter a gathering of intelligent men, nor would they dare to reveal their noble beliefs in their presence; but whenever they see adolescent boys and a crowd of slaves and a company of fools, they push themselves in and show off.

In the narrative of Acts 17, Luke has Paul so charged, but Paul's later behavior refutes the allegation.

Others say, "He sounds like a promoter of foreign divinities" (v. 18). They take this line because he preaches about "Jesus" (a masculine term) and the "Resurrection" (a feminine term). His auditors assume he is preaching about a divine couple of whom they have never heard. Socrates, of course, faced the same charge: promoting foreign divinities (Xenophon, *Memorabilia* 1.1.1; Plato, *Apology* 24B).

The philosophers take Paul along to the Areopagus, the council (Aristotle, *Rhetoric* 1.1354A; Lysias, *Oration* 7.22) not the place. This is probable because (a) v. 22 says Paul stands in the midst of the Areopagus; (b) v. 33 says Paul goes out from among them; (c) v. 34 says an Areopagite believes. In Diogenes Laertius, *Lives of Eminent Philosophers*, the Areopagus is regularly the scene for the trial of a philosopher (2.101; 2.116; 7.169; cf. also Lucian, *Double Indictment* 4-12). They then say, "May we learn what this new teaching is that you speak of? For you bring some strange notions to our ears; we should like to know what these things mean" (vv. 19-20). In a culture that values, in matters of religion, the old and the traditional, the charge of newness and strangeness constitutes the ultimate refutation of a religion. Even if a pagan did not like a teaching, if it was old it had its own vindication (e.g., Tacitus, *History* 5.5, expressed his disdain for Jewish rites but had to admit that "Jewish worship is vindicated by its antiquity"). By contrast Suetonius, *Nero* 16.2, speaks of Jesus' followers as "a class . . . given to a new . . . superstition." Of course, Socrates had been charged with teaching new and strange things by the Athenians (Plato, *Euthyphro* 1C; 2B; 3B; *Apology* 24B-C; Diogenes Laertius 2.40; Justin, *1 Apology* 5.4; *2 Apology* 10.5). The Lukan Paul stands before the body responsible for the regulation of religion in Athens, faced with the same type of question Socrates had faced and that had led to his death. By reputation, Athens was severe in its treatment of religious deviation (e.g., Josephus, *Against Apion* 2.38 §§ 262-67). In Paul's case, however, the motivation is portrayed as far different. The Athenians of his time "used their time for nothing else but telling or hearing something new" (v. 21). Curiosity was a part of the Athenian reputation (Demosthenes, *Oration* 4.10; Chariton, *Chareas and Callirhoe* 1.11.6-7). According to Luke, Paul is not on trial but is being used to

satisfy the insatiable curiosity of the court. The Athenian Areopagus are portrayed by Luke as effete intellectuals violating by their own behavior the
very standards they are charged to protect (cf. 16:21; 17:5b–6; 23:3).

(2) The second of the three parts of the mission at Athens, the proclamation, comes in vv. 22–31. The speech has three parts: (a) the introduction
(vv. 22–23); (b) the common core (vv. 24–29); and (c) the Messianist conclusion (vv. 30–31). (a) In the introduction Paul says he will tell the Athenians about the unknown god they worship. "You Athenians, I see that in
every respect you are very religious" (v. 22b). This was their reputation:
(e.g., Sophocles, *Oedipus Tyrannus* 260–Athens is held of states the most
devout; Pausanias 1.17.1–Athenians more than others venerate the gods;
Josephus, *Against Apion* 2.12 § 130–the Athenians are the most religious of
the Greeks; Strabo 10.471–the Athenians welcomed many of the foreign
rites). For example, Paul says, "as I walked around . . . I even discovered an
altar inscribed 'To an Unknown God'" (v. 23a). Pausanias 1.1.1–3 speaks
about altars of gods called "unknown gods" near one of the harbors of
Athens. Diogenes Laertius 1.110 mentions altars in Athens that had no name
on them because the deity was unknown. Philostratus, *Apollonius* 6.3, has
the philosopher say, "It is a much greater form of prudence to speak well of
all the gods, especially in Athens, where altars are set up in honor even of
unknown gods." In fact, there were altars to unknown gods all over the
Mediterranean world (Horst 1989, 1426–56). Jerome, *Commentary on
Titus* 1.12, says, "In actuality, the altar inscription read 'to the unknown,
foreign gods of Asia, Europe, and Africa,' not 'to the unknown god,' as Paul
would have it." To change a plural inscription to the singular for the sake of
argument would not be unusual in antiquity. Philo, *On Sobriety* 150, quotes
Hesiod's *Works* 289–92 in a monotheistic form by changing *theoi* (gods) to
theos (God). Using the altar inscription as his point of departure, Paul says,
"What therefore you unknowingly worship, I proclaim to you" (v. 23b).
This was a conventional technique in an argument: for example, Pseudo-
Heraclitus, *Fourth Epistle,* takes the text of an altar inscription that could
be read in two ways as the point of departure for reflections on true worship. The selection of this inscription may have been facilitated by the fact
that the deity of the Jews was sometimes called an/the unknown god: for
example, Lucan, *Pharsalia* 2.592–93, says, "Judea [is] given over to the
worship of an unknown god"; the *Scriptores Historiae Augustae*,
"Claudius," 2.4, speaks about Moses receiving a revelation from "the
unknown god"; Josephus, *Against Apion* 2.167, says Moses represented
God as one who in His essence is unknown. A Messianist Jew sees an Athenian inscription and takes it as his point of departure for a speech that will
wind up attacking idolatry. Paul claims that, unlike Socrates, he is not teaching anything new or strange. What he proposes to do is not to tell them

about a new deity but to acquaint them with the one already honored but not understood by them. Justin Martyr, *2 Apology* 10.5-6, says Socrates in his teaching urged the Athenians to know the unknown god. Perhaps here is yet another Socratic echo.

(b) The core of the speech comes in vv. 24-29. Any proper understanding must take account of its organization. Verses 24-25 are arranged in a chiastic pattern: ABB'A' (Tannehill, 2.219); vv. 26-29 continue the pattern: A"B". "A" in each case concerns who God is; "B" deals with the implications for worship of who God is. The pattern looks like this:

A—Who God is: creator (v. 24a)
    B—Implication for worship: no temples (v. 24b)
    B'—Implication for worship: no sacrificial cult (v. 25a)
A'—Who God is: giver of life, breath, everything (v. 25b)
A"—Who God is: maker of humans to seek after Him (vv. 26-28)
    B"—Implication for worship: no idols (v. 29)

This attack on temples, idols, and sacrifices reflects the best of pagan philosophy, echoes Hellenistic Judaism, and is generally in continuity with the theology of Luke-Acts.

Verse 24a, "A," states who God is: "the God who made the world and all that is in it, the Lord of heaven and earth." God is creator. The Athenian philosophical audience would have resonated with this claim: for example, Epictetus 4.7.6—"God has made all things in the universe." A Hellenistic Jew would have felt it truly reflected his beliefs: for example, Bel and the Dragon 5—Daniel gives his reason for not worshipping Bel: "Because I do not revere man-made idols, but the living God, who created heaven and earth and has dominion over all flesh." It is also a conviction of the author of Acts (e.g., 4:24; 14:15—"a living God who made the heaven and the earth and the sea and all that is in them").

What is the consequence for worship of God's being creator? Verse 24b, "B," gives the answer: God "does not dwell in sanctuaries made by human hands." This is a rejection of temples and the worship that takes place within them. Many philosophers would feel comfortable with this critique: for example, Seneca (according to Lactantius, *Institutes* 6.25): "Temples are not to be built to Him with stones piled up on high"; Zeno (according to Plutarch, *Moralia* 1034B) taught, "One should not build temples for gods." Some Hellenistic Jews would have affirmed the sentiment: for example, Josephus, *Antiquities* 8.4.3 § 114: God cannot be confined to shrines made by humans. Stephen's speech in 7:48 reflects Luke's use of the same tradition (cf. Talbert 1992b, 87-94).

Verse 25b, "A'," states who God is: "It is He who gives to everyone life and breath and everything." God is the giver in the divine–human relationship.

Contacts with this assertion are found in the philosophic tradition: for example, Seneca, *Epistle* 95.47: "God seeks no servants; He himself serves mankind." Hellenistic Jews would have also heard a compatible concept: for example, Josephus, *Against Apion* 2.23 § 190: "God is self-sufficient and supplies all other beings." The assertion is also at home in Lukan theology: for example, Acts 14:17: "He gave you rains from heaven and fruitful seasons, and filled you with nourishment and gladness for your hearts."

What is the implication for worship of God's being the giver in the relationship with humans? Verse 25a, "B'," gives the answer: "nor is He served by human hands because He needs anything." The philosophic tradition made similar claims: for example, Euripides, *Hercules* 1345–46: "God has need of nothing"; Plutarch, *Moralia* 1052D: God is self-sufficient. Hellenistic Jews held to the same tenet: for example, Josephus, *Antiquities* 8.4.3 § 111: "It is not possible for men to return thanks to God by means of works, for the Deity stands in need of nothing and is above any such recompense"; 2 Macc 14:35; 3 Macc 2:9. Acts 7:41 reflects the same theme. The disobedient Israelites in the wilderness offered sacrifice to the golden calf and reveled in the works of their hands, an act that assumes God's need of something. Because God is the giver in the divine–human relationship, He has no need of sacrifices being offered to meet some divine need.

Verses 26–28, "A"," again focus on who God is: the one who makes humans seek after Him. There are four assertions combined in this picture: (a) God is the maker from one of the whole human race (v. 26a); (b) God has fixed the ordered seasons and zones of the earth so that people might seek Him (v. 26b–27a); (c) God is not far from us (v. 27b–28a); (d) we are God's offspring (v. 28b). The philosophic tradition contains similarities to these assertions. (a) Seneca, *Epistle* 44.1: "all persons, if they are traced back to their origins, are descendants of the gods"; Dio Chrysostom, *Oration* 30.26: It is from the gods that the race of men is sprung. (b) Cicero, *Tusculan Disputations* 1.28.68–69: Seasons and zones are evidence of God's existence. (c) Seneca, *Epistle* 41.1–2: "God is near you, He is with you, He is within you." (d) Clement of Alexandria, *Miscellanies* 1.19, says the quote "For we too are His offspring" comes from the Greek poet Aratus (ca. 310 B.C.). Hellenistic Jews would have felt comfortable with much of what is said here. (a) Josephus, *Antiquities* 1.1.2 § 34; 1.6 §§ 122–53: Adam is created first; from him come all the nations. (b) Wis 7:17–19; *1 Enoch* 2:1–5:3: the structure of the universe is due to God. (c) Josephus, *Antiquities* 8.4.2 § 108: "Thou art present and not far removed." Eusebius, *Preparation for the Gospel* 13.12.3, says Aratus's quote had already been used by the Hellenistic-Jewish author Aristobulus to interpret the biblical creation story. Lukan theology also reflects these assertions: (a) and (d) Luke 3:23–38; (b) Acts 14:17; and (c) Acts 14:17.

What are the implications for worship of this view of God as our maker? Verse 29, "B",," offers the Lukan Paul's answer: "Since therefore we are the offspring of God, we ought not to think that the divinity is like an image fashioned from gold, silver, or stone by human art and imagination." The philosophic tradition shared this perspective: for example, Zeno, according to Clement of Alexandria, *Miscellanies* 5.76, taught that "men shall neither build temples nor make idols"; Dio Chrysostom, *Oration* 12.83, says that the living can only be represented by something that is living. Similar assertions are found in Hellenistic Judaism: for example, Wis 15:16-17: "The Creator is not to be represented by the created"; *Epistle of Jeremiah* 8, 24, 26, 34-40: idols are lifeless. Acts 7:41-43 and 14:15 reflect Luke's hostility to idolatry. Lifeless idols cannot represent a living God.

In each and every statement made so far in the core of his proclamation, the Lukan Paul uses the common Mediterranean philosophic critique of temples, sacrifices, and idols. Thereby he says that the popular religion in Athens does not live up to the insights of the pagan philosophers and poets. In all of this, he has sought the common ground. There is nothing he has said yet that would appear ridiculous to his philosophic audience. Furthermore, there is nothing he has said yet that would violate the conscience of a Hellenistic Jew or a Lukan Messianist.

(c) The ending of Paul's speech before the Areopagus is a Christian conclusion (vv. 30-31). Its structure is simple. There are two points: first, repent now (v. 30), and second, because of who God is: the cosmic judge (v. 31). There is first the call for repentance. "God has overlooked the times of ignorance (of Gentiles—14:16; of Jews—3:17; 13:27; cf. Rom 3:25), but now He demands that all people everywhere repent" (2:38; 3:19; 14:15; Luke 24:47). Second, there comes the basis for the call to repentance: "because He has established a day on which He will judge the world with justice (24:25; cf. Rom 2:5, 16; 1 Thess 5:2, 4) through a man He has appointed (10:42), and He has provided confirmation for all by raising him from the dead" (2:24; 10:40; 13:33). Paul contends that the creator will hold a cosmic trial. The time has been set. The judge has been chosen. The notice has been posted. Repent (1 Thess 1:9-10). The audience would have had minimal trouble with the notion of divine judgement. Two examples suffice. Lucian, *Zeus Catechized*, has a doctrine of rewards and punishments after death based on one's life here and now. Justin, *1 Apology* 20, says, "When we assert that the souls of the wicked living after death will be sensibly punished, and that the souls of the good, freed from punishment, will live happily, we believe the same things as your poets and philosophers." It is only with the statement about the resurrection of Jesus that the Lukan Paul's speech goes beyond the bounds of the familiar for his auditors. In a very real sense, it is the resurrection of Jesus that is distinctive for the Messianists (cf. 23:6; 24:21; 26:6, 8).

(3) The conclusion of the entire mission to Athens comes in vv. 32–34. There is the usual division. On the one hand, "When they heard about the resurrection of the dead, some began to scoff, but others said, 'We should like to hear you on this some other time'" (v. 32). Postponement of a decision until another time is the equivalent of unbelief in Acts (cf. 24:25). Scoffing is a typical response to speeches by fringe figures (cf. the mocking response to the speeches of the Cynic in Lucian, *Peregrinus* 7–8, 34). Given the assumptions of Paul's auditors, scoffing is an entirely appropriate response. Aeschylus, *Eumenides* 647–48, relates how, on the occasion of the inauguration of the court of the Areopagus, the god Apollo says: "When the dust hath drained the blood of man, once he is slain, there is no return to life."

On the other hand, "some did join him, and became believers. Among them were Dionysius, a member of the court of the Areopagus, a woman named Damaris, and others with them" (v. 34). At least one prestigious convert is made, a member of the Areopagus. The Lukan emphasis on the high social standing of converts continues. Female as well as male converts are noted. Messianist Judaism has put down its roots in the intellectual center of the world. (For information about the church in Athens at a later time, see the letter of Dionysius from Corinth to Athens in Eusebius, *Church History* 4.23.2–3.)

Paul in Corinth and Beyond
Acts 18:1–18, 19–23

Acts 18:1–23 is a composite unit whose components can be recognized if the overall structure of the second journey is reviewed.

The commission (16:6–10)
Visits to Philippi (16:11–40), Thessalonica (17:1–9), Beroea (17:10–14),
        Athens (17:15–34), Corinth (18:1–18), and Ephesus (18:19–21a)
To Antioch and Jerusalem (18:21b–22)
Return (18:23)

Acts 18:1–18a is a large thought unit dealing with Paul's visit to Corinth. It begins with Paul's going there (v. 1); it ends with his departure (v. 18a). References to Aquila and Priscilla frame the narrative (vv. 2, 18b), just as references to Lydia frame Paul's visit to Philippi (16:14, 40). It contains two scenes (vv. 1–8 and vv. 9–18), whose components loosely correspond to one another.

SCENE ONE: 18:3-8
Paul's preaching: a contrast scene (vv. 4 and 5)
   The results of Paul's preaching (vv. 6-8)
      1. Jewish resistance in the synagogue (v. 6a)
      2. Pauline responses, nonverbal (v. 6a) and verbal (v. 6b)
      3. Remedy for the situation (v. 7)
      4. Good results (v. 8)

SCENE TWO: 18:9-18
Paul's long-term preaching (v. 11) in response to a vision (v. 9)
   The results of Paul's preaching (vv. 12-18)
      1. Jewish opposition in court (vv. 12-13)
      2. Pauline response is unnecessary (v. 14a)
      3. Remedy for the situation (vv. 14b-17)
      4. Good results (v. 18a)

This pattern is a variant of that used by Luke for Paul's earlier visit to Antioch of Pisidia (13:14-52).

When Paul leaves Athens, he comes to Corinth. The Corinth of Paul's time was not the classical city. That was destroyed by the Romans in 146 B.C. It was rather the Roman colony founded by Julius Caesar in 46 B.C., which eventually became the capital of the Roman province of Achaia in 27 B.C. Its geographical location resulted in its great wealth. Ships could avoid the dangerous trip around the southern tip of Greece by using either the port of Cenchreae on the Aegean side or that of Lechaeum on the Adriatic side. The contents of these vessels could then be transferred from one side to the other. Of course, duties were collected from such transfers, enriching the city. The site also resulted in a diverse population of almost every imaginable stripe (Cf. Talbert 1987, xvi-xviii).

In Corinth Paul meets a couple, Aquila and Priscilla (Rom 16:3; 1 Cor 16:19; 2 Tim 4:19), Jewish Christians who have recently come from Italy because Claudius had ordered all the Jews out of Rome (v. 2). Such expulsions had a history. In 139 B.C. Jews were expelled from Rome for attempting "to infect the Roman manners with the worship of Jupiter Sabazius" (Valerius Maximus 1.3.3). In A.D. 19, during Tiberius's reign, thousands of Jews were expelled from Rome because of a moral scandal involving four Jews' exploitation of a Roman lady named Fulvia (Josephus, *Antiquities* 18.3.5 §§ 81-84; Tacitus, *Annals* 2.85.4; Suetonius, *Tiberius* 36). The expulsion mentioned in Acts 18:2 during the reign of Claudius is likely that referred to by Suetonius, *Claudius* 25.4: "Since the Jews were continually making disturbances at the instigation of Chrestus, he [Claudius] expelled them from Rome." Many scholars think that Chrestus is a garbled spelling of Christus and that the disturbances referred to are the result of conflicts in the synagogues between Messianists and non-Messianists. Orosius 7.6.15-16 dates the event to about A.D. 49 (Claudius's ninth year). This event is separate from that in A.D. 41 when Claudius both confirmed the rights of Jews to live in their traditional way and warned them not to engage in a massive campaign of proselytism (Dio Cassius 60.6.6) (Tajra 1989, 53).

Because Aquila and Priscilla practice the same trade as Paul, he stays with them and works at tentmaking (v. 3). The early tradition depicted Paul as one who worked with his hands (1 Thess 2:9; 2 Thess 3:6-8; 1 Cor 4:12; 9:6). Luke follows suit (20:34-35—"You know well that these very hands have served my needs and my companions. In every way I have shown you that by hard work we must help the weak"). Such behavior reflects a rabbinic ideal (e.g., *m. Aboth* 2:2—"Excellent is the study of the Law together with worldly occupation"; *Abot de Rabbi Nathan* 11), as well as that of certain Cynic philosophers (Diogenes Laertius 7.168; Epictetus 3.26.23).

Verses 4-8 is the first of two similar scenes depicting the Pauline mission in Corinth. It falls into two parts: (a) Paul's preaching (vv. 4-5) and (b) the results of that preaching (vv. 6-8). (a) Paul's preaching is described in two stages. In the first (v. 4), his overt attempts at evangelization of the synagogue are limited to the sabbath. "Every sabbath, he entered into discussions in the synagogue, attempting to convince both Jews and Greeks" (Gentile God-fearers). This limitation is owing to the fact that he must work every other day of the week. It is difficult to imagine that Paul would have forgone any opportunity to bear witness to Jesus even while he worked at his trade (cf. Cynic epistles, Socratics 13, Aristippus to Simon—"I admire you because although you are a shoemaker, your wisdom attracts noteworthy people like Socrates, noble youths, men of public affairs, and even Pericles to sit with you"). In the second stage (v. 5), "when Silas and Timothy came down from Macedonia (presumably with financial aid—cf. 2 Cor 11:8-9), Paul began to devote himself totally to preaching the word." Because of financial assistance from Macedonia, he is able to do nothing but evangelize the Jews. His message is, "The Messiah is Jesus."

The results of Paul's preaching come in several stages in vv. 6-8. First, there is opposition from the synagogue establishment. They oppose and revile him (v. 6a). Second, Paul makes two responses, one verbal and the other nonverbal (v. 6b-c). He shakes out his garments (i.e., breaks off fellowship—Neh 5:13; Luke 10:11; Acts 13:51). He says, "Your blood be on your heads (2 Sam 1:16; Ezek 33:4; Matt 27:25; Acts 20:26). I am clear of responsibility. From now on I will go to the Gentiles" (13:46; 28:28). Paul's first responsibility is to testify to Israel (13:46). That having been done and its having been rejected, in this place he now turns to Gentiles. In so doing, he is guiltless. Third, the remedy proposed for Paul's mission, given the synagogue's rejection of his message, is transference of the location of his preaching from the synagogue to a house next door belonging to a God-fearer named Titius Justus, who is now a Messianist (v. 7; cf. 19:8-9). This does not mean that Jews will no longer be converted (see v. 8) any more than it means that in the future in other cities he will not go to the synagogue first (see v. 19). Paul means here that he is now moving his site of preaching in this city from the synagogue to a Gentile house. This gives the appearance that Messianists are separate from Judaism, an inference that Acts will seek to deny later on (21:20-25; 22:1; 23:6; 24:14-17; 25:8; 26:5; 28:17, 22). Fourth, the results of Paul's separation from the synagogue are good. "Crispus (1 Cor 1:14–one of the few baptized by Paul himself), the synagogue official, came to believe in the Lord along with his entire household, and many of the Corinthians who heard believed and were baptized" (v. 8). Resistance from the synagogue establishment cannot stop the progress of the gospel. Even the leader of the opposition is converted.

Verses 9-18a constitute the second scene depicting the Pauline mission in Corinth. It too focuses on Paul's preaching and its results. A significant difference between the two scenes is that the second involves a prophecy-fulfillment schema: (1) the prophecy is in two parts (vv. 9-10)–(a) "speak and do not be silent" (v. 9) and (b) "no one shall attack you to harm you" (v. 10); and (2) the fulfillment is in two parts–(a) "And he stayed a year and six months, teaching the word of God" (v. 11), and (b) the Gallio episode, which shows no one will harm Paul (vv. 12-17). Literarily, this prophecy-fulfillment schema functions to set the stage for what follows. At the end of Acts the narrative flow is controlled even more than before by the prophecy-fulfillment pattern (21:11; 23:11; 27:24). The occurrence of so obvious an instance of fulfillment here following closely on the heels of the prophecy alerts the auditors to what will follow and gives them confidence that what is prophesied later will also have its fulfillment. This is akin to Luke 22:10-12 (prophecy) and 22:13 (fulfillment) which both prepare for Jesus' prophecies to follow and instill confidence in their ultimate fulfillment (Luke 22:14-38; 22:69; 23:29-31; 23:43; 24:49; Acts 1:8). This schema needs to be kept in mind as the various components of scene two are investigated.

Scene two falls into two parts: (a) Paul's preaching (vv. 9-11) and (b) the results of that preaching (vv. 12-18). (a) Paul's preaching is set forth as part of a commissioning story with five parts (Hubbard, 1977; 1978):

Introduction (v. 9b): One night in a vision
Confrontation (v. 9a): The Lord (= Jesus) said to Paul
Commission (v. 9c): Do not be afraid, but speak
Reassurance (v. 10): No one will harm you
Conclusion (v. 11): He stayed 18 months, teaching.

Such a dream of promise is typical of Mediterranean visions. For example, an inscription from Delos, carved about 200 B.C., tells of the growth of the cult of Serapis on the island.

> But when certain people opposed us and the god, and brought a public suit against the temple and me, claiming punishment or damages, the god announced to me in a dream that we would win. When the contest was finished and we won in a manner worthy of the god, we praised the gods by returning proper thanks. (Grant, 38–39)

Reassured by the divine promise (Jer 1:5–8, 19), Paul is obedient to his commission. He settles in Corinth for a year and a half and teaches the word of God among them (v. 11).

The results of Paul's preaching in the second scene come in vv. 12–18. The same four points that were made in the first scene reappear. First, Paul meets Jewish opposition when Gallio is proconsul of Achaia (v. 12). Gallio was born in Cordova, Spain, the son of a Spanish orator. When his father moved the sons to Rome, Gallio was adopted by a wealthy benefactor whose name he took. His younger brother, Seneca, was a famous Stoic philosopher and the tutor of the emperor Nero. It was Seneca who was influential in getting Gallio the post as proconsul of Achaia. An inscription in the museum at Delphi mentions Gallio as proconsul during Claudius's reign, probably A.D. 51 or 52. The nine fragments, taken together, deal with the depopulation of Delphi. One translation runs as follows:

> Tiberius Claudius Caesar Augustus Germanicus, 12th year of tribunician power, acclaimed emperor for the 26th time, father of the country, sends greetings to_____. For long have I been well-disposed to the city of Delphi and solicitous for its prosperity, and I have always observed the cult of the Pythian Apollo. Now since it is said to be destitute of citizens, *as my friend and proconsul L. Iunius Gallio recently reported to me*, and desiring that Delphi should regain its former splendor, I command you to invite well-born people also from other cities to come to Delphi as new inhabitants, and to accord them and their children all the privileges of the Delphians as being citizens on like and equal terms. . . . (Murphy-O'Connor 1983, 141–42; Greek text and discussion of it, 173–76)

Gallio served in this post only briefly. "When in Achaia, he (Gallio) began to feel feverish, he immediately took ship, claiming that it was not a malady of the body but of the place" (Seneca, *Epistle* 104.1). Gallio's brief rule, which may have been as brief as a summer or as long as nearly one year, coincided with Paul's presence in Corinth (Murphy-O'Connor 1993, 315–17).

During Gallio's brief tenure, the synagogue establishment brings Paul to the tribunal (*bēma*, the raised platform that served as the proconsul's judgment seat and from which justice could be decided; cf. 25:6). The charge against Paul is "This man is inducing people to worship God contrary to the Law" (v. 13). How should the term "law" be taken: as Roman law or Jewish law? If the former, then the issue would be a criminal one; if the latter, it would not be criminal.

Second, a Pauline response is unnecessary. "When Paul was about to reply, Gallio spoke to the Jews" (v. 14a). Third, the remedy for the situation is given in vv. 14b–17. Gallio takes law to mean Jewish law and so views the dispute as one between two Jewish parties, which is exactly how Luke sees it (23:1–10; 24:1–21; 26:2–23; Luke 23). The proconsul says, "If it were a matter of some crime or malicious fraud, I should with reason hear the complaint of you Jews; but since it is a question of arguments over doctrine and titles and your own law, see to it yourselves. I do not wish to be a judge of such matters" (vv. 14–15). The Roman proconsul states that he is not competent to serve as judge in theological disputes within Judaism. Thereupon he drives them away from the tribunal (v. 16). Then the narrative reads, "They all seized Sosthenes, the synagogue official, and beat him in full view of the tribunal" (v. 17a). The Western text makes the probable meaning even more explicit: "All of the Greeks seized Sosthenes and beat him." This is an expression of pagan anti-Semitism. It was not an isolated incident in antiquity: for example, Josephus, *Antiquities* 16.2.4 §§ 58–60—Ionians use violence against Jews; *Antiquities* 19.5.2 §§ 284–85—Alexandrians use violence against Jews. "But none of this was of concern to Gallio" (v. 17b). The Roman ruler in Corinth ignores mob violence against the Jews after having prevented their violence against Paul.

Why the anti-Jewish sentiment displayed by both people and ruler here? Lukan pagans manifest a general hostility to Jews (e.g., 16:20–"These people are Jews"; 19:34–"when they recognized that he was a Jew, they all shouted in unison for about two hours, 'Great is Artemis of the Ephesians'"). The Lukan portrait stands in continuity with the views expressed widely in the culture (e.g., Diodorus Siculus 34–35.1.1–Jews look upon all people as their enemies; Josephus, *Against Apion* 2.68 § 121–Apion says Jews show no good will to Greeks; Tacitus, *Histories* 5.4.1–Jews regard as profane all that we hold sacred; Philostratus, *Apollonius* 5.33–Jews have long been in revolt against humanity in general). There may also be the additional fact that Claudius has only recently expelled disorderly Jews from Rome. The climate created by recent events reinforces a general antipathy toward Jews among the pagan people and proconsul in Corinth. Philo, *Flaccus* 4 § 24, regarded the refusal of Flaccus to listen to the Jews a subtle, and therefore particularly insidious, form of hostility. That is the case in Acts 18.

Fourth, there are good results stemming from the aborted session before the tribunal: "Paul remained for quite some time" (v. 18a). He is not run out of town as in 17:10, 14. Indeed, the promise that the risen Lord made to him in 18:10 has been fulfilled in Paul's vindication by Gallio. He is unharmed. The state has once again given protection against hatred of Christians.

One tactic taken by Hellenistic-Jewish apologists when faced with the hostility of the pagan populace was to contrast the favorable stance of rulers toward Jews with the hostility of citizens toward them (e.g., Josephus, *Against Apion* 2.4 §§ 33–47). Acts uses this very apologetic device in chap. 18's visit to Corinth as a protection against the hostility of the synagogue establishment. Gallio, the ruler, is favorable toward Messianists even if establishment Jews are not.

If Acts 18:1–18a constitutes the Pauline visit to Corinth, 18:18b–21 gives a brief summary of an initial visit to Ephesus. After saying his farewells to the Corinthian church, Paul sails with Priscilla and Aquila. Luke's inversion of the names of the couple (cf. 18:2—Aquila and Priscilla) so that Priscilla comes first is as significant as his earlier inversion of the names of Barnabas and Saul (13:2, 7) to Paul and his company (13:13) or Paul and Barnabas (13:43, 46, 50). To put one's name first seems to be the evangelist's way of indicating who has the leadership role. If so, then this detail fits into the general Lukan emphasis on women and their ministries (Luke 8:1–3; 10:38–42; 23:49, 55–56; 24:1–11, 22–23; Acts 1:14; 9:36–43; 12:12–17; 16:14–15; 17:4, 12, 34, etc.). Since they are heading for Ephesus, they depart from the port of Cenchreae (cf. Rom 16:1—Phoebe, a deaconess of Cenchreae). There Paul has his hair cut because he has taken a vow. Here again, the Pauline observance of Jewish custom is noted (16:3), giving the lie to the charges of his opponents (21:21). Upon arrival in Ephesus, Paul follows his usual custom. He goes to the synagogue to discuss with the Jews there. "Although they asked him to stay for a longer time, he did not consent, but as he bade farewell he promised, 'I shall come back to you again, God willing'" (cf. James 4:15; 1 Cor 4:19) (vv. 20–21a). This legitimates the return visit to Ephesus (19:1–20:1). It says that this part of the missionary outreach, like every other part, is according to the divine plan (8:26; 11:17; 13:2; 15:14–18; 16:6–10).

After visits to Corinth (told as a specific situation) and Ephesus (given as a brief summary), Paul sails from Ephesus (v. 21b). "Upon landing at Caesarea, he went up (Luke 2:4, 42; 18:31; 19:28; Acts 11:2; 15:2) and greeted the church (Jerusalem) and then went down to Antioch (of Syria)" (18:22). At the end of his missionary journeys, Paul reports to Jerusalem (15:1–29; 18:22), just as Peter had done (11:1–18). Among the laws of agency is one which says that the agent must report back (*Mekilta Exodus* 12:1; *p. Hagigah* 76d). There is a certain unity to the Messianist movement, with Jerusalem as the visible symbol of that unity. This the Lukan Paul respects.

Acts 18:23 introduces the return part of the second missionary journey, the full picture of which begins in 18:24–20:1. As in the first journey of Paul, after the outreach is finished and the missionaries report to Jerusalem, there is an expressed desire to return to strengthen the disciples touched by the initial outreach. So "after staying there (Antioch) some time, he left and traveled in orderly sequence through the Galatian country and Phrygia, bringing strength to all the disciples." Once again, the emphasis is on the need to nurture converts (14:21–23; 15:36, 41; 16:40).

In Ephesus
Acts 18:24–20:1

Acts 18:24–20:1 is a large thought unit held together by its geographical focus: Ephesus (Apollos arrives in Ephesus—18:24; Paul leaves Ephesus—20:1). It has dual functions within the Lukan plot. (1) It is the fulfillment of Paul's promise made in 18:21 ("I shall come back to you again, God willing"). This means, in Luke's scheme of things, that Paul's ministry in Ephesus, narrated in Acts 19, is according to God's will. (2) It constitutes the main part of the "return" section of the second missionary journey. Paul's two missionary journeys in Acts (13:1–16:5 and 16:6–20:3a) are constructed according to a common pattern:

(a) commission (13:1–3 and 16:6–10);
(b) outreach (13:4–14:26 and 16:11–18:18a);
(c) to Antioch and Jerusalem (14:26–28; 15:1–35 and 18:18b–22); and
(d) return (15:36–41; 16:1–5 and 18:23; 18:24–19:41; 20:1–3a).

Acts 18:24–20:1 functions as (d) in the pattern. The unit has two foci: (1) 18:24–19:20, dealing with the correction of eccentric forms of religion, and (2) 19:21–20:1, focusing on the encounter with popular paganism. Each must be examined in turn.

Scene one, Acts 18:24–19:20, gives attention to how to deal with eccentric forms of religion. There are four paragraphs: (1) 18:24–28; (2) 19:1–7; (3) 19:8–10; (4) 19:11–19. In the first two, the need is for something to be added; in the last two, the need is for something to be removed.

(1) Acts 18:24–19:1a deals with the matter of a doctrinal deficiency's being remedied by accurate knowledge. The paragraph is held together by an inclusion (18:24c—well versed in the scriptures; 18:28b—showing by the scriptures). Its organization is in terms of two patterns: ABCB'A' and ABB'A'.

A—Apollos came to Ephesus (*eis Epheson*) (18:24a)
  B—He had been instructed in the Way of the Lord; he taught accurately (*akribōs*), though he knew only the baptism of John (18:24b-25)
    C—He spoke boldly in the synagogue (18:26a)
  B'—Priscilla and Aquila expounded to him the Way of God more accurately (*akribesteron*) (18:26b)
A'—When Apollos wished to go to Achaia (*eis tēn Achaian*), the Ephesian disciples supported him (18:27a)
A—When he arrived in Achaia (18:27b)
  B—He helped the church (18:27c)
  B'—For he refuted the Jews (18:28)
A'—While Apollos was at Corinth (19:1a)

An itinerant preacher from Alexandria, Apollos, arrives in Ephesus speaking accurately about Jesus though he knows only the baptism of John. At most, Apollos knew of Jesus' life before Jerusalem; at least, he knew only the teaching of John the Baptist. "The Way of the Lord" (18:25) echoes Luke 1:76; 3:4; 7:27 (repentance). "The things concerning Jesus" echoes Luke 3:15-17 (Jesus as the coming messianic judge). "The baptism of John" echoes Luke 3:3 (baptism of repentance for the forgiveness of sins). If so, then Apollos is not fully a Messianist when he comes to Ephesus. His mission, like that of the Baptist, is preparatory (Pereika, 59).

When Priscilla and Aquila hear Apollos teach in the synagogue, they take him aside and explain to him "the Way of God more accurately" (18:26). This is a truth encounter leading to a correct understanding. Apollos's deficiency has been remedied by instruction in the Pauline tradition. Although the *Textus Receptus* lists Aquila first, the best manuscript tradition gives Priscilla first. In Lukan practice, whichever of a pair is listed first is regarded as the dominant authority (cf. 11:30; 12:25; 13:2; 13:7; 13:13!; 13:50!). Here, then, not only is a male preacher instructed by a woman but the wife is regarded by the narrator as the dominant religious authority. This shows that in the post-Pauline period, the statement in 1 Tim 2:12 ("I permit no woman to teach or to have authority over men") was not regarded as the guideline for all circumstances.

When the fully instructed Apollos wants to go to Achaia, the Ephesian disciples give him a letter of recommendation (cf. 2 Cor 3:1-3). There was a church in Ephesus before Paul's arrival in 19:1. It doubtless goes back to 18:19-21 and the continuing presence of Priscilla and Aquila in Ephesus. Acts gives hints on a number of occasions about pre-Pauline churches (Antioch—11:20-26; Corinth—18:1-4; Rome—18:2 and 28:15; Puteoli—28:13-14). Apollos is not only a teacher now instructed in the Pauline tradition, he is also one endorsed by a Pauline church. His work in Achaia is effective (1 Cor 1:12; 3:4, 5-6, 22; 4:6; 16:12). "He vigorously refuted the Jews in public, establishing from the scriptures that the Messiah is Jesus" (18:28; i.e., the Pauline gospel, 17:3).

(2) Acts 19:1-7 deals with the matter of an experiential deficiency's being remedied by full participation in the life of the Spirit. The paragraph falls into an ABCC'B'A' pattern (Nelson, 18).

A—Some disciples (v. 1)
  B—Holy Spirit not yet received (v. 2)
    C—John pointed to Jesus (vv. 3-4)
    C'—Recipients of John's baptism are baptized in the name of Jesus
      (v. 5)
  B'—Holy Spirit came on them (v. 6)
  A'—There were about twelve disciples (v. 7)

When Paul returns to Ephesus he finds some disciples who have never even heard of the Holy Spirit (vv. 1-2). They had been baptized only "with the baptism of John" (v. 3; cf. Luke 3:3), that is, they are disciples of John the Baptist (Luke 5:33; 7:18-19; 11:1). Paul then instructs them: "John baptized with a baptism of repentance, telling the people to believe in the one who was to come after him, that is, in Jesus" (v. 4). When they hear this, the disciples of the Baptist are baptized in the name of Jesus (v. 5). A correct understanding leads to a correct transfer of allegiance. "When Paul laid [his] hands on them, the Holy Spirit came upon them, and they spoke in tongues and prophesied" (v. 6). Those who belong to Jesus receive the Holy Spirit given by Jesus (2:33). In 19:6 the Holy Spirit is not tied to baptism but is linked with the postbaptismal laying on of hands. Here Paul exercises the same function that Peter and John did in 8:14-17. This indicates that for Luke the experience of the Spirit cannot be confined to sacramental impartation (cf. Luke 3:21-22; Acts 10:44; 11:15). The Spirit, who is free, confirms the shift of allegiance. That there are twelve of these disciples is probably symbolic. Those whose preparatory work was on behalf of the twelve tribes now transfer their allegiance to Jesus. With full participation in Messianist experience, their deficiency is remedied.

(3) In Acts 19:8-10 a communal deficiency is remedied by separation from an unbelieving synagogue. This paragraph is a stylized summary.

(a) Paul goes into the synagogue (v. 8; cf. 18:4-5; 13:14-41)
(b) He meets resistance from the synagogue establishment (v. 9a; cf. 18:6a; 13:45)
(c) Paul withdraws to a nonsynagogue setting (v. 9b; cf. 18:6b-7; 13:46-47)
(d) Successes follow the separation (v. 10; cf. 18:8; 13:48-49)

As usual Paul begins in the synagogue. After three months "some in their obstinacy and disbelief disparaged the Way before the assembly" (v. 9). When this happens, Paul takes the Messianists with him and begins to hold "daily discussions" in the lecture hall of Tyrannus (cf. 18:7). In this he reflects the practice of some philosophers: for example, Dio Chrysostom 32.10 speaks about philosophers who "exercise their voices in what we call lecture halls." He continues for two years with the result that "all the inhabitants of the province of Asia heard the word of God, Jews and Greeks alike" (v. 10). Institutional separation does not imply cessation of a mission to non-Messianist Jews. That continues. The deficiency of having only a hostile environment in which to teach is remedied by institutional separation.

(4) Acts 19:11–19 deals with a behavioral deficiency that is remedied by separation from magical practices. This section has two parts: (a) a summary of healings associated with Paul (vv. 11–12), and (b) a parody of a miracle story (vv. 13–19).

(a) "So extraordinary were the mighty deeds God accomplished (4:30) at the hands of Paul that when face cloths or aprons that touched his skin were applied to the sick, their diseases left them and the evil spirits came out of them" (vv. 11–12). This is similar to a statement made about Peter in Acts 5:15 and about Jesus in Luke 6:19 and 8:43–48. The miraculous power to heal is, as in the case of Peter and Jesus, linked in some way to Paul's body and clothing. Since this has, on first glance in antiquity as well as in modern times, a magical cast to it, it is followed by a story about Jewish magicians (vv. 13–19).

(b) This parody of a miracle story has the usual three components of such accounts: the problem (v. 13a), the cure (vv. 13b–16), and the reactions (vv. 17–19, 20). First, the problem is that some itinerant Jewish exorcists try to perform their work by invoking the name of Jesus (v. 13a). The existence of Jewish exorcists is well known from antiquity (e.g., Matt 12:27//Luke 11:19; Josephus, *Antiquities* 8.2.5 §§ 45–49; a Jewish magical text, quoted by A. Deissmann, *Light from the Ancient East*, 259–63, reads, "for those possessed by demons"; Justin, *Dialogue* 85.3; 80.9–10; Irenaeus, *Against Heresies* 2.6.2; Origen, *Against Celsus* 4.33). The use of names in healing is also widespread (e.g., Josephus, *Antiquities* 8.2.5 § 47; Justin, *Dialogue* 85.3; *2 Apology* 6.6; Irenaeus, *Against Heresies* 2.6.2; 2.32.4; Origen, *Against Celsus* 1.6; 3.24; Lucian, *Lover of Lies* 9). The practice of exorcists from one tradition using the authoritative names from another is known in antiquity. Origen, *Against Celsus* 1.22, mentions pagan exorcists who appropriate the names of Solomon and even Jesus Christ in their formulas. Pseudo-Cyprian, *On Rebaptism* 7, refers to people outside the church who are able to drive out demons using the name of Christ.

Second, there is the exorcism in reverse (vv. 13b–16). The Jewish exorcists say to an evil spirit, "I adjure you by the Jesus whom Paul preaches." The spirit replies, "Jesus I recognize, Paul I know, but who are you?" Whereupon the person with the evil spirit leaps upon them, so that they flee naked and wounded from the house. Since a magician has no personal relationship with the power involved but simply uses it for his own purposes, these exorcists who are not disciples of Jesus attempt to use the name of Jesus, with whom Paul has the relationship. The Lukan point is that the spiritual power manifest through Jesus' disciples like Paul is not appropriated or dispensed as a commodity (see 8:18-24) but is the result of a personal relationship with the risen Lord.

Third, the mishap with the demon produces a number of reactions (vv. 17-20). When the exorcists' fate becomes known to all the Jews and Greeks who live in Ephesus, "fear fell upon them all, and the name of the Lord Jesus was held in great esteem" (v. 17). Some believers come forward, openly acknowledging their former practices. A large number of those who formerly practiced magic gather their books and burn them in public. This is a significant act because the value of the books is fifty thousand silver pieces (vv. 18-19). The use of incantations and magical formulas was so prevalent in Ephesus that books or rolls of such formulas were referred as *Ephesia grammata* (e.g., Plutarch, *Table Talk* 7.5, refers to *Ephesia grammata* as a magical formula against demons; Clement of Alexandria, *Miscellanies* 5.8, quotes Androcydes the Pythagorean: "the far-famed so-called Ephesian letters").

Book burning in antiquity was not uncommon (Pease, 145-60). On the one hand, most of it was politically motivated; most of it was forced: for example, Jewish–Jer 36:1-32; Josephus, *Antiquities* 10.6.2 § 95, Jeremiah's roll is burned by the king; 1 Macc 1:56, Antiochus Epiphanes has the books of the law burned; Greek–Diogenes Laertius 9.52, Protagoras is condemned to exile and his books are burned in the Agora; Roman–Livy 39.16.8, magistrates seek out and burn books of seditious prophecies; Suetonius, *Augustus* 31.1; Dio Cassius 56.27.1, Augustus orders slanderous pamphlets searched for and burned in Rome and elsewhere; Augustine, *On Baptism* 5.1, in the persecution under Diocletian, gospels, Bibles, and other sacred writings are burned; Christian–Socrates, *Church History* 1.8, Constantine has the books of Arius burned; *Code of Justinian* 1.1.3, in the fifth century the anti-Christian writings of Porphyry are burned. On the other hand, some of the book burning was an expression of a renunciation of an old life. Two examples suffice. Diogenes Laertius 6.95 relates that Metrocles, after his conversion from the Peripatetic to the Cynic school, burned his notes of the lectures of Theophrastus. The *Life of Barlaam and Ioasaph* 32.302 describes how the converted magician, Theudas, burned his books on magic. The book burning in Acts 19 is akin to these last two examples. It is voluntary; it is an expression of repentance, symbolizing one's leaving the old life behind. The aborted exorcism produces a renunciation of magic by Jesus' disciples.

This is a power encounter. It is necessary because believers continue to seek spiritual power from sources other than Jesus. They have not yet given up their pre-Messianist allegiances in the area of spiritual power. They practice a bifurcated religion characterized by dual allegiance and a syncretistic understanding of truth. Luke's renunciation of magic (8:19-24; 13:6-12; 19:13-19) is part of a trajectory continuing into the ancient church: for example, Ignatius of Antioch, *Ephesians* 19:3, says that with Christ's birth all magic is abolished; *Didache* 2:2 says, "you shall not practice magic; you shall not use enchantments"; *Barnabas* 20:1 says that the way of darkness and death includes enchantment and magic; Tertullian, *On Idolatry* 9, says that in the Gospel one will find enchanters, diviners, and magicians nowhere mentioned except as punished; Justin, *1 Apology* 14, states the church's posture: "we who formerly used magical arts, dedicate ourselves to the good and unbegotten God." The fourth form of eccentric religion is now dealt with. The evangelist sums up the situation after the four forms of deficient religion have been corrected: "Thus did the word of the Lord continue to spread with influence and power" (v. 20; cf. 2:47; 6:7; 9:31; 12:24; 16:5).

Scene two, Acts 19:23-20:1, focuses on an encounter with popular paganism. Before the riot scene, 19:21-22 has Paul resolving "in the Spirit" to travel through Macedonia (cf. 20:1b-2a) and Achaia (20:2b-3), and then to go on to Jerusalem (20:16; cf. Luke 9:51). His sights are already set far beyond Jerusalem, however: "After I have been there, I must visit Rome also." Like Jesus in Luke 9:52, Paul then sends two of his assistants on before him: Timothy and Erastus (Rom 16:23; 2 Tim 4:20) go to Macedonia while Paul stays in Ephesus. This brief notice functions as the introduction to 20:1-21:17. Its location in the previous thought unit reflects the chain-link principle of organization: units should not lie side by side but should overlap like a chain (Lucian, *How to Write History* 55). Together with 20:1-3, 19:21-22 serves as a bracket around the riot scene. It guarantees that Paul's leaving Ephesus is not because of the riot but because of the Spirit (19:21).

Acts 19:23-20:1 is the riot scene (cf. Acts 21 for another riot scene, in Jerusalem). Paul, the preacher of monotheism (19:26; see 14:15-17; 17:16, 29; 1 Thess 1:9-10), evokes mob action from the devotees of Artemis of the Ephesians (cf. *Acts of John* 37, 39, 42, 43, 46—a story of the apostle John's power encounter with the goddess Artemis and the temple of the goddess). The section falls into three parts: (1) the cause of the riot (vv. 23-27); (2) the riot (vv. 28-34); and (3) the official response to the riot (vv. 35-41). Each component needs attention.

(1) A silversmith named Demetrius, who makes miniature silver shrines of Artemis, providing considerable work for the craftsmen, calls a meeting of these and other workers in related crafts and says in effect, Jesus' disciples are dangerous. The reasons are two. First, there is the economic argument. "Men, you know well that our prosperity derives from this work" (v. 25). "The danger grows . . . that our business will be discredited" (v. 27a). Second, there is the religious argument. "This Paul has persuaded and misled a great number of people by saying that gods made by hands are not gods at all" (v. 26; cf. 17:29; 14:15; Justin, *1 Apology* 9; Minucius Felix, *Octavius* 8; Arnobius, *Against the Heathen* 39). "The danger grows . . . that she whom the whole province of Asia and all the world worship will be stripped of her magnificence" (v. 27b).

The temple of Artemis was the foremost of the Ionian temples of that time (Pausanias 7.5.4), one of the seven wonders of the world. The epigrammist Antipater says,

> I have set eyes on the wall of lofty Babylon on which is a road for chariots, and the statue of Zeus by Alpheus, and the hanging gardens, and the colossus of the sun, and the huge labor of the high pyramids, and the vast tomb of Mausolus; but when I saw the house of Artemis that mounted to the clouds, those other marvels lost their brilliancy, and I said, "Lo, apart from Olympus, the sun never looked on aught so grand." (*Greek Anthology* 9.58)

The temple was a central pillar in the banking structures of Asia (Dio Chrysostom 31.54), as well as an asylum offering protection and relief to debtors and the helpless (Pausanias 7.2.7; Achilles Tatius, *Leucippe and Clitophon* 7.13). The goddess and her devotees had worldwide aspirations for the cult (Pausanias 4.31.8; Strabo 4.1.4-8; 3.4.6; Xenophon, *Anabasis* 5.3.4-13) (Oster, 24-44; Horsley, 105-68).

Luke portrays the trouble as due to the threat that Pauline monotheism posed for the business interests tied to the pagan cult (echoing a similar situations in Acts 16:19 and Luke 8:37). Demetrius appeals to both economic and religious reasons for his opposition to Paul and his party. Wisdom 14:18 gives a Hellenistic-Jewish estimation of such pagan religion, an opinion with which Luke agrees: it is the "ambition of the craftsman" that fosters idol worship.

Demetrius has every reason to be nervous. Pliny's letter to Trajan (10.96) says that the large number of conversions to Christ in Bithynia in the early second century A.D. had left the sellers of sacrificial animals for pagan temples bankrupt. Only a rare individual could be found buying sacrificial meat or frequenting the temples while Christianity was growing. But after Pliny's attention to the Christian problem, "the temples, which had been almost deserted, begin now to be frequented; and the sacred festivals, after a long intermission, are again revived; while there is a general demand for

sacrificial animals, which for some time past have met with few purchases."
The *Martyrdom of Polycarp* 12.2 gives as a charge against Polycarp, "This
is the teacher of Asia, the father of the Christians, and the overthrower of
our gods, he who has been teaching many not to sacrifice, or to worship the
gods." Tertullian, *Apology* 42, says, "Every day, you complain, the temple
receipts are dwindling away. How few people nowadays put in their contributions"; Tertullian, *On Idolatry* 5.1, indicates that artisans who manu-
facture idols, when converted to Christ, are forced to find a new trade.
Pagan greed (16:19; 19:25, 27) like Jewish zeal (13:45; 17:5) is a match to
ignite the fires of mob action.

(2) Verses 28-34 describe the riot (cf. Achilles Tatius, *Leucippe and Clitophon* 7.7-12, for an Ephesian trial that becomes unruly). The paragraph
is held together by the refrain, "Great is Artemis of the Ephesians" (vv. 28
and 34; an expression known to Xenophon, *Ephesians* 1.11.5). The combination of greed and piety produces social chaos. The people rush into the
theater, seizing Gaius and Aristarchus, Paul's traveling companions. Paul
wants to go before the crowd but the Asiarchs (government officials), who
are friends of his, will not permit it. "Meanwhile, some were shouting one
thing, others something else; the assembly was in chaos, and most of the
people had no idea why they had come together" (v. 32).

Alexander, a Jew, tries to speak to the crowd; but when he is recognized
as Jewish, the crowd "all shouted in unison, for about two hours, 'Great is
Artemis of the Ephesians'" (v. 34; for Judaism in Ephesus, see Josephus,
Antiquities 14.10.12 § 225; 14.10.16 § 234; 14.10. 18-19 §§ 237-40;
14.10.25 §§ 262-64). Pagan anti-Semitism again rears its head (16:20; 18:17;
for pagan hostility to Jews in Asia, cf. Josephus, *Antiquities* 16.2.3-4
§§ 27-65). The refusal to allow a Jewish spokesman to speak was regarded
by Philo as a particularly insidious form of hostility in Mediterranean cities
(Philo, *Flaccus* 4 § 24). The description of the mob is similar to what Dio
Chrysostom says he had experienced in such cities. In *Oration* 48.3, he says
sarcastically to the assembly that when they meet again "then . . . you will
have the opportunity not only to speak but also to shout others down." In
Oration 7.25, he tells of an occasion in a theater in Euboea when the crowd
"kept up a shouting . . . with vehemence and in wrath . . . [that] I . . . was
once almost knocked over by the shouting, as though a tidal wave or thun-
derstorm had suddenly broken over me."

(3) The official response to the riot comes in vv. 35-41. The town clerk
(one of the top officials) makes four points. First, the reputation of Artemis
is unassailable. "Since these things are undeniable, you must calm yourselves and not do anything rash" (v. 36; similar advice is given by a government official in Heliodorus, *An Ethiopian Story* 4.20.1-3).

Second, the Messianists are not guilty of criminal acts like temple robbing

or desecration of the deity (v. 37). This is a major assertion by the city official. It reflects the ideal verbalized by Josephus for Hellenistic Jews: for
example, "Our legislation has expressly forbidden us to deride or blaspheme the gods recognized by others, out of respect for the word 'God'"
(*Against Apion* 2.34 § 237); "Let none blaspheme the gods which other
cities revere, nor rob foreign temples, nor take treasure that has been dedicated in the name of any god" (*Antiquities* 4.8.10 § 207).

Third, any complaints are to be handled in a regular assembly or official
court (v. 38–39). Chrysostom says the Ephesian assembly (*ekklēsia*) met
three times a month (*Homily* 42.2). The gathering in Acts 19 is not a regular assembly and is, therefore, not a lawful one. The clerk says, What you do,
do it legally. Demetrius should bring those against whom he is aggrieved
before a lawful assembly.

Fourth, today's behavior puts Ephesus in the position of being charged
with rioting (v. 40). A city charged with riotous behavior could suffer severe
consequences. (a) In 20 B.C. Cyzicus lost its freedom as a city after having
permitted some Roman citizens to be put to death, apparently in connection with a riot (Dio Cassius 54.7.6). (b) In A.D. 59, a riot in Pompeii led to
a Roman suspension of assemblies for ten years. Associations were dis-
solved and the leaders of the outbreak were executed (Tacitus, *Annals*
14.17). (c) Dio Chrysostom (*Oration* 34.39), speaking to his home town of
Prusa, thanks the proconsul for his permission "to hold an assembly once
more." It had apparently been suspended because of riots. The town clerk
(*grammateus*) in Acts 19 is depicted as an ideal official. Dio Chrysostom
(*Oration* 34.33) says that one who is fit to be a leader of a city should "be
prepared to withstand . . . especially the vilifications and anger of the mob."
He should "stand out against the violence of the people." This the town
clerk does. "With these words he dismissed the assembly" (v. 40b).

How would an ancient Mediterranean auditor have heard the narrative of
the Ephesian riot in Acts 19? There are several probabilities. (a) Hellenistic
Jews had by Luke's time an established argument for such situations. Josephus gives a number of instances where mob violence leads to a confirmation of the rights of its victims, the Jews (*Antiquities* 14.10.21 §§ 244–46;
16.2.5 §§ 58–60; 19.5.2 §§ 284–85; *War* 7.5.2 §§ 107–11). The crucial question is, Who started the violence? If the Jews did, they deserve punishment
(*War* 2.27.7–8 §§ 487–98). If the pagans did, the rights of the Jews should
be confirmed. In such an argument the following principle was applied:
The rights of the victims of riots should be confirmed. Luke follows this
Hellenistic-Jewish pattern. Since the pagans in Ephesus started the social
chaos, the rights and privileges of the Messianists ought to be confirmed.
The riot scene is a legitimation technique for the Messianists' mission
(Stoops, 73–91).

(b) The Cynic tradition says that Heraclitus had been exiled from Ephesus for his critiques of popular religion (Pseudo-Heraclitus, *Epistle* 7). An auditor of Acts may have heard Acts 19's riot scene as a continuation of Acts 17's link of Paul with the respectable philosophic tradition and its critique of corrupt, superstitious, popular paganism.

(c) The enlightened state is here portrayed as the protector of the Messianists against violence stemming from the vested economic interests hiding behind religious devotion. Moreover, governmental officials' positive attitude toward the Messianists is contrasted with the crowds' hostility (remember Acts 18). The Asiarchs, highly respected officials from the first families of the country, are sympathetic with the Messianists and intervene on Paul's behalf (v. 31). Roman order is the best defense against the dangers of hostile mobs.

"When the disturbance was over, Paul had the disciples summoned and, after encouraging them, he bade them farewell and set out on his journey to Macedonia" (20:1). Paul does not leave Ephesus because of the riot. Acts 19:21 has already alerted the reader to the fact of Paul's plans for the future, plans dictated by the Spirit: "Paul decided in the Spirit to travel through Macedonia." The missionary's plans are due not to pagan opponents but to the leading of the Spirit. God controls the movement of the gospel.

To Jerusalem
Acts 20:1-21:26

Acts 20:1-21:26 carries out Paul's declaration in 19:21: to go to Jerusalem after having passed through Macedonia and Achaia. Its functions are three: (1) to depict as a model for ministry Paul's care of his churches as he is leaving them (20:2; 20:7-12; 20:17-35); (2) to parallel Jesus' journey to Jerusalem in Luke 9:51-19:44 and his acceptance of God's will in Luke 22:42 as a way of interpreting Paul's sufferings; and (3) to show Paul's spirit of accommodation in his quest for church unity (21:18-26). The narrative alternates between four travel summaries and four concrete episodes.

Travel summary: Paul encourages his churches (20:1-6)

    Episode in Troas: Paul cares for his church (20:7-12)

Travel summary: Paul hastens to Jerusalem (20:13-16)

    Episode in Miletus: Paul makes provision for his church after his departure; he goes to Jerusalem amidst prophecies of trouble (20:17-38)

Travel summary: Through the Spirit, Paul is told not to go to Jerusalem
        (21:1–8a)

Episode in Caesarea: Agabus's prophecy of Paul's binding in
                Jerusalem is met by Paul's willingness to die
                for Jesus there (21:8b–14)

Travel summary: Paul's reception by disciples in Jerusalem is cordial
        (21:15–16 [17])

Episode in Jerusalem: Paul acts in a spirit of accommodation
        (21:18–26)

Each segment of the narrative deserves attention.

Acts 20:1–6 is a travel summary focusing on Paul's encouragement of his churches (cf. v. 2–"as he traveled throughout those regions, he provided many words of encouragement for them"). From Ephesus Paul goes to Macedonia and then to Greece. Because of a plot made against him by Jews (cf. 23:12–15), instead of sailing directly for Syria, he returns through Macedonia and eventually arrives at Troas where he spends a week. With him are seven representatives of his churches: Sopater from Beroea (Rom 16:21?), Aristarchus (Phlm 24; Col 4:10) and Secundus from Thessalonica, Gaius from Derbe, Timothy from the Derbe-Lystra-Iconium area (16:1–2; Rom 16:21; 1 Cor 4:17; 16:10; 2 Cor 1:1, 19; Phil 1:1; 2:19; 1 Thess 1:1; 3:2, 6; Phlm 1; 1 Tim 1:2), and Tychicus (Eph 6:21; Col 4:7; 2 Tim 4:12; Titus 3:12) and Trophimus (2 Tim 4:20) from Asia. The number seven implies completeness, so these seven brothers represent the Gentile churches outside Palestine. Verse 6 implies that Paul observes the feast of Passover and so is an observant Jew. This refutes the charges of 21:21 (cf. 18:18; 20:16; 21:26).

Acts 20:7–12 is an episode from Paul's week in Troas, again with the focus on Paul's care for his church but with auxiliary aims besides. The paragraph is a modified miracle story with its usual three points: (1) problem (vv. 7–9); (2) miracle (v. 10); and (3) reactions (vv. 11–12).

(1) The problem is stated only after the cause of the problem is mentioned. The cause: On the first day of the week (the Lord's Day = Sunday— cf. 1 Cor 16:2; Rev 1:10; *Didache* 14:1; Ignatius, *Magnesians* 9:1; Melito [Eusebius, *Church History* 4.16.2]; Dionysius of Corinth [Eusebius, *Church History* 4.23.11]; Clement of Alexandria, *Miscellanies* 7.12; Tertullian, *Chaplet* 3; *Gospel of Peter* 35 and 50), there is an evening eucharist (v. 1a; cf. Pliny, *Epistle* 10.96, for a Sunday evening eucharist in Bythinia about A.D. 112). The celebration includes a sermon which lasts until midnight (v. 7b; cf. Pliny, *Epistle* 2.11–"My speech lasted for nearly five hours"; *Epistle* 4.9–"I had spoken for three and a half hours and still had one and a half to go"). The problem: "a young man (Philo, *On the Creation* 105, says

a *pais* is a youth between nine and fourteen) named Eutychus who was sitting on a window sill was sinking into a deep sleep as Paul talked on and on. Once overcome by sleep, he fell down from the third story and when he was picked up, he was dead" (v. 9).

(2) The miracle is stated very simply: "Paul went down, threw himself upon him, and said as he embraced him, 'Don't be alarmed; there is life in him'" (v. 10). There are a number of echoes: of 1 Kgs 17:21–Elijah stretched himself out upon the dead child; of 2 Kgs 4:34–Elisha lay upon the dead child on the bed; of Luke 7:11-17–Jesus raises the widow's son at Nain; of Luke 8:40-42, 49-56–Jesus raises Jairus's daughter; of Acts 9:36-43–Peter restores Tabitha to life. These echoes indicate that Paul is in continuity with prophets, Jesus, and Peter. The same power is operative in all.

(3) The reactions are two. First, Paul does not let the mishap interrupt the more important purpose of the assembly: "he returned upstairs, broke the bread, and ate; after a long conversation that lasted until daybreak, he departed" (v. 11; cf. 20:20, 27, 31). Like Jesus (Luke 22:14-38), Paul has a last meal with his disciples. Second, the believers are "immeasurably comforted" that the lad is alive (v. 12). Overall, the story speaks of Paul's nurturing of his church at Troas. (Cf. *Acts of Paul* 1-2–the boy Patroclus falls from a high window while listening to Paul and is killed, but Paul raises him.)

An auxiliary aim may also be operative within the story, an aim signaled by v. 8 ("There were many lamps in the upstairs room where they were gathered") and by the resuscitation of the young boy. One can only hear the story with the ears of an ancient Mediterranean auditor if sufficient background is provided. The important thing to know is that nocturnal meetings were perceived negatively by Mediterranean society. On the one hand, nocturnal meetings were associated with political conspiracy: for example, Cicero, *Catiline* 1.1; 3.5-6; Juvenal, *Satires* 8.231-35; Pliny, *Epistles* 10.96–Christians had ceased their night meetings after Pliny's edict in which, in accordance with Trajan's orders, he had forbidden secret societies. On the other hand, night gatherings were thought to be connected with human sacrifice and sexual immorality. The following examples make this clear (so Daniel Hilty).

(1) Pagan charges against pagans–(a) Euripides, *Bacchae* 215-20, voices concern over women's participation in nocturnal Bacchic rituals. The danger is immorality. (b) Cicero, *Laws* 2.35, mentions a concern about "the performance of sacrifices by women at night." In 2.37, Marcus proposes to Atticus that the Romans make careful provision for the reputation of our women. This would involve having their worship in the clear light of day when they can be observed by many eyes.

> And, that we may not . . . seem too severe, I cite the fact that in the very center of Greece, by a law enacted by Diagondas of Thebes, all nocturnal rites were

abolished forever; and furthermore that Aristophanes . . . attacks strange gods and the nightly vigils which were part of their worship.

(c) Livy 39.8 records a "secret conspiracy" that involves a nameless Greek, "a priest of secret rites performed at night." These rites involve men and women, wine and feasts, and end up with debauchery and murders. (d) Philostratus, *Apollonius* 8.7.12–14, tells of the philosopher's defense before Domitian. It includes a defense against the charge that Apollonius had killed a boy as part of a ritual of divination held at night. His response is that at the time of the child's death, he was with a sick friend "praying for a man's life." Such claims of ritual killing of a child in a religious or magical context are not uncommon in antiquity: for example, Lollianos, *Phoinikika* (ritual murder of a boy who is then eaten); Horace, *Epode* 5 (a boy is killed to make a magical potion); Tertullian, *Apology* 22–23 (magicians strangle boys in order to make an oracle speak).

(2) Pagan charges against Jews—(a) As early as the fourth century B.C., Theophrastus reports, according to Porphyry (*On Abstinence* 2.26), that Jews were involved in terrible things during nocturnal sacrifices. (b) Plutarch (*Questions of a Feast* 4.6.2) also makes mention of the nocturnal festivals of the Jews. "The time and character of the greatest, most sacred holiday of the Jews clearly befit Dionysius. . . . What they do after entering we do not know, but it is probable that the rite is a Bacchic revelry."

(3) Jewish charges against pagans—Wis 14:23–24a accuses pagans of the kind of immorality commonly associated with nightly meetings:

For whether they kill children in their initiations,
    or celebrate secret mysteries
    or hold frenzied revels with strange customs,
they no longer keep either their lives
    or their marriages pure.

(4) Pagan charges against Christians—(a) Minucius Felix, *Octavius*, has Fronto make charges against Christians such as:

They . . . with nocturnal assemblies . . . and inhuman feasts seal their pact . . . with desecrating profanation; they are a crowd that furtively lurks in hiding places, shunning the light. (8.4)

their clandestine and nocturnal ceremonies. (9.3)

The . . . initiation of new recruits. . . . A young baby is covered with flour, . . . to deceive the unwary. . . . The recruit is urged to inflict blows onto it. . . . Thus the baby is killed. . . . It is the blood of this infant . . . that they lick with thirsty lips . . . by which they seal their covenant. (9.5)

We all know, too, about their banquets. . . . There, flushed . . . after such feasting and drinking, they begin to burn with incestuous passions. They provoke a dog tied to a lampstand to leap. . . . By this means the light is overturned and . . . incest [follows]. (9.6-7)

(b) Theophilus of Antioch, *To Autolycus* 3.4, also refers to pagan charges that Christians in their gatherings are guilty of sexual immorality and cannibalism. (c) Justin Martyr, *Dialogue* 10, is yet another who mentions the pagans' belief that during worship Christians "extinguish the lights and indulge in unbridled sensuality." (d) Athenagoras, *Plea for the Christians* 3, 35, likewise mentions the pagan accusations against Christians associated with nocturnal festivals. (e) Origen reports a similar charge leveled by Celsus against Christians: eating the flesh of little children and indulging in unrestrained sexual intercourse (*Against Celsus* 6.40). (f) Tertullian argues eloquently against such charges: killing children and sexual immorality (*Apology* 7.13-8.5). (g) Eusebius, *Church History* 5.1.14, speaks about pagan slaves who, when arrested, accuse their Christian masters of Thyestean feasts and Oedipean intercourse.

(5) Jewish charges against Christians—Origen, *Against Celsus* 6.27, mentions certain Jews who spread the rumor that Christians sacrifice a child and partake of its flesh and that they turn out the light and engage in illicit sexual intercourse.

(6) Christian charges against Christians—(a) Jude 12-13 speaks about questionable forms of worship. "These are blemishes on your love feasts, as they carouse fearlessly and look after themselves." (b) Justin, *1 Apology* 26, in his remarks about the heretics, says,

All who follow these men [i.e., Simon of Samaria, Menander, and Marcion] are, as we said above, called Christians, just as those who do not share the same doctrines share among philosophers the name of philosophy. We do not know whether they are guilty of those disgraceful and fabulous deeds, the upsetting of the lamp, promiscuous intercourse, and anthropophagy.

Charges of nocturnal assemblies and associated immoralities were a cultural commonplace among and within religious groups of the ancient Mediterranean world. The charges and countercharges existed from pre-Christian times well into our era. It would have been difficult for an ancient auditor not to have heard Acts 20:7-12 as a protection of Messianist disciples against at least implicit charges connected with nocturnal meetings: in particular, love of the darkness and killing of a child. In contrast, Luke's narrative shows that a Messianist Sunday evening eucharist involves lots of lights (and so nothing immoral) and restoration of a child to life (rather than child sacrifice). The story, so told, would function as a legitimation device for Lord's Day worship.

Acts 20:13-16 is another travel summary whose point is that Paul is hastening to Jerusalem. From Troas Paul's company sails to Assos (a coastal town south of Troas) where they meet up with Paul who had come by land. The entire party then sails for Mitylene (a town on the island of Lesbos). The next day they sail past Chios (an island where Homer was born and the chief city on the island) to Samos (an island where Pythagoras was born and its chief city). The next day they arrive in Miletus (a coastal city south of Ephesus). The impression is that of one-day hops from one spot to another. Paul bypasses Ephesus because he is "hurrying to be in Jerusalem, if at all possible, for the Day of Pentecost" (v. 16). What better time than the feast of the first fruits for introducing his seven traveling companions (20:4) as the first fruits of the Gentile mission!

Acts 20:17-38 is an episode about Paul's visit with the Ephesian elders (*presbyterous*; cf. 14:23) at Miletus. Elders were a standard feature of Jewish community organization. There were (a) teaching elders (Mark 7:5, 13); (b) ruling elders (Luke 7:3; 22:66; Acts 22:5); and (c) a ruling elder of a synagogue (Luke 8:41, 49; 13:14). The early church reflects these three types of elders: (a) 2, 3 John; Papias; (b) Acts 20:17-35; Titus 1:5-9; Phil 1:1; 1 Thess 5:12-13; Heb 13:17; and (c) 1 Tim 3:1-7. The elders of Acts 20 are a group who rule the Ephesian church. During his speech, Paul makes provision for his church in the time after he has gone.

Verses 18b-35 are his farewell speech. A farewell-speech form was frequently used in ancient Judaism (e.g., Genesis 49; Deuteronomy; Joshua 24; 1 Samuel 12; Tobit 14; *Testaments of the Twelve Patriarchs;* 1 Macc 2:49-68) and in the early church (e.g., for Jesus—Mark 13; John 13-17; Luke 22:14-38; for apostles—2 Timothy; 2 Peter). In Acts 20, one meets a farewell speech put into the mouth of Paul. Farewell speeches are alike in that the hero knows he is about to die; he calls his primary community around him and gives them a speech. It includes first a prediction of what is going to happen after he is gone. This can be done because in antiquity it was believed that at the time of death, one was given prophetic powers (e.g., *Iliad* 16.843-54—Patroklos; *Iliad* 22.355-60—Hector; Diodorus Siculus 18.1—Alexander of Macedon; *Aeneid* 210.739-41—Orodes and Mezentius; Diogenes Laertius 1.117-18—Pherecydes; Genesis 49—Jacob; 50:24—Joseph; Deuteronomy 32—Moses; Joshua 23—Joshua). Then there follows an exhortation of how to behave after the hero's departure. The basis for the exhortation in farewell speeches of apostles is what they taught and how they behaved.

The farewell speech of Paul in Acts 20:18b-35 falls into a chiastic pattern: ABCDC'B'A' (Pereira, 201).

A—Past record: You yourselves know/*epistasthe* (v. 18b)
   B—Present activity: and now/*kai nyn* (v. 22a)
      C—Prophetic future: I know/*egō oida* (v. 25a)
         therefore (*dioti*) (v. 26a)

D—The charge (v. 28)
  C'—Prophetic future: I know/*egō oida* (v. 29)
    therefore (*dio*) (v. 31a)
  B'—Present activity: and now/*kai nyn* (v. 32a)
A'—Past record: you yourselves know/*ginōskete* (v. 34a)

Paul's past record, "A," is given in vv. 18b–21. It is known to the Ephesian elders; it involves suffering from plots of the Jews (9:23, 29; 13:50; 14:5, 19; 17:5, 13; 18:12; 20:3; 21:28–31; 23:12); it conforms to the Greek ideal of a good citizen (Plutarch, *Moralia* 60C–"Since we are free men, we must speak with boldness and may conceal nothing nor pass over in silence what is profitable"); it includes both Jews and Greeks; it concerns the necessity of repentance toward God and faith in our Lord Jesus.

His present activity, "B," comes in vv. 22–24. Compelled by the Spirit (cf. 19:21), Paul is going to Jerusalem (20:1–21:17). He is aware, from prophetic messages in every city, that hardships and imprisonment await him. "Yet I consider life of no importance to me, if only I may finish my course and the ministry that I received from the Lord Jesus, to bear witness to the gospel of God's grace" (v. 24).

Verses 25–27, "C," begin with Paul's prediction of the future: "I know that none of you . . . will ever see my face again" (v. 25). His ministry in their area is complete. Since that is so, he spells out his innocence: "I am not responsible for the blood of any of you (cf. 1 Sam 12:2–5; *T. Levi* 10:1–2), for I did not shrink from proclaiming to you the entire plan of God" (vv. 26–27). Paul has done his part. Now it is time for the elders to do theirs.

The charge to the elders, "D," comes in v. 28: "Keep watch over yourselves and over the whole flock (people of God, Isa 40:11; Ezekiel 40; Psalm 23; Luke 15:3–7; 12:32) of which the Holy Spirit has appointed you overseers (*episkopous*; so in Acts 20 elders and bishops are synonymous, in contrast to the monepiscopacy found in Ignatius, *Ephesians* 4:1–2; 6:1; *Trallians* 3:1), in which you tend the church of God that He acquired with the blood of His own Son" (cf. Luke 22:20–"new covenant in my blood"). At the center of the chiasmus is this exhortation which shows that the pastoral care of the Ephesian church is central in this farewell speech.

In vv. 29–31, "C'," there is a second prediction of the future. "I know that after my departure savage wolves (false teachers; *4 Ezra* 5:18; *1 Enoch* 89:13–14; *Didache* 16:3; *2 Clement* 5:2–5; Ignatius, *Philadelphians* 2.2) will come among you, and they will not spare the flock. And from your own group, men will come forward perverting the truth to draw the disciples away after them." This calls for vigilance on the part of the elders/bishops who need to remember Paul's unceasing instruction of them. This is a prediction of the emergence of heresy in Ephesus after Paul's departure (cf. 1 Tim 1:19-20; 4:1-3; 2 Tim 1:15; 2:15-18; Rev 2:2, 6).

The notion of a period during which evil was under control being followed by one in which evil is unrestrained is known in Judaism. Josephus (*Antiquities* 13.1.1 § 2) says about the Maccabean era that Judas Maccabeas gained the Jews their freedom from the Seleucids,

> but after he was dead, all the wicked, and those that transgressed the laws of
> their forefathers, sprang up again in Judea, and grew upon them, and distressed
> them on every side.

The same type of schema is known from the early church. Hegesippus (Eusebius, *Church History* 3.32.7-8) says that until the deaths of the apostles, "the church remained a pure and uncorrupted virgin, for those who attempted to corrupt the healthful rule of the Savior's preaching . . . lurked in obscure darkness." But when the apostles died, the "godless error took its beginning through the deceit of false teachers." Acts reflects this schema. This is not to say that there were no problems in the apostolic age. There were. These problems, however, were solved under the authority of the apostles, and false teaching was not allowed to thrive among the churches. After Paul's death, he predicts, the false teachers will come out of obscurity and attempt to disturb the flock. The elders/bishops are to tend the flock and prevent any damage to God's people.

Verse 32, "B'," reverts to Paul's present activity. "Now I commend you to God and to the gracious word of His that can build you up and give you the inheritance (Luke 20:14; 10:25) among all who are consecrated" (*hagiasmenois*; cf. 1 Cor 1:2; 6:11). When Paul leaves, he leaves the elders in the hands of God (cf. John 17:11-15).

The farewell speech ends on the note of Paul's past record, "A'" (vv. 33-35). "I have never wanted anyone's silver or gold or clothing" (v. 33). Disavowing love of money was a stock apology of philosophers in antiquity (e.g., Dio Chrysostom, *Oration* 32.9, 11; Philostratus, *Apollonius* 1.34; Lucian, *Nigrinus* 25-26; Cynic epistles, Socrates 1, of Socrates—"I do not consider it at all right to make money from philosophy. . . . For no one will ever find that I have taken anything from anyone ever since I applied myself to the philosophic life at the command of God"; cf. 1 Thess 2:5). Instead Paul supports himself by working with his own hands (v. 34; cf. 18:3; 1 Thess 4:11; 2 Thess 3:6-13; *Didache* 12:3-5). In this he has been an example.

The use of a life of a philosopher as an example was widespread in antiquity. Xenophon, *Memorabilia* 4.1.1, speaks of Socrates as an example both in his presence and in his absence. Seneca, *Epistle* 6.5-6, says the way to wisdom is long if one follows precepts only but short if one follows the examples of moral heroes. Lucian, *Demonax* 1, appeals to the use of an example from one's own time. With this Seneca agrees. Examples may come from the living (*Epistle* 52.8-9) or the dead (*Epistle* 25.6). Dio Chrysostom, *Oration* 55.4-5, sums it up: "That is precisely, it seems, what the pupil does—by imitating his teacher and paying heed to him he tries to acquire his art." It was in these terms that Philo understood the patriarchs. In *On Abraham* 1.3-5, he says that the patriarchs are men who have lived good and blameless lives and

> whose virtues stand permanently recorded in the most holy scriptures . . . for the instruction of the reader and as an inducement to him to aspire to the same; for in these men we have laws endowed with life and reason.

Musonius Rufus, Fragment 11, relates the appeal to a teacher's example to the sphere of work. When banished to Gyara, he thought it valuable to work with his hands so his students would be benefitted by seeing him at work in the fields, demonstrating by his own labor the lesson not to depend upon another for sustenance. Paul's labor, which serves as an example for the Ephesian elders and Luke's auditors, also fulfills the saying of Jesus: "It is more blessed to give than to receive" (v. 35b; cf. *1 Clement* 2:1).

The Ephesian elders are called upon to do three things in this speech: (1) they are to feed the church (v. 28); (2) they are to be alert to the dangers threatening the church (vv. 29-31); and (3) they are not to be greedy for gain (vv. 33-35). In all three areas, Paul is set up as an example: (1) Paul says three times that he did not shrink from declaring to them the word of God (vv. 20, 27, 31); (2) the farewell speech as a whole represents Paul's alertness to the dangers to come (vv. 29-30); and (3) Paul says he coveted no one's wealth (v. 33).

Since Acts roots what the church does in the Lukan Jesus, it is no surprise to find the same three concerns in the Third Gospel: (1) the Lukan Jesus says church leaders must give the household their food at the proper time (Luke 12:41-48); (2) they must be alert (Luke 12:35-40); and (3) in the speech of Acts 20, Jesus is quoted as saying, "It is more blessed to give than to receive" (v. 35b). The Lukan Paul has been faithful to the Lukan Jesus.

The things called for in the behavior of the Ephesian elders, moreover, are a part of the general parenesis of the time of Luke-Acts, especially in the Pauline circle represented by the Pastoral epistles. (1) The leaders are called upon to feed the church (1 Tim 3:2; 4:13-14, 16; 2 Tim 4:2; Titus 1:9). (2) The Pastorals as a whole reflect the need to be alert to the emergence of error in the church in the province of Asia. (3) The church leaders are exhorted to avoid greed (1 Tim 3:3; Titus 1:7, 11). These parallels show that the farewell speech in Acts 20 reflects the general concern at the end of the first century that church leaders do their jobs properly and with integrity. This concern is expressed in terms of the changing of the guard. The older generation (Paul) is departing; the mantle of leadership is passing to the younger generation; and the new leadership is challenged to be as faithful as its predecessors.

Following the speech, Paul prays with them all. Greatly distressed because "he had said that they would never see his face again" (v. 38), they escort him to the ship. Acts 21:1-8a is the third travel summary in this large thought unit. From Miletus Paul's company sails to Cos (an island and the chief city of the island) and on the next day to Rhodes (an island and the main city on the island) and from there to Patara (a coastal city). From Patara they sail to Tyre (a coastal city in Phoenicia), where they stay a week with the disciples. The disciples in Tyre (Luke 6:17; Acts 11:19; 15:3) keep "telling Paul through the Spirit (a word of prophecy, cf. 13:2) not to embark for Jerusalem" (v. 4). Nevertheless, after a week Paul's company catches a ship to Ptolemais (a coastal city just south of Tyre). After a day's visit with disciples there, they come to Caesarea (v. 8a).

Acts 21:8b-14 gives an episode in Caesarea (remember Acts 10). Paul and his company are offered hospitality by Philip the evangelist (Acts 8:40; cf. Eph 4:11; 2 Tim 4:5), one of the Seven (6:1-6). Philip's four daughters are "gifted with prophecy" (v. 9; cf. Eusebius, *Church History* 3.31.39). In the scriptures of Israel only four women are mentioned as being prophetesses: Miriam (Exod 15:20), Deborah (Judg 4:4), Huldah (2 Kgs 22:14), and Noadiah (Neh 6:14). Also Ezek 13:17-23 speaks of both prophets and prophetesses, while Joel 2:28 looks forward to both sons and daughters prophesying. Luke 2:36-37 sketches Anna as an ideal for prophetesses under the new covenant. In Acts, both men and women prophesy (2:17-18). Prophecy appears in the church both as the occasional utterance of various members of the community and as a continual ministry of some. They conduct their ministry in one congregation or throughout a region (15:22, 32; cf. *Didache* 11), singly or in groups (Acts 11:27; 13:1; cf. Rev 22:9). Their message is tested by other prophets and only afterward is received as the word of the Lord (cf. 1 Cor 14:29; 1 Thess 5:19-20; 1 John 4:1). False prophets appear (Acts 13:6; cf. Matt 7:15; Mark 13:22; *Didache* 11:3-6; Hermas, *Mandate* 11.7). Because of the problem of false prophecy and the uncertainties involved in discerning it, the gift of prophecy itself gradually fell into disuse and disrepute (Ellis 1976, 700-701).

After several days, a prophet named Agabus (11:27-28) comes down from Jerusalem. He performs a symbolic act and gives an interpretive word (cf. Isa 8:1-4; 20:2; Jer 13:1-11; 27:1-7; Ezekiel 4). He takes Paul's belt (the long cloth that was wound several times around Paul's waist to carry money and other things in) and binds his own hand and feet with it. Then he says, "Thus says the Holy Spirit: This is the way the Jews will bind the owner of this belt in Jerusalem, and they will hand him over to the Gentiles" (v. 11).

The language echoes that of the Third Gospel (Luke 9:44–to be handed over; 18:32–will be handed over to the Gentiles), although in Acts actually the Romans rescue Paul from the hands of the Jews (Acts 21:33).

When Paul's companions and the local residents hear the prophecy, whose truth is assured by an earlier fulfillment of a prophecy of Agabus (11:27–28), they beg him not to go up to Jerusalem (v. 12). But Paul resists them. "I am prepared not only to be bound but even to die in Jerusalem for the name of the Lord Jesus" (v. 13; cf. Socrates' resistance of his followers' pleas to avoid his death–Plato, *Phaedo* 116E-117A). Since Paul will not be dissuaded, his cohorts say, "The Lord's will be done" (v. 14; Luke 22:42; *Martyrdom of Polycarp* 7:1). The paragraph shows that for Luke what will happen in Jerusalem is a part of the divine plan. That Paul and his friends know ahead of time what to expect allows them the opportunity to submit to the divine will, as Jesus did. This is the Pauline Gethsemane. It shows that suffering may be a part of the divine will for His servants, even though they be Spirit-empowered (Luke 3:21–22; 4:16–19; Acts 9:17). It shows, moreover, the Spirit-filled person's submission to the divine will, whatever that may be. If it is to return to Ephesus (18:21), that is fine; if it is to be imprisoned and die in Jerusalem, that must be done (21:13).

Acts 21:15–17 constitutes the fourth and final travel summary in this section. "After these days we saddled our horses (*episkeuasamenoi*) . . . , then went up to Jerusalem" (v. 15). The translation of *episkeuasamenoi* as saddling horses is possible linguistically and would allow the sixty-mile journey from Caesarea to Jerusalem to be made in a day. Walking, one could cover seventeen to twenty-three miles per day; by horseback, up to three times that (Rapske 1994, 10). Some of the Caesarean disciples go along to lead Paul and his company to the house of Mnason, a Cypriot Messianist, who offers them hospitality (v. 16). "When we reached Jerusalem, the brothers welcomed us warmly" (v. 17).

Acts 21:18–26 is the final episode in this section. In it Paul acts with a spirit of accommodation in order to preserve the unity of the church. The form of the meeting of Acts 21 mirrors that of the Jerusalem council of Acts 15:1–16:5.

Paul goes to Jerusalem (15:4; 21:17)

Paul meets the elders and James (15:4, 6, 13; 21:18)

Paul relates what God has done among the Gentiles through him (15:12; 21:19)

The Jerusalem decree states the obligations of Gentile Messianists with regard to the law (15:20, 29; 21:25)

Paul acts in an accommodating way on behalf of the unity of the church (15:30–35; 16:4; 21:23–24, 26)

The content is different. In 11:1–18 the issue had been, Is baptism of Gentiles all right? Can ethnic Jewish Messianists stay in the house of a Gentile Messianist? In 15:1–31 the issue was, Should Gentile Messianists be required to be circumcised and to keep the Law of Moses? In 21:18–26 the issue is, Should Jewish-born Messianists abandon their ethnic way of life? In particular, is Paul advocating that they do so (cf. 16:3; 18:18; 20:5, 17)?

The Jerusalem Messianist leadership is positive about Paul's missionary activities among the Gentiles (v. 20a). Their concerns, however, are about how the Jerusalem Messianists who are zealous for the law will react to Paul, given the rumors circulating about him. "They have been informed that you are teaching all the Jews who live among the Gentiles to abandon Moses and that you are telling them not to circumcise their children or to observe their customary practices" (v. 21). The rumors claim that Paul is the moral equivalent of the Jews in Maccabean times who gladly adopted Gentile practices and of Antiochus Epiphanes who actively promoted the abolition of Jewish religion and customs (1 Macc 1:43–50—e.g., profane sabbaths and feasts, defile sanctuary and priests, leave their sons uncircumcised). If the Jewish Messianists are zealous for the law, they are like Mattathias who resisted the Hellenization of the Jews in Maccabean times (1 Macc 2:15–28, 50, 54, 58). "What is to be done?" (v. 22). The suggestion of the Jerusalem leadership is that Paul not only purify himself (Num 6:9) but also pay for the vows of four men (v. 24; as Herod Agrippa I did in order to show his Jewish piety—Josephus, *Antiquities* 19.6.1 § 294). "In this way everyone will know that there is nothing to the reports they have been given about you but that you yourself live in observance of the law" (v. 24). So Paul purifies himself with the four and enters the Temple (Num 6:13) to give notice of the day when the purification will be completed and the offering made for each one (v. 26). In doing this, the Lukan Paul acts in an accommodating way to foster the unity of the church.

Justin Martyr dealt with a similar problem in the mid-second century in his *Dialogue with Trypho the Jew* 47. Trypho asks, Can one be saved if he believes in Christ and observes Jewish institutions? Justin's answer is twofold. On the one hand, Jewish Messianists who observe the ethnic dimensions of the law can be saved if they do not try to persuade Gentiles to be observant, telling them that they will not be saved unless they are observant. Although some in the church disagree, Justin thinks such Jewish Messianists are brethren with whom he should associate. On the other hand, if Gentiles who believe in Christ are led to live according to the law along with their Christian profession, they will probably be saved. But if they deny Christ, they will not. On his first point, Justin reflects the stance of Acts 21:18–26. Those who are born Jews may continue to observe their ethnic customs after they have become Messianists. Gentiles who believe in

Jesus have no such obligation to observe the law of Moses. All that is expected of them is the minimum behavior necessary to enable Jew and Gentile Messianists to live and eat together without compromising Jewish ethnic consciences (21:25). On his second point, Justin appears to stand in contradiction to Paul, who regards a converted Gentile's adding the law to Christ as a denial of Christ and a fall from grace (Gal 5:1–4).

Witness in Jerusalem
Acts 21:26–23:10

Beginning with chap. 21, the narrative of Acts relates Paul's final arrest and imprisonments. This section is slightly longer than that describing his earlier missionary travels. Acts 21–28 depicts Paul as a prisoner-missionary, fulfilling the prophecy of the risen Jesus in Acts 9:16 ("what he will have to suffer for my name"). The significance of Luke's expansive narration at the end of Acts is indicated by Lucian, *On How to Write History* 56–57. He says that a writer must take care not to waste words on unessential matters but must pass over them quickly in order to concentrate on what is most important for his purposes. Acts, while coherent, is highly selective. That to which space is devoted (amplification) is that to which emphasis is given (cf. the threefold repetition of Paul's conversion and the threefold mention of Cornelius's conversion). This section, Acts 21–28, is told in a way that makes it seem, on one level, as if Paul is caught up in a swirl of events beyond his control and by which he is swept along with a loss of all self-determination. On another level, however, the narrative is presented in a way that indicates that all is happening according to the divine plan, which is made known by a series of three prophecies and visions: (1) prophecies (20:23; 21:4; 21:11); (2) prophecy (23:11); (3) prophecy (27:23–26).

Acts 21:26–23:10 is a large thought unit subdivided into three scenes (21:26–40; 21:40–22:29; 22:30–23:10), each consisting of the same three components:

(1) Paul's actions (21:26–27a; 21:40–22:21; 22:30–23:6)
(2) the danger to Paul (21:27–31a, 36; 22:22–23; 23:7–10a)
(3) intervention by the tribune (21:31b–40; 22:24–29; 23:10b)

According to Acts 23:11, this section constitutes Paul's witness in Jerusalem. The discussion of 21:26–23:10 will take up the three scenes in order.

Scene one (21:26–40) opens with (a) Paul's actions. They are those of a pious Jew (21:26–27a). Paul purifies himself with the four men who have a Nazarite vow and enters the Temple with them in order to give notice of the day when he will make the offering for each of them. To pay a Nazarite's expenses expressed great piety. Agrippa I, for example, at his accession in A.D. 41, paid the expenses of a number of Nazarites to signal his Jewish devotion (Josephus, *Antiquities* 19.6.1 § 294). The person who paid such a vow incurred a considerable expense (Num 6:13–21; Josephus, *Antiquities* 4.4.4 §§ 72–73; *m. Nazir* 6:6–11).

(b) In spite of his good intentions, Paul's actions place him in danger (21:27–31, 36). Jews from the province of Asia (20:18–19) stir up the crowd and lay hands on Paul. The presence of Diaspora Jews at a feast like Pentecost was customary (Josephus, *Antiquities* 14.13.4 § 337; 17.10.2 § 254; *War* 2.3.1 §§ 42–43; Philo, *Special Laws* 1.69, who speaks of countless people going up to the Temple from many thousands of cities). Non-observance among Jews of the Diaspora was a problem (Philo, *Migration of Abraham* 89–92). Those who cared enough to make the trip to Jerusalem would have had little patience with deviancy. They cry out, "Fellow Israelites, help us. This is the man who is teaching everyone everywhere against the people and the law and this place (6:13–14), and what is more, he has even brought Greeks into the Temple and defiled this sacred place" (v. 28). The first charge, Paul's alleged anti-Judaism, has been shown to be false by the previous narrative (16:3–4, 13; 18:18; 20:16; 21:24). It will be denied explicitly in what follows (23:6; 24:11–12, 17–18; 25:8; 26:4–5; 28:17). The evangelist with an aside refutes the second: "they had previously seen Trophimus the Ephesian (20:4) in the city with him and supposed that Paul had brought him into the Temple" (v. 29).

The second charge reflects the fact that non-Jews were not permitted to go beyond the Court of the Gentiles. This is confirmed by both literary (Philo, *Embassy to Gaius* 31 § 212; Josephus, *Antiquities* 12.3.4 § 145; *War* 5.5.2 §§ 193–94) and archaeological evidence (e.g., a slab with an inscription discovered in Jerusalem in 1871 by C. S. Clermont-Ganneau and now in Istanbul reads, "Let no one of another nation penetrate beyond the balustrade and into the inner precinct around the sanctuary. Whoever is caught will himself be to blame for what ensues: death"; a second inscription on a slab discovered in 1935 near St. Stephen's Gate has a text similar to the preceding one).

"The whole city was in turmoil with people rushing together" (v. 30). This is another riot scene (cf. 19:28–34). They seize Paul and drag him out of the Temple so the Temple will not be defiled with blood when he is killed. The gates are closed to keep the violence outside the Temple. How should this Jewish action against Paul be understood? It is an example of establishment violence, that is, the use of violence by Jews to maintain or defend the status quo. Philo offers evidence of such vigilantism directed against nonconformers to the Torah in the first century A.D. (Seland).

(1) *Special Laws* 1.54–57 deals with idolatry. In 1.55 Philo says, "And it is well that all who have a zeal for virtue should be permitted to exact the penalties offhand and with no delay." (2) *Special Laws* 2.252–54 deals with perjury. In 2.253 Philo says that such a one will never escape the chastisements of men.

> And these he will never escape: for there are thousands who have their eyes upon him full of zeal for the laws, strictest guardians of the ancestral institutions, merciless to those who do anything to subvert them.

(3) *Special Laws* 1.315–18 deals with false prophecy or seduction of the people. In 3.316 Philo says,

> We must punish him as a public and general enemy, taking little thought for the ties which bind us to him; and we must send round a report of his proposals to all lovers of piety, who will rush with a speed which brooks no delay to take vengeance on the unholy man, and deem it a religious duty to seek his death.

Such references from Philo help explain the extralegal behavior of zealous establishment Jews at a number of other points in Acts as well (e.g., 7:54–60; 14:19; 23:12–15) as well as here. In certain contexts, establishment Jews actually had governmental permission to act in this way (e.g., 3 Macc 7:10–14, where the Ptolemaic king grants Jews permission to punish those of their number who had become apostates). In Acts 21, Paul is viewed as an apostate who is rightly subject to establishment violence.

Furthermore, riots at festivals were common occurrences. Josephus generalizes, "the Jews made an insurrection . . . at a festival; for at those feasts seditions are generally begun" (*War* 1.4.3 § 88). The narrative of Acts makes clear here as elsewhere that disorderly assemblies and incidents of riotous behavior are caused by opponents of the Messianists, beside whom the followers of Jesus emerge as peaceable people (6:10–14; 13:50–52; 14:5–7, 19; 16:19–24; 17:5–9; 19:23–40; 21:27–34; 23:12–15; 25:1–3).

(c) The tribune's intervention is related in three stages. First, there is the officer's act. "While they were trying to kill him, a report reached the cohort commander (tribune, a commander of one thousand men) that all Jerusalem was rioting. He immediately took soldiers and centurions (commanders of one hundred men) and charged down on them" (vv. 31–32). Roman soldiers were permanently stationed near the Temple with the responsibility of watching for and suppressing any disturbances. Josephus, *Antiquities* 2.12.1 § 224, says that at festival time a Roman cohort (one thousand men) stood over the cloisters of the Temple "for they always were armed and kept guard at festivals, to prevent any innovation which the multitude thus gathered together might make." To reach the affected area the soldiers would have had to come down a flight of steps into the Temple precincts (Josephus, *War* 5.5.8 § 243). The tribune's intervention stops the beating of Paul. He then arrests Paul and has him secured with two hand chains (i.e., Paul is chained between two soldiers, one on each side). He is unable to find out who Paul is and what he has done because of the uproar (v. 33). So he orders Paul to be brought into the barracks (*eis tēn parem-bolēn*—v. 34). The barracks are the Fortress of Antonia, built by Herod the Great on the foundation of an earlier Hasmonean fortification (Josephus, *Antiquities* 18.4.3 §§ 91–92; *War* 5.5.8 §§ 238–47). It stood to the north-west of the Temple and was connected to the Temple precinct by steps. Paul has to be carried up the steps by the soldiers "because of the violence of the mob" (v. 35), some of whom shout, "Away with him" (v. 36; cf. Luke 23:18). At this point, Lycias does not intervene to rescue Paul. He inter-venes to maintain public order. Paul's safety is a by-product.

Second, there is an interchange between Paul and the tribune (vv. 37–39). Just as Paul is about to be taken into Antonia, he asks the tribune, "May I say something to you." The tribune is surprised: "Do you speak Greek?" From Paul's speech he draws a conclusion: "So you are not the Egyptian who started a revolt some time ago and led the four thousand assas-sins into the desert?" Josephus mentions the Egyptian (*War* 2.13.3–5 §§ 254–63; *Antiquities* 20.8.6 §§ 169–72). During Felix's rule, about A.D. 54, he led thousands to believe that on his command the city walls would fall down. The Romans killed or captured many of his followers, but he escaped. The tribune has to this point apparently assumed that Paul is this man, still around and still causing trouble. Now a question is raised for him by Paul's speech. Paul's response clarifies the matter: "I am a Jew of Tarsus in Cilicia, a citizen of no mean city" (a boast; v. 39a). Then he makes a request: "Per-mit me to speak to the people" (v. 39b).

Third, the outcome is permission for Paul to speak to the crowd. Why would the tribune give his permission (v. 40)? Vergil, *Aeneid* 1.148–53, sup-plies at least one reason:

> When rioting breaks out in a great city,
> and the rampaging rabble goes so far that stones fly . . .
> for anger can supply that kind of weapon—
> if it so happens, they look round and see
> some dedicated . . . man, . . .
> they quiet down, willing to stop and listen.
> Then he prevails in speech over their fury . . .
> and placates them. (cf. Acts 19:35–40)

The tribune hopes Paul's speech to the crowd will end the rioting. Perhaps it will reveal the cause of the disturbance as well.

Scene two (Acts 21:40–22:29) also begins with (a) Paul's actions (21:40–22:21). Paul stands on the steps, motions with his hand to the people like an orator to gain their silence (19:33), and addresses them in

Hebrew (i.e., Aramaic) with his defense (22:1). Defense speeches are found in a variety of ancient Mediterranean sources (e.g., Livy 3.45.6-11; 26.30.11-31.11; 40.9.1-15.16; 42.41-42; 45.22-24; 38;47-49; 39.47-49; 39.36.7-37.17; Dionysius of Halicarnassus 9.29-32; Appian, *Roman History* 3.52-61; Q. Curtius Rufus, *Alexander* 6.10.1-37; 7.1.18-2.11; Tacitus, *Annals* 6.8; 13.21; 16.21-35; Josephus, *Antiquities* 16.4.1-4 §§ 91-126). This one is arranged in a chiastic pattern (Bligh, 97).

A—Paul comes from the Gentile world to Jerusalem (v. 3)
   B—Paul persecuted the Way (vv. 4-5a)
      C—Paul's journey from Jerusalem to Damascus (v. 5b)
         D—Paul's vision on the road to Damascus (vv. 6-11)
            E—Ananias restores Paul's sight (vv. 12-13)
               F—Ananias tells Paul of his mission (vv. 14-15)
            E'—Ananias urges Paul to receive baptism (v. 16)
         D'—Paul's vision in Jerusalem (vv. 17-18a)
      C'—Paul is commanded to leave Jerusalem (v. 18b)
   B'—Paul speaks of his days as a persecutor (vv. 19-20)
A'—Paul is sent from Jerusalem to the Gentiles (v. 21)

The chiastic pattern's center indicates the speech's main point: Paul's mission to be Jesus' witness before all people of what Paul has seen and heard (v. 15).

The speech begins with Paul's summary of his life before his conversion. As to race, he is a Jew. His hometown is Tarsus in Cilicia, a great metropolis. Strabo 14.5.13 says that Tarsus not only had a flourishing population but also was most powerful. Dio Chrysostom 33.17, 28 and 34.7-8, 37 regards Tarsus as the greatest of the cities of Cilicia, possessed of size and splendor. As to education, Paul was brought up at the feet of Gamaliel, educated according to the strict manner of the law. Paul was apparently one of those natives of Tarsus described by Strabo (14.5.13) who completed their education abroad and then lived abroad instead of returning home. His teacher was the greatest of the rabbis of his time, Gamaliel (Acts 5:34). His education was in the Pharisaic tradition. Josephus, *Life* 38 § 191, speaks about the Pharisees as having the reputation for excelling in the accurate knowledge of the law (cf. Acts 26:5—"I have lived my life as a Pharisee, the strictest party of our religion"). As for his deeds, Paul had persecuted the Way even unto Damascus on orders from the Sanhedrin (*m. Makkoth* 1:10 says, "The Sanhedrin may conduct its office either within the land of Israel or outside the land of Israel"). There is at least the possibility that here Paul claims to have been a member of the Sanhedrin. It would have been possible. From the mid-first century B.C., scribes of the Pharisees were admitted to the Sanhedrin (cf. John 3:1). Verses 3-5 constitute a typical exordium of an ancient defense speech, presenting the character of the speaker as favorably as possible.

Verses 6-16 recount Paul's conversion in the region of Damascus. The story is one the reader has already heard in Acts 9. Verses 17-21, however, offer new data about Paul's early Messianist experience after his conversion. In Jerusalem, while praying in the Temple as a good Jew, he fell into a trance (10:10) and saw the Lord (i.e., Jesus) saying to him, "Hurry, leave Jerusalem at once" (v. 18). Paul's reluctance was overcome by yet another word from the Lord. "Go, I shall send you far away to the Gentiles" (v. 21; cf. Isa 6:1-9). Verses 6-21 comprise an incomplete *narratio* (a statement of the facts in which the true issue is stated). Before Paul can make his point, his speech is interrupted (cf. 10:44).

(b) Paul's mention of "Gentiles" causes the crowd to erupt again. "They listened to him until he said this, but then they raised their voices and shouted, 'Take such a one as this away from the earth. It is not right that he should live'" (v. 22; cf. 17:32). They yell, throw off their cloaks, and fling dust into the air, indicating that Paul is once more in danger. One stream of the Pharisaic movement was hostile to Gentile converts, namely the school of Shammai (e.g., Rabbi Eliezer ben Hyrcanus [ca. A.D. 90] says, "No Gentile will have a part in the world to come" [*t. Sanhedrin* 13.2]; and "The people of Sodom will not rise again" [*Abot de Rabbi Nathan* 36]). Paul's affinities are more with the school of Hillel, which welcomed Gentile proselytes. In Acts, Paul is not only a Pharisee but also a certain type of Pharisee: one from the stream that flowed from Hillel through Gamaliel. The people's hostility to the word "Gentiles" here is, however, more likely because of the growing Jewish nationalism that preceded the revolt against Rome in A.D. 66-70, which rejected everything Greek.

(c) The tribune intervenes once again (vv. 24-29). This paragraph has the same three components as the first scene's equivalent. First, the tribune acts in a twofold way. On the one hand, the tribune orders Paul to be brought into barracks (*eis tēn parembolēn* = Tower of Antonia) (v. 24a). Paul is rescued. On the other hand, he gives orders that Paul be interrogated "under the lash to determine why they were making an outcry against him" (v. 24b). The use of torture by the Romans to obtain information was not unusual (Chariton, *Chaereas and Callirhoe* 1.5.2; 3.4; Pliny, *Epistle* 10.96; Achilles Tatius 7.12.2-3—the hero Clitophon, about to be tortured for information, says, "I was therefore at once fettered, stripped naked of my clothes, . . . the attendants were some of them bringing the scourges"). Information gained by such means was considered good evidence by Romans (Quintilian, *Institutes* 5.4.1). Such methods were used only after other forms of inquiry had been exhausted. The tribune so far has used non-coercive means to no avail. Now he turns to coercion.

Second, there is an interchange (vv. 25–28). "But when they had stretched him out for the whips, Paul said to the centurion on duty, 'Is it lawful for you to scourge a man who is a Roman citizen and has not been tried?'" (v. 25). Torture was not to be used on Roman citizens before trial, although it was permitted on non-Romans. Livy 10.9.4 says, "the Porcian law alone seems to have been passed to protect the persons of the citizens, imposing, as it did, a heavy penalty if anyone should scourge or put to death a Roman citizen." Cicero, *Verres* 2.5.170, says the following about the case of Verres, who had flogged and executed Roman citizens without regard for their repeated cries of citizen status: "To bind a Roman citizen is a crime, to flog him is an abomination, to slay him is almost an act of murder; to crucify him is—what? There is no fitting word that can possibly describe so horrible a deed." The *Lex Julia* prohibited torture of Roman citizens. Josephus, *Antiquities* 18.6.6 § 189, says that when Tiberius ordered Macro to bind the Jewish prince Agrippa, Macro waited until he was ordered to do so a second and even a third time before he would act. Part of his hesitancy arose from the cost of arresting or chaining a Roman citizen, especially of high status. Although such law was not always followed, it is a factor in Acts 22. "When the centurion heard this, he went to the cohort commander and reported it, saying, 'What are you going to do? This man is a Roman citizen'" (v. 26).

The tribune then comes and asks Paul, "Tell me, are you a Roman citizen?" Paul replies, "Yes." What follows is an attempt of the tribune to determine Paul's social status relative to his own. Paul wins the battle of status. Citizenship could come in one of several ways: by birth, by being honored for some special service rendered to the government, by purchase. The tribune says: "I acquired this citizenship for a large sum of money" (v. 28a). Cicero, *Philippics* 5.4.2, charges Antony with selling citizenship for money. Dio Cassius 60.17.6 says that Claudius's wife, Messalina, and the members of her court would sell citizenship rights for their own personal gain. At first the price was high but gradually degenerated to the point where citizenship could be had for a few scraps of glass. Since it was customary to take the name of the emperor in whose reign citizenship was acquired, the tribune's name, Claudius Lysias (23:26), may suggest the time of his purchase, namely, during Claudius's reign. The practice of selling citizenship was continued into the time of Nero (Tacitus, *Annals* 14.50.1). It was with much money that the tribune had secured his citizenship. Not so Paul. Paul says, "But I was born one" (v. 28b).

Third, there is the outcome (v. 29). When Paul's Roman citizenship possessed from birth becomes known to the soldiers, "those who were going to interrogate him backed away from him, and the commander became alarmed when he realized that he was a Roman citizen and that he had him bound."

Actually a Roman citizen sometimes secured a lighter sentence than an alien, even for the same offence. Several examples make the case. In A.D. 17 when astrologers were rounded up by order of the Senate, the citizens among them were banished while the noncitizens were executed (Dio Cassius 57.15.8; Tacitus, *Annals* 2.32.3). When the attempt to incriminate Agrippina, the mother of Nero, failed, the perpetrators were punished. Calvisius and Iturues, freeborn citizens, were banished, but Atimetus, who was not a citizen, was executed (Tacitus, *Annals* 13.22). During the governorship of Pliny in Bithynia in Trajan's time, Pliny separated the accused Christians citizens from the noncitizens. The former were held until a judgment could be received from the emperor, but the latter were executed forthwith (Pliny, *Epistles* 10.96). In the reign of Marcus Aurelius, the governor of Lugdunum separated Christians from aliens and sent only the former to the beasts, with the exception of Attalus, a Roman citizen (Eusebius, *Church History* 5.1.47). Paul's appeal to his citizenship carried benefits beyond protection from flogging.

Scene three (Acts 22:30–23:10) also begins with (a) Paul's actions (22:30–23:6). Since interrogation of a Roman citizen by torture is not an option open to the tribune, the commander turns to another means to determine the truth about why Paul is being accused by the Jews. Freeing him (from chains), he convenes the Sanhedrin and brings Paul before them (22:30). Paul then defends himself.

The Sanhedrin was the Jewish supreme court. It had seventy-one members: seventy plus the president (*m. Sanhedrin* 1:6). It was presided over by the reigning High Priest (1 Macc 14:44). Its members came from three categories: High Priests, elders, scribes (Mark 14:53). It had the right to judge noncapital cases involving Jews and to inflict punishment on them (Mark 14:65; Josephus, *War* 6.5.3 §§ 300–309). It could not carry out the death penalty without the ratification of the Roman governor (John 18:31; Josephus, *Antiquities* 20.9.1 §§ 197–203). The governor was under no constraint to carry out a death penalty decided by the Sanhedrin (John 19:10). The sole instance in which the Sanhedrin had the right to punish by death, even if the offender was a Roman citizen, was when a non-Jew entered the inner precincts of the Temple.

There are analogies to the tribune's convening the Sanhedrin in the papyri of the Ptolemaic period (Tajra 1989, 91). The closest thing to what is reported here that is found in Josephus comes in *Antiquities* 20.9.1 § 202, where the procurator says it is not right for the High Priest to assemble the Sanhedrin without the governor's consent.

Paul's defense begins with his identification with his fellow Jews and with a claim of innocence: "My brothers, I have conducted myself with a perfectly clear conscience before God to this day" (23:1). Whereupon the High Priest, Ananias (Josephus, *War* 2.12.6 § 243; 2.17.6 §§ 426–29; *Antiquities* 20.5.2 § 103; 20.9.4 §§ 213–14), orders his attendants to strike Paul in the mouth (v. 2). Paul offers a quick rejoinder: "God will strike you, you whitewashed wall (Matt 23:27–28). Do you indeed sit in judgment upon me according to the law and yet in violation of the law order me to be struck?" (v. 3). Paul is being treated unjustly by an official who does not follow the law. Ananias has treated Paul as guilty before having heard the defendant (Deut 1:16–17; *Exodus Rabbah* 21.3–"Men pass judgment on a man if they hear his words; if they do not hear his words they cannot establish judgment on him") or the witnesses (*m. Sanhedrin* 3:6–8). Ananias received his just desserts, later dying a violent death at the hands of brigands at the outbreak of the first Jewish revolt (Josephus, *War* 2.17.9 §§ 441–42).

The attendants are just as quick to judge Paul. They ask, "Would you revile God's High Priest?" (v. 4). Paul's rationale is given, again prefaced by his identification with them: "Brothers, I did not realize he was the High Priest. For it is written, 'You shall not curse a ruler of your people'(Exod 22:27)" (v. 5). Paul, in contrast to the High Priest, makes an effort to follow the law.

Aware that some in the Sanhedrin were Sadducees and some Pharisees, Paul says, again with an opening identification with the audience, "My brothers, I am a Pharisee (26:5; Phil 3:5), the son of Pharisees; [I] am on trial for hope in the resurrection of the dead" (v. 6; cf. 24:15, 21; 26:6–8, 23–24; 28:20; 17:32). The Messianist proclamation is presented as the fulfillment of the Pharisaic eschatological expectation. The missionary Paul is here, moreover, presented as a resourceful witness from whom other missionaries can learn.

(b) Paul's defense again puts him in danger (vv. 7–10a). The statement about the resurrection from the dead serves as a catalyst to cause the long-standing dispute between Sadducees and Pharisees about life after death to erupt (v. 7). "For the Sadducees say that there is no resurrection or angels or spirits (Josephus, *War* 2.8.14 §§ 164–65; *Antiquities* 18.1.4 § 16; Luke 20:27–38), but the Pharisees (Josephus, *War* 2.8.14 § 163; *Antiquities* 18.1.3 § 14; *m. Sanhedrin* 10:1) acknowledge all three" (v. 8). What is involved is an intra-Jewish religious dispute. The tribune gains his desired end: accurate information about the issues (22:20; 23:28–29!). The long-standing dispute divides the Sanhedrin. "Some scribes belonging to the Pharisaic party stood up and argued sharply, 'We find nothing wrong with this man. Suppose a spirit or an angel has spoken to him'" (v. 9). These Pharisees reckon with the abstract possibility of resurrection. They are a long way, however, from belief in the concrete resurrection of Jesus. The result of Paul's ploy is a "great uproar" (v. 9). The dispute between Sadducees and

Pharisees is so serious that the tribune is afraid that Paul will "be torn to pieces by them" (v. 10a). The Sanhedrin acts no better than the Jewish mob at the Temple in 21:30-31, 34-36 and 22:22-23 or the pagan mob in Ephesus (19:28-34).

(c) The tribune then "ordered his troops to go down and rescue him from their midst and take him into the barracks" (*eis tēn parembolēn*). Confinement served various purposes for the Romans. It could offer protection (Tacitus, *History* 1.58, 71); it could secure the appearance of the accused at a trial (Suetonius, *Julius* 17.2); it could keep the prisoner available until sentence could be pronounced (Josephus, *Antiquities* 18.5.6 § 178); it could offer the place of execution (Tacitus, *Annals* 5.9); it could function as an instrument of coercion (Suetonius, *Tiberius* 57.2); it could serve as punishment (Suetonius, *Tiberius* 37.3) (Rapske 1994b, 10-20). At this point, Paul's confinement functions as his protection from violence (23:10). Custody, moreover, had various degrees of severity. The most severe was confinement in prison. Less severe was military custody, either in a barracks or in one's own home (Rapske 1994b, 20-32). Paul in Jerusalem has been in military custody in a barracks setting throughout. The degree of severity, however, has lessened in each scene. Now he is simply in protective custody, with no chains, and with the tribune aware that he is deserving of neither death nor imprisonment (23:28-29).

The narrative in Acts 21:26-23:10 is illustrative of a number of Lukan themes. (1) The non-Messianist Jews, Diaspora and Palestinian, people and leaders, are portrayed as unruly and violent, just as they have been throughout Acts (9:23, 29; 13:45, 50; 14:5, 19; 17:5-8, 13; 18:6, 12; 19:9; 20:3, 19). (2) Paul, by contrast, is depicted both as a faithful Jew (21:21-26; 22:1, 2, 3, 4-5, 17; 23:3, 5, 6), as elsewhere in Acts (16:3, 4, 13; 17:2; 18:18; 20:16), and as an obedient citizen (21:37-39) who claims his rights (22:24-29), as elsewhere (16:37-39; 19:31). His circumstances are also described as a fulfillment of Luke 21:12-19 and Acts 9:16. He is a faithful witness. (3) The Romans are described in a nuanced way. On the one hand, they are shown to be the best protection from violence the Messianists have ("he brought him into the barracks" in 21:34-37; 22:24; 23:10), as elsewhere in Acts (18:12-17; 19:23-40). On the other hand, the officials are painted in all their human frailty and fallibility, as elsewhere in Acts (16:22-24; 18:17; 24:26; 25:9). (4) Overall the events are presented, by means of a prophecy-fulfillment schema, as happening within the divine plan (19:21; 20:22-23; 21:11), as elsewhere in Acts (1:8; 9:15-16; 13:1-3; 16:6-10; 18:9-10, 21). (5) Above all, the Gentile mission is shown to be the result of the will of the risen Christ (22:15, 18, 21), as elsewhere in Acts (1:8; 10:1-11:18; 14:27; 15:11, 17).

Declared Innocent by Rulers
Acts 23:11–26:32

Acts 23:11–26:32 is a large thought unit subdivided into four scenes (23:12–35; 24:1–27; 25:1–12; 25:13–26:32), each dealing with Paul's status before Roman authorities. The overall thrust of the unit is that Paul is declared innocent by human authorities (23:29; 25:25; 26:31, 32). The four scenes are preceded by a prophecy of the risen Jesus promising Paul's witness in Rome (23:11). This prophecy indicates that in spite of all the chaos at the human level, the narrative is guided by "omnipotence behind the scenes." (The language is that of Meir Sternberg, 106.) The plan of God cannot be blocked.

The night after Paul's narrow escape from Sanhedrin violence (23:1–10), the Lord stands by him (in a dream/vision) and says, "Take courage. For just as you have borne witness to my cause in Jerusalem, so you must (*dei*) also bear witness in Rome" (23:11; cf. 18:9–10; 22:17–18; 27:23–24). Ancient auditors would have taken the vision with its promise about the future as an indication of Paul's favored status with the Lord. The philosopher Apollonius of Tyana expresses the general cultural belief: "I know better than any man that the gods reveal their intentions to holy and wise men" (Philostratus, *Life of Apollonius* 8.7.10). Regardless of what follows, the auditors now know that Paul will bear witness in Rome.

Scene one (23:12–35) consists of three paragraphs: (a) the plot (23:12–15); (b) the plot discovered (23:16–22); and (c) the plot foiled (23:23–35) and Paul declared innocent (23:29). (a) Verses 12–15 tell of a plot by more than forty Jews to kill Paul. The conspirators go to the chief priests and elders and say, "We have bound ourselves by a solemn oath to taste nothing until we have killed Paul. You, together with the Sanhedrin, must now make an official request to the commander to have him bring him down to you, as though you meant to investigate his case more thoroughly. We on our part are prepared to kill him before he arrives." There were such oaths, to do a certain deed or starve to death (*m. Shebuoth* 3:1–5). Of course, there were also provisions for release from such vows, if circumstances made them unfulfillable (*m. Nedarim* 3:3). Stories of plots, conspiracies, and intrigues are widespread in ancient literature (e.g., Daniel 3 and 6; *Joseph and Aseneth* 23–28; Chariton, *Chaereas and Callirhoe* 1.2–4; Achilles Tatius, *Leucippe and Clitophon* 7; Philostratus, *Apollonius* 4.35–47; 5.7–13). Given what Josephus says about the behavior of various Jewish groups toward one another in first-century Palestine, such a vow is in character (Josephus, *Life* 40 §§ 201–3; *War* 2.17.4–5 §§ 418–23; 4.3.2 §§ 129–34; 4.5.3 §§ 326–33).

(b) Verses 16–22 tell of the discovery of the plot. The son of Paul's sister hears about the plot and reports it to Paul, who is in Antonia (v. 16). Access to prisoners by family members or associates was not uncommon (Phil 2:25; 2 Tim 1:16–17; *Acts of Paul* 18–19; Lucian, *Peregrinus* 12–13). Paul then asks one of the centurions to take the young man to the tribune (v. 17). When the tribune speaks with him privately (v. 19), the young man tells him of the plot of the "more than forty" (vv. 20–21). The tribune dismisses the young man with a word of caution: "Tell no one that you gave me this information" (v. 22). In order to understand both Paul's access to Roman officers in Antonia and the tribune's subsequent actions, one must remember that at this point Paul is only in protective custody designed to guarantee the safety of a Roman citizen (23:10).

(c) Verses 23–35 tell how the plot is foiled. First, there are the preparations. The tribune summons two centurions and gives them instructions: "Get two hundred soldiers ready to go to Caesarea by nine o'clock tonight, along with seventy horsemen, and two hundred auxiliaries. Provide mounts for Paul to ride, and give him safe conduct to Felix the governor" (vv. 23–24). "The display intends to illustrate the importance of the prisoner, the enormity of the danger, and the quality of the measures taken by Roman military officials" (Conzelmann, 194).

Second, there is the letter from the tribune, Claudius Lysias, to the governor, Felix (vv. 25–30). The letter has five parts. (1) The introduction follows the usual form: "Claudius Lysias to his excellency the governor Felix, greetings" (v. 26; cf. 15:23). (2) The description of Paul's being taken into custody is self-serving. The tribune says he rescued Paul from the Jews after learning that he was a Roman citizen (v. 27; contrast 21:31–34; 22:25–29). (3) The summary of the procedure of inquiry is equally self-serving (v. 28). The tribune omits the aborted torture tactics (22:24–25) and mentions only the Sanhedrin episode (23:1–10). (4) The tribune's findings in the matter are crucial. "I discovered that he was accused in matters of controversial questions on their law and not of any charge deserving death or imprisonment" (v. 29; cf. 18:14–15; 25:19; 26:3). Here is the first of a series of four pronouncements of Paul's political innocence. The issue, the tribune says, is an intra-Jewish dispute. (5) The reason for remitting the prisoner is given: the plot against Paul (v. 30). The tribune also says he has notified Paul's accusers that they may state their case against Paul before Felix.

Third, there is the completion of the task (vv. 31–35). The soldiers escort Paul by night to Antipatris, about thirty-five miles from Jerusalem (v. 31), and return to Jerusalem the next day (v. 32). The horsemen complete the journey with Paul to Caesarea, some twenty-five miles farther (vv. 32–33). When Paul and the letter from the tribune are presented to Felix, the governor asks to what province he belongs. A governor had the right to extradite a prisoner to the governor of the province in which the accused was

born for trial there (Luke 23:7). Cilicia being too distant, Felix accepts jurisdiction. "I will hear your case when your accusers arrive" (v. 35). The comment sounds like Felix will begin all over, as though the tribune's findings
were of no value. He then holds Paul in custody in Herod's praetorium, the
palace built by Herod the Great (Josephus, *Antiquities* 15.9.6 § 331; *War*
1.21.5 § 408). Herod the Great's son, Antipater, had earlier been imprisoned
there (*Antiquities* 17.7 §§ 182–87).

Scene two (Acts 24:1–27) is comprised of three parts: (a) Felix hears the
charges against Paul (vv. 1–9); (b) Felix hears Paul's defense (vv. 10–21);
and (c) Felix disposes of Paul's case (vv. 22–27). (a) Verses 1–9 present the
charges against Paul. Five days later the high priest, Ananias, came down
with some elders and an advocate, Tertullus, to present formal charges
against Paul before Felix (v. 1; cf. Luke 23:1–2 where Jewish leaders accuse
Jesus before Pilate; Josephus, *War* 6.5.3 §§ 303–4, where Jewish rulers
bring a prophet before the Roman procurator). The use of an orator to present the charges is shrewd. Quintilian 5.1.57 says,

> the judges themselves demand the most finished and elaborate speeches, think-
> ing themselves insulted, unless the orator shows signs of having exercised the
> utmost diligence in the preparation of his speech, and desire not merely to be
> instructed but to be charmed.

Tertullus's speech begins with an exordium (vv. 2b–3), in which he
attempts to ingratiate himself with Felix. "Since we have attained much
peace through you, and reforms have been accomplished in this nation
through your provident care, we acknowledge this in every way and everywhere, most excellent Felix, with all gratitude." This was standard procedure (Winter, 505–31). Tertullus's statements are far from true. Felix had a
bad reputation among the Romans. Tacitus says he, "backed by vast influence, believed himself to be free to commit any crime" (*Annals* 12.54) and
he "practiced every kind of cruelty and lust, wielding the power of a king
with all the instincts of a slave" (*Histories* 5.9). During his administration
Jewish social chaos reached new heights (Josephus, *War* 2.13.2–7 §§ 252–
70). Toward the end of his procuratorship there were riots in Caesarea,
resulting in Felix's sending troops against the Jews. Many were killed and
their property plundered. This led to Jewish delegations to Nero to plead
the case against Felix (Josephus, *War* 2.13.7 § 270). Nevertheless, Tertullus
attempts to curry favor.

The issues at hand are described in vv. 4–7. Paul is "a pest" (v. 5a), that
is, a troublemaker (cf. 16:20; 17:6). He creates dissension among Jews
worldwide. He is a ringleader of the sect of the Nazoreans. He tried to des-
ecrate the Temple, and was arrested by the Jews. This is precisely the type
of charge that would have been most effective against a Jew in the time of

Claudius or the early years of Nero. During Claudius's reign, Jews had been expelled from Rome for disturbing the peace (Suetonius, *Claudius* 25.4; cf. Acts 18:2). During Claudius's reign, the emperor had written to Alexandria in the wake of civil disturbances there. He not only rebuked the Alexandrians for molesting the Jews but also warned the Jews against civil disturbances. (The papyrus from Egyptian Philadelphia, discovered in 1924, is published in English translation in Cadbury 1955, 116.) Rome, moreover, was protector of the Jewish Temple as a holy site (Josephus, *War* 6.2.4 § 128). Paul, then, is accused of being a disturber of the peace and a desecrator of holy sites.

The speech ends with Tertullus's claim that if Felix would examine Paul (by torture?), he would learn for himself from Paul everything of which he has been accused (v. 8). "The Jews also joined in the attack and asserted that these things were so" (v. 9).

(b) Felix then hears Paul's defense (vv. 10-21). In what follows, Paul reflects the confidence that a rhetorician was encouraged to display (Quintilian 5.21.51, cites Cicero in support of his contention that "our orator must . . . adopt a confident manner"). He begins with the same type of ingratiating comment as that used by Tertullus, but less untruthful. "I know that you have been a judge over this nation for many years and so I am pleased to make my defense before you" (v. 10b). "For many years" may reflect the knowledge that Felix served as an administrator in Palestine together with Cumanus before succeeding him as governor (Tacitus, *Annals* 12.54). Or it may merely reflect the fact that this event takes place toward the end of Felix's tenure. In any case, Felix is supposed to know the Jewish nation. That makes him a good judge for Paul, so the introduction claims.

What follows of Paul's defense falls into an ABA'B' pattern.

A—Narrative of real facts and denial of charges (vv. 11-13)
    (answering the charge of v. 5—disturber of the peace)
    B—Confession (vv. 14-16): I believe in resurrection
A'—Narrative of real facts and repudiation of charges (vv. 17-19)
    (answering the charge of v. 6—desecrator of Temple)
    B'—Confession (v. 20-21): I believe in resurrection

In A, vv. 11-13, Paul gives an account of the true facts of what happened in Jerusalem. Since the governor only has jurisdiction over things within the province of Judea, Paul limits his comments to events in Jerusalem (vv. 11-12). His behavior there, he says, can be verified by Felix (v. 11a; by the tribune?). He then denies the charges and impugns the witnesses. On the one hand, at no time did Paul argue with anyone or instigate a riot in the city (v. 12). On the other hand, he discredits the witnesses, following normal procedure: "Nor can they prove to you the accusations they are now making against me" (v. 13).

In B, vv. 14–16, Paul does confess, "But this I do admit to you" (v. 14a). To what does he confess? He worships the Jewish God, albeit according to the Way (v. 14b); he believes the Law and the Prophets (v. 14c); he has the same hope as they that there will be a resurrection of the righteous and the unrighteous (v. 15), a conviction that causes him always to keep his conscience clear (v. 16). He is a Jew, a certain kind of Jew: one who believes in the resurrection of the dead.

In A', vv. 17–19, Paul comes back to the true facts and once again repudiates the charges made against him. He came to Jerusalem to bring alms and offerings for his people (v. 17). This was a normal act of piety (Philo, *Embassy to Gaius* 216, 313). While he was so engaged (21:26–27), some Jews from Asia made charges (v. 19a; 21:27–29). But where are these Jews from Asia? They are the ones who should be present to make whatever accusation they might have against Paul (v. 19b). Roman law was strong against accusers who abandoned their charges. With these comments, Paul has dismissed the charge of desecration of the Temple. If that is gone, what is left?

In B', vv. 20–21, Paul offers to have the Jews who are present with Tertullus say what crime they discovered when Paul stood before the Sanhedrin (23:1–10). He will confess and they can confirm it. It was his one outcry: "I am on trial before you today for the resurrection of the dead" (v. 21). The defense speech attempts to reduce the charges from disturbance of the peace and desecration of the Temple to the theological issue of the resurrection from the dead (23:6, 29; 26:6, 8; 28:20b).

(c) Verses 22–27 relate Felix's disposal of Paul's case. On the one hand, he puts the Jews off: "Then Felix, who was accurately informed about the Way, postponed the trial, saying, 'When Lysias the commander comes down, I shall decide your (plural) case'" (v. 22). Of course, Felix already has the tribune's report in his letter (23:26–30). On the other hand, "he gave orders to the centurion that he [Paul] should have some liberty, and that he should not prevent any of his friends from caring for his needs" (v. 23). This represents a lessening of the severity of custody in Caesarea (cf. 23:35b) but an increase of severity over the protective custody Paul had experienced at the end in Jerusalem from the tribune.

Felix uses the delay and Paul's relative freedom to have more contact with Paul. Several days later he and his wife, Drusilla, a Jewess, listen to Paul speak about faith in Christ (v. 24). Drusilla was the youngest daughter of Agrippa I. She was seduced away from her husband by Felix through the use of a magician (Josephus, *Antiquities* 20.7.2 §§ 141–44). When Paul begins to speak about righteousness, self-restraint, and the coming judgment, Felix becomes frightened and says, "You may go for now; when I find an opportunity I shall summon you again" (v. 25). It is not a sermon that Felix wants. It is a bribe. "At the same time he hoped that a bribe would be offered him by Paul, and so he sent for him very often and conversed with him" (v. 26).

Bribery was widespread in the Mediterranean world. Cicero, *Pro Caecina* 73, says there were three major hindrances in civil litigation: excessive favor, possession of resources, and bribery. Petronius, *Satyricon* 14, has one of his plaintiffs ask, "Of what avail are laws to be where money rules alone . . . ? So a lawsuit is nothing more than a public auction." Propertius, *Elegies* 3.13.48–50, says, "Piety is vanquished and all men worship gold. Gold has banished faith, gold has made judgment to be bought and sold, gold rules the law." The practice seemed to be especially bad in the provinces, in spite of the *Lex Repetundarum,* which forbade anyone in power to solicit or accept a bribe. Cicero, *In Pisonem* 87, chronicles the evils of the Roman governor Piso: "What need for me to adduce . . . your bargains with defendants, your selling of justice, your savage condemnations and your capricious acquittals?" Albinus, the governor who succeeded Festus, accepted bribes to release individuals who had been imprisoned for trifling offenses (Josephus, *Antiquities* 20.9.5 § 215; *War* 2.14.1 § 273). Florus, who succeeded Albinus, was worse. "He thought it but a petty offense to get money out of single persons, so he spoiled whole cities" (Josephus, *War* 2.14.2 § 278). How could this happen? Agrippa told the Jews that it was not by Rome's command that a governor was oppressive but rather that Palestine was so far from Rome that such acts could not be seen or heard of easily by Rome (Josephus, *War* 2.16.4 §§ 351–52). The practice of bribery was, however, sometimes manipulated even by the emperor. Suetonius, *Vespasian* 16, says the emperor Vespasian

> thought nothing of . . . selling pardons to the innocent and guilty alike; and is said to have deliberately raised the greediest procurators to positions in which they could fatten their purses satisfactorily before he came down hard on them for extortion.

Assuming that Paul is wealthy or at least has access to the funds he had brought to Jerusalem, Felix tries to play the bribery game. Not being successful he leaves Paul in custody for two years (v. 27a).

Then, when he is departing office, he leaves Paul in prison "wishing to ingratiate himself with the Jews" (v. 27b). Given the fact that immediately after his replacement Felix was charged before Nero with various injustices to the Jews by a Jewish delegation (Josephus, *Antiquities* 20.8.9 § 182), Felix may very well have had good reason to seek to ingratiate himself with the Jews by leaving Paul in jail. It was after a governor left office that he could be accused and brought to trial for his wrongful deeds (e.g., Marius

Priscus, ca. A.D. 98, following his term as proconsul of Africa, was charged with taking bribes—Pliny, *Epistles* 2.11).

Scene three (Acts 25:1–12) is composed of three parts: (a) Festus hears the charges against Paul (vv. 1–7); (b) Festus hears Paul's defense (v. 8) and appeal to Caesar (vv. 9–11); and (c) Festus disposes of Paul's case by agreeing to send him to Caesar (v. 12). (a) Verses 1–7 tell of Festus's hearing the charges against Paul. Festus seems to have taken over for Felix about A.D. 60, after the riots in Caesarea. Given the troubles of his predecessor, he is eager not to offend the Jews. Three days after his arrival in the province, Festus goes up to Jerusalem. This visit is necessary, both for protocol and because of the recent Caesarean riots under Felix. There the chief priests and Jewish leaders present their case against Paul. Their request is that Festus send Paul to Jerusalem, their intent being to kill him along the way (vv. 1–3). Festus resists, saying that Paul is in custody in Caesarea, so the Jews should send their authorities there to make their accusations (vv. 4–5). Upon returning to Caesarea, Festus takes his seat upon the tribunal (the elevated platform from which a ruler would hear cases and deliver judgment; cf. 18:12) and has Paul brought in. The Jews from Jerusalem then make "many serious charges against him," which they cannot prove (vv. 6–7).

(b) Paul's defense is given in condensed form. "I have committed no crime either against the Jewish Law or against the Temple or against Caesar (by now, Nero)" (v. 8). He denies three charges: the first is religious; the second, religious and political; and the third, purely political. Then, "wishing to ingratiate himself with the Jews" (v. 9a; cf. 24:27, where the same language is used of Felix), Festus asks Paul, "Are you willing to go up to Jerusalem and there stand trial before me on these charges?" (v. 9b). 1 Maccabees 15:21 indicates a Roman understanding of their relationship with the Jews in terms of which "any pestilent men from their country" should be handed over "to Simon the high priest, that he may punish them according to their law." Paul is adamant: "I am standing before the tribunal of Caesar; this is where I should be tried. I have committed no crime against the Jews, as you well know . . . if there is no substance to the charges they are bringing against me, then no one has the right to hand me over to them. I appeal to Caesar" (vv. 10–11).

By Paul's time the right of appeal had been extended to Roman citizens living in the provinces. For example, Tacitus, *Annals* 16.10.2, tells of a Roman citizen in A.D. 64 being sent in chains for an unknown offense to the tribunal of Nero by the proconsul of Asia. Pliny sends certain condemned Bithynians who are citizens to the emperor Trajan in Rome (*Epistles* 10.96). Deinias, arraigned on murder charges, is sent by the governor of Asia to the emperor (Lucian, *Toxaris* 17). The right to appeal was reaffirmed by the promulgation in Augustus's reign of the *Lex Iulia de vi publica et privata*.

This law basically forbade an official to bind, torture, or kill a Roman citizen who had appealed to Rome (Tajra 1989, 146). Paul knows his rights and uses them for his protection. Of course, appeal to Caesar was a costly business. The appellant would personally have to undertake the costs of travel to Rome, the living costs while there, and perhaps the costs of actually litigating the case, including securing witnesses. "The status which granted the citizen the right of appeal never implied the means to carry it out" (Rapske 1994b, 55).

(c) Then Festus, after conferring with his council, replies, "You have appealed to Caesar. To Caesar you will go" (v. 12). Festus's council is a group of advisers used by magistrates (e.g., 4 Macc 17:17; Philo, *Gaius* 254; Josephus, *Antiquities* 16.6.2 § 163). The new governor continues to play it safe politically, even if it makes life difficult for Paul.

Scene four (Acts 25:13–26:32) is comprised of three parts: (a) Agrippa hears charges against Paul, privately (25:13–22) and publicly (25:23–27), including a statement of his innocence by Festus (25:25); (b) Agrippa hears Paul's defense (26:1–23); and (c) Agrippa and others give their judgment that Paul is innocent (26:24–32). (a) When King Agrippa and Bernice arrive in Caesarea for a visit, Festus refers Paul's case to the king (25:13–14). This Agrippa, the son of Herod Agrippa I, was born in A.D. 27 and was educated in Rome. Claudius gave him the kingdom of Chalcis in A.D. 50 (Josephus, *Antiquities* 20.5.2 § 104; *War* 2.121 § 223). In A.D. 53, Claudius granted him the tetrarchy of Philip together with Batanaea and Trachonitis, but deprived him of Chalcis (*Antiquities* 20.7.1 § 138; *War* 2.12.8 § 247). In A.D. 54 he obtained parts of Galilee and Perea from Nero (*Antiquities* 20.8.4 § 159; *War* 2.13.2 § 252). When possible, he promoted Judaism; yet his policy was one of unconditional subordination to Rome. Paul, then, appears before a man who was well known in the Roman court. Bernice was the daughter of Agrippa I and the sister of Drusilla (24:24). She was the widow of her uncle, Herod of Chalcis. At this point she is living with her brother (Josephus, *War* 2.11.5 § 217; *Antiquities* 20.7.3 § 145). Such an incestuous relationship was frowned upon by most Mediterranean peoples (Jewish law—Deut 27:20; Lev 18:9; Philo, *Special Laws* 3.22–28; *m. Yebamoth* 2:3; Greek tradition—Macareus, who committed incest with his sister, ended in disgrace/death; Plato, *Laws* 838ABC; Roman opinion—Juvenal, *Satires* 6.155–60).

After granting Paul's appeal, Festus would be required to write letters that would accompany Paul to Rome in order to inform the imperial tribunal of the particulars in the case. Acts 25:26 indicates Festus did not know what to write. He, therefore, enlists a Jewish expert to assist him. Such a practice has analogies: e.g., Herod the Great invited Varus, the Roman governor, and others to consult on the matter of Antipater (Josephus, *Antiquities* 17.5.3 § 93); Marcus Agrippa involves Roman officials and those kings and princes present in a key decision (Josephus, *Antiquities* 16.2.3 § 30).

First, Agrippa hears about Paul privately (25:14b–22). Festus's report begins in a self-serving way. He had followed the Roman practice of not handing over an accused person until he had the opportunity to defend himself (v. 16). He had acted speedily to deal with the matter (v. 17). The report then gives an outsider's view of exactly what is involved with Paul. "His accusers . . . did not charge him with any of the crimes I suspected. Instead they had some issues with him about their own religion and about a certain Jesus who had died but who Paul claimed was alive" (vv. 18–19). This is crucial! The issues are religious, not political. The self-serving report continues. Festus wanted Paul to go to Jerusalem to stand trial on these religious charges since he [the governor] was at a loss how to investigate the matter (v. 20). When Paul appealed to Caesar, Festus complied (v. 21). Agrippa's interest is piqued. He says to Festus, "I too should like to hear this man" (v. 22).

The next day Agrippa hears from Festus publicly about Paul (25:23–27). The audience hall is filled with noteworthy people: Agrippa and Bernice, cohort commanders, prominent men of the city, and Festus (v. 23). When Paul is brought in, Festus speaks to Agrippa and all those assembled. Paul is a man who the Jews say should be given the death penalty (v. 24). "I found, however, that he had done nothing deserving death, and so when he appealed to the Emperor, I decided to send him" (v. 25). The problem is that Festus does not know what to write to Rome (v. 26–27). That is why Festus has brought Paul before the gathered assembly, especially the Jewish expert, Agrippa (v. 26b). Twice, privately (25:18–19) and publicly (25:25), Festus has pronounced Paul innocent of criminal charges. The issue is a theological matter (25:19). Festus agrees with the Lukan Paul about what is at stake (23:6; 24:15, 21). Shaped by private and public briefings, Agrippa is ready to hear Paul himself.

(b) Paul's defense involves a long speech (26:1–23). It begins with the usual attempt to ingratiate the speaker into the good graces of the auditor. "I count myself fortunate, King Agrippa, that I am able to defend myself before you today . . . especially since you are an expert in all the Jewish customs and controversies" (vv. 2–3). Agrippa, a Jew, is even better informed than Felix, who was married to a Jewess, had been. That is an acknowledged advantage for Paul.

What follows in Paul's speech falls into an ABA'B' pattern.

A—Autobiographical: Paul's life as a Jew (vv. 4–5)
  (*men oun*)
  B—The issue: resurrection (vv. 6–8) (*hestēka*)

A'—Autobiographical: Paul's life as a Jew, his conversion, and his preaching—the last of which is why he was seized in the Temple (vv. 9–21)
(*men oun*)
B'—The issue: resurrection of Christ (vv. 22–23) (*hestēka*)

A, vv. 4–5, is an autobiographical section in which Paul gives his Jewish
credentials. From his youth Paul has lived among Jews and in Jerusalem as
a Pharisee, "the strictest party of our religion." This is known by the Jews
who are accusing him.

B, vv. 6–8, focuses the issue. "But now I am standing on trial because of
my hope in the promise made by God to our ancestors." What is that hope?
"Why is it thought unbelievable . . . that God raises the dead?" The issue is
theological. It is belief in the resurrection of the dead, a good Pharisaic
doctrine.

A', vv. 9–21, is also autobiographical. It begins with an account of Paul's
persecution of followers of Jesus. In Jerusalem he acted on the authority of
the chief priests to imprison Messianists. When they were to be put to
death, he voted against them (v. 10). He was so enraged against them that
he pursued them outside of Jerusalem (v. 11). On one such occasion, when
he was going to Damascus with the authorization of the chief priests (v. 12),
he was converted. At midday, a bright light shone around him and he fell to
the ground. A voice said to him, "Saul, Saul, why are you persecuting me? It
is hard for you to kick against the goad" (vv. 13–14). "Goads" were sharp
pointed sticks used to move cattle in the desired direction. The expressing
"kicking against the goads" was a Greek proverb (e.g., Pindar, *Pythian Odes*
2.94; Aeschylus, *Agamemnon* 1624; *Prometheus* 324–25; Euripides, *Bacchae* 794; Julian the Apostate, *Oration* 8.246B). Philo, *Decalogue* 17 § 87,
uses the imagery for conscience's prodding humans to proper behavior.
Paul, by his persecution of Messianists, is resisting the direction that Jesus
has for his life. When Paul asks the identity of the voice, he hears, "I am
Jesus whom you are persecuting." During this christophany, Paul receives
his commission from Jesus in language that echoes that of Israel's prophets.

> Get up now, and stand on your feet (Ezek 2:1). I have appeared to you for this
> purpose, to appoint you as a servant and witness of what you have seen [of me]
> and what you will be shown. I shall deliver you (Jer 1:8) from this people and
> from the Gentiles to whom I send you (Jer 1:7), to open their eyes that they may
> turn from darkness to light (Isa 42:6–7) and from the power of Satan to God, so
> that they may obtain forgiveness of sins and an inheritance among those who
> have been consecrated by faith in me (vv. 16–18).

Paul "was not disobedient to the heavenly vision" (v. 19). He has everywhere preached the need to repent and to do works giving evidence of

repentance (v. 20). It is because of his preaching that the Jews seized him and are trying to kill him.

Paul's behavior is described in terms that a Roman would understand. When one receives a heavenly vision, it is imperative that the person obey. Two examples suffice. First, Livy 2.36 and Plutarch, *Caius Marcius Coriolanus* 24, tell of one Titus Latinius, quiet and modest, free from superstitious fears and vain pretensions, who had a vision of Jupiter appearing to him, bidding him to tell the Senate a certain message. After having the vision, Titus gave it no thought at first. After he had seen it a second and third time and still neglected it, he suffered the loss of an excellent son by death and himself became suddenly palsied. He was then brought to the Senate on a litter. No sooner had he told his message than he felt the strength return to his body. He rose up and walked away without aid. Second, in the *Scriptores Historiae Augustae*, "Hadrian" 25, a woman was warned in a dream to convey a message to Hadrian. When she did not, she became blind. A second time she was told what to do and say. When she did it, she recovered her sight. In Mediterranean antiquity, it is proper piety to obey a heavenly vision. This Paul did.

B', vv. 22–23, once again focuses on the true issue: the resurrection of Jesus. "I stand here testifying to small and great alike . . . that the Messiah must suffer and that, as the first to rise from the dead, he would proclaim light both to our people and to the Gentiles."

(c) Agrippa and others, after dialogue with Paul (vv. 24–29), give their judgment that Paul is innocent (vv. 30–32). While Paul is speaking (cf. 10:44; 24:25), Festus interrupts him: "You are mad, Paul; much learning is driving you mad" (v. 24). The charge of madness in antiquity was sometimes leveled at philosophers: for example, Cynics (Ps-Socratic, *Epistles* 6.1; 9.3; Dio Chrysostom, *Orations* 8.36; 9.8) and Dio Chrysostom (*Oration* 12.8–9; 34). When so charged, Dio Chrysostom responded that he was not mad but rather spoke the truth (*Oration* 77/78.41–42). Paul shares the stock charge against philosophers. He is accused by the proconsul of being mad. The cause of his madness is his great learning. This fits into the Lukan concern overall to portray Messianists as people with relatively high social standing (6:7; 8:26–39; 10:1–48; 13:6–12; 16:14–15; 18:8). Festus is a witness to the fact not only that Paul is innocent but that he is not ignorant as some of the church's opponents claimed Jesus' followers were (e.g., Minucius Felix, *Octavius* 5.4; 8.4; Origen, *Celsus* 6.13). Paul's response is essentially that of Dio Chrysostom. "I am not mad, most excellent Festus; I am speaking words of truth and reason" (v. 25).

Turning to Agrippa, Paul says, "The king knows about these matters and to him I speak boldly, for I cannot believe that any of this has escaped his notice; this was not done in a corner (in secret)" (v. 26). The Romans had fears about secret societies and secret rites and teaching (Pliny, *Epistles* 10.96; Origen, *Celsus* 1.3). Paul denies the Messianist movement is in any way a secret society. What it stands for, the king knows. Then Paul presses, not his defense, but for an evangelistic decision: "King Agrippa, do you believe the prophets? I know you believe" (v. 27). The Jewish scriptures with their prophetic oracles functioned as a bridge by which many Gentiles (e.g., Tatian, *Oration* 29; Justin, *Dialogue* 7ff.; preaching of Peter [so Clement of Alexandria, *Miscellanies* 6.15]; Theophilus of Antioch, *To Autolycus* 14) as well as Jews crossed to the Messianist camp. To which the king responds, "In so short a time do you think you will make me a Christian (a lackey of Christ)?" Agrippa joins a host of ancients in deriding the possibility of instantaneous conversion (e.g., Plutarch, *Progress in Virtue* 75C-E; Lucian, *Nigrinus* 1). Paul replies: "I would pray to God that sooner or later not only you but all who listen to me today might become as I am except for these chains" (v. 29; cf. Justin Martyr, who after his conversion says, "And, further, I could wish that all should form a desire as strong as mine, not to stand aloof from the Savior's words"—*Dialogue* 8.2). "Except for these chains" refers to his loss of honor and dignity (Josephus, *War* 4.10.7 §§ 628-29). The long speech before King Agrippa fulfills the promise of Acts 9:15 that Paul would be a witness before kings, just as his chains fulfill the prediction of suffering.

The king, Bernice, Festus, and the others then rise and depart. After conversation among themselves, they say to one another, "This man is doing nothing [at all] that deserves death or imprisonment" (v. 31). The expert then gives his opinion. Agrippa says to Festus, "This man could have been set free if he had not appealed to Caesar" (v. 32).

The main point of 23:11–26:32 is found in the official verdicts. Paul is declared innocent by human authority of any crime for which the state is responsible: the tribune (23:29), the governor Felix by implication (24:23, 26, 27), the governor Festus (25:25; 26:31), and the king, Agrippa (26:32). The matter at issue concerns intra-Jewish debates (23:29; 25:18), in particular, the claim that Jesus, who was dead, is now alive (25:19b; 26:23). Paul is faithful to Judaism's hope of the resurrection and is innocent of any criminal acts against Rome. The Messianist movement is a branch of Judaism that believes in the resurrection and that is politically responsible.

The narrative also makes clear what Jesus' disciples are and are not to expect from the state. On the one hand, the state is available to offer disciples protection against violence (23:17–22). The state respects a disciple's Roman citizenship (22:27–29; 25:16), often sparing no expense to guarantee a citizen's physical safety (23:23). On the other hand, one must be realistic about what can be expected in the way of implementation of Roman justice. If Paul is deemed completely innocent, why does he remain a prisoner? At one level, Paul's continuing imprisonment is viewed as due to human evil. Both Felix (24:27) and Festus (25:9) dilute the justice due to Paul by their desire to please the Jews (cf. 12:3). Moreover, Felix's desire for a bribe (24:26) gives him an additional reason to keep Paul in custody. Even though Roman officials recognize his innocence, they do not give Paul full justice because of their own personal failings. Whereas the disciples of Jesus may expect to benefit from Roman justice, contingent on the character of the individual administrators, there is one area in which they should not expect anything from the State. The Roman state is not competent to judge religious or theological matters about which Messianists and non-Messianists clash (25:20a, 26; 26:24; see 18:15). The matter of resurrection is incomprehensible to the state.

An auxiliary point in the narrative concerns the suffering of Jesus' followers (cf. Heb 10:32-34; 1 Pet 4:4). Paul in this narrative acts to protect himself from senseless violence. He does not rush into martyrdom but uses his legal options. He makes use of the Roman legal system to preserve his life (23:17-22; 25:10-12; cf. 16:37-39). He manifests no lust for death as Ignatius of Antioch and the young Origen do later. Messianists may die as martyrs, Luke thinks, but this is only after they have exhausted every legal recourse. Martyrdom is not suicide.

Declared Innocent By God
Acts 27:1-28:16

Acts 27:1-28:16 is a large thought unit dealing with Paul's journey from Caesarea to Rome. It consists of introductory (27:1-8) and concluding (28:11-16) itineraries enclosing three scenes (27:9-20; 27:21-44; 28:1-10). It functions in a twofold way: (1) to indicate God's declaration of Paul's innocence, and (2) to show that nothing can hinder the unfolding of God's plan, in particular, Paul's bearing witness in Rome.

The introductory itinerary (27:1-8) consists of two paragraphs (vv. 1-5 and vv. 6-8). The first, vv. 1-5, narrates Paul's journey from Caesarea to Myra in a ship of Adramyttium (a town on the coast of Asia Minor near Troas). When Festus decides that Paul and his associates should sail to Italy, he hands Paul over to a centurion named Julius (v. 1; cf. 24:23). They go on board a ship bound for ports in the province of Asia (v. 2a). With "us" (another of the "we" sections of Acts) is Aristarchus, a Macedonian from Thessalonica (v. 2b; 19:29; 20:4; cf. Col 4:10; Phlm 24). For Paul's associates to endanger themselves by accompanying him is a sign of true friendship. Lucian, *Toxaris* 18, in speaking of friendship says of Agathocles that he "alone of all [Deinias's] friends kept with him, sailed with him to Italy, went to the trial with him, and failed him in nothing." This was in contrast to Apollonius's disciples who, fearing imprisonment and death themselves if they followed their teacher to Rome, are reduced from thirty-four to eight (Philostratus, *Life* 4.37). Paul, by contrast, has true friends who will stand with him no matter what. He also has friends along the way. The next day they put in at Sidon where "Julius was kind enough to allow Paul to visit his friends who took care of him" (v. 3). From Sidon the ship sails to Myra in Lycia (v. 5).

The second paragraph (vv. 6–8) narrates Paul's journey from Myra on the southern coast of Asia Minor to Fair Havens in Crete on a ship of Alexandria. In Myra the centurion finds an Alexandrian ship sailing for Italy and puts Paul and his company on board (v. 6). Alexandria was the granary of the empire. Since grain was so desperately needed in Rome, Claudius had attempted to insure a regular supply by means of financial guarantees. He assumed the expense of any loss that a ship might suffer from storms (Suetonius, *Claudius* 18.2). The ship on which Paul is now traveling is one of the grain ships that plied the Mediterranean even in dangerous seasons. With difficulty they arrive at Cnidus at the southwestern tip of Asia Minor. Because of unfavorable winds, with difficulty they sail past Salmone at the northwestern tip of Crete to a place called Fair Havens (v. 8). The itinerary is little more than stops on the way. There are, however, intimations already present in the narrative of difficulties due to weather.

Scene one (Acts 27:9–20) and scene two (27:21–44) together comprise a sea storm and shipwreck type-scene. Narratives of storm and shipwreck are widespread in Mediterranean antiquity. (1) Greek—for example, Homer, *Odyssey* 4.499–511; 5.291–453; 12.403–28; Herodotus 7.188–92; 8.12–14; Apollonius Rhodius, *Argonautica* 2.1093–1121; Dio Chrysostom, *Oration* 7.2–7; Lucian, *Toxaris* 19–21; *The Ship* 7–9; Aelius Aristides, *Sacred Tales* 2.12–14; 2.64–68; Achilles Tatius, *Leucippe and Clitophon* 3.1–5. (2) Roman—for example, Plautus, *The Rope* 62–78; Vergil, *Aeneid* 1.122–252; 3.253–275; 5.14–43; Ovid, *Metamorphoses* 11.477–574; Seneca, *Agamemnon* 456–578; Lucan, *Civil War* 4.48–120; 5.560–677; 9.319–47; Statius, *Thebaid* 5.360–421. (3) Jewish—for example, Jonah 1:3–17; *T. Naphtali* 6:1–10; Josephus, *War* 1.14.2–3 §§ 279–80; *Life* 13–16.

Practice in composing such narratives was part of the rhetorical training in the Roman imperial period. Such stories shared numerous elements: for example, (1) a warning not to sail; (2) sailing in a bad season; (3) unusually chaotic winds; (4) darkness during the storm; (5) horrendous waves; (6) sailors scurrying about; (7) cargo or tackle thrown overboard; (8) control of the ship given up so that it is driven by the winds and waves; (9) the ship's breaking up; (10) passengers abandoning all hope; (11) the ship's wrecking on rocks or a shallow beach; (12) survivors drifting on planks; (13) swimming to shore or to another ship; (14) helpful, simple folk on shore. It is these common elements that justify calling such accounts type-scenes. So predictable were these accounts that they became the object of satire (Juvenal, *Satires* 12.17–82; Lucian, *On Salaried Posts in Great Houses* 1–2) and parody (Lucian, *True Story* 1.5–6).

Some of these sea stories functioned merely as a record of historical events (e.g., Tacitus, *Annals* 2.23–24); others served primarily as entertainment (e.g., Petronius, *Satyricon* 114). Certain of the narratives, however, served to teach either theological or moral lessons. Examples of moral lessons taught by sea narratives include (a) reckless pride leads to destruction (e.g., Polybius, *Histories* 1.37; cf. Acts 27:9–12); (b) wealth is a burden and is a transient possession (e.g., Phaedrus, *Fables* 4.23; cf. Acts 27:18, 38); (c) a true friend is willing to risk his life for the other (e.g., Lucian, *Toxaris* 19–21; cf. Acts 27:31–32); (d) only the true philosopher is calm in a crisis (e.g., Lucian, *Peregrinus* 43–44; Diogenes Laertius 9.68; cf. Acts 27:33–36); (e) when in crisis pray (e.g., *T. Naphtali* 6:1–10; cf. Acts 27:23–26). Most of these moral points function in subsidiary roles in Acts 27.

The theological functions of sea narratives are best seen when the stories are looked at in terms of causality. Viewed in terms of causality, the narratives fall into four categories of the sea storm type-scene: (a) a storm is caused by gods or God//the outcome is due also to gods or God, whether deliverance or death (Homer, *Odyssey* 4.499–511; 5.291–453; Aeschylus, *Agamemnon* 647–66; Herodotus 7.188–192; Euripides, *Daughters of Troy* 77–86; *Iphigeneia in Taurica* 1391–1489; Apollonius Rhodius 2.1093–1121; Chariton 3.3; Vergil, *Aeneid* 1.122–252; Seneca, *Agamemnon* 456–578; Statius, *Thebaid* 5.360–421; Valerius Flaccus 1.614–58; Silius Italicus 17.244–90; Jonah 1:3–17); (b) a storm is caused by gods or God//outcome is due to mortals on the ship (e.g., Euripides, *Helen* 400–413; Plautus, *The Rope* 62–78); (c) the storm is due to natural causes//the outcome is due to the gods or God (e.g., *Herpyllis*; Lucian, *On Salaried Posts* 1–2; *The Ship* 7–9; Aelius Aristides, *Sacred Tales* 2.12–14; Achilles Tatius 1.1; 3.1–5; Vergil, *Aeneid* 3.253–75; Ovid, *Tristia* 1, 2.1–110; *T. Naphtali* 6:1–10; Josephus, *Life* 13–16); (d) the storm is due to natural causes//the outcome is due to natural or human agents (e.g., Apollonius Rhodius, *Argonautica* 4.1228–47; Polybius 1.37; *Ninus* C; Chion 4; Dio Chrysostom, *Oration* 7.2–7; Xenophon, *Ephesian Tale* 2.11; 3.2; 3.12; Lucian, *Toxaris* 19–21; *True Story* 1.5–6; 2.47; Aelius Aristides, *Sacred Tales* 2.64–68; *Apollonius King of Tyre* 11–12; Heliodorus 1.22; 5.27; Vergil, *Aeneid* 5.14–43; Ovid, *Metamorphoses* 11.472–574; Quintus Curtius, *Alexander* 4.3.16–18; Phaedrus, *Fables* 4.23; Petronius, *Satyricon* 114; Lucan 5.560–677; 9.319–47; Tacitus, *Annals* 2.23–24; Josephus, *War* 1.14.2–3 §§ 279–80).

From a reading of Acts 27, it ought to be possible to discern where it fits in this typology of sea storm and shipwreck type-scenes. Scene one (27:9–20) is organized in terms of Paul's prediction and its fulfillment.

> Paul's prediction (27:10), based on the time of year (27:9), is overridden by greed (27:11) and an unsatisfactory harbor (27:12)–that is, the storm and shipwreck are not due to Paul's wickedness.

Paul's prediction is fulfilled in three paragraphs:

(a) 27:13–the south wind blew gently
(b) 27:14–17–a tempestuous wind struck
(c) 27:18–20–violently storm-tossed so that all hope is abandoned.

The first paragraph of scene one (vv. 9–12) is organized around Paul's prediction. "Much time had now passed and sailing had become hazardous because the time of the fast (the Day of Atonement, 10th Tishri, i.e., September/October) had already gone by" (v. 9). After mid-September, sailing on the Mediterranean was regarded as unsafe. Paul's warning is prophetic: "Men, I can see that this voyage will result in severe damage and heavy loss not only to the cargo and the ship, but also to our lives" (v. 10). Seneca (*Epistle ad Lucilium* 14.8) says that the more careful pilot consults and heeds the advice of those on ship who have maritime knowledge. Paul would have been one of those (2 Cor 11:25)–"Three times I have been shipwrecked; a night and a day I have been adrift at sea"). The centurion, however, pays more attention to the pilot and the owner of the ship than to Paul (v. 11). Since the harbor is unfavorable for spending the winter, the majority plan to put out to sea in the hopes of reaching Phoenix, a favorable port in Crete where they could spend the winter (v. 12).

The second paragraph of scene one (27:13–20) is organized around the fulfillment of Paul's prediction. The story is told in a stock fashion: for example, Chion of Heraclea's mid-first-century novel in letters has a warning not to sail because of weather signs, but the warning is overridden by the crew; a fair wind blew initially promising a fine trip, but then there was a terrible gale (letter 4); or the surviving fragment of the second-century A.D. romance *Herpyllis* contains a prediction of bad weather and a warning not to sail that is overridden; the sun appears initially but then there is darkness, thunder, and winds with no prospects of coming out alive. So in Acts 27:13 the south wind blows gently, leading the sailors to weigh anchor and sail along the coast of Crete. Before long, however, a tempestuous wind strikes (v. 14) and the ship is helpless in the wind's fury (v. 15). Fearful that they will be driven aground on the shoal of Syrtis, they lower the anchor and are dragged along (v. 18). Then they jettison cargo and even some of the ship's tackle (v. 19). "Finally, all hope of our surviving was taken away" (v. 20).

Scene two (27:21-44) is organized very much like scene one. There is a prediction of Paul followed by its fulfillment.

Paul's prediction (27:21-22, 26), based on an angelic message (27:23-25)—that is, deliverance is due to divine protection of Paul.

Paul's prediction is fulfilled in three stages:

(a) 27:27-32—about midnight, a Pauline warning
(b) 27:33-38—as day was about to dawn, Pauline encouragement
(c) 27:39-44—when it was day, all escaped to land.

The first paragraph of scene two (vv. 21-26) is organized around Paul's prediction. When many would no longer eat, Paul speaks. He first says in effect, "I told you so" (v. 21). Then he calls for courage because no life will be lost, only the ship (v. 22). How does he know?

Last night an angel of the God to whom [I] belong and whom I serve stood by me and said, "Do not be afraid, Paul. You are destined (*dei*) to stand before Caesar; and behold, for your sake, God has granted safety to all who are sailing with you" (v. 24).

Paul trusts in God that it will be as he has been told (v. 25). What he has been told apparently includes, "We are destined (*dei*) to run aground on some island" (v. 26).

Paragraph two (vv. 27-44) is organized around the fulfillment of Paul's prophecy. It unfolds over three periods of time. First, on the fourteenth night, about midnight, the sailors suspect they are nearing land. Their soundings confirm their suspicion (v. 28). Because of the danger, the sailors try to abandon ship by taking the dinghy (v. 30), a stock motif in antiquity (e.g., Petronius, *Satyricon* 102; Achilles Tatius, *Clitophon and Leucippe* 3.3). Paul says to the centurion and soldiers, "Unless these men stay with the ship, you cannot be saved" (v. 31). This indicates that on ship Paul is kept above deck (in a lenient custody). Only thereby can he address the centurion and soldiers. "So the soldiers cut the ropes of the dinghy and set it adrift" (v. 32).

Second, as day is about to dawn, since they have not eaten for fourteen days, Paul encourages the travelers to take some food (cf. Aelius Aristides, *Sacred Tales* 2.68, who tells of being adrift for fourteen days with no one on board being able to eat during that time). He himself then "took bread, gave thanks to God in front of them all, broke it, and began to eat" (v. 35). Encouraged by his example the others, some 276 (Josephus, *Life* 15, says there were six hundred with him when he was shipwrecked), did likewise. This is not a eucharist despite the language. Those involved are not all believers, and it is not a common meal. Then, having eaten enough, they throw the wheat into the sea (v. 38).

Third, when it is day they try unsuccessfully to run the ship ashore. Instead they strike a sandbar, running the ship aground. The stern of the ship then begins to break up under the pounding of the waves. "The soldiers planned to kill the prisoners so that none might swim away and escape, but the centurion wanted to save Paul and so kept them from carrying out their plan" (v. 42–43). Some swim, others on planks and debris from the ship make it to land. "In this way, all reached shore safely" (v. 44b).

Scenes two and three (27:9–44) belong to category three of ancient sea storm type-scenes: the storm is due to natural causes; the outcome is due to the divine will. In Acts 27 the narrator makes no mention of divine action in sending the storm. Rather there are references that indicate the natural causes of the storm: (a) the time of the year (27:9–"the time of the fast had already gone by, so Paul warned them"); (b) the apparent greed of the pilot and owner of the ship who want to sail despite the bad time of year (27:11–"the centurion paid more attention to the pilot and the owner of the ship than to what Paul said"; cf. Pliny, *Natural History* 2.47.125–"not even the fury of the storms closes the sea; pirates first compelled men by the threats of death to rush into death and venture on the winter seas, but now avarice exercises the same compulsion"); (c) the search for a suitable harbor in which to spend the winter (27:12–"since the harbor was unfavorably situated for spending the winter, the majority planned to put out to sea . . . in the hope of reaching Phoenix, a port in Crete"); (d) the fact that other ships had spent the winter in a safe harbor (28:11–"three months later we set sail on a ship that had wintered at the island"). All of these details make the same point. The storm and shipwreck were not due to divine judgment but to a natural cause, namely, the time of the year.

Such a depiction of Paul's experience could be understood as a protection against possible misunderstanding in terms of category one: you cannot escape divine Justice; the storm is caused by God as a judgment on a guilty party, Paul. That the narrator was aware of such a possibility is evidenced by the views espoused by his characters in 28:4b: "This man must certainly be a murderer; though he escaped the sea, Justice has not allowed him to remain alive."

Over against any impression that Paul was judged guilty by God because he was involved in a storm and a shipwreck, Acts 27 makes explicit that the storm and shipwreck are due to the time of the year (27:9). Over against any claim that Paul's escape from the dangers of the deep was due to human prowess, Acts 27 makes explicit that the deliverance is in accord with the divine plan (27:23–25; 19:21–22; 23:11). The effect of the former is to declare that Paul's involvement in storm and shipwreck is not evidence of any guilt on his part. The effect of the latter is to say that Paul's preservation is part of the divine plan to carry the gospel to Rome by means of this innocent one. You cannot stop the divine plan! This seems to be the way an ancient Mediterranean auditor would have heard the narrative, given the cultural conventions about sea storms and shipwrecks.

Acts 28:1–10 constitutes scene three in the thought unit 27:1–28:16. It consists of two parts: 28:1–6 and 28:7–10. In the first part, Paul is bitten by a viper (v. 3), which causes the natives to think he is a murderer who, though he escaped from the sea, has now been caught by divine Justice (v. 4). When he is not affected by the snake bite, the natives change their opinion (v. 5). He is not a murderer; he is a god. Two things emerge from vv. 3–4. First, there is an explicit statement by the characters of the Mediterranean assumption that the animal kingdom, often a serpent, functioned as a vehicle of divine Justice. Second, the serpent bite is explicitly understood as a corollary to involvement in storm and shipwreck. Both are believed by the natives to function in the same way, as divine judgment.

Three examples from the Greco-Roman world illustrate one or the other or both of the dimensions of the case. (a) In the *Greek Anthology* 7.290, we read:

> The shipwrecked mariner had escaped the whirlwind and the fury of the deadly sea, and as he was lying on the Libyan sand not far from the beach . . . naked and exhausted by the unhappy wreck, a baneful viper slew him. Why did he struggle with the waves in vain, escaping then the fate that was his lot on the land?

Here both dimensions are combined: snake bite and shipwreck as vehicles of divine destiny.

Heliodorus, *An Ethiopian Story* 2.20, tells of a brigand, Themouthis, making his escape, who lay down to sleep, "but the sleep he slept was the final sleep, the brazen sleep of death, for he was bitten by a viper."

An Egyptian papyrus of the fourth–fifth centuries A.D. offers a similar perspective:

> A son having murdered his own father and fearing the laws fled into the desert. As he passed through the mountains he was pursued by a lion; and being pursued by a lion he went up into a tree, and finding a snake as he went up into a tree and being unable to go up on account of the snake, he came down again. Wrong doing does not escape the attention of god. The divine always brings the wicked into Dike. (Cadbury 1955, 27)

Similar assumptions are found in Jewish sources as well. (a) In the *Tosefta,* Sanhedrin 8:3 [E], R. Simeon ben Shatah (ca. 80 B.C.) said he saw a man with a sword running after a fellow. The two ran into a deserted building. When Simeon entered, he saw the one slain and the other with the sword dripping blood. The rabbi comments, "but He who knows the thoughts of man will exact punishment from the guilty. He did not move from the spot before a snake bit him and he died." (b) In the Jerusalem Talmud, *Berakoth* 5:1 [XIV.D], there is a tradition about R. Haninah ben Dosa (before A.D. 70), who, when praying, was bitten by a snake but did not interrupt his prayers. Not only was the rabbi not affected by the bite but the snake died at the entrance to its den. In the Babylonian Talmud, after these events Hanina is reported to have said, "It is not the snake that kills, but sin" (*b. Berakoth* 33a). A righteous man is unaffected by snake bite, just as a wicked man is punished by it (cf. Mark 16:18).

The latter point corresponds to the Jewish mindset found in Dan 6:22, where Daniel says to the king, "My God sent His angel and shut the lions' mouths . . . *because* I was found blameless before Him." That this is not limited to a Jewish context is evidenced by the Greco-Roman tradition found in Horace, *Odes* 1.22. There the poet proves his righteousness with the news that while he was strolling unprotected through the woods, a wolf fled from him, leaving him unharmed. The animal kingdom, like the sea, punishes the wicked as the agent of divine Justice. It does not, however, harm the righteous.

There seems to be no other way to read Acts 28:1–6 in a Mediterranean context. The natives think Paul guilty when he is bitten; they change their minds when he is unaffected. So Paul is declared innocent by God! Neither storm nor serpent bite is to be taken as God's judgment on Paul. Quite the contrary. God protects and vindicates his upright one.

Acts 28:7–10 functions in two ways. First, it refutes the natives' wrong belief that Paul is a god (v. 6). How? In v. 8, in connection with the healing of Publius's father, Paul "prays" for the healing. A god does not pray for a healing but heals out of Himself (cf. Luke 8:46). Likewise, a magician with pretensions of deity would not pray but would regard the miracle as his own doing. This is made clear by Philostratus, *Life of Apollonius* 8.7.9. In Apollonius's defense before Domitian, he contends that he is no magician even though he has eradicated the disease causing a plague in Ephesus. Why? Because he "prayed" to Hercules for the healing. A magician would not do this because he would consider it his own achievement. Contrary to the natives' opinion, Paul is neither a god nor a pretender to divine honors (a magician; cf. 8:10).

Second, it indicates that Paul is a righteous man. James 5:16b–18, in the context of prayers for healing, uses Elijah as an example to indicate that "the fervent prayer of a righteous person is very powerful." John 9:31, again in the context of healing, has the formerly blind man declare, "We know that God does not listen to sinners, but if one is devout and does His will, He listens to him." That Paul's prayer is answered is an indication that he is a righteous man. Acts 28:1–10 declares Paul innocent by God's decree. This goes hand in glove with the same point being made in chap. 27. Acts 27 says Paul is not guilty even if he was in a storm and shipwreck. Acts 28 says Paul is not guilty even if he was bitten by a serpent. Both affirm Paul is God's servant, a righteous man to whom God discloses His will and whose prayers are answered. By God's decree, Paul is innocent. If so, Acts 27:1–28:16 functions to declare divine vindication of Paul just as 23:11–26:32 functions to declare Paul innocent before human authorities.

At the same time that Acts 27:1–28:10 functions to show Paul is pronounced innocent by God, it also serves to show that what transpires happens according to the divine plan. According to Luke-Acts, there is a divine plan that stands behind the events of history. It is spoken of in various ways: for example, the plan of God (*boulē tou theou*) in Luke 7:30; Acts 2:23; 4:28; 5:38–39; 13:36; 20:27; God's will (*thelēma*) in Luke 22:42; Acts 21:14; 22:14; God's authority (*exousia*) in Acts 1:7. Events of history happen according to God's plan in Luke-Acts. This is often described with the term *dei* ("it is necessary," "must," "be destined"; Luke 2:49; 4:43; 9:22; 13:33; 17:25; 21:9; 22:37; 24:7; 24:26; 24:44; Acts 1:16; 1:21; 3:21; 4:12; 9:16; 17:3; 23:11; 27:24). The realization of the divine plan is often spoken of in terms of fulfillment: Luke 1:20; 4:21; 21:24; Acts 1:16; 3:18; 13:27 all use *plēroun*; Luke 9:51 uses *symplērounthai*; Luke 18:31 and 22:37 employ *telein*.

The divine plan can be known by humans. The scriptures of Israel make it known: for example, Luke 4:18–19; 24:45–47; Acts 13:23, 32–33, 37; 15:15; 28:25–27. Angelic announcement reveals it as well: for example, Luke 1:13–17; 1:30–33; Acts 10:3–8, 22, 30–33; 27:23–25. Living humans prophesy in ways that make the divine will known: for example, Luke 1:29–32, 34–35; Acts 21:10–11. Both the pre-Easter Jesus (e.g., Luke 9:22, 44; 18:31–33; 24:6–7) and the risen Jesus (e.g., Luke 24:49; Acts 1:4–5; 1:8) express the divine purpose for others to know. Sometimes God's will is made manifest by special appointment, as in Acts 22:14. In various ways, the will of God, which lies behind and determines the course of history, is made known to humans.

This Lukan understanding of the divine plan would have been intelligible to a Mediterranean auditor. (a) The belief that a divine necessity controls human history, shaping the course of events, was a widespread assumption in Mediterranean antiquity. A pagan like Polybius (1.4.1–2) and a Jew like Josephus (*Antiquities* 10.8.2–3 § 142) would hold very similar views. A Jew would have heard it in terms of his belief in a personal deity, but the cultural context was agreed that history unfolds according to a divine plan. (b) It was also believed that this divine will could be disclosed to and known by humans. This was often connected with oracles in the pagan sphere and with prophecy in Jewish culture. History moved along its appointed course as a fulfillment of oracles/prophecy.

Within this overall scheme, the narrative of Acts 23:11–28:16 fits nicely. In Acts 23:11 there is prophecy of the risen Jesus that controls the rest of the book: "The following night the Lord stood by him and said, 'Take courage. For just as you have borne witness to my cause in Jerusalem, so you must (*dei*) also bear witness in Rome.'" In Acts 27:23–26 Paul speaks to the terrified sailors and passengers on board the driven ship about his vision in which God's messenger told him, "You are destined (*dei*) to stand before Caesar; and behold, for your sake, God has granted safety to all who are sailing with you." If the storm and shipwreck of Paul's journey to Rome are shown to be due to natural causes and not divine judgment, his deliverance is depicted as part of the divine plan that he preach the gospel in Rome before Caesar.

The concluding itinerary (28:11–16) is organized in terms of two paragraphs (vv. 11–14 and vv. 15–16). In the first, Paul travels to Puteoli aboard a ship of Alexandria that had wintered at the island of Malta. It had the Dioscuri as its figurehead (v. 11). The Dioscuri were the twin sons of Zeus, Castor and Pollux, who were associated with protection at sea (Homeric Hymns 33; Euripides, *Orestes* 1635–37; Diodorus Siculus 4.43.1–2). Theocritus, *The Hymn to the Dioscuri* 14–22, speaks of them with awe.

> Night comes, and with it a great storm from the sky, and the broad sea rattles and splashes with the battery of the blast and of the irresistible hail. But for all that, ye, even ye, do draw both the ship and the despairing shipmen from out of hell; the winds abate, the sea puts on a shining calm, the clouds run asunder this way and that; till out comes the Bears peeping, and betwixt the Asses lo! that Manger so dim, which betokens all fair for voyaging on the sea.

A figurehead of the Twins, saviors from the sea, was carved from wood and located at the front of the ship (v. 11). The Wisdom of Solomon ridicules such pagan idolatry, speaking of prayers "for a prosperous journey" to "a thing that cannot take a step" (13:18). "Again, one preparing to sail and about to voyage over raging waves calls upon a piece of wood more fragile than the ship which carries him" (14:1). Deliverance from the sea comes from the Creator: "O Father . . . thou hast given it [the ship] a path in the sea, and a safe way through the waves, showing that thou canst save from every danger" (14:3–4). Is Luke reflecting such sarcasm when he says the ship protected by the Dioscuri spent the winter safely in the harbor while Paul and his companions were rescued from their peril at sea by the living God who has power even over storms? (cf. Luke 8:22–25; Talbert and Hayes 1995, 321–36)

The initial leg of Paul's trip comes to an end at Puteoli (the port city on the bay of Naples where passengers disembarked in order to pick up the

Appian Way into Rome; v. 13). "There we found some brothers and were urged to stay with them for seven days. And thus we came to Rome" (v. 14; cf. 23:11). The Jesus movement is already in Italy when Paul arrives. What is more, it is hospitable to Paul. A rest from the sea travel and preparation for the next leg of the journey are in order. Both would be necessary given that the *Acts of Peter* 2:6 says the road from Puteoli to Rome was rough and flinty, making significant demands on travelers.

In the second paragraph of the concluding itinerary (vv. 15–16), fellow believers from Rome come as far as the Forum of Appius (forty-three miles from Rome) and Three Taverns (thirty miles from Rome) to meet Paul (v. 15). They then accompany Paul back to the city (v. 16). Sometimes Christians would come to a prisoner from a distance (e.g., Ignatius, *Trallians* 1:2; *Ephesians* 2:1; *Magnesians* 2:1; *Philippians* 11:2; Lucian, *Peregrinus* 13). With Paul, it is more. Paul's reception by Messianists in Rome is that accorded to visiting dignitaries in antiquity. Cicero, *Ad Atticum* 5.16, says that at the outset of his judicial tour in 51 B.C. "extraordinary throngs of people have come out to meet me." Josephus, *War* 7.4.1 §§ 70–71, says that when Vespasian returned to Rome as emperor, the populace went to the roadsides outside the city to receive him. In *War* 7.5.2 §§ 100–102, Josephus says that when the people of Antioch heard Titus was approaching, they were so glad that they proceeded as far as thirty furlongs to meet him and then returned with him to the city. It is this type of welcome that Paul receives from Roman Messianists. His reception by Roman authorities is likewise auspicious. He is allowed to live by himself, with the soldier who guards him (v. 16b). This reflects Rome's view of Paul as a minimal risk.

The journey to Rome from Caesarea functions in the narrative in two main ways: (1) to show that from a divine point of view Paul is innocent, and (2) to depict his deliverance from multiple perils and his arrival in Rome as fulfillments of the divine plan. Acts 27:1–28:16 is no secular narrative. It is one controlled by "omnipotence behind the scenes" (Sternberg, 106).

Witness in Rome
Acts 28:16–31

Acts 28:16–31 is a thought unit held together by an inclusion (v. 16—Paul is allowed to live by himself; v. 30—he remains in his lodgings, receiving those who come to him). It is composed of three scenes: vv. 17–22; vv. 23–28; and vv. 30–31. Its main thrust is Paul's witness to Jews in Rome. When this is recognized, it is possible to see the overall organization of Acts 21–28.

Paul's witness to Jews in Jerusalem (21:26-23:10)
  Paul is pronounced innocent by rulers (23:12-35; 24:1-27; 25:1-12;
    25:13-26:32)
  Paul is pronounced innocent by God (27:1-44; 28:1-10)
Paul's witness to Jews in Rome (28:17-31)

Scene one (Acts 28:17-22) gives Paul's first interview with the leaders of the Roman Jews. It consists of two paragraphs (vv. 17-20 and vv. 21-22). The first paragraph (vv. 17-20) offers a speech of Paul that indicates his Jewishness ("my brothers"; "our people"; "my own nation") and emphasizes his innocence. The paragraph is organized in a chiastic pattern.

A—v. 17a: Paul calls together the leaders of the Jews.
  B—v. 17b: Paul identifies himself as a Jew who, though he had done
        nothing against "our ancestral customs," was handed over to
        the Romans as a prisoner.
    C—v. 18: The Romans wanted to release Paul because they found
        nothing against him deserving the death penalty.
  B'—v. 19: Paul, although he had no accusation to make against "my own
        nation," was forced to appeal to Caesar because the Jews
        would not accept the Roman verdict.
A'—v. 20: Paul's reason for requesting to see the Jews is to explain that he
        is in chains because of the hope of Israel.

The central member of the chiasmus (C—v. 18) indicates its main point: Paul's innocence (23:29; 25:18-19; 26:31; 26:32). Other Lukan themes are also present: for example, Paul's Jewishness (16:3; 17:2; 18:18; 20:16; 21:23-26; 22:3; 23:6; 24:17-18; 26:5) and the fact that the issue in his imprisonment is the resurrection from the dead (23:6; 24:21; 25:19; 26:6).
  The second paragraph of scene one (vv. 21-22) gives the reply of the Jewish leaders of Rome to Paul. The pattern is ABA'.

A—v. 21: Roman Jews have received neither letters nor oral reports from
        Judea with negative comments about Paul personally.
  B—v. 22a: The Jewish leaders would like to hear Paul present his views.
A'—v. 22b: Roman Jews know the Messianist sect of Judaism is denounced
        everywhere.

Again the central member indicates the central point. After hearing Paul speak the first time, the Jewish leadership is open to hearing Paul's views. Why? They know nothing negative about Paul personally, although they know the movement he is a part of has a bad reputation (e.g., Luke 21:17, "you will be hated by all for my name's sake"; Tacitus, *Annals* 15.44, "a class hated for their abominations, who are commonly called Christians"; 1 Pet

2:12, "they speak against you as wrongdoers"; 4:4, "they abuse you"; Heb 10:33, "publicly exposed to abuse").

Why would Paul immediately (after three days–v. 17a) seek to converse with the leaders of the Roman Jewish community? After all, he is in Rome to appear before Caesar. The most obvious Lukan answer is theological: Paul goes first to Israel (Acts 3:26; 10:36). Another more significant reason has to do with sociological factors. The Jewish community in Rome was large and powerful in Paul's time. It was not uncommon for Roman Jews to try to influence the decisions of Roman authorities on matters of interest to them. Three examples illustrate this: (a) Cicero, *Pro Flacco* 28.66-69, notes how Roman Jews attempted, successfully, to use their influence against the governor and in favor of their co-religionists' interests in the courts. (b) Josephus, *Antiquities* 17.11.1 § 300 and *War* 2.6.1 §§ 80-92, tells how some eight thousand Roman Jews supported their Judean brethren's complaint against Archelaus presented before Augustus. (c) Josephus, *Life* 3 §§ 13-16, tells how he went to Rome to try to secure acquittal by the emperor of certain Jewish priests sent as prisoners by Felix. He did this by using a Jewish actor, Aliturius, who was much beloved by Nero, to make the acquaintance of Poppea, Nero's mistress and a Jewish sympathizer. He then entreated Poppea on the priests' behalf and was successful in gaining their release. Intervention by Roman Jews was often provoked by appeals from Jerusalem. Paul would have had every reason to wonder whether such an appeal had already been made. Justin Martyr, *Dialogue* 17, 108, and 117, says that Jewish delegates were sent throughout the world in his time to speak against the Messianists. Eusebius, *In Isaiah* 18.1-2, says that in the writings of the ancients he found that the priests and elders of the Jews in Jerusalem sent letters to Jews of every country slandering the doctrine of Christ. The characters in Acts 28 seem to assume that such was a possibility in Paul's time. It has, however, not happened, at least so far. Being so forewarned would be an indispensable part of Paul's defense.

Scene two (Acts 28:23-28), Paul's second interview with the Jewish leadership in Rome, is made up of three parts. First, there is a summary of Paul's day-long preaching. When on the scheduled day the Jews come to Paul's lodgings in great numbers, "from early morning until evening, he expounded his position to them, bearing witness to the kingdom of God and trying to convince them about Jesus from the law of Moses and the prophets" (v. 23; 17:2-3; 18:4-5). Second, there is a mixed response to Paul's proclamation. "Some were convinced by what he had said, while others did not believe" (v. 24). When agreement is not reached and the leaders begin to leave (v. 25a), there is, third, Paul's final speech (vv. 25b-28).

This speech indicates Paul's distance from the unbelieving Jews ("your fathers") and justifies the Gentile mission. It has three parts. (a) The introduction comes in v. 25b. "Well did the Holy Spirit speak to *your* ancestors through the prophet Isaiah." What is to come from Isaiah 6 applies to unbelieving Jews. (b) There is a citation of LXX Isa 6:9–10 in vv. 26–27.

> You shall indeed hear but not understand.
> You shall indeed look but never see.
> Gross is the heart of this people:
> They will not hear with their ears; they have closed their eyes;
> So they may not see with their eyes
> > and hear with their ears
> > and understand with their heart
> > and be converted, and I heal them.

If, in Acts, the positive promises of Israel's scriptures are fulfilled in the Jesus movement, the negative prophecies like Isa 6:9–10 are fulfilled in Jewish unbelief.

(c) The conclusion of Paul's speech is given in v. 28: "Let it be known to you that this salvation of God has been sent to the Gentiles; they will listen" (13:46–47; 18:6). Two questions are raised by what Paul has just said: (1) Is the Gentile mission due to Jewish belief or unbelief? and (2) Why is so much attention devoted, in Acts, to Jewish unbelief and Gentile belief when, in fact, both Jewish and Gentile auditors divide over the Messianists' proclamation? What follows attempts answers to these two questions.

(1) Is the Gentile mission in Acts understood as due to Israel's rejection or acceptance of the gospel? The answer to this question is not an either/or but a both/and. Mediterranean peoples believed that a divine plan controls the movement of human affairs. This divine plan is revealed through oracles/prophecy. Indeed, oracles/prophecy not only reveal the divine plan but also advance it. History moves along its appointed course as a fulfillment of oracles/prophecy.

Three examples from the pagan world give one a feel for that segment of the culture. (a) Lucian's *Alexander the False Prophet* tells of one Alexander who wanted to start a new religion. As a first step to this end, he and a companion go to Chalcedon and bury bronze tablets which state that in the near future Asclepios and his father, Apollo, would migrate to Pontus. These tablets are found and, as a result, the people set about building a temple. Alexander, dressed like Perseus, then goes to Abonutichus, declaiming an oracle that says he is a scion of Perseus. A Sibylline prophecy of his activity is then produced. As a result of two written prophecies and one oral oracle, the stage is set for the emergence of a new religion. Events follow oracles. (b) Suetonius's *Life of Vespasian* contains a section of omens that prophesy his ascendancy as emperor. Among these references are not only Josephus's declaration that he would soon be released by the same man who would then be emperor but also mention of antique vases dug up by soothsayers that had on them an image of Vespasian. History develops along lines indicated by prophecy/oracles. (c) Apuleius's *Golden Ass* moves to its climax with Lucius trapped in the form of a donkey as a result of his experimentation with magic. Despairing over his plight, he cries out to Isis to save him. The goddess appears to him by night and gives an oracle (11.7). The next day Lucius does exactly as Isis had said. He eats the roses that are a part of the procession in Isis's honor and is miraculously changed back into a human being. Having been saved from his fate, Lucius is initiated into the Isis cult. He says, "I was not deceived by the promise made to me" (11.13). In all three of these examples from the pagan world, the fulfillment of oracles legitimates the religious or political authority of the person referred to by the prophecy or the deity that gave it. What happened in each case was in line with what the divine realm had allegedly revealed before the fact.

Three examples from the Jewish milieu should also suffice. (a) The Deuteronomic history uses the device of prophecy and fulfillment. For example, in Deuteronomy 28 Moses says that if Israel does not keep the covenant and obey the commandments, then it will go away into exile (vv. 25, 36–37). In 2 Kings 17 the northern kingdom falls to the Assyrians and the Israelites are taken away into bondage. Verse 7 says the exile was because of Israel's sins; v. 23 says what was done was "as the Lord spoke by all his servants the prophets." In 2 Kings 25 the southern kingdom is taken away into Babylonian exile. Moses' prophecy in Deuteronomy 28 about what would happen if Israel proved disobedient is shown to have been fulfilled in the subsequent narrative of 2 Kings. History moves along according to the divine plan as disclosed and effected through prophecies. (b) At Qumran one finds a community that believes its own history is the fulfillment of the prophecies of the scriptures of Israel. In the commentaries on Isaiah, Micah, Psalm 37, and especially Habakkuk, there are statements of this position. When the people of Qumran interpret the prophets and Psalms as prophecies that are fulfilled in the wickedness of Qumran's enemies and in the righteousness of Qumran's covenanters, they are saying not only that the time of fulfillment has come but also that they are heirs of the promises to Israel, the true people of God. Again, what happens in history is the fulfillment of the divine plan for history as revealed and effected by prophecies. (c) In his *Antiquities* Josephus uses the motif of prophecy and fulfillment as evidence of the providence of God (2.16.5 § 333). In 8.4.2 §§ 109–10, the fact that the prophecy of David is fulfilled makes clear the providence of God. In 10.11.7 §§ 278–81, the fulfillment of Daniel's prophecies of the destruction of the Temple by Antiochus Epiphanes and later the Romans is said to demonstrate, against the Epicureans, the providence of God. The pattern of prophecy–fulfillment in the history of Israel constitutes evidence for the providence of God. Again, history moves according to the divine purpose as revealed and effected by prophecies.

Of course, in Luke-Acts the fulfillment of prophecy is a major motif. The prologue speaks of "the things fulfilled (*peplērophorēmenōn*) among us" (Luke 1:1). There follows a narrative that is literally controlled by a prophecy-fulfillment pattern. Prophecy is given by the scriptures of Israel, by living prophets, and by heavenly beings. The prophecies disclose the divine will, and the fulfillment of prophecy moves the story along to another stage. In this regard, the Lukan writings would have been perfectly intelligible to the Mediterranean hearer whether pagan or Jewish.

It was also a part of the Mediterranean mindset that viewed history as the fulfillment of oracles/prophecies to hold that an oracle could be misunderstood as well as understood. The very act of misunderstanding could be the means by which the oracle/prophecy was fulfilled. Herodotus's *History* is a storehouse of examples. The classic example is the story of Croesus, who, after acknowledging the Delphic oracle to be the only true place of divination, asks it if he should send an army against the Persians. The oracle replies that if he should send an army, he would destroy a great empire. Mistaking the meaning of the oracle, Croesus goes to war against the Persians and loses. Sending his chains to Delphi, Croesus asks if it is the manner of Greek gods to be thankless. The priestess replies that the oracle was right. Croesus should have sent to ask whether the god spoke of Croesus's or Cyrus's empire. "But he understood not that which was spoken, nor made further inquiry: wherefore now let him blame himself" (1.91). When Croesus receives the answer, he confesses that the sin was not the god's but his own.

The similarity of this way of thinking to Acts 13:27 would not be lost on Luke's auditors.

> Those who live in Jerusalem and their rulers, because they did not understand the utterances of the prophets which are read every sabbath, fulfilled these by condemning him.

Here, in a speech made by Paul to the synagogue in Pisidian Antioch, the claim is made that the death of Jesus, which was a part of the divine plan (Luke 9:22, 44; 18:31–33; 24:26–27, 46; Acts 2:23; 3:18), happened according to divine plan because of the people's failure to understand the oracles/prophecies of scripture. A similar note is sounded in Peter's speech in Acts 3:17–18:

> And now, brethren, I know that you acted in ignorance, as also did your rulers. But what God foretold by the mouth of all the prophets, that his Christ should suffer, He thus fulfilled.

In Luke-Acts, as in Mediterranean culture generally, the divine purpose for history can be effected by human misunderstanding and ignorance as well as by human understanding and cooperation. Once this fact is grasped, the question of whether the Gentile mission originated due to Jewish belief or unbelief can be answered.

Since Mediterranean culture assumed that behind the events of history was a divine plan that moved along in terms of oracles/prophecies and their fulfillment, and since the divine purpose could be accomplished both by human understanding and cooperation with prophecy and by human misunderstanding/ignorance of it, it ought not to be difficult to believe that in Acts both Jewish belief and Jewish unbelief are grounds for the Gentile mission.

It is indisputable that Gentiles are included in God's people in Acts after some in Israel believe the gospel and because they believe it. The believing Jews interpret their inclusion of the Gentiles as action in line with the revelation of the divine will in scriptural prophecy (Acts 15:13-21). Inclusion of the Gentiles after Jewish belief is understood as part of the divine plan. It is something that is done and approved by those who know the meaning of scripture and, therefore, cooperate with the divine will revealed in it. History moves along according to the will of God because of human understanding and cooperation.

It is also indisputable that Gentiles are included in God's people after Jewish rejection of Jesus and the gospel and because of such rejection (Acts 13:27-29; 13:46; 18:6; 28:24-28). The missionaries interpret their inclusion of the Gentiles as action in line with the revelation of the divine will in scriptural prophecy (Acts 13:46-47–going to the Gentiles is in line with the prophecy of Isa 49:6; Acts 28:25-27–Jewish rejection is in line with the prophecy of Isa 6:9-10). Inclusion of the Gentiles after Jewish unbelief is interpreted as part of the divine plan. The very rejection of Jesus and the gospel by certain Jews, although done in ignorance and out of misunderstanding of the meaning of scriptural prophecies, serves but to advance the divine plan's accomplishment in history. Ignorance of God's intent and failure to cooperate with the divine will serve to advance God's purposes just as understanding and cooperation do.

For Acts to assert that the Gentile mission originated *both* because of Jewish belief and in accordance with the meaning of scriptural prophecy *and* because of Jewish unbelief due to failure to understand scriptural prophecy properly is something that Mediterranean hearers would have understood. It was a common cultural conviction that the divine purpose behind history that determines history's movement is effective not only in connection with human understanding and cooperation but also in spite of human misunderstanding and opposition. Both dimensions of the matter would have been expected by the auditors.

(2) Why is there a disproportionate amount of attention given to Jewish rejection of the gospel in Acts? A cursory reading of Acts reveals that when Jews are confronted with the gospel, some believe and some do not. The same phenomenon is present in the Gentile mission. Some believe and some do not. Both audiences are divided when confronted with the message about Jesus. Yet the narrative of Acts makes much of Jewish rejection and little of Gentile disbelief. Why is this the case?

In the Third Gospel there is a general theme of status reversal. The new age will overturn the values and structures of the present evil age. We meet this motif in the birth narratives (1:51-53) and in the Sermon on the Plain (6:20-26), for example. In the central section of Luke (9:51-19:44), Jesus' teaching anticipates this eschatological reversal by overturning the common estimate of what is virtue and what is vice. Consider 10:29-37 (good Samaritan//bad priest and Levite); 10:38-42 (good inactive Mary//bad active Martha); 11:37-41 (good unclean//bad clean); 12:13-34 (good poor//bad rich); 14:7-11 (good humble//bad exalted); 15:11-32 (good prodigal//bad elder brother); 16:19-31 (good beggar//bad rich man); 18:9-14 (good tax collector//bad Pharisee); 18:18-30 (good poor//bad rich). The Lukan focus in Acts on Jewish rejection and Gentile acceptance of the gospel, in spite of the fact that both groups are divided in their response, is yet another part of the general theme of status reversal connected with eschatological fulfillment and its inauguration.

The positions taken in Luke that we described as status reversal are rarely explicitly described as such by the narrator. The Magnificat (Luke 1:51-53) is explicit.

> He has shown strength with His arm, he has scattered the proud in the imagination of their hearts, He has put down the mighty from their thrones, and exalted those of low degree; He has filled the hungry with good tidings, and the rich He has sent empty away.

The same is true of the beatitudes and the woes (Luke 6:20-23, 24-26). That the evangelist is explicit in places like these enables the reader to say for certain that the reversal theme is intended and that one should anticipate it later in the narrative when it is not explicitly signaled.

What enables the reader to say that various passages that have no explicit designation as such reflect the reversal motif is a knowledge of the common cultural assumptions that lie behind a given text. Only because the reader knows the general Jewish cultural estimate of priests, Levites, and Samaritans can one hear the parable of the Good Samaritan as a reversal of values (bad priest and Levite//good Samaritan). It is not spelled out explicitly in the text. Yet because of the reversal motif that is explicit elsewhere and because of a knowledge of general cultural assumptions not spelled out in the text, one does not hesitate to read or hear the parable in terms of the reversal motif.

It was a widespread Jewish conviction that when the law was revealed at Sinai, it was offered to all nations. When the nations refused it, God gave it to Israel. Three examples illustrate the position. (a) The *Mekilta,* "Bahodesh" 1, on Exod 19:2, says that although God gave the Torah openly, the nations were unwilling to accept it. So God declared His word unto Jacob. (b) *Sifre on Deuteronomy* § 343 says that when God revealed Himself he did so not only to Israel but to all the nations who rejected the revelation. So when the Lord saw that, He gave the law to Israel. (c) *Pesikta Rabbati* 30.4 says that before the Lord gave the Torah to Israel He went around offering it to all the seventy nations. Since no one of them would accept it, it was finally offered to Israel. G. F. Moore contends that this teaching was the position of both great schools of the second century A.D., the schools of Ishmael and Akiba, and is therefore presumably part of the earlier common tradition from which they drew (1.277). It was Jewish convention that God's revelation had been offered first to the Gentiles; after their rejection of it, God had turned to Israel, who accepted it.

Acts 2 tells of a new communication from God analogous to the Sinai events that is intended to be understood by all. Just as a revelation of God was disseminated from Sinai, so a new communication goes forth at Pentecost. This is the key signature for the composition that follows. Unlike the events at Sinai, where God goes first to the Gentiles and only after their rejection of the revelation turns to Israel, the new divine disclosure goes first to Israel, and only after her rejection of the gospel do the messengers turn to the Gentiles who listen. The narrative of Acts continues the Lukan reversal theme. In connection with the inauguration of the new age, there is a status reversal. Whereas it was formerly rejection by Gentiles//acceptance by Israel, now it is rejection by Israel//acceptance by Gentiles. Just as in the Third Gospel's use of the reversal motif, so here too reversal is ironic. The disproportionate attention given to Israel's rejection of the gospel is an expression of the irony of status reversal in connection with the end times (Talbert 1991, 99–110).

Scene three (Acts 28:30–31) provides a summary of Paul's two years of preaching in Rome. (a) Paul remains for two full years in his own lodgings (v. 30a). This probably means he rented an apartment in one of the thousands of tenement buildings in Rome. If so, it would have been an expensive proposition. Juvenal 3.164–66 says that in Rome one must pay a big rent for a wretched lodging; 3.223–25 says that one could buy an excellent house outside Rome for what in Rome it costs to rent a dark garret for one year. How such a dwelling was paid for by Paul is unclear. (b) "He received all who came to him" (v. 30b). That such accessibility would have been possible is indicated by the *Martyrdom of Justin* 3.3A, where the Christian philosopher says,

> I have been living above the baths of Myrtinus for the entire period of my sojourn at Rome . . . and I have known no other meeting-place but here. Anyone who wished could come to my abode and I would impart to him the words of truth.

(c) Being a citizen and having a registered domicile would enable Paul to receive the grain ration. His being a prisoner would not affect it (Seneca, *Beneficiis* 4.28.2—"the good and the bad share alike"). (d) The two-year delay was likely due to the volume of court business (Rapske, 317). Dio Cassius 60.28.6 says that during the reign of Claudius the number of law suits was beyond all reckoning. The reign of Nero would have been no different. (e) "With complete assurance (*parrēsias*) and without hindrance (*akōlytōs*) he proclaimed the kingdom of God and taught about the Lord Jesus Christ" (v. 31). That Paul speaks with *parrēsia* (2:29; 4:13, 29, 31) is significant. He speaks with boldness because he has a good conscience (23:1; 24:16): For example, Wis 5:1 says that the righteous man will stand with great confidence (*en parrēsia*) in the presence of those who have afflicted him; Josephus, *Antiquities* 2.6.7 § 131, says that Joseph's brothers spoke with assurance (*parrēsia*) because they were conscious of having committed no crime. Paul's boldness then has its roots in his innocence. That he preached "without hindrance" (*akōlytōs*) indicates that such religious issues were not a concern to Rome.

How is the ending of Acts to be understood? Three types of answers have been offered. (a) A historical explanation goes back to the Muratorian fragment.

> The Acts of all the Apostles, however, were written in one volume. Luke described briefly "for" most excellent Theophilus particular [things], which happened in his presence, as he also evidently relates indirectly the death of Peter and also Paul's departure from the city as he was proceeding to Spain. (Theron, 109)

According to the Muratorian fragment, Luke told only what he was involved in. The ending with Paul's imprisonment is due to the fact that Luke was no longer with Paul after these two years.

(b) A theological explanation has also been offered. In 2 Kgs 25:27–30, the ending of Deuteronomic history, Jehoiachin, the exiled Davidic king, is given relative freedom. His circumstances symbolize not only the exile and deprivation of his people but also their hope. Paul's relative freedom at the end of Acts 28, likewise, symbolizes hope for the Jesus movement (Trompf, 225–39).

(c) A rhetorical explanation was offered as early as Chrysostom.

The author (i.e., Luke) conducts his narrative up to this point, and leaves the hearer thirsty, so that he fills up the lack by himself through reflection. The outsiders (i.e., non-Christian writers) do also likewise. . . . Consider indeed that what follows is absolutely identical with what comes before. (*Homily on Acts 55*)

Chrysostom believes that the ending of Acts requires the reader to fill it out by extrapolation from the previous narrative. In Mediterranean antiquity suspended endings were not uncommon: For example, the *Iliad*, the *Odyssey*, and Herodotus's *History* end without narrative closure. Dionysius of Halicarnassus criticizes Thucydides because Thucydides does not carry his work to a suitable end (*Epistle to Pompeius* 3.771). Narrative suspension is a literary device whereby the author, by failing to bring certain narrative data to their resolution, hinders the closure of the narrative world for the reader. The closure must be achieved by the reader, who does so by finishing the story in consonance with its plot (Marguerat, 74–89).

If auditors of Acts complete the ending for themselves based on the plot offered earlier in the narrative, what would they infer? (a) Paul stood before Caesar (cf. 25:12; 27:24). (b) He was innocent (23:29; 25:18–19; 26:31–32). (c) He met his death (20:25, 38). The narrative has not led the reader to expect that Paul would be released. At the same time that Paul's innocence is recognized, his release is denied. (d) It was not due to Roman Jewry (28:21). If Jews were involved, it would probably have been those from the Aegean basin (18:12; 20:3, 19; 21:27). (e) It was likely due to corrupt Roman officials (24:26–27; 25:9), who would be following expediency rather than justice.

If the preceding points are those inferred from the plot of Acts, how do they relate to non-Lukan tradition about Paul's life after Acts 28? They run counter to some claims of ancient church tradition: For example, (a) Paul was released after the two years of imprisonment in Acts 28 (so Eusebius, *Church History* 2.22.1–2—probably an inference from 2 Tim 4:17); and (b) Paul went to Spain (Muratorian fragment; *Acts of Peter* 3.1; *Acts of Xanthippe and Polyxena*—probably an inference from Rom 15:24, 28). They fit or do not conflict with other claims of ancient tradition: For example, Paul suffered martyrdom under Nero by beheading (Eusebius, *Church History* 2.22.1–2; 2.25.5–8; *Acts of Paul* 10; *Acts of Peter* 3.1; Tertullian, *Prescription against Heretics* 36); and (b) Paul was beheaded at *Tre Fontane* on the Ostian Way (however, this is a sixth-century tradition, totally legendary, born of a desire to enhance the prestige of the Abbey of Three Fountains; so Tajra 1994, 26) and was buried on the Ostian Way (which is questionable, however, because there is a rival early tradition—i.e., he was buried at the site of St. Sebastian on the Appian Way, as well as a rival tradition from the sixth-century chronicler John Malalas—i.e., Paul remained unburied after his martyrdom by order of Nero; so Bruce, 262–79; Tajra 1994, 26).

APPENDIX A

What Is Meant by the Historicity of Acts?

Of what value is the Acts of the Apostles for the study of early Christianity? This question demands answers on two levels: (1) Of what value is Acts for our knowledge of Christianity near A.D. 100 (i.e., for the time when the book was written)? and (2) Of what value is Acts for our knowledge of Christianity during the apostolic age (i.e., for the time of the events narrated, before A.D. 64)? The latter is the focus of this appendix. Our query is about the historicity of Acts, that is, Acts' value for our knowledge of Christianity up through Paul.

The question of the historicity of Acts has been neglected since the early years of this century (Hemer 1989, 1). Two reasons for this neglect seem to be primary: (1) There has been in this century a shift of focus in the study of Acts from historical to theological concerns, and (2) the complexity of the problems and the extent of the knowledge from multiple fields required to deal with the issues are so threatening as to make scholars look to less demanding areas of study.

If one agrees that such neglect should be remedied, one then faces the further question: *What* do we really mean by the historicity of Acts? One's answer to this question determines *how* one goes about arguing either for or against the historicity of Acts. So *what* and *how* are two sides of the same coin. In fact, one can see the *what* assumed by noting the *how* of the argument.

A survey of the secondary literature reveals three levels of argument about *what* and *how*, plus three specific issues crucially related to the matter of the historicity of Acts. The purpose of this appendix is to describe these three levels and three issues in order to define as precisely as possible what one means when one speaks about the historicity of Acts. Until the nature of the problem is clearly defined, progress toward the larger matter of the value of Acts for the study of early Christianity is delayed.

We begin with an overview of the three levels of argument about the historicity of Acts: (1) contemporary color, (2) historical sequence, and (3) individual events and episodes. These three levels of argument will be taken up in the order mentioned here.

Contemporary Color

The argument from contemporary color assumes that a document is not historically accurate if it contains errors and anachronisms. (Smallwood, 312, gives an example of this type of argument in denying historicity to a purported letter from Hadrian to his brother-in-law about the emperor's visit to Egypt in A.D. 130.) By inference, a document must be historically accurate if one does not find errors and anachronisms. Hence, the quest to show or to deny the historicity of Acts involves the search for signs of the presence or absence of contemporary color, that is, the fitness of details in Acts to our knowledge of its environment.

Let us begin with a few representative examples of Acts' congruence with its milieu. (1) Titles of officials. (a) The title "proconsul" (*anthypatos*) is correctly used for the two governors of senatorial provinces named in Acts: Sergius Paulus, governor of Cyprus (Acts 13:7–8), and Gallio, governor of Achaea (Acts 18:12). (b) Inscriptions confirm that the city authorities in Thessalonica in the first century A.D. were called *politarchs* (Acts 17:6, 8). (c) According to inscriptions, *grammateus* is the correct title for the chief executive magistrate (town clerk) in Ephesus (Acts 19:35). (d) Felix (Acts 23:24, 26) and Festus (Acts 24:27; 25:1) are correctly called procurators (*hēgemōn*) of Judea. (e) Acts correctly refers to Cornelius (10:1) and Julius (27:1) as centurions (*hekatontarchēs*) and to Claudius Lysias (Acts 21:31; 23:26) as a tribune (*chiliarch*).

(2) Administrative divisions. Unlike other provinces, Macedonia was divided into four administrative districts. If one follows the Greek text of the Nestle 26th edition (*protēs meridos* instead of *protē tēs meridos*, assuming dittography of *tē*), Acts 16:12 reflects this division when it calls Philippi a colony and a city of the first district of Macedonia.

(3) Town assemblies. Acts 19:29–41 and (possibly) 17:5 describe the function of town assemblies in the operation of a city's business. This is characteristic of the first and perhaps early second centuries. In the second century A.D., however, these town assemblies were replaced by town councils.

(4) Details about the administration of affairs associated with the Jewish temple in Jerusalem. (a) Both inscriptions (cf. Barrett, 50, for an example)

and literary sources (e.g., Philo, *Embassy* 212; Josephus, *Antiquities* 14.11.5 § 417; *War* 5.5.2 §§ 193–94; 6.2.4 §§ 125–26) speak about the prohibition against Gentiles in the inner areas of the temple. Acts 21:27–36 presupposes this. (b) A Roman tribune had to possess Roman citizenship. During the reign of Claudius citizenship could be bought with a sufficient number of bribes (e.g., Dio Cassius 60.17.5–6). The tribune in Acts 21:28, Claudius Lysias, who had bought his citizenship, apparently had gained it during the time of Claudius, when bribes were in fashion. (c) Roman soldiers were permanently stationed in the tower of Antonia with the responsibility of watching for and suppressing any disturbances at the festivals of the Jews (e.g., Josephus, *War* 5.5.8 § 244). To reach the affected area they would have had to come down a flight of steps into the Temple precincts (Josephus, *War* 5.5.8 § 243). The events of Acts 21:31–37 reflect these details precisely.

(5) Synchronization of historical details. R. P. C. Hanson gives an example.

He (Luke) tells us that Paul encountered the high priest Ananias shortly before he met the procurator Felix (Acts 23:2, 33, 24:2, 3); that Felix was at that time married to Drusilla (24:24); that some time afterwards (whether as long as two years or not is uncertain) Felix was superseded by Festus, who shortly after reaching Palestine attended to Paul's case and gave him, among other measures, a hearing before King Agrippa II, with whom the King's sister Bernice was at that time living (25:1–27). (p. 8)

Hanson concludes, "This is a very remarkable piece of synchronization on the part of the author" (p. 8). It would have been easy to miss the fact that Ananias was priest at just that time. He was deposed sometime during the procuratorship of Felix. It would have been difficult to get Drusilla rightly related to Felix. She had already been married to one husband, and even more so to get Bernice correctly associated with Festus. She lived with her brother, Agrippa, for only a limited time during Festus's procuratorship.

This type of evidence has been assembled carefully by a host of scholars. One of them, the Roman historian A. N. Sherwin-White, concludes,

For Acts, the confirmation of historicity is overwhelming. Yet Acts is, in simple terms and judged externally, no less of a propaganda document than the Gospels, liable to similar distortion. But any attempt to reject its basic historicity even in matters of detail must now appear absurd. Roman historians have long taken it for granted. (p. 189)

There are those, however, who believe the same type of evidence argues against the historicity of Acts. A few typical examples should suffice. (1) Gamaliel's speech. Acts 5:33–39 gives an account of a speech by the first-century Pharisee Gamaliel, in which he refers to two movements other than the Way: one led by Theudas (v. 36), and "after him" (v. 37) one led by

Judas the Galilean. Josephus places Judas about A.D. 6 (*Antiquities* 18.1.1 §§ 4-10; 20.5.2 § 102; *War* 2.8.1 § 118; 2.17.8 § 433; 7.8.1 § 253). He places Theudas under the procurator Fadus, A.D. 44–46 (*Antiquities* 20.5.1 §§ 97–98). Two problems emerge. First, the order of Judas and Theudas is reversed in Acts 5. Second, Theudas's movement comes after the time when Gamaliel is speaking. There is not much to be said about this unless Josephus is wrong or there was an earlier Theudas.

(2) Geography of Palestine. First, Acts 9:31, which says, "So the church throughout all Judea and Galilee and Samaria had peace and was built up," has been taken to mean that Judea was understood to have been directly connected to Galilee. If so, then Luke had an incorrect understanding of Palestinian geography. In response, one must note first that Luke does not always use Judea in the same way. (a) Sometimes Judea refers to the Roman province which, in contrast to Galilee, was subject to Roman procurators (Luke 3:1; 23:6). (b) At other times it refers to the whole of Palestine (Luke 1:5; 7:17; 23:5; Acts 10:37). (c) In still other places Judea refers to the part of Palestine inhabited by Jews, excluding Samaria (Acts 1:8) and Galilee (Acts 9:31) and even Caesarea (Acts 12:19). (d) Sometimes Luke distinguishes between Judea and Jerusalem (Acts 1:8; 8:1). In Acts 9:31 Judea is used as in instance (c). One must note secondly, given Acts 8:1 ("scattered throughout the region of Judea and Samaria") and 15:1-3 (which has the journey pass from Antioch through Phoenicia and Samaria to Jerusalem), that Luke knows the proper arrangement of Palestine's component regions. The order of the regions mentioned in 9:31 must be due to other than geographical reasons (Hengel, 99).

A second example is Acts 23:31, which says the soldiers brought Paul from Jerusalem to Antipatris, a distance of some forty-five miles, overnight. Thirty miles constituted a suitable day's journey whether by land or by sea. Both the numbers involved (two hundred soldiers, seventy horsemen, two hundred spearmen) and the speed of the journey (thirty-eight to forty-five miles in a night) are exaggerated to emphasize the importance of the person being accompanied and the extent of the danger.

There are certainly points at which the contemporary color of Acts can be challenged, but they are few and insignificant compared to the overwhelming congruence between Acts and its time and place. What is one to make of such evidence?

There is widespread agreement that an exact description of the milieu does not prove the historicity of the event narrated. Henry J. Cadbury's *The Book of Acts in History* makes two points: (1) Acts fits beautifully into its contemporary setting (Greco-Roman, Jewish, and early Christian), and (2) accurate local color in no way proves general historical accuracy (p. 120). This has prompted a strong response from Ward Gasque.

Cadbury's statement . . . that Greek and Latin novels are often as full of accurate local and contemporary color as are historical writings is misleading. . . . Whereas the author of Acts is carefully accurate in his representation of the time and places of which he writes, the local and contemporary color contained in the writers of fiction is that of the time and places in which they write. (p. 193 n. 94)

One level on which the argument about the historicity of Acts is carried on is that involving the quest for contemporary color. Taken alone, however, its results are indecisive.

Historical Sequence

The argument from historical sequence assumes that a document is not historically reliable if it lacks a correct sequence of the events narrated. By inference, a document must be historically trustworthy if the events it relates are given in their proper chronological order. Scholars involved in this type of argument, therefore, look for evidence to corroborate or correct the historical sequence given by Acts. This evidence comes from Greco-Roman and Jewish sources on the one hand and the Pauline epistles on the other.

Greco-Roman and Jewish sources speak about certain events also mentioned by the narrative of Acts. They enable one to check the relative chronology of the events in Acts. Five such events are usually noted (e.g., Jones; Donfried; Caird).

(1) The reference to the death of Herod Agrippa I in Acts 12:23 has a counterpart in Josephus (*Antiquities* 19.8.2 §§ 343-51). From Josephus, Herod's death can be dated to A.D. 44.

(2) Acts 11:28 and 12:25 speak of a famine under Claudius (A.D. 41-54). The famine is mentioned in Acts before the death of Herod (12:20-23). Josephus (*Antiquities* 20.2.5 §§ 51-53; 20.5.2 §§ 100-101) mentions a famine in Jerusalem relieved by the good graces of Queen Helena of Adiabene connected with the procuratorship of Tiberius Julius Alexander (A.D. 46-48) and possibly with that of his predecessor, Fadus. Josephus, however, locates the famine after the death of Herod. Assuming Josephus's accuracy, Agabus's prophecy is, therefore, not precisely placed in the sequence of Acts (11:28). It may belong to the period when the signs of trouble were first apparent in Egypt (Hemer 1980, 6; Gapp). Or the order of the two events may have been inverted due to some Lucan tendency (Talbert 1967).

(3) Acts 18:2 mentions an edict of Claudius expelling the Jews from Rome. Suetonius (*Claudius* 25.4) mentions the same event. The fifth-century historian Orosius (7.6.15-16) places the edict in the ninth year of

Claudius (A.D. 49), citing Josephus as an authority. Two matters cause some pause. First, we know of no such reference by Josephus in his extant materials. Second, Dio Cassius (60.6.6) mentions Claudius's embargo on Jewish meetings in Rome in A.D. 41, but there is no hint of actual expulsion. As a result, some have wanted to identify the embargo on public meetings with the expulsion and regard them as two references to the same event and then to date the event to A.D. 41. If so, then the relative chronology of Acts at this point is problematic. If, however, as seems preferable, one takes the references to be to two different events and accepts Orosius's date of A.D. 49, the relative chronology is correct.

(4) The proconsulship of Gallio is mentioned in Acts 18:12. On the basis of an inscription found at Delphi, Gallio's stay in Corinth can be dated to about A.D. 51-52 (Haacker, 2.901-3). This fits the relative chronology of Acts.

(5) The procuratorship of Festus mentioned in Acts 24:27 is also referred to by Josephus (*Antiquities* 20.8.9 § 182). Eusebius in his chronological tables places the arrival of Festus in the tenth year of Agrippa II. Josephus (*War* 2.14.4 § 284) places the beginning of Agrippa's reign in A.D. 50. His tenth year would have been A.D. 59 (contra Lake 5.464-67, who puts the date at 55). If so, then the relative chronology of Acts is appropriate.

In addition to these five points in the relative chronology of Acts corroborated or corrected by Greco-Roman and Jewish sources, scholars who work at this level seek further clarification from a comparison of Acts with Paul's letters.

T. H. Campbell, in a rarely noticed article of 1955, argues that the sequence of Paul's missionary activities that can be inferred from his letters is remarkably compatible with the information from Acts. (His schema is approved by Kümmel 1966, 179, and Fitzmyer, 83.) His schema as developed from the letters runs as follows:

persecution of Christians (Gal 1:13-14; cf. Acts 9)
conversion (Gal 1:15-17a; cf. Acts 9)
to Arabia (Gal 1:17b; cf. Acts makes no mention)
to Damascus (Gal 1:17c; cf. Acts 9)
to Jerusalem (Gal 1:18-19; cf. Acts 9)
to regions of Syria and Cilicia (Gal 1:21; cf. Acts 11:25)
to Jerusalem after fourteen years (Gal 2:1-10; cf. Acts 11 or 15?)
to Philippi (1 Thess 2:1-2; Phil 4:15-16; cf. Acts 16)
to Thessalonica (1 Thess 2:1-2; Phil 4:15-16; cf. Acts 17)
to Athens (1 Thess 3:1-3; cf. Acts 17)
to Corinth (2 Cor 11:7-9; cf. Acts 18)
to Ephesus (1 Cor 16:8-9; cf. Acts 19)

to Troas (2 Cor 2:12; Acts does not mention)
to Macedonia (2 Cor 8-9; cf. Acts 20)
to Corinth (2 Cor 12; cf. Acts 20:2b-3)
to Jerusalem (Rom 15:22-25; cf. Acts 21)
to Rome (Rom 15:22-25; cf. Acts 28)

"When the sequence of Paul's movements as revealed by his letters is put side by side with that recorded in Acts, there is a correspondence which is very striking, especially in view of the probability that the author of Acts had not read Paul's letters" (Campbell, 84).

There are, of course, some details Acts does not mention just as there are some things the epistles do not mention. The most serious gap in the sequence is that in Paul's letters one finds no clue as to when his work in the province of Galatia should be placed. We learn only that Paul had been among the Galatians twice when he wrote them (Gal 4:13). In spite of these gaps, the overall correspondence between the relative order of events in Acts and in Paul's letters is remarkable.

The major problem in any attempted correlation between Paul's letters and Acts is that of Paul's visits to Jerusalem. The situation can be simply stated. In Paul's letters one hears explicitly about three visits of the apostle to Jerusalem: (a) Gal 1:18-19; (b) Gal 2:1-10; (c) Rom 15:25-32. In Acts there are five such visits described: (a) Acts 9:26-29; (b) Acts 11:27-30; 12:25; (c) Acts 15:1-29; (d) Acts 18:22; and (e) Acts 21:15-17. The first visits mentioned in Paul's letters and in Acts are usually thought to be the same, in spite of certain difficulties. It is Paul's first visit to Jerusalem after his conversion. The last visits in Paul's letters and in Acts are usually thought to be the same, in spite of certain differences. It is his visit to deliver the collection, at which time he is arrested and eventually sent to Rome. The problem lies in the attempted correlation between the second visit mentioned in Galatians (2:1-10) and the three visits in Acts (chaps. 11; 15; 18).

There are multiple solutions proposed. A partial list is instructive.

(a) Galatians 2 = Acts 15 (Lightfoot, 123-28)
(b) Galatians 2 = Acts 11 (Ramsay, 57-59)
(c) Galatians 2 = Acts 11 = Acts 15 (Enslin, 228-29)
(d) Galatians 2 = Acts 18 (Knox)
(e) Galatians 2 = a visit nowhere mentioned in Acts (Manson, 176-78)

If one assumes the first solution, the implications about the historical sequence of Acts are negative. Acts is not simply silent about events; it is simply wrong about a certain key event (Acts 11). If one assumes the second solution, the implications are more favorable for Acts. The first two visits dovetail nicely. A certain later visit merely goes unmentioned in the epistles. At present the entire discussion is stalemated.

At this point one needs to become aware of an assumption that controls virtually the entire discussion. It is decisive in the evaluation of the data. This assumption runs as follows: Paul's letters are primary sources for a knowledge of Paul; Acts is a late secondary source. Of the two sources, Paul's letters are obviously the more trustworthy. This is true not only for Paul's ideas but also for Paul's career (Knox). So one starts from Galatians 1–2. The trustworthiness of the narrative outline of Paul's career in this autobiographical section is underscored by his oath of truthfulness in 1:20 ("In what I am writing to you, before God, I do not lie!").

In spite of its apparent truth (a primary source is to be preferred over a secondary source), this assumption is in need of careful reconsideration given the nature of autobiography in antiquity (Misch). George Lyons states the case:

> Caution is in order in reaching historical conclusions on the basis of ancient autobiographical literature. . . . Persuasion, not truth, was its overriding concern. . . . The emphasis upon ethical characterization and idealization permitted exaggeration and/or suppression of certain aspects of the real life as legitimate autobiographical devices. Protests of truthfulness often were made precisely at the point where truth was most seriously compromised. . . . Autobiographical documents scarcely ever have the value of truthful records or objective narratives. (p. 65)

Scholes and Kellog take the same line. "First person narrative in antiquity seems to have been used mainly not for factual representation but for highly unreliable and one sided *apologiae*" (p. 244). For this reason, Jack Sanders can say that Paul's remarks in Galatians 1–2 should be considered suspect and so unreliable as to the sequence of events and details of the apostolic council (p. 335). If one operates out of expectations conditioned by ancient autobiography (e.g., Cicero, *Letters* 5.12–"An autobiographer must needs . . . pass over anything that calls for censure"), there must be much less certainty about the absolute reliability of the sequence of events derived from Galatians 1–2, especially as regards Paul's visits to Jerusalem. The implications of this consideration have yet to be worked out in terms of Paul's visits to Jerusalem in Acts.

From the point of view of Greco-Roman and Jewish history, the relative sequence of events in Acts is sound. The one possible exception is the date of the famine. From the perspective of Paul's letters, the relative sequence of events is also generally sound. The one sticking point is the possible correlation of Paul's visits to Jerusalem in Galatians and Acts, especially Galatians 2:1–10's counterpart in Acts (11? or 15?). This is not to claim historicity for every detail; it is to claim soundness for the overall sequence of events in Acts with rare exception, insofar as comparative materials allow one to check.

Nevertheless, the ongoing debate about the correlation of Paul's visits to Jerusalem in Galatians and in Acts prevents decisive conclusions from this level of argument.

Confirmed Facts and Episodes of Integrity

It is assumed that a document cannot be regarded as historically reliable if its individual events cannot be confirmed by external evidence and if its individual episodes do not manifest integrity/unity. By inference, a document whose events can be confirmed by external means and whose episodes can be shown to possess integrity must be considered historically reliable. Scholars who argue at this level search for external confirmation for individual facts in Acts' narrative and seek to show that the individual episodes of the account do, in fact, possess integrity/unity. The two sides of this argument need explanation.

(1) Excursus I of Adolf Harnack's *The Acts of the Apostles* is entitled "Survey of the narratives of St. Luke concerning the Primitive Community and the earlier history of St. Paul (Acts i-xiv), which are confirmed by the Pauline Epistles." In this appendix, Harnack gives thirty-nine examples of facts in Acts 1-14 that can be confirmed from the Pauline epistles. A few examples suffice.

(a) Jerusalem, not some town in Galilee, is the seat of the primitive community (Acts *passim*; Galatians 2; Romans 15).

(b) Christian communities were also in existence outside Jerusalem, especially in Judea, at a very early date (Acts 9:31; 1 Thess 2:14; Gal 1:22).

(c) The churches of Jerusalem and Judea had to endure persecution at the hands of their compatriots (Acts *passim*; 1 Thess 2:14).

(d) Barnabas is an important missionary to the Gentiles from the Jerusalem church, especially as regards Antioch of Syria (Acts 11:22-26; Gal 2:13). He worked side by side with Paul (Acts 11:25-26; Gal 2:1, 13).

(e) Baptism was an act of entry into the Christian community (Acts 2:38; 8:12; 1 Cor 1:14; Rom 6:1-4). It was in the name of Jesus (Acts 2:38; 1 Cor 1:13).

(f) The resurrection of Jesus was at the core of Christian proclamation (Acts 1:22; 2:32; 3:15; 5:30; 1 Cor 15:14, 17).

(g) Paul fled secretly from Damascus after escaping over the wall (Acts 9:23–25; 2 Cor 11:32–33).

Harnack concludes,

> The agreement which in these numerous instances exists between the Acts (chaps. i–xiv) and the Pauline epistles . . . is so extensive and so detailed as to exclude all wild hypotheses concerning those passages of the Acts that are without attestation in those epistles. The Acts is *an historical work* that has nothing in common with the later "Acts of the Apostles," and is not to be judged by the standard nor criticized by the method which suits these. (p. 272)

(2) The second aspect of this level of work has to do with the challenges to the integrity of various episodes in the narrative of Acts. It is sometimes argued that a single episode in Acts is actually a combination of more than one event and hence is not to be taken as historically reliable (Lüdemann, 130–33, 176, 178, 194, 200).

Acts 18, Paul's visit to Corinth, is a prime example. Does Acts 18 conflate two or more Pauline visits to Corinth into one? Jerome Murphy-O'Connor seems to think so (1983, 129–52). On the one hand, Acts 18:2 says that Aquila and Priscilla had lately come to Corinth from Italy because Claudius had commanded all the Jews to leave Rome. As we have seen, this expulsion is confirmed by Suetonius (*Claudius* 25.4), who says, "Since the Jews were continually making disturbances at the instigation of Chrestus, he (Claudius) expelled them from Rome." The question about the expulsion relates to its date.

The fifth-century historian Orosius (7.6.15–16) says,

> Josephus refers to the expulsion of Jews by Claudius in his ninth year. But Suetonius touches me more in saying, "Claudius expelled from Rome the Jews constantly making disturbances at the instigation of Chrestus."

If Orosius is taken at face value, then the event is linked to A.D. 49.

Dio Cassius, a third-century historian, speaks of an event that happened in A.D. 41. He says,

> As for the Jews, who had increased so greatly by reason of their multitude that it would have been hard without raising a tumult to expel them from the city, he did not drive them out, but ordered them, while continuing their traditional mode of life, not to hold meetings. (60.6.6)

The question is, Are Orosius and Dio Cassius speaking about the same event or two separate events? Murphy-O'Connor contends they are referring to one and the same event: namely, as a result of a disturbance in a Roman synagogue concerning Christ, Claudius expelled the missionaries who were not Roman citizens and temporarily withdrew from that Jewish community the right of assembly (1983, 136).

On the other hand, Acts 18:12 says that when Gallio was proconsul of Achaea, the Jews brought Paul before the tribunal. From an inscription found at Delphi, Gallio's presence in Corinth can be dated to A.D. 51–52 (Deissmann 1912, 261–86; Murphy-O'Connor 1983, 141–52). If this is so, then Acts 18 actually contains in its narrative about Paul's coming to Corinth two separate visits of the apostle to the city, one in A.D. 41 and the other in A.D. 50–52. A document that conflates separate events into a narrative and treats them as one is obviously not historically reliable.

Stephen Benko, however, concludes that the accounts of Claudius's dealings with the Jews in Rome cannot be convincingly conflated into a single episode, but that trouble did arise on two occasions during his reign: A.D. 41 and A.D. 49 (p. 18). The main reason for refusing to conflate the events is that the one denies what the other affirms. Dio Cassius says Claudius in 41 did not expel the Jews; Orosius agrees with Suetonius that Claudius did expel the Jews and dates it to 49. The most natural way to take accounts that are diametrically opposite is to regard them as referring to different events. If so, then the unity of Acts 18 is upheld. Priscilla and Aquila arrived in Corinth sometime after their expulsion from Rome in 49. Paul joined them and was there during Gallio's tenure in 51–52. A document that narrates episodes that have integrity has a high claim to historicity; one that conflates separate events into one does not.

From this cursory survey of the types of argument having to do with individual events and episodes one can see the nature of the issues. Regarding the evidence assembled by Harnack, an opponent might say, Yes, a number of details in Acts 1–14 are confirmed by Paul's letters, but what about those that are not? Is it legitimate to infer historicity for uncorroborated details because some details check out? Regarding the debates about the unity of individual episodes, one can see that every issue is debatable and that what is probable appears different to various scholars.

This appendix so far has sought, by a hasty survey, to indicate the three levels on which the debates about the historicity of Acts are carried on. No one is sufficient to carry the day, either for or against the historical value of the Acts of the Apostles. Any successful argument must involve all three levels of evidence: accurate contemporary color, sound historical sequence, and confirmed facts and individual episodes with integrity. Even then the argument is incomplete. This is because the matter of Acts' historicity also involves three specific issues: (1) the speeches, (2) the portrait of Paul, and (3) the miracles. No argument for or against the historicity of Acts is adequate that omits even one of these issues. The second part of this paper, therefore, will survey these issues and how they play a role in the overall case one way or the other.

The Speeches of Acts

Since Dibelius and Cadbury (5.402-26), most scholars have regarded the speeches of Acts after the analogy of the speeches used in ancient historical writings. Thucydides (1.22.1) is most often quoted:

> As to the speeches that were made by different men, either when they were about to begin the war or when they were already engaged therein, it has been difficult to recall with strict accuracy the words actually spoken, both for me as regards that which I myself heard, and for those who from various other sources have brought me reports. Therefore, the speeches are given in the language in which, as it seemed to me, the several speakers would express, on the subjects under consideration, the sentiments most befitting the occasion, though at the same time I have adhered as closely as possible to the general sense of what was actually said.

Tacitus (*Annals* 15.63) remarks on the occasion of Seneca's death that the farewell speech of that philosopher had been published literally so that the historian did not need to reproduce it in Seneca's own words. Pliny (*Epistle* 1.16) says regarding Pompeius Saturninus, "his histories will please you . . . for the words he puts into the mouths of his characters are as vivid as his own public speeches, though condensed into a simpler and terser style." Lucian (*On the Art of Writing History* 58) says, "If a person has to be introduced to make a speech, above all let his language suit his person and his subject." Such statements from Thucydides to Lucian have been taken to mean that ancient speeches were an author's compositions based on what he deemed appropriate for the particular individual in his particular time, place, and circumstances.

This conclusion is reinforced by two additional strands of evidence. On the one hand, comparison of different versions of ancient speeches seems to confirm the conclusion reached. (a) Josephus (*Antiquities* 1.6.3 §§ 279-84) gives the farewell speech of Mattathias in a very different form from that in 1 Macc 2:50-68. (b) Also Herod's speech to his soldiers is found in two very different forms in two different places in Josephus (*Antiquities* 15.5.3 §§ 127-46 and *War* 1.19.4 §§ 373-79). (c) Plutarch (*Otho* 15) and Tacitus (*Histories* 2.47) manifest extensive agreement in their accounts of Otho but offer entirely different versions of his last address. (d) Dio Cassius's report of Caesar's speech to his soldiers (38.36-46) is very different from that reported by Caesar himself (*Gallic War* 1.40). On the other hand, recognition that biographers since the time of Xenophon (Cox, 63), as well as Jewish writers (Kaplan, 154), followed the same practice offers confirmation to the widely held conclusions of Cadbury and Dibelius. If so, what does this imply about the historicity of Acts?

A minority voice contends that it is "by no means true that all ancient historians felt free to put fictitious speeches in the mouths of historical characters" (Hemer 1989, 75). Polybius is the example cited. In book 12, Polybius gives a contrast between history as he understands it and as one Timaeus practices it. Polybius is critical of Timaeus because his "pronouncements are full of dreams, prodigies, incredible tales, and to put it shortly, craven superstitions and womanish love of the marvelous" (12:24). His speeches are "untruthfully reported" and "on purpose" (12.25a). Timaeus "actually invents speeches," while it is the function of history to discover first of all what was actually spoken (12.25b). The brief speeches in Acts, moreover, bear no resemblance to the rhetorical compositions of Josephus. "This is not to say they are to be simply fitted into a 'Polybian' alternative" (Hemer 1989, 78). It does mean, however, that the possibility exists that some or all of the speeches of Acts are a digest or summary of what was actually said. The matter needs examination. In confronting this first specific problem, one meets yet again the divide between scholars about the historicity of Acts.

The Portrait of Paul

With the shift in focus from the historicity to the theology of Acts, certain scholars sharpened their descriptions of Lucan theology by contrasting it with Paul's as known from his epistles. Out of this emerged the contention that there is a discrepancy between the portrait of Paul in Acts and that in the genuine letters. Representative points in the comparison may be noted (derived from Haenchen, 112–16, and Vielhauer).

(1) In Acts, Paul is a great miracle worker. In the epistles, he is a suffering apostle (e.g., 2 Cor 12:10).

(2) In Acts, Paul is an outstanding orator. In the epistles, he is called a feeble speaker (2 Cor 10:10).

(3) In Acts, Paul is not on an equal footing with the Twelve. In the epistles, he is an apostle of equal standing with the Twelve (1 Cor 9:1; 15:1–11).

(4) In Acts, Jewish opposition to Paul is due to his teaching about the resurrection from the dead. In the epistles, Jewish opposition is over the law (Gal 2:11–16).

(5) In Acts, natural theology is used to portray Greco-Roman culture as a true preparation for Christianity. In the epistles, natural theology is used to hold the Gentiles responsible before God (Romans 1–3).

(6) In Acts, Paul is pro-Jewish law. In the epistles, he wages an anti-Jewish polemic against the law.
(7) In Acts, Paul's Christology is adoptionistic. In the epistles, Paul holds a Christology of preexistence.
(8) In Acts, Paul does not hold to an imminent eschatology. In the epistles, there is an imminent expectation.

These contrasts are taken by scholars like Haenchen and Vielhauer as irreconcilable differences between the portrait of the historical Paul and the Lucan Paul. Given these discontinuities, the historical reliability of Acts is called into question.

These sharp distinctions between the picture of Paul gained from his genuine letters and that found in Acts have not gone unchallenged. Granted, there are at least three portraits of Paul found in the New Testament: that of the genuine epistles, that of the Deuteropaulines like the Pastorals, and that of Acts. Granted, each has its own distinctive elements. To call the discontinuities irreconcilable differences, however, is something many scholars will not accept. A typical response to Haenchen and Vielhauer runs something as follows (a composite taken from Wilckens, Borgen, and Kümmel).

(1) In Paul's letters, his ministry includes miracles (2 Cor 12:12; Rom 15:19; 1 Cor 2:1-4; Gal 3:1-5; 1 Thess 1:5). In Acts, Paul's ministry also involves suffering (Acts 14:5, 22; 16:19-40; 17:5-9, 13; 18:12-17; 20:1, 3; 21:4, 11-14, 27-36).
(2) In Paul's letters, one finds evidences of rhetorical skills and techniques characteristic of the orators of his time (e.g., diatribe, *inclusio, chiasmus*). The specific charge in 2 Cor 10:10 refers to Paul's withdrawal at an earlier time rather than risk the loss of the church in Corinth (Talbert 1987, 111-12). It has nothing to do with his lack of rhetorical skill. Nor does 1 Cor 2:1-5 imply that Paul was oratorically deficient. It says rather that Paul's converts' confidence lay in the evidences of the Spirit in their midst rather than in Paul's verbal pretenses.
(3) In Acts, the Twelve represent the true Jesus tradition while Paul stands for the vitality of religious experience of the risen Lord. Acts' schema makes the latter subservient to the former. In his letters, one also finds Paul subservient to the authentic tradition, which came down to him from the apostles before him (1 Cor 11:23-25; 1 Cor 15:1-11), at the same time that he claims his equal status based on his religious experience (Galatians 1).
(4) Jewish opposition to Paul in Acts is due not only to his teaching about the resurrection (Acts 23:6; 24:21; 26:6) but also because of

Paul's perceived opposition to the law and Temple (15:5; 21:21; 21:28).

(5) Both the Paul of Acts and of the genuine epistles hold to a natural theology or general revelation. The functions of this natural theology vary, depending upon the context in which it is used.

(6) In Acts, Paul expresses reservations about the soteriological value of the Law (Acts 13:39) at the same time that he, as a Jewish Christian, lives by its rules amidst Jews (18:18; 21:23-24). This is similar to the Paul of the epistles who is critical of the law's soteriological role (Gal 2:19-21) at the same time that he lives by its tenets when necessary (1 Cor 9:19-23).

(7) Paul's picture of Jesus in Acts 13:33 belongs not to preexistence Christology but rather to exaltation Christology; in Acts 17:30-31 it resembles two-foci Christology. In the epistles, an epiphany Christology (Gal 4:4) lies side by side with exaltation Christology (Phil 2:6-11) and probably a two-foci Christology (1 Thess 1:9-10). (The categories are those of Fuller.)

(8) In the epistles, Paul sometimes seems to hold to an imminent expectation and believes he will be alive when the end arrives (1 Thess 4:15; 1 Cor 15:51-52); in other places he seems to reckon with his death before the parousia (Phil 1:19-26; 2 Cor 5:1-10?).

Two observations need to be made at this point. First, given these adjustments to the claims made for irreconcilable differences between Acts and the epistles in their portraits of Paul, Ulrich Wilckens can say that "it is Paul, interpreted existentially, who is so sharply set against Luke. . . . But the existentially interpreted Paul is not the historical Paul" (p. 77). Second, given the different historical situations of Paul and Acts, one should not expect theological identity. There would be continuity in doctrine, but the doctrines would be expected to function differently in different contexts.

If the discontinuities in the portraits of Paul in the genuine epistles and in Acts are taken to be irreconcilable differences, then the historicity of Acts may be called into question. If the discontinuities are seen merely as different shadings due to variation in historical contexts, then the historical reliability of Acts fares better.

Miracles

Since the nineteenth century the historical value of Acts has been called into question because of the presence of miracles in its narrative. This posture is still dominant. Gerd Lüdemann is a typical representative of this perspective in the current generation. Regarding the healing of the lame man in Acts 3, he writes,

> There is no historical nucleus to the tradition of the miracle story in vv. 1-10. Those who are lame from their childhood are (unfortunately) not made whole again. But the story reflects the existence of a Christian community which reported great things of Peter's activity in Jerusalem and/or miracles performed by him. (54)

Regarding the story of Peter's release from prison by an angel in Acts 12, Lüdemann writes,

> the miraculous release bears within itself its own historical refutation. However, we may still presuppose a historical nucleus in it, namely that Agrippa had Peter arrested. (p. 145)

For someone with this presupposition about miracles, Acts is indeed a questionable entity.

Over against Lüdemann, one finds a scholar like the late Colin Hemer. Hemer (1989) says,

> I am content to operate in a framework where the possibility of miracle is accepted and its appearance is not an automatic cue for reinterpretation or special interpretation. (p. 443)

> Within that framework we may still require reasonably rigorous testimony . . . but their possibility may be accepted in principle (p. 443 n. 52).

Are miracles possible? The possible is always a function of one's worldview. Worldviews are highly resistent to disconfirmation. The materialistic worldview, represented by Lüdemann, dictates that the world was and is ruled by iron physical laws that not even God could or can bend. Walter Wink comments:

> In the last decade, advances in the understanding of the placebo effect, the functioning of the immune system, empirical studies of the control yogis can exercise over their internal organs, and above all, the shift from Newtonian lawfulness to Heisenberg's uncertainty principle have changed the way many people look at the possibility of healing. We simply no longer know for certain what is within the realm of possibility. Consequently, some scientists are beginning, *through* science, to jettison the materialistic worldview as reductionist. (p. 213)

Wink points out that these changes in attitude are not based on a single scrap of new evidence from the ancient world but on shifting evaluations of what is possible. What one considers possible determines one's stance on the miraculous in the Acts of the Apostles (p. 214). On the matter of what is considered possible, scholars differ. These differences, of course, affect their evaluations of the historicity of Acts.

Having looked at the three levels of argument and the three specific issues associated with the question of the historicity of Acts, what can be concluded? *What* does one mean by the historicity of Acts? Judging from *how* the argument is conducted, it possible to say that an affirmation of the historical worth of the Acts of the Apostles can be given only if and when certain answers are possible on the levels of contemporary color, historical sequence, and individual episodes on the one hand, and to the issues of speeches, portrait of Paul, and miracles on the other. Confidence in the historicity of Acts requires a certain type of answer to be given in all six cases.

Even then the issue is not settled because of a final matter, namely, the burden of proof demanded. Lüdemann poses the problem. He says,

> The real question is whether Luke's information has to be proved to be true or rather whether it is only false if it can certainly be shown to be so. (p. 51)

If one can show that external evidence confirms the accuracy of Acts' contemporary color at numerous points, does that give one the right to assume the accuracy of points that cannot be checked? If one can show that at a significant number of points the historical sequence of Acts' narrative checks out as sound, does that mean that one can assume the soundness of sequence at those points that cannot be checked? If one can show that many individual matters of fact can be confirmed and the unity of a number of episodes can be established, should one infer that matters of fact that cannot be confirmed externally can be assumed to be accurate and that other episodes that are unverified by external data are indeed possessed of integrity?

One group of scholars believes it is responsible to infer the accuracy of unconfirmed material because of the accuracy of confirmed material. F. F. Bruce serves as spokesman for this position. He says,

> When a writer's accuracy is established by valid evidence, he gains the right to be treated as a reliable informant on matters coming within his scope which are not corroborated elsewhere. (1985, p. 2578)

The other group thinks it is not responsible to accept anything in Acts as historically reliable unless it has been corroborated by other data, either external or internal. The former feel free to speak globally about the historicity of Acts; the latter are willing to speak about Acts' historical reliability in a much more limited sense. Martin Dibelius says, "the historical reliability of Acts must be measured in each individual case" (107; cf. Talbert 1989, 311). Assumptions matter.

Enough corroborating data has been assembled already by scholars to enable one to conclude that Acts is not mere fiction and that its record is reasonably reliable in areas where it can be checked. There are, however, enough unchecked areas and enough problems in areas that can be checked to keep professors and graduate students in work for the indefinite future.

Of what value is the Acts of the Apostles for the study of early Christian history, in particular the period prior to A.D. 64? That depends on what one thinks about Acts' historicity. How is the historicity of Acts determined? If the thesis of this appendix is correct, the historical value of Acts is determined by an argument that includes the three levels and that addresses the three specific issues described above. Ultimately, the pervasiveness of one's argument will depend on the burden of proof demanded of it.

APPENDIX B

Aspects of Biography
in Mediterranean Antiquity

In a number of respects ancient history and biography are similar (Talbert 1996). (1) History is prose narration. The dominant type of biography is also prose narration. This sets them apart from epic. (2) Both history and biography are about real people and real events. This sets them apart from romance. (3) Varieties of both share certain aims: apologetics, instruction, entertainment.

Indeed, histories often contain biographical sections (Polybius 9.22; 10.2.2; Dionysius of Halicarnassus 5.48.1; Diodorus Siculus 17; Josephus, *Antiquities* bks. 14-17; Dio Cassius 45-56; 73 at beginning; 73.11.2-4; Eusebius, *Church History* 6). Biographies often include a narrative of events. The dominant type of biography is prose narrative, which is similar to history except that it is anecdotal and mostly unconcerned about cause and effect. This is in contrast to biographies that are dialogues (e.g., Satyrus, *Life of Euripides*; Palladius, *Life of Chrysostom*; Sulpicius Severus, *Life of St. Martin*) and the biographical collections of sayings like Plutarch's "Sayings of Kings and Commanders" (e.g., in D, Plutarch says, "their pronouncements and unpremeditated utterance . . . afford an opportunity to observe . . . the working of the mind of each man").

At the point of a historical monograph about a single individual, especially if told in eulogistic terms, the line between history and biography is most blurred. In Cicero's *Letters to His Friends* 5.12 is a request addressed to Lucceius. Cicero desires that his name gain celebrity through Lucceius's works. Lucceius is about finished with the account of the Italian and civil wars he has been writing and is looking forward to writing about subsequent events. Cicero asks him to do one of two things: either to weave his affairs along with those of the rest of the period into a single narrative, or to detach the material relating to Cicero from the continuous history and to treat it eulogistically. "Waive the laws of history for this once." Cicero's preference is for the latter because "in the doubtful and various fortunes of an outstanding individual we often find surprise and suspense, joy and distress, hope and fear." Lucceius has often promised that he will "compose the record of my public career, its policies and events." Now Cicero is impatient because he wants to enjoy a modicum of glory before he dies. It is not a biography that Cicero wants written but a historical monograph about his public career, and he wants it done in eulogistic terms. In this case, as with Sallust's *Catiline* and *Jugurtha*, the aim is not to set forth the individual's distinctive essence but to narrate political events with which the individuals were associated.

In spite of the similarities between history and biography, some ancients spoke about a difference between them. On a number of points the difference is noted. (1) History claims completeness (Cicero, *Orator* 34.120); biography incompleteness (Plutarch, *Alexander* 1.2-3).

(2) History deals with grand events (Herodotus 1.177; Xenophon, *Hellenica* 5.1.4; Polybius 10.21.5-8; Dionysius of Halicarnassus 5.56.1; Statius, *Silvae* 1.2.96-97). Cicero, *Orator* 34.120, speaks about history as "omitting no important event." Biography, however, deals with incidental matters as well as grand events (Plutarch, *Demosthenes* 11.7). Plutarch, *Alexander* 1.2-3, puts it this way:

> It is not Histories that I am writing, but Lives; and in the most illustrious deeds there is not always a manifestation of virtue or vice, nay, a slight thing like a phrase or a jest often makes a greater revelation of character than battles where thousands fall.

(3) In history there is an attempt to discern causes (Polybius 3.32; 12.25b.1; Cicero, *Orator* 2.15.63). As Dionysius of Halicarnassus put it, "The readers of histories do not derive sufficient profit from learning the bare outcome of events, but . . . everyone demands that the causes of the events be related." In biography the aim is to reveal character (Plutarch, *Alexander* 1.2-3; *Nicias*; Lucian, *Demonax* 67). Cornelius Nepos, *Pelopidas* 16.1, says, "I do not know exactly how I should describe his character, and I am afraid that if I begin to tell you of his deeds, I will appear not a biographer but a historian."

It is true that sometimes histories included material about an individual's character. Polybius 9.22, for example, says that "Since the course of affairs has called out attentions to the character of Hannibal, I think I am called upon at present to state my opinion regarding those peculiar traits in it which are the subject of most dispute." When history included a section on an individual's character, it was subsumed under the general explanations of why events happened as they did. Character is one cause among others. In biography, character is the end sought. Events are but one means of the illumination of character. In biography "character is studied in its own right, almost independently of the political framework of historiography in which it had served a functional purpose" (Fornara, 187).

(4) Much history was designated as instruction for political figures as political figures. Dionysius of Halicarnassus 5.56.1 is to the point. "For statesmen I perceive that the knowledge of these things is absolutely necessary, to the end that they may have precedents for their use in the various situations that arise." Much biography aimed to shape the life of the reader as a human being (Plutarch, *Pericles* 21.4; *Cimon* 2.3–5; Tacitus, *Agricola* 46; Lucian, *Demonax* 2). Plutarch, *Aemilius Paulus* 1, says, "I try in one way or another to order my own life and to fashion it in accordance with the virtues of these lives." In *Aratus* 1, he contends that his readers should do the same.

(5) The subject matter of history was states, that is, political and military events. The subject matter of biography was the character of individuals and/or peoples. *Bios* was written of peoples as well as individuals. Dikaiarchus in the fourth century B.C. wrote *Bios Hellados*, a life of Greek culture from the Golden Age to his own time, as well as *bioi* of individuals like Plato and other philosophers. Varro, in the first century B.C., wrote *De vita populi Romani*, a social treatment of the Roman people. Although these two *bioi* are not extant, it is possible to discern something about their ethos from a statement by Cornelius Nepos. In his preface, Nepos says,

> If these could only understand that what is honorable in one land is often disgraceful in another and that all manners must be judged in the light of national customs, they would not be surprised that in our description of Greek character we carefully consider local practices and conventions.

Whether a *bios* dealt with an individual or a people, the focus was on character, the individuality of the subject: what sort of person he was, what sort of people they were. It was this focus on the individuality, the distinctiveness of the subject, that set biography apart.

These guidelines provided by the ancient authors serve to clarify how Plutarch's *Parallel Lives*, Philostratus's *Life of Apollonius of Tyana*, the *Life of Aesop*, or the *Life of Secundus the Silent Philosopher*, for example, can be said to be biography. There are other documents, however, that perplex the reader, raising questions about their genre. Two types are especially problematic. (1) Those writings that possess great brevity: for example, Philostratus's *Lives of the Sophists* (which is said by Eunapius 454 to be *bioi*) and his predecessors Hermippus, *Lives of Distinguished Men* (third century B.C.), and Nepos, *Lives of Illustrious Men* (contemporary with Cicero); the Jewish *Lives of the Prophets* (first century A.D.); and the *Lives of Illustrious Men* by Jerome and Gennadius (fifth century A.D.). The brevity (some sketches are no more than one sentence while others are a long paragraph) raises the question in what sense these sketches convey character, individuality, distinctiveness. The same may be said for the first-century B.C. biography of Aristotle that served to introduce his works and its later derivatives. Can anything this sketchy be said to be *bios*? They can, I think, be said to be *bioi* in the same way that biography in the modern world covers not only a long, fully developed treatment of an individual's personality but also the sketches of people that appear in volumes like the *Dictionary of International Biography*. Even the sketches convey something of an individual's uniqueness. So also in antiquity.

(2) Another type of writing sometimes said to be biographical are the catalogues of philosophical schools such as are found in the Herculaneum papyri (Scott). Here there is a catalogue of the members of the school broken at a number of points by anecdotes about this or that individual within the philosophical community. Are these catalogues history (e.g., institutional histories)?* They do not fit what the ancients said about history: they are not about states; they do not deal with grand events; they do not seek for causes; they are not complete; they do not seem to serve an instructional purpose. Are they biography? If so, in what sense? Their closest analogies are to the biographies of peoples/groups. This would establish their type: biography of a group rather than an individual. They are also analogous to the sketches of individuals in the *Lives of Illustrious Men*. They are characterized by brevity, but their brevity still enables one to recognize the distinctiveness of the group. This school is distinctive in that it was composed of these individuals whose essence is shown at points by selected anecdotes associated with certain of them. This establishes their aim: to expose the individuality, uniqueness, character, essence of the subject, which, in this case, is a philosophical school.

* Marcello Gigante, *Philodemus in Italy: The Books from Herculaneum,* trans. D. Obbink (Ann Arbor: University of Michigan Press, 1995), 20–23, regards these catalogues as parts of Philodemus's *Syntaxis of Philosophers* from the first century B.C. and calls them historiographical. The *Syntaxis,* he contends, is constructed in the style of a large "institutional" manual. He builds on the work of T. Dorandi: (1) *Index Academicorum,* P.Herc. 1021 and 164 (*Filodemo: Storia dei filosofi: Platone e l'Academia* [Naples: Bibliopolis, 1991]); (2) *Index Stoicorum,* P.Herc. 1018 (*Storia dei filosofi: La Stoa da Zenone a Panezio, P.Herc. 1018* [Leiden, 1994]); (3) *De Stoiciis,* P.Herc. 339 and 155 ("Filodemo. Gli stoici [PHerc.155 e 339]," *CErc* 12 [1982], 91–133).

WORKS CITED

Alexander, Loveday
  1993   "Acts and Ancient Intellectual Biography." Pp. 31-64 in *The Book of Acts in Its Ancient Literary Setting*. Ed. B. W. Winter and A. D. Clarke. Grand Rapids: Eerdmans.
Arrighetti, Graziano
  1964   "Satiro Vita di Euripide." *Studi Classici e Orientali* 13:1-168.
Bailey, Shackleton
  1978   *Cicero's Letters to His Friends*. Atlanta: Scholars Press.
Barrett, C. K.
  1961   *The New Testament Background: Selected Documents*. New York: Harper.
Bauckham, Richard
  1995   "James and the Jerusalem Church." Pp. 415-80 in *The Book of Acts in Its Palestinian Setting*. Ed. R. Bauckham. Grand Rapids: Eerdmans.
Beardslee, W. A.
  1960   "The Casting of Lots at Qumran and in the Book of Acts." *Novum Testamentum* 4:245-52.
Benko, Stephen
  1984   *Pagan Rome and the Early Christians*. Bloomington: Indiana University Press.
Black, Robert Allen
  1985   "The Conversion Stories in the Acts of the Apostles." Ph.D. dissertation, Emory University.
Bligh, John
  1969   *Galatians*. London: St. Paul's Publications.
Blinzer, Josef
  1970   "The Jewish Punishment of Stoning in the New Testament

Period." Pp. 147–61 in *The Trial of Jesus*. Ed. E. Bammel. London: SCM.

Blomberg, Craig
1984   "The Law in Luke-Acts." *Journal for the Study of the New Testament* 22:53–80.

Borgen, Peder
1969   "From Paul to Luke." *Catholic Biblical Quarterly* 31:168–82.

Bruce, F. F.
1968   "St. Paul in Rome, 5: Concluding Observations." *Bulletin of the John Rylands Library* 50:262–79.
1985   "The Acts of the Apostles: Historical Record or Theological Reconstruction." Vol. 2.25.3, pp. 2569–2603 of *Aufstieg und Niedergang der römischen Welt*. Ed. H. Temporini and W. Haase. New York and Berlin: de Gruyter.

Burridge, Richard A.
1992   *What Are the Gospels? A Comparison with Graeco-Roman Biography*. Cambridge: Cambridge University Press.

Buss, Septimus
1901   *Roman Law and History in the New Testament*. London: Rivingtons.

Cadbury, Henry J.
1955   *The Book of Acts in History*. London: Adam & Charles Black.
1958   *The Making of Luke-Acts*. London: SPCK.
1966   "The Speeches in Acts." Vol. 5, pp. 402–26 in *The Beginnings of Christianity*. Ed. F. J. Foakes Jackson and Kirsopp Lake. Grand Rapids: Baker.
1979   "The Tradition." Vol. 2, pp. 209–64 in *The Beginnings of Christianity*.

Caird, G. B.
1962   "Chronology of the New Testament." Vol. 1, pp. 603–7 in *Interpreter's Dictionary of the Bible*. Ed. G. A. Buttrick. Nashville: Abingdon.

Callan, Terrance
1993   "The Background of the Apostolic Decree (Acts 15:20,29; 21:25)." *Catholic Biblical Quarterly* 55:284–97.

Camparetti, Domenico
1875   "Papiro ercolanese inedito." *Rivista di Fililogia* 3:449–555.

Campbell, T. H.
1955   "Paul's Missionary Journeys as Reflected in His Letters." *Journal of Biblical Literature* 74:80–87.

Carrubba, R. W.
1967   "The Technique of Double Structure in Horace." *Mnemosyne* Series 4. 20:68–75.

Conzelmann, Hans
1987   *Acts of the Apostles*. Hermeneia. Philadelphia: Fortress.
Cox, Patricia
1983   *Biography in Late Antiquity*. Berkeley: University of California Press.
Dean, J. E.
1935   *Epiphanius' Treatise on Weights and Measures, the Syriac Version*. Chicago: Oriental Institute of the University of Chicago.
Deissmann, Adolf
1912   *Paul: A Study in Social and Religious History*. New York: Harper.
1922   *Light from the Ancient East*. New York: Harper.
Dibelius, Martin
1956   *Studies in the Acts of the Apostles*. Ed. H. Greeven. New York: Scribner's.
Donfried, Karl P.
1992   "Chronology." Vol. 1, pp. 1016–22 in *Anchor Bible Dictionary*. Ed. D. N. Freedman. New York: Doubleday.
Duckworth, G. E.
1962   *Structural Patterns and Proportions in Vergil's Aeneid*. Ann Arbor: University of Michigan Press.
Dupont, Jacques
1964   *The Sources of Acts: The Present Position*. London: Darton, Longman & Todd.
1979   "Community of Goods in the Early Church." Pp. 85–102 in *The Salvation of the Gentiles*. New York: Paulist.
Düring, Ingemar
1957   *Aristotle in the Ancient Biographical Tradition*. Göteborg: Göteborg Universitet Arsskrift.
Ellis, E. Earl
1976   "Prophecy in the Early Church." Pp. 700–701 in *Interpreter's Dictionary of the Bible: Supplementary Volume*. Ed. K. Crim. Nashville: Abingdon.
1991   "The End of the Earth (Acts 1:8)." *Bulletin for Biblical Research* 1:123–32.
Enslin, Morton S.
1938   *Christian Beginnings*. New York: Harper.
Ethridge, J. W.
1968   *The Targums of Onkelos and Jonathan ben Uzziel of the Pentateuch*. New York: Ktav.
Fitzmyer, J. A.
1988   "The Pauline Letters and the Lucan Account of Paul's Missionary Journeys." Pp. 82–89 in *SBL 1988 Seminar Papers*. Ed. D. J. Lull. Atlanta: Scholars Press.

Fornara, Charles William

1983   *The Nature of History in Ancient Greece and Rome*. Berkeley: University of California Press.

Fritz, Kurt von

1940   *Pythagorean Politics in Southern Italy: An Analysis of the Sources*. New York: Columbia University Press.

Fuller, R. H.

1965   *The Foundations of New Testament Christology*. New York: Scribner's.

Gapp, K. S.

1935   "The Universal Famine under Claudius." *Harvard Theological Review* 28:258–65.

Gasque, Ward

1975   *A History of the Criticism of the Acts of the Apostles*. Tübingen: Mohr.

Gill, David

1974   "The Structure of Acts 9." *Biblica* 55:46–48.

Gillard, Frank

1993   "More Silent Reading in Antiquity." *Journal of Biblical Literature* 112: 689–96.

Goodspeed, E. J.

1950   *The Apostolic Fathers*. New York: Harper.

Grant, Robert M.

1986   *Gods and the One God*. Philadelphia: Westminster.

Haacker, Klaus

1992   "Gallio." Vol. 2, pp. 901–3 in *Anchor Bible Dictionary*. Ed. D. N. Freedman. New York: Doubleday.

Haenchen, Ernst

1971   *The Acts of the Apostles*. Philadelphia: Westminster.

Hanson, R. P. C.

1967   *The Acts*. Oxford: Clarendon.

Harnack, Adolf

1909   *The Acts of the Apostles*. New York: G. P. Putnam's Sons.

Hemer, Colin J.

1980   "Observations on Pauline Chronology." Pp. 3–18 in *Pauline Studies*. Ed. D. A. Hagner and M. J. Harris. Grand Rapids: Eerdmans.

1989   *The Book of Acts in the Setting of Hellenistic History*. Ed. C. H. Gempf. Tübingen: Mohr.

Hengel, Martin

1985   *Between Jesus and Paul*. Philadelphia: Fortress.

Horsley, G. H. R.
  1992   "The Inscriptions of Ephesus and the New Testament." *Novum Testamentum* 34:105-68.

Horst, P. W. van der
  1977   "Peter's Shadow: The Religio-Historical Background of Acts 5:15." *New Testament Studies* 23:204-12.
  1989   "The Altar of the 'Unknown God' in Athens (Acts 17:23) and the Cult of 'Unknown Gods' in the Hellenistic and Roman Periods." Vol. 2.18.2, pp. 1426-56 in *Aufstieg und Niedergang in der römischen Welt*. Ed. H. Temporini and W. Haase. Berlin: de Gruyter.

Hubbard, Benjamin
  1977   "Commissioning Stories in Luke-Acts: A Study of Their Antecedents, Form and Content." *Semeia* 8:103-26.
  1978   "The Role of Commissioning Accounts in Acts." Pp. 187-98 in *Perspectives on Luke-Acts*. Ed. Charles H. Talbert. Edinburgh: T. & T. Clark.

Hunt, A. S.
  1912   *The Oxyrynchus Papyri: Part IX*. London: Egypt Exploration Fund.

Jervell, Jacob
  1972   *Luke and the People of God*. Minneapolis: Augsburg.

Johnson, Luke T.
  1983   *Decision Making in the Early Church*. Philadelphia: Fortress.
  1992   *The Acts of the Apostles*. Collegeville, Minn.: Liturgical Press.

Jones, Donald L.
  1989   "Luke's Unique Interest in Historical Chronology." Pp. 378-87 in *SBL 1989 Seminar Papers*. Ed. D. J. Lull. Atlanta: Scholars Press.

Kaplan, Julius
  1933   *The Redaction of the Babylonian Talmud*. New York: Bloch.

Kee, H. C.
  1995   "Defining the First Century C.E. Synagogue." *New Testament Studies* 41:481-500.

Kilgallen, John
  1988   "Acts 13:38-39: Culmination of Paul's Speech in Pisidia." *Biblica* 69:480-506.

Knox, John
  1950   *Chapters in the Life of Paul*. Nashville: Abingdon.

Korn, Manfred
  1993   *Die Geschichte Jesu in veränderter Zeit*. Tübingen: Mohr.

Krodel, Gerhard
  1986   *Acts*. Minneapolis: Augsburg.

Kümmel, W. G.
1966 *Introduction to the New Testament*. Nashville: Abingdon.
1972 "Lukas in der Anklage der heutigen Theologie." *Zeitschrift für die neutestamentliche Wissenschaft* 63:149-65.
Kurz, William S.
1993 *Reading Luke-Acts*. Louisville: Westminster/John Knox.
Lake, Kirsopp
1966 "The Ascension." Pp. 16-21; "The Death of Judas." Pp. 22-30; "The Gift of the Spirit on the Day of Pentecost." Pp.111-21; "The Chronology of Acts." Pp. 464-67 in vol. 5 of *The Beginnings of Christianity*. Ed. F. J. Foakes Jackson. Grand Rapids: Baker.
Lightfoot, J. B.
1890 *Saint Paul's Epistle to the Galatians*. 10th ed. London: Macmillan.
Lohfink, Gerhard
1971 *Die Himmelfahrt Jesu*. Munich: Kösel.
Lüdemann, Gerd
1984 *Paul, Apostle to the Gentiles*. Philadelphia: Fortress.
1989 *Early Christianity according to the Traditions of Acts*. Minneapolis: Fortress.
Lyons, George
1985 *Pauline Autobiography*. Atlanta: Scholars Press.
MacRae, George W.
1973 "Whom Heaven Must Receive Until the Time: Reflections on the Christology of Acts." *Interpretation* 27:151-65.
Malherbe, A. J.
1989 "Not in a Corner: Early Christian Apologetic in Acts 26:26." Pp. 147-63 in *Paul and the Popular Philosophers*. Minneapolis: Fortress.
Manson, T. W.
1962 *Studies in the Gospels and Epistles*. Philadelphia: Westminster.
Marguerat, Daniel
1993 "The End of Acts (28:16-31) and the Rhetoric of Silence." Pp. 74-89 in *Rhetoric and the New Testament*. Ed. S. E. Porter and T. H. Olbricht. Sheffield: JSOT.
Mason, Steve
1991 *Flavius Josephus on the Pharisees*. Leiden: Brill.
1993 "Greco-Roman, Jewish, and Christian Philosophies." Pp. 1-28 in *Approaches to Ancient Judaism. New Series 4*. Ed. J. Neusner. Atlanta: Scholars Press.
1995 "Chief Priests, Sadducees, Pharisees and Sanhedrin in Acts." Pp.

115-78 in *The Book of Acts in Its Palestinian Setting*. Ed. R. Bauckham. Grand Rapids: Eerdmans.

Mejer, Jørgen
1978   *Diogenes Laertius and His Hellenistic Background*. Wiesbaden: Franz Steiner.

Misch, George
1951   *A History of Autobiography in Antiquity*. 2 vols. Cambridge: Harvard University Press.

Mitchell, A. C.
1992   "The Social Function of Friendship in Acts 2:44-47 and 4:32-37." *Journal of Biblical Literature* 111:255-72.

Momigliano, Arnaldo
1971   *The Development of Greek Biography*. Cambridge: Harvard University Press.

Moore, George F.
1958   *Judaism*. 3 vols. Cambridge: Harvard University Press.

Moyter, S.
1987   "The Rending of the Veil: A Markan Pentecost?" *New Testament Studies* 33:155-57.

Murphy-O'Connor, Jerome
1983   *St. Paul's Corinth*. Wilmington, Del.: Michael Glazier.
1992   "Lots of God-Fearers?" *Revue Biblique* 99:418-24.
1993   "Paul and Gallio." *Journal of Biblical Literature* 112:315-17.
1995   *Paul the Letter Writer*. Collegeville, Minn.: Liturgical Press.

Nelson, Edwin S.
1982   "Paul's First Missionary Journey as Paradigm." Ph.D. dissertation, Boston University.

Nolland, John
1993   *Luke 18:35-24:53*. Word Biblical Commentary. Dallas: Word Books.

Oster, Richard
1976   "The Ephesian Artemis as an Opponent of Early Christianity." *Jahrbuch für Antike und Christentum* 19:24-44.

O'Toole, R. F.
1981   "Activity of the Risen Jesus in Luke-Acts." *Biblica* 62:471-98.

Palmer, Daryl W.
1993   "Acts and the Ancient Historical Monograph." Pp. 1-30 in *The Book of Acts in Its Ancient Literary Setting*. Ed. B. W. Winter and A. D. Clarke. Grand Rapids: Eerdmans.

Pease, A. S.
1946   "Notes on Book Burning." Pp. 145-60 in *Munera Studiosa*. Ed. M. H. Shepperd. Cambridge, Mass.: Episcopal Theological School.

Pereira, Francis

1983   *Ephesus: Climax of Universalism in Luke-Acts*. Anand, India: Gujarat Sahitya Prakash.

Porten, B.

1967   "The Structure and Theme of the Solomon Narrative (1 Kings 3–11)." *Hebrew Union College Annual* 38:93–128.

Ramsay, W. M.

1960   *St. Paul the Traveller and the Roman Citizen*. Grand Rapids: Baker.

Ramsey, A. M.

1965   "What Was the Ascension?" Pp. 135–44 in *Historicity and Chronology in the New Testament*. Ed. D. E. Nineham. London: SPCK.

Rapske, Brian M.

1994   "Acts, Travel and Shipwreck." Pp. 1–47 in *The Book of Acts in Its Greco-Roman Setting*. Ed. D. W. J. Gill and C. Gempf. Grand Rapids: Eerdmans.

1994b   *Paul in Roman Custody*. Grand Rapids: Eerdmans.

Reynolds, Joyce, and Tannenbaum, Robert

1987   *Jews and God-fearers at Aphrodisias. Greek Inscriptions with Commentary*. Cambridge: Cambridge Philological Society.

Riesner, Rainer

1995   "Synagogues in Jerusalem." Pp. 179–211 in *The Book of Acts in Its Palestinian Setting*. Ed. R. Bauckham. Grand Rapids: Eerdmans.

Sanders, E. P.

1991   "Defending the Indefensible." *Journal of Biblical Literature* 110:463–77.

Sanders, Jack T.

1966   "Paul's Autobiographical Statements in Galatians 1–2." *Journal of Biblical Literature* 85:335–43.

Sandmel, Samuel

1979   *Philo of Alexandria*. New York: Oxford University Press.

Sandnes, Karl Olav

1993   "Paul and Socrates: The Aim of Paul's Areopagus Speech." *Journal for the Study of the New Testament* 50:13–26.

Scholes, Robert, and Kellog, Robert

1966   *The Nature of Narrative*. New York: Oxford University Press.

Scott, Walter

1885   *Fragmenta Herculanensia*. Oxford: Clarendon Press.

Seifrid, M. A.
1987   "Jesus and the Law in Acts." *Journal for the Study of the New Testament* 30:39–57.

Seland, Torrey
1995   *Establishment Violence in Philo and Luke.* Leiden: Brill.

Setzer, Claudia J.
1994   *Jewish Responses to Early Christians: History and Polemics 30–150 C.E.* Minneapolis: Fortress.

Sherwin-White, A. N.
1978   *Roman Society and Roman Law in the New Testament.* Grand Rapids: Baker.

Smallwood, E. Mary
1976   *The Jews under Roman Rule: From Pompey to Diocletian.* Leiden: Brill.

Spencer, F. Scott
1992   *The Portrait of Philip in Acts.* Sheffield: JSOT.

Squires, John T.
1993   *The Plan of God in Luke-Acts.* Cambridge: Cambridge University Press.

Sternberg, Meir
1987   *The Poetics of Biblical Narrative.* Bloomington: Indiana University Press.

Stoops, Robert F., Jr.
        "Riot and Assembly: The Social Context of Acts 19:23–41." *Journal of Biblical Literature* 108:73–91.

Tajra, Harry W.
1989   *The Trial of St. Paul.* Tübingen: Mohr.
1994   *The Martyrdom of St. Paul.* Tübingen: Mohr.

Talbert, Charles H.
1966   *Luke and the Gnostics.* Nashville: Abingdon.
1967   "Again: Paul's Visits to Jerusalem." *Novum Testamentum* 9:26–40.
1970   "Artistry and Theology: An Analysis of the Architecture of John 1:19–5:47." *Catholic Biblical Quarterly* 32:341–66.
1974   *Literary Patterns, Theological Themes and the Genre of Luke-Acts.* Missoula: Scholars Press.
1974b   "An Introduction to Acts." *Review and Expositor* 71:437–49.
1982   *Reading Luke.* New York: Crossroad.
1984   *Acts.* Knox Preaching Guides. Atlanta: John Knox.
1987   *Reading Corinthians.* New York: Crossroad.
1988   Review of *The Narrative Unity of Luke-Acts* by Robert Tannehill. *Biblica* 69:135–38.

1989   "Luke-Acts." Pp. 297–320 in *The New Testament and Its Modern Interpreters*. Ed. E. J. Epp and G. W. MacRae. Atlanta: Scholars Press.

1991   "Once Again: The Gentile Mission in Luke-Acts." Pp. 99–110 in *Der Treue Gottes Trauen*. Ed. C. Bussmann and W. Radl. Freiburg: Herder.

1992   "Reading Chance, Moessner, and Parsons." Pp. 229–40 in *Cadbury, Knox, and Talbert*. Ed. M. C. Parsons and J. B. Tyson. Atlanta: Scholars Press.

1992b   *Reading John*. New York: Crossroad.

1996   "The Acts of the Apostles: Monograph or *Bios*?" Pp. 58–72 in *History, Literature and Society in the Book of Acts*. Ed. Ben Witherington, III. Cambridge: Cambridge University Press.

Talbert, Charles H., with J. H. Hayes
1995   "A Theology of Sea Storms in Luke-Acts." Pp. 321–36 in *SBL 1995 Seminar Papers*. Ed. E. H. Lovering, Jr. Atlanta: Scholars Press.

Tannehill, Robert C.
1986,   *The Narrative Unity of Luke-Acts*. 2 vols. Minneapolis: Fortress
1990   Press.

Theron, Daniel J.
1958   *Evidence of Tradition*. Grand Rapids: Baker.

Thiering, Barbara
1963   "The Poetic Forms of the Hodayot." *Journal of Semitic Studies* 8:189–209.

Traversa, Augustus.
1952   *Index Stoicorum Herculanensis*. Genova: Instituto di Filologia Classica.

Trebilco, Paul R.
1989   "Paul and Silas–'Servants of the Most High God' (Acts 16:16–18)." *Journal for the Study of the New Testament* 36:51–73.

Trompf, G. W.
1984   "On Why Luke Declined to Recount the Death of Paul: Acts 27–28 and Beyond." Pp. 225–39 in *Luke-Acts: New Perspectives*. Ed. Charles H. Talbert. New York: Crossroad.

Vanderkam, James C.
1992   "Calendars, Ancient Israelite and Early Jewish." Vol. 1, pp. 814–20 in *Anchor Bible Dictionary*. Ed. D. N. Freedman. New York: Doubleday.

Vielhauer, Philip
1966   "On the 'Paulinism' of Acts." Pp. 33–50 in *Studies in Luke-Acts*. Ed. L. E. Keck and J. L. Martyn. Nashville: Abingdon.

Vogel, C. J.
  1960   *Greek Philosophy: A Collection of Texts*. 2 vols. Leiden: Brill.
Ward, Roy Bowen
  1973   "James of Jerusalem." *Restoration Quarterly* 16:174–90.
Wehrli, F.
  1967   *Die Schule des Aristoteles*. Vol. 2. Basil: Schwabe.
Whitman, Cedric H.
  1958   *Homer and the Heroic Tradition*. Cambridge: Harvard University Press.
Wilckens, Ulrich
  1966   "Interpreting Luke-Acts in a Period of Existentialist Theology." Pp. 60–83 in *Studies in Luke-Acts*. Ed. L. E. Keck and J. L. Martyn. Nashville: Abingdon.
Wills, Lawrence M.
  1991   "The Depiction of the Jews in Acts." *Journal of Biblical Literature* 110:631–54.
Wilson, Stephen G.
  1992   "Jewish-Christian Relations 70–170 C.E." Vol. 3, pp. 834–39 in *Anchor Bible Dictionary*. Ed. D. N. Freedman. New York: Doubleday.
Wink, Walter
  1993   "Our Stories, Cosmic Stories, and the Biblical Story." Pp. 209–22 in *Sacred Stories*. Ed. Charles and Anne Simpkinson. San Francisco: Harper.
Winter, Bruce
  1991   "The Importance of the *Captatio Benevolentiae* in the Speeches of Tertullus and Paul in Acts 24:1–21." *Journal of Theological Studies* 42:505–31.